Career Counseling

Career Counseling

Theory, Practice, and Application

Written and Edited by

Janet Hicks, Brandé Flamez, and Mary Mayorga

Belmont University

cognella®

SAN DIEGO

Bassim Hamadeh, CEO and Publisher
Amy Smith, Senior Project Editor
Abbey Hastings, Associate Production Editor
Jess Estrella, Senior Graphic Designer
Stephanie Kohl, Licensing Coordinator
Ken Whitney, Interior Designer
Natalie Piccotti, Director of Marketing
Kassie Graves, Vice President of Editorial
Jamie Giganti, Director of Academic Publishing

cognella® ACADEMIC PUBLISHING
3970 Sorrento Valley Blvd., Ste. 500, San Diego, CA 92121

I dedicate this book to the authors who were so great to work with. My colleagues and former students are the best! Also, Matt, you are so patient during these projects. I couldn't do any of this without you.

—Janet

To my children, Evelyn and Braeden, you have been a gift from the beginning. Wherever you may go on this beautiful journey we call life, may you go with all your heart and carry that amazing childlike enthusiasm I see in you daily. I love you more than all the stars in the sky and the sand on the beach.

—Brandé

I dedicate this book to those colleagues who have inspired me to reach further than I thought I could. I thank you. And to the best support system I could ever ask for, I thank my husband Armando.

—Mary

BRIEF CONTENTS

DETAILED CONTENTS

Part II   Career Counseling With Diverse Populations 99

CHAPTER 7

Career Counseling for Diverse Populations 119

Part III   Practical Aspects for Working With Clients: Assessment and Theoretical Integration 139

CHAPTER 11

CHAPTER 14

Marriage, Couples, and Family Therapy: Treating Vocational Issues Systemically ... 265

CHAPTER 15

Building Career Counseling Programs ... 281

PREFACE

Jobs offered ten years ago no longer exist, interview and application strategies now encompass technological interventions, and the integration of technology in society has impacted couple, family, and personal counseling issues. Every year while teaching our career counseling courses we struggle to find a textbook that contains all of the information covered in the Council for the Accreditation of Counseling and Related Programs assessment standards (CACREP, 2020) and that actually prepares students for the National Counseling examination. Even more difficult to find than this, however, are practical applications of career counseling techniques and strategies. We find it interesting that, although we claim to be teaching a class based on how to use vocational counseling as part of sessions, few resources exist that demonstrate these skills. *Career Counseling: Theory, Practice, and Applications* provides both the theoretical basics, emerging trends, and actual practice/practical applications.

Whether you are working specifically with couples and families, in a school, private practice, or an agency setting, this text covers all the bases of career counseling theory to practical application. We often hear students say, "I don't want to do career counseling; I want to do *real* counseling." As a result, *Career Counseling: Theory, Practice, and Applications* highlights practical applications and demonstrations that show career counseling as a specialty but also how it overlaps with couples and family counseling, personal counseling, and addictions counseling and how it infuses with counseling theory and even vocationally related diagnosis requirements.

The aim of *Career Counseling: Theory, Practice, and Application* is to provide readers with a strong foundation in career counseling history, theory, and clinical assessment that will allow them to develop the skills and competencies needed to become effective, ethical counseling practitioners in today's diverse society. We want students to be able to visualize the process of career counseling. In other words, when a client comes to see you for career counseling, what does this look like? How do you do career counseling? This book, while it discusses all the major premises, provides the reader with practical applications of career counseling and demonstrates to the reader how to do career counseling from multiple perspectives. We even have a chapter on using art and play therapy and spiritual techniques to help with vocational discernment. As an added bonus, we have an entire chapter dedicated to building career counseling programs in schools and work settings. Along with programmatic information, this chapter covers specific activities school counselors can use when conducting vocational counseling with all ages. Readers will find the case illustrations, guided practice activities, and expert reflections that accompany each chapter interesting, relevant, and helpful. Currently, there are no textbooks on the market that emphasize the practical application piece.

To further meet these goals, our textbook is divided into three main sections. The chapters are arranged to flow from knowledge to more extensive application. The first section covers the history and major theories of career counseling. The reader will learn how historical and political events shaped the practice of career counseling and career assessment. Students will understand how career counseling emerged, why it is a needed counseling specialty today, how vocational issues impact counseling sessions and relationships, and future directions predicted for the field.

The second section focuses on career counseling with diverse populations. Readers will learn about age-related career issues and best practices when working with diverse clients of all ages. Sections discuss particular issues, theories, and methods for helping clients overcome age-related oppression, and unequal opportunities and stress particular interventions depending on client age. Strategies for helping youth establish career goals in elementary, middle, and high schools are discussed and followed by specific interventions for working adults and retirees. Career issues faced by those coming from diverse populations are thoroughly discussed in this section and further enhanced in the epilogue. Authors focus on particular issues, theories, and methods for helping clients overcome oppression and unequal opportunities and stress particular interventions. Strategies for helping minorities, women, LGBTQ persons, individuals with disabilities, displaced workers, the economically disadvantaged, military veterans, and ex-offenders are discussed, and strategies are given to help with career- and advocacy-related issues.

The third section focuses on practical applications. Readers will learn how to approach career counseling assessment as a holistic process that begins with intake assessment and ranges from informal, non-standardized assessments to formal, standardized assessments. You will learn about the types of assessments and how and why they are used, as well as reliability, validity, and ethical issues involved in career assessment. As the book comes to an end, readers learn about the practical aspects of working with clients and how assessment and one's theoretical orientation all come together. The reader will gain information needed to create career counseling programs in schools and work settings.

In addition, each chapter includes the following:

- **Learning objectives** based on the CACREP standards
- **Guided practice exercises**, which include mini case studies, tables, charts, and activities
- Rich **case illustrations** to demonstrate the applied practice of the content
- **Author reflections** in which authors share how they apply and use the material in their practice
- **Keystones**, which contain bulleted main summary points
- **Additional resources**, including readings, websites, and videos for additional study

Each chapter is written by experts in our field who have been recognized nationally for their publications and leadership in counseling. Students introduced to the topics in this text have the unique and unusual advantage of exposure to not only expert knowledge but also to their personal reflections, strategies, and unique case illustrations. Where else can students hear so many personal reflections and stories and even read advice from so many top counselors in the field?

We realize that this text alone cannot adequately address all the issues one may come across with career counseling. However, we hope that exposure to the rich, substantive, and interesting material not only increases learning but answers the questions "What does career counseling look like? How might I use it with my clients to improve client services and outcomes." We hope you enjoy reading the many differing views and strategies in the text as much as we did!

ACKNOWLEDGMENTS

I can't thank Brandé Flamez and Mary Mayorga enough for helping make this project successful. I couldn't ask for better colleagues. I also want to thank the chapter authors for enduring all the edits and requests with a smile. You are the reason this book made it to the finish line. To Kassie, Amy, and the entire Cognella staff, thank you for everything you did to help make this book the best it can be. I feel honored and blessed to have the support and help of so many!

—Janet Hicks

Completing a project of this scope would not have been accomplished without the perseverance, dedication, hard work, and wonderful help from the contributing authors. To each of you, I extend my sincere appreciation for helping create a career counseling book that truly shows what career counseling looks like.

A special thank you to my dear friend and coeditor, Janet Hicks, for inviting me to be a part of this project. There are friends and there are family and then there are "framily"—those friends who become our family. Your work ethic and how you approach everything with kindness is awe inspiring! I am grateful for Janet and Mary's friendship.

I would like to thank those at Cognella who helped turn our vision into reality, especially my first editor, Kassie Graves, now vice president of editorial. Your support, patience, and encouragement are invaluable, and this book would not have been possible without your involvement and your continued support throughout the years. Finally, I would like to give a warm thank you to Amy Smith, our senior project editor, for her helpful and enthusiastic responses.

Each and every one of you has my sincere appreciation and gratitude.

—Brandé Flamez

I want to thank Janet Hicks who has been a colleague and a great friend and who is welcoming and willing to share her knowledge and success with me and always takes the time to introduce me to others in our field who have turned into exceptional colleagues and friends. Thank you Brandé for your friendship. To my husband, daughters, grandchildren, family and friends who have stood by me in my career journey and foray into professional writing, thank you all for always saying "You can do this."

—Mary Mayorga

1

Foundations and Major Theories of Career Counseling

CHAPTER

The History and Future of Career Counseling

Janet Hicks, Brande Flamez, Mary Mayorga, DeAnna Green,

and Garrik Dennis

The best way to predict the future is to create it.
—Abraham Lincoln

As evidenced in this quote, Abraham Lincoln realized that change occurs when people decide to make a difference. Fortunately, those who came before us decided to make the changes needed to advance career counseling and created a number of assessments and technological systems that influence how we find jobs and advance our careers today. From the ideas and practices of Frank Parsons to assessments created by Cattel, Strong, and others, we have a foundation on which to build our profession. Because career counseling must morph in response to changing career demands, politics, and the global economy, we know we must build on this foundation and change with the future if we are to meet client needs. This chapter begins our voyage through the foundations and future of career counseling that will continue throughout this textbook.

CHAPTER OVERVIEW

Career counselors, and the counseling profession itself, owe much to our predecessors who took risks and shared their knowledge. These people set the stage for career counseling, created new processes, and, because of their input, we can successfully move our profession forward and into the future. Keep reading to discover the historical and political events that shaped the practice of career counseling and career assessment. The following sections will expose you to the beginnings of career counseling, why it is a needed counseling specialty today, how vocational issues impact counseling sessions and relationships, and future directions predicted for the field.

LEARNING OBJECTIVES

After reading this chapter you will be able to do the following:

- Understand the history and origins of career counseling
- Know the origins of career assessment
- Recognize current issues in the career counseling field
- Discover websites and technology that aid in career exploration
- Identify impending future job, career, and career counseling trends

Historical Background

Knowledge of the origins of career counseling is important if we are to best understand its significance. Looking back to the end of the 19th century and beginning of the 20th century, the United States was transitioning from an economy primarily based on agriculture to one advancing with the industrial revolution (Herr, 2001). These economic changes brought on new job opportunities, and Americans moved into urban areas to find these opportunities. These things, along with an influx of immigrants coming to the United States for job opportunities, created an increased need for vocational guidance (Herr, 2001).

This new vocational guidance was influenced by several key people. These individuals wanted to go beyond just helping others find a paying job. They wanted to help them find an occupation that matched interests and skills. Some of those visionaries who played a role in the development of career counseling included Jesse Buttrock Davis, Frank Parsons, Harry Kitson, and Donald Super. Let's read more about these historic persons in the sections that follow.

Jesse Davis

Jesse Buttrick Davis was passionate about education and advocated for access to free public schools, a belief that led to his career in education. He is often considered the first school counselor in the United States because he developed the first guidance program in public schools (Pope, 2009). Let's look at Davis's background and vocational contributions in more detail.

Davis graduated from Colgate University in 1895 and accepted his first job as a teacher at Detroit Central High school. He later became Detroit Central High School's 11th-grade principal, where he saw a need to conduct vocational and moral guidance sessions for his students. Today, these sessions are largely viewed as being the forerunner to current school counseling programs (Pope, 2009).

Davis also impacted vocational counseling through publications, school development, and counseling associations. His stance on vocational awareness was published in his book, *Vocational and Moral Guidance* in 1914 (Davis, 1914). This book was widely used when incorporating vocational guidance in schools during the beginning of the 20th century (Pope, 2009). Davis also went on to create the first junior high school as well as the first junior college in Michigan. Finally, he became one of the founders of the National Vocational Guidance Association (NVGA), a group discussed later in this chapter (Pope, 2009).

Frank Parsons

Parsons is widely considered to be the father of vocational guidance (Herr, 2001). He believed finding the right job was crucial and, in fact, stated that choosing a vocation was equally as important as choosing a husband or wife (Parsons, 1909). He was so emphatic about helping clients, particularly immigrants, with career choice that, in 1908, he developed a center called the Vocation Bureau in Boston. This Vocation Bureau is often equated as being the foundation upon which all professional counseling in the United States began (Gummere, 1988).

Parsons's vocational program involved knowledge and understanding as part of a three-factor process: (a) knowledge of self, (b) knowledge of different lines or work, and (c) understanding of the relationship between self, work, and independent decision making. Zytowski and Swanson (1994) stated that this three-part vocational planning process was an important piece of career counseling and is pertinent even today. You will learn more about Parson'ss premises in Chapter 2 where we discuss trait and factor theories.

National Vocational Guidance Association (NVGA)

The National Vocational Guidance Association (NVGA) is forerunner to the National Career Development Association (NCDA). This organization, a division of the American Counseling Association (ACA), is a leader in career development and counseling and has over 5,000 members (Pope, 2009). Its origins can be traced back to November of 1910 when the Boston Chamber of Commerce, the Vocational Bureau, and Boston schools held the first national vocational guidance conference (Smith et al., 1985).

The first few NVGA conferences focused on developing the organization and furthering career counseling issues. For example, the first conference focused on the importance of vocational guidance and on helping students make transitions to work. The second national conference focused on vocational guidance in schools. During the third conference, held in October 1913 in Grand Rapids, Michigan, the organization's constitution was adopted and officers were elected (Smith et al., 1985).

Since its inception, NVGA sought to meet the needs of society and provide vocational guidance. Following are a couple of examples that illustrate this involvement. First, during the Great Depression, the organization prepared and published relevant information on vocational decision making. Second, when soldiers were returning from WWII in the 1940s, NVGA assisted returning veterans needing help finding job information (Smith et al., 1985). Today, the NCDA continues to assist through online publications, trainings, resources, standards, and authoring/disseminating ethical codes (NCDA, 2015).

Donald Super

Donald E. Super (1980) said it well when he stated that "a career is defined as the combination and sequence of roles played by a person during the course of a lifetime" (p. 282). According to William C. Bingham (2001), Super was one of the leading experts in career development, and he offered two major and popular contributions: the life career rainbow and the archway of career determinants (Bingham, 2001). The life career rainbow considers an individual's career journey, including internal and external factors, and is a representation of the life space that covers an individual's life span (Bingham, 2001). The archway of career determinants represents the resources that an individual has available (Bingham, 2001; Super, 1980). Chapter 4 describes Super's theories and these components in greater detail.

Shaping Career Assessment

Career assessment also played a major role in the development of vocational counseling and was shaped by several major historical figures. Read along and you will learn some fascinating information about those who designed and influenced career assessment.

James Cattell is remembered as being the person who coined the term *mental test* (Sokal, 1980). He grew up in an upper middle–class home and attended Lafayette College in 1876 (Sokal, 2016). With the help of his parents, he was awarded a fellowship at Johns Hopkins University in 1882, where he went on to work in the university's psychological laboratory (Sokal, 2016). While working in this lab, Cattell measured how long it took people to identify letters as well as read words in the Latin alphabet. Cattell placed words and letters on a drum (kymograph), placed the drum behind a screen, and asked participants to read the letters. By altering speed and letter size, he was able to assess the processing time of different individuals (Cattell, 1886; Sokal, 2016).

Cattell continued his research through his employment at Cambridge and Columbia University. Measuring intelligence became his focus, and his quantitative experiments helped establish psychology as a legitimate science. Cattell's experiments also formed much of the foundation upon which today's vocational testing is based (Sokal, 1980).

Hugo Münsterberg is regarded as being the founder of applied psychology. He dedicated himself to the application of psychology with industry and believed psychology could contribute to quality of life (Moskowitz, 1977; Spillman & Spillman, 1993). He believed one way to use psychology and also impact industry and improve lives was through vocational counseling. For example, his focus on vocational counseling is illustrated through his famous quote,, "the best possible man, the best possible work, and the best possible effect" (Spillman & Spillman, 1993, p. 331).

From these vocational premises, Münsterberg developed a system of career guidance, including factors such as job satisfaction, high achievement, and psychological factors like prediction and control. He called this new science psychotechnics, which preceded ergonomics and industrial psychology (Spillman & Spillman, 1993). He also wrote *Vocation and Learning* (Münsterberg, 1912), a five-part book including a three-part triangular psychological theory on vocation which consisted of (a) thinking or knowledge, (b) feeling or demands and desire, and (c) willing or a combination of action and motive (Porfeli, 2009). He combined this theory with a trait-and-factor approach and created a correspondence course that would help individuals find fitting vocations (Porfeli, 2009).

The Army Alpha/Beta Tests

When the United States declared war on Germany on April 2, 1917, the American Psychological Association felt compelled to help with the war effort. As a result, they formed a committee called the Psychological Examination of the Recruits, which included members such as Robert Yerkes, Arthur Otis, and Lewis Terman (Richardson & Johanningmeier, 1998). This committee wrote a letter to the Surgeon General stating they had the ability to help distinguish unfit military recruits from those possessing higher intelligence (Richardson & Johanningmeier, 1998). Two weeks later, the committee created two different tests: the Army alpha, a verbal test, and the Army beta, a nonverbal test (Richardson & Johanningmeier, 1998). This new testing program was put into effect, and by January 1919, over 1.7 million men had been tested and assigned military duties based on their scores (Richardson & Johanningmeier, 1998). These tests are forerunners of tests still used today.

Strong Interest Inventory

Edward Kellog Strong, Jr., developed his original interest inventory, the Strong Vocational Interest Blank, in 1927 (Donnay, 1997). The basis of Strong's inventory fits with Parsons's principle of matching people with jobs (Donnay, 1997). Since its first release, it has been edited six times and is now known as the Strong Interest Inventory. It is the most commonly used psychological instrument and boasts the longest history (Donnay, 1997). Chapter 8 will discuss career assessment and the Strong Interest Inventory in greater detail.

Donald G. Paterson

Donald Paterson enlisted in the Army during WWI and served on the Army's Psychological Examining of Recruits' Committee where, for over 2 years, he administered the Army alpha and Army beta tests ((Erdheim et al., 2007). Upon leaving the military, he was hired by the Scott Company to help create its file clerk test (Erdheim et al., 2007). His focus was on job fit from the perspective of the individual and the employer. He strove to create assessments that employers could use to select the best employees, hopefully leading to company efficiency and employee satisfaction (Erdheim et al., 2007).

Clark Hull

The opening line of Clark Hull's (1928) book *Aptitude Testing* is "THE most accurate method of determining the aptitude of an individual for a vocation or other activity is the test of life itself" (p. 1). In other words, being able to observe how well a person learns a vocation and performs would be the most ideal test of aptitude (Hull, 1928). Hull's writing impacted society and, in response, a new need for aptitude tests emerged.

John Crites

The Career Maturity Inventory (CMI), developed by John Crites, was first administered in 1961 and was the first pencil and paper assessment of vocational development (Savickas & Porfeli, 2011). The instrument intends to measure student occupational readiness through 50 true-or-false items. The instrument is still widely used to assess career maturity today. More information on the Career Maturity Inventory, assessment, and recent instruments will be addressed in Chapter 8. Guided Practice Exercise 1.1 asks you to consider the Career Maturity Inventory and its development.

Guided Practice Exercise 1.1

Pretend you know nothing about career assessment. Now assume someone just came to you and asked if you could determine which children in grades 5 through 12 are "where they should be" regarding career development. How would you assess this? How would you determine what is "on track" for these children? Crites was probably discussing many of your responses years ago when he developed the Career Maturity Inventory.

Now that we understand the roots of career counseling and testing, let's look at the current directions in the field.

Current Directions

The following section discusses some of the current directions the field of vocational counseling is taking. Let's begin by discussing the use of technology in career counseling.

Technology

"What do you do?" This is an intuitively posed career question often asked when meeting a stranger today. As illustrated by this question, the close tie between career and personal identity has long been established in our culture and seems to provide healthy pride in meaningful positions or existential quandaries for those not employed in fulfilling roles. With the rapidly growing technological marketplace providing new forms of career search and interview processes, a disparate environment exists where finding a suitable position can be difficult and time consuming. Fortunately, many modern tools and techniques exist to help find the best-suited positions, thus offering our clients career and life fulfillment. Let's look at some of these tools.

O*Net

The *Occupational Information Network*, otherwise known as the *O*Net*, is a massive data collection site where one finds large swathes of information about most positions and titles in the American workforce. It is sponsored by the U.S. Department of Labor/Employment and Training Administration (USDOL/ETA) (O*Net, n.d.). Used by both job seekers and human resource managers to find a person/job fit, the O*Net presents information about job positions within its unique content model (i.e., worker oriented, occupation specific, job oriented, or cross occupational; O*Net, n.d.). Further classification divides positions by categories such as worker characteristics, worker requirements, experience requirements, occupational requirements, workforce characteristics, and occupation-specific information (O*Net, n.d.). This system lays the groundwork for a precise job-listing codification and is the most refined job search experience using the *Standard Occupational Classification* (SOC) system as developed by the Department of Labor (O*Net, n.d.).

The SOC is a classification system for almost 1,000 jobs in the American market. It is organized into categories of major groups, minor groups, broad occupations, and specific, individual occupations (U.S. Bureau of Labor Statistics, 2018). "The codification of each job is accomplished with the use of a six-digit system; the first two digits are separated from the other four and represent the major group of the job; the third digit shows the minor group, the fourth and fifth digits show the broad occupation, and the final digit represents the specific occupation" (U.S. Bureau of Labor Statistics, 2018, p. 3). Data is collected on these listed positions in order to share valuable job information with the public (O*Net, n.d.). This data guides job seekers to either the ideal position or at least to the right area in which to continue their detailed search. The classification system claims to encompass "all occupations in the US economy" and includes an "all other" category for those not specifically addressed in other listings (U.S. Bureau of Labor Statistics, 2018, p. 4).

In addition to a comprehensive classification system, the O*Net presents search functions for three broad areas, enveloping job seekers from all backgrounds. One can search for a suitable position using the "Find Occupations" function, searching for jobs by category of "Bright Outlook," "Industry," "Job Zone," and so on. (O*Net, n.d.). The "Advanced Search" function enables one to search for a job by sought abilities, interests, skills, and so on, and the "Crosswalks" search lets one find positions that translate in and out of military service (O*Net, n.d.). Regardless of a client's background or sought position, the O*Net provides information career counselors can use to help clients find fulfilling careers. Guided Practice Exercise 1.2 asks you to peruse the O*Net for better understanding.

Guided Practice Exercise 1.2 The O*Net

Take a moment and look up the following website: www.onetonline.org. Using the search box, type in "counselor" and see what information you can find. Familiarize yourself with this site, locating as much information as possible about your future career. What is the outlook for counseling as a vocation? How much do counselors make on average? What other information can you find?

Internet Job Search Engines and Interviews

When a client has narrowed their vision down to a specific type of position, the next step is to find where that particular job is located and which companies are currently hiring for that position. Job search engines and application processes can be vast and intimidating, but they also present opportunities for job seekers. Many existing job search engines offer a way for employees to connect with employers. Most search engines allow a client to search for their desired position and directly upload resumes or resume information on the site. Human resource personnel can then peruse information and schedule interviews. Career Coach Robert Hellman (as cited in Adams, 2012), advises spending as little time as possible wading through the online job searches; instead, he suggests spending time in some form of direct communication with desired companies.

A newer element in the world of resumes is the video format. A short film is produced by a job-seeking candidate who seeks to showcase a more personalized portrayal of their skills and characteristics. Much like meeting someone in person, the video resume adds some context to one's technical abilities and is becoming more popular in today's technologically saturated marketplace. Loft Resumes (n.d.) offers some examples of compelling video resumes that are posted online and suggests do's and don'ts for building one's product. Advice in building a video resume includes knowing the audience to whom the video will be sent, showcasing the specific skills and qualifications a company lists as being sought after, and presenting a well-produced, brief, and professionally appearing representation (Loft Resumes, n.d.). Guided Practice Exercise 1.3 asks you to examine sample video resumes.

Guided Practice Exercise 1.3 Video Resumes

Search "Video Resumes" online. Take a few minutes and listen to some samples. What are some advantages of this form of resume? What are some disadvantages? Do you feel competent to assist today's clients with these newer forms of interviewing? What skills do you need to improve on to be the best source of information for your clients?

Once a desired position is found, and the company fortress has been penetrated, career counseling clients will need to focus on preparing for the interview process. Interviews can be face to face or conducted over technology. They can also be the most intimidating, and yet most pivotal, component to gaining employment. The Muse (2020) lists many useful interview preparation methods, ranging from asking the hiring manager what method of interview will be used to dressing in a modern (and tailored) business outfit, pampering yourself so as to smooth over those seemingly less-noticed smaller details, creating an interview cheat sheet, and getting enough sleep. It definitely seems that preparation for interviews cannot be underestimated.

Technology and Assessment

Counselors have what may be viewed as an overwhelming array of career tools and techniques at their disposal. Helping clients gain self-awareness and insight into their own inherent nature and habits is an important factor in career counseling. Today's clients have the ability to gain this insight in part through online assessment or through pencil/paper tests. Read on as we discuss some of the pros and cons of both of these forms of assessment.

Both online and paper/pencil assessments offer advantages and disadvantages. For example, Internet testing relies on technology with inherent connection issues, clients may have technological learning deficits, and assessments may not have been normed for Internet use. Further, some clients may have disabilities that affect the ability to use technology. For example, vision problems may make seeing small print or lighting on a screen difficult. For this reason, counselors should always consider accessibility when choosing a testing format. Pencil/paper tests are also imperfect since they may also have accessibility issues, require long wait times, and are not instantaneously scored. Finally, it is important to consider cultural issues when deciding which form of assessment is best for your client. Instruments should be normed for use with the age, culture, and gender of the client tested (Hayes, 2013). Guided Practice Exercise 1.4 asks you to further compare online and paper/pencil assessments. Chapter 8 will go into greater detail on the limitations of these assessments.

Guided Practice Exercise 1.4 Assessment

The passage describes a few advantages and disadvantages of Internet and pencil/paper assessments. What might be additional advantages and disadvantages of online versus pencil/paper assessments? Can you think of some ethical or multicultural issues that might arise with either or both types of assessment? Have you ever taken an online assessment? Did you have any problems? What are some potential issues that test takers might experience?

The Integration of Career and Family/Personal Issues

Career issues impact family and personal issues. For this reason, the next section discusses some factors that must be considered when working with clients and their career issues. Let's begin by discussing stress and burnout.

Stress and Burnout

Stress can be loosely defined as a response to a demand; good stress is known as *eustress* and is characterized by focused energy (arguably being "in the zone"). It often feels exciting and is perceived as within one's coping abilities (Mills et al., 2019). Conversely, bad stress is known as *distress*, and is, perhaps, all too well known for causing anxiety, feeling beyond one's coping abilities, decreasing performance, and ultimately leading to mental and physical issues (Mills et al., 2019). Suffice to say then, that it is the goal of most job seekers to find the least distressing career, with the inclusion of a balance of a healthy load of positive stressors (eustress). A primary goal in finding a properly stressful position is to find one that does not lead to *burnout* or *rust out*, familiar terms in today's high-paced,

> *Burnout is nature's way of telling you, you've been going through the motions your soul has departed; you're a zombie, a member of the walking dead, a sleepwalker. False optimism is like administering stimulants to an exhausted nervous system.*
> —Sam Keen (n.d.)

caffeinated workplace. According to Mayo Clinic Staff (2018), burnout can be defined as "a state of physical or emotional exhaustion that also involves a sense of reduced accomplishment and loss of personal identity." Rust out, while not as debilitating as burnout, still results in lack of passion and excitement for one's position (Keen, 1991). According to the Mayo Clinic Staff (2018), the path that leads one to burnout includes having a lack of control over one's workload or schedule, a lack of clear expectations, the need to apply constant energy in order to keep up with ever-changing activities, and more personal issues such as having a lack of social support and simply not taking time to enjoy activities outside of the workplace.

Counseling Today senior writer Laurie Meyers (2015) notes that "workplace pressure has become so prevalent that both the World Health Organization and the National Institute for Occupational Safety and Health consider job stress to be a significant risk to public health." She continues by sharing input from Brenda Ramlo (LPC) who posits that her clients in private practice are seemingly faced with higher workloads, including the heightened expectation that communication (namely e-mail) be maintained at a higher level, essentially meaning that workers are more stressed while at work, but then taking it home with them and not regulating from the workday itself (Meyers, 2015). With the modern workplace becoming increasingly demanding and communication methods making time away from work fewer and farther between, counselors will likely see an increase in work (and stress) related issues for years to come. This may include increases in the secondary issues of substance use, social isolation, and depression.

The career counselor may find great benefit in bringing a client back to the basics of motivation in life. For example, helping a client map their overall life values may directly highlight how they wish to spend their time, both in and out of work. Meyers (2015) echoes Cristi Thielman, a licensed mental health counselor who sees many clients from employee assistance programs (EAPs), and notes that clients experiencing stress or burnout can benefit from assessing how they identify outside of their work life, and then in deciding how much time they would like to be spending in those areas.

Career counselors might assist clients through mindfulness techniques in order to facilitate a more desired work-life balance. Dr. B. Grace Bullock (2017) concluded that techniques such as meditation and body scans produced reduced stress and anxiety in the workplace, which also correlated to increased experiences of job satisfaction. It seems that Dr. Jon Kabat-Zinn (n.d.), founding executive director of the Center for Mindfulness in Medicine, Health Care, and Society at the University of Massachusetts Medical School, phrases this issue equally well: "You can't stop the waves, but you can learn to surf" (p. 1). Through this lens, a client's workload woes are less focused on finding the perfect stress-free position, but rather on balancing an acceptable position with the appropriate use of mindfulness techniques in order to soften the blow of the challenges it inevitably presents.

The Impact of Work and Work Issues on Relationships

With such exhaustion taking place in a way that transcends work and digs into one's core being, career counselors should note that work stress and burnout can lead to acute and profound client relationship issues (Lacovides et al., 2003). It is no surprise to most people in today's fast-paced work culture that relationship problems can quickly arise from work-derived stressors, and counselors must be armed with the tools necessary to facilitate clients' safe passage through them. One such tool presented by Dr. Elizabeth Hall is the *spillover-crossover model*, in which a client's tendency to bring work home (*spillover*) and stress about it results in transferring that negative stress to their spouse, subsequently causing mutual stress and even burnout (*crossover*; Hall, 2018). It is easy to see that if one were spending the majority of their waking hours in a position that exceeds their stress tolerance (or is frankly unchallenging and leaving one unfulfilled), they may tend to bring that discomfort home with them. The few remaining waking hours each day after work will likely be spent ruminating on the day's previous negative experiences, transitioning throughout the night and even repeating the occasion the following day.

Alexandra Katehakis, relationship therapist and clinical director for the Center for Healthy Sex in Los Angeles, California, presents this issue by stating that work stress results in an activated yet unresolved nervous system (as cited in Levi, 2018). Dr. Katehakis continues to note that this negative work energy is essentially channeled into one's spouse, and negative affect or emotion regarding a supervisor or coworker can quickly be handed off to a significant other at home.

Thankfully, though, there is light at the end of the work-stress tunnel. Dr. Hall (2018) also reminds us that work satisfaction and fulfillment can lead to a more positive vibe at home (positive spillover), which facilitates positive crossover and leads to a more fulfilled and satisfied home life. Dr. Katehakis suggests that those seeking to find a better balance at home turn to using a small dose of verbal discipline. Instead of unloading on a significant other about the intricate details of the day, she suggests sharing emotions about the events of the day. Chapter 14 will discuss couple, family, and career issues in greater detail. Case Example 1.1 asks you to categorize a client's experience based on spillover.

Case Example 1.1 Spillover

Linda and Manuel have been married for 30 years. Linda is a nurse and Manuel is a realtor. Linda walks in the door after work and angrily runs into the kitchen to start dinner. When Manuel enters the house a few minutes later, he asks what is for dinner. Linda says, "Please don't start. I don't need you pressuring me to cook tonight." Manuel looks at her and says, "I'm sorry. I didn't mean to upset you." Linda starts to cry and says she just needs some time to unwind.

What type of spillover might be occurring in this case? What would you suggest that might help Linda and Manuel?

Diagnosis and Occupation

The realm of career counseling does not inherently come with its own groupings of diagnoses to assist clinicians in helping clients gain desired employment. Thus, the themes of diagnoses in career counseling seem to revolve around either workaholism or diagnoses more common in the "non-career" counseling session such as depression and anxiety. *Workaholism*, although not a DSM-5 diagnosed mental health disorder at the time of this writing, is a potential issue for many clients. A broad definition of workaholism might include the unhealthy execution of work beyond one's ability to maintain physical/mental/emotional health, the recognition that work habits are continuously unhealthy, and that the person does not enjoy working excessively.

In today's fast-paced and competitive workplace, it is likely this issue will increase in frequency and intensity and will likely be a focus for many career counselors well into the future. A key reason that workaholism may be around for the long haul is the apparent social acceptance of its prevalence and symptoms. Because many cultures today appear to revolve around strong work ethic, it will become more useful for all counselors to share concepts such as mindfulness, relaxation, and self-care to ensure their clients have the needed resources to overcome the workplace challenges that the future will surely present.

Ethical Issues

Career counseling seeks to abide by a governing code of ethics and must consider issues related to their niche profession, given the unique circumstances clients face (ACA, 2014). The National Career Development Association (NCDA) is currently a division within the American Counseling Association (ACA) and maintains an independent code of ethics specific to those in the career counseling and career development professions (NCDA, n.d., 2015). Despite a separate document outlining the career counselor's ethical considerations, it coincides with the overarching ACA code of ethics. Both the ACA (2014) and NCDA (2015) ethical codes advise counselors to confront questionable decisions or practices through professional consultation. Career counseling ethical standards also reflect the ACA in encouraging adherence to the "fundamental principles of professional ethical behavior" throughout counseling a client, including *autonomy, non-maleficence, beneficence, objectivity, accountability, and veracity* (NCDA, 2015, p. 1). The NCDA, similar to the ACA, makes clear that the mission of the code of ethics is to protect the client and that situations will inevitably arise that require a sound decision-making process and an effective consultative network.

> *Each man is questioned by life; and he can only answer to life by answering for his own life; to life he can only respond by being responsible.*
> —Viktor Frankl

Another important ethical consideration for the career counselor is found in rather existential themes. When someone of the modern age begins ruminating on how they would like to spend most of their waking hours at work, they are also inherently digging to the root of their perceived purpose in life, the meaning they seek to create or find. Well-known career counselor, professor, and author Dr. Mark Savickas echoes sociologist Anthony Giddens in reflecting that modern people lack certain traditional aspects of life found in earlier eras, leaving them more prone to existential questions and perhaps crises (Savickas et al., 2009). Savickas, Nota, Rossier, Dauwalder, Duarte, Guichard, Soresi, Van Esbroeck, and van Vianen (2009) continue to urge the career counselor to help clients understand their unique life situations throughout career development by building for them a "contextualized model" from which they may begin to define and build their life. The profession of career counseling seems, then, to combine both the science of assessment and personality identification with the art of existential, solution-focused, and other approaches to therapy and help clients construct and find their desired life meanings.

Future Directions

Competent counselors do not live in a static world. We must always focus on changes occurring in the field. For this reason, let's delve into issues we must consider in the future. We begin with a discussion on the global economy as follows.

The Global Economy

As the world continues to move toward a global stage, the future direction of career development must move with it. Career education and career development is now being viewed from a global perspective, and one of the biggest issues in the minds of adults may be how to compete on the global stage (NAFSA, 2010). As early as the 1990s, educators and the economic industry recognized how career trends were changing to include a more global reach. Society became concerned with how to strengthen the competitive abilities of the incoming workforce (Kerka, 1993).

Preparing the workforce to function within a global economy has become a new mantra. The economy continually expands and interconnects, making it imperative that counselor educators understand and teach from a global perspective. New competitive frameworks may require clients to learn a new set of skills, including technical and interpersonal skills. These skills allow for a vital, innovative, and competitive economic future that plays out on a global stage.

As the world shrinks and the global economy increases, adults transitioning into a new career will be faced with learning a new set of rules and skills required to compete (NAFSA, 2010). For this reason, we can agree that examination of the globalization of the economy demonstrates a continued impact on individuals who are looking to start a career or transition into a new career. We can also agree that globalization of the economy and counseling is not frequently a concept that is discussed or addressed in the arena of counseling (Lorelle et al., 2012).

As the field of counseling, and especially career counseling, continues to expand and develop, counselor educators need to transform counseling from a Western-based practice to a more globally encompassing medium (Heppner, 1997). Lorelle et al. (2012) state that viewing the field of counseling from a global perspective places the field on the cusp of growth and innovation, especially in the field of career counseling. As changes continue to occur in the nature and structure of the economic systems in which society exists, individuals' values and beliefs about themselves, others, and the world will change (Gysbers et al., 2009).

To meet the changing trends of a global society and global economy, career counseling must broaden its scope and purposes. This involves the inclusion of numerous adult career transitions throughout the life span. Futuristic views of a changing global economy may well include expanding the existing career counseling theories to include theories that consider a global view of the economy and how best to prepare clients to enter this new change. Such a change involves not only a willingness but also an ability to refine and redefine current career counseling theories, along with a continued understanding of an international attitude of change and inclusion (Lorelle et al., 2012).

Because many of today's youth acquired technology skills at an early age and communicated exclusively via the Internet and texting, they may lack the ability to communicate without these forums. On the other hand, the older generation may have excellent verbal communication skills, but may not have the needed technology skills to compete in a global economy. Working with different age groups who may be miles apart in their abilities to compete in a global economy warrants examination of the impact of economic globalization on the field of career counseling.

Diversity and Multicultural Competence

Just as career counseling needs to be aware of global economics and its effects on career development, career counselors must prepare to work with a diverse population. This ability to work with and understand diverse populations who seek career direction includes the ability to be multiculturally competent.

Counselors must be well versed in applying appropriate services to help diverse people make career decisions (Lee, 2012).

The term *multiculturalism* was first coined in the early 1980s and 1990s and began to be referred to as the fourth force in the field of counseling (Sue et al., 2012). In spring 1991, the Association for Multicultural Counseling and Development (AMCD) approved a document outlining justifications for promoting a multicultural perspective in counseling. Since that time, multicultural counseling and the competencies continue to make an impact on the counseling profession in all areas, including career counseling. Cultural diversity is no longer a small part of counseling; instead, it has become a major factor in understanding counseling in all forms. Career counselors must provide services to help diverse populations make career decisions in an ever-changing world (Lee, 2012). Chapters 6 and 7 in this text discuss issues and methods for working with diverse clients in more detail.

The Changing Job Market

As the economy becomes more globally focused and the population continues to become more diverse, career counselors and clients must embrace lifelong learning. This is important not only for the counselor, but for the client who must deal with the changing economic landscape (Campanella, 2018). This changing landscape includes a constantly morphing job market that alternates economically between more workers and less jobs and vice versa. Clients will need strong skills and an education that lends itself to better outcomes. Career counselors must work diligently to help clients understand the need for transferable skills so that they meet job qualifications and have the ability to compete amongst other qualified job candidates (Green, 2014).

Competent career counselors must also provide accurate labor market information to clients if they are to be successful. Career counselors are expected to provide relevant information that describes a realistic job market and helps the client explore the information efficiently and effectively. Understanding the changing job market, determining occupational outlook, and deciphering job compensation are necessary when making career decisions. Career counselors can perform the needed but stressful task involved with keeping clients focused (NCDA, 2014).

Data from the U.S. Bureau of Labor Statistics indicates that while jobs are currently available, employers have problems finding job seekers whose skills align with available job opportunities (Gimbel & Sinclair, 2018). If employers are to find these qualified applicants, credentialed career counseling clients need access to career information, including (a) compensation and benefit packages, (b) the culture of the work environment, (c) and clear and appealing job opportunities (Lopez, 2018). Transparency seems to be key in appropriately matching employees with employers.

What does this mean for career counseling services? Simply put, it means staying abreast of the changing trends in employment availability and being cognizant that some jobs will be either harder or easier to fill. We might consider that a career counselor needs to work closely with both the client and the employer. As career counselors continue to play an important part in the global economy, we may begin to see a change in the field of career counseling from a dyad to a triad: moving from counselor-client to counselor-client-employer and evolving into a collaborative relationship that creates a win-win situation for everyone.

SUMMARY

Career counseling was formed by visionaries such as Jesse Buttrock Davis, Frank Parsons, Harry Kitson, Donald Super, James Cattell, and others. These people established the foundation of career counseling, created assessments, and set the stage for techniques we use today. Technological advancements such as the O*Net, search engines, and other Web-based career processes allow us to compete in our global economy and improve career-related issues affecting our families and relationships closer to home.

Keystones

- Jesse Davis is considered by many to be the first school counselor in the United States.
- Frank Parsons is widely considered the father of vocational guidance.
- The National Vocational Guidance Association (NVGA) is the forerunner to the National Career Development Association.
- Cattell, Munsterberg, Otis, Strong, Patterson, Hull, and Crites played a major role in the development of career assessment.
- The O*Net is a data collection site where one finds information about positions and titles in the American workforce.
- Work stress and burnout can lead to acute and profound client relationship issues.
- Career counselors abide by professional codes of ethics.
- Preparing the workforce to function in a global economy, working with a diverse population, and morphing with a changing job market are important future considerations.

Author Reflections

Beginning counselors often misunderstand the importance of career counseling and don't value its importance and background when working with clients. Career counseling and personal counseling are so related that they cannot be separated. In fact, career counseling formed the foundation of today's counseling profession. As you read this text, I hope you see how career happiness and success impacts personal factors and vice versa. As you continue to read, you will see that our careers are such an important part of our lives that they affect every aspect of our happiness. Yes, career counseling *is* personal counseling and personal counseling involves aspects of a person's career identity. —Janet Hicks

Additional Resources

The following resources provide additional information about the content provided in this chapter.

Websites

Business News Daily: www.businessnewsdaily.com

This news site offers updated career information on a routine basis. The site addresses topics such as employee behaviors that impact careers, current business climate, and skills for success.

Career Research: http://career.iresearchnet.com/career-counseling/

This site offers a summary of career counseling, its practices, and its clientele.

Indeed Hiring Lab: www.hiringlab.org

This site offers up-to-date career and labor information.

National Association of Colleges and Employers: www.naceweb.org

This site offers career readiness resources relevant to college student, graduates, and employers.

National Career Development Association (NCDA): www.ncda.org

This is the website of the NCDA, a division of the American Counseling Association.

O*Net: https://www.onetonline.org

This government website gives details about careers and the labor market and assists with career exploration.

References

Adams, S. (2012, January 18). *Secrets of making the most of job search websites.* Forbes. https://www.forbes.com/sites/susanadams/2012/01/18/secrets-of-making-the-most-of-job-search-websites/#600dcb7637fe

American Counseling Association. (2014). *2014 ACA Code of ethics.* https://www.counseling.org/resources/aca-code-of-ethics.pdf

American Psychological Association. (n.d.). *Industrial and organizational psychology.* https://www.apa.org/ed/graduate/specialize/industrial

Bingham, W. C. (2001). Donald Super: A personal view of the man and his work. *International Journal for Education and Vocational Guidance, 1*(1), 21–29.

Bullock, B. G. (2017, August 14). *How mindfulness beats job stress and burnout.* Mindful. https://www.mindful.org/mindfulness-beats-job-stress-burnout/

Campanella, E. (2018). *To succeed in a changing job market, we must embrace lifelong learning.* We Forum. Retrieved from https://www.weforum.org/agenda/2018/07/the-cognitive-limits-of-lifelong-learning/

Cattell, J. M. (1886). The time it takes to see and name objects. *Mind, 11*(46), 63–65.

Davis, J. B. (1914). *Vocational and moral guidance.* Ginn.

Donnay, D. A. (1997). E.K Strong's legacy and beyond: 70 years of the Strong Interest Inventory. *Career Development Quarterly, 46,* 2–22.

Erdheim, J., Zickar, M. J., & Yankelevich, M. (2007). Remembering Donald G. Paterson: Before the separation between industrial-organizational and vocational psychology. *Journal of Vocational Behavior, 70*(1), 205–221.

Gimbel, M., & Sinclair, T. (2018). *State of the labor market: The US labor market is changing fast—but job seekers are keeping up.* https://www.hiringlab.org/2018/09/20/us-labor-market-changing/

Green, A. (2014). *8 ways the economy is still affecting the job market.* U.S. News & World Report. https://money.usnews.com/money/blogs/outside-voices-careers/2014/01/08/8-ways-the-economy-is-still-affecting-the-job-market

Gummere, R. M. (1988). The counselor as prophet: Frank Parsons 1854–1908. *Journal of Counseling & Development, 66*(9), 402–405.

Gysbers, N. C., Heppner, M. J., & Johnston, J. A. (2009). *Career counseling: Contexts, processes, and techniques.* American Counseling Association.

Hall, E. D. (2018, March 3). *Why work stress is bad for your relationships.* Psychology Today. https://www.psychologytoday.com/us/blog/conscious-communication/201803/why-work-stress-is-bad-your-relationship

Hayes, D. (2013). *Assessment in counseling: A guide to the use of psychological assessment.* American Counseling Association.

Heppner, P. P. (1997). Building on strengths as we move into the next millennium. *The Counseling Psychologist, 25*(1), 5–14.

Herr, E. L. (2001). Career development and its practice: A historical perspective. *Career Development Quarterly, 49*, 196–211.

Hull, C. L. (1928). *Aptitude testing.* World Book Company.

Kabat-Zinn, J. (n.d.). *You can't stop the waves, but you can learn to surf.* Counseling and Mindfulness Group. https://counselingand-mindfulness.com/you-cant-stop-the-waves-but-you-can-learn-to-surf-jon-kabat-zinn/

Keen., S. (n.d.). AZQuotes.com. https://www.azquotes.com/quote/794043

Keen, S. (1991). *Fire in the belly: On being a man.* Bantam.

Kerka, S. (1993). *Career education for a global economy.* US Department of Education.

Lacovides, A., K. Fountoulakis, K., S. Kaprinis, S., & Kaprinis, G. (2003). The relationship between job stress, burnout, and depression. *Journal of Affective Disorders, 75*(3), 209–221. https://doi.org/10.1016/S0165-0327(02)00101-5

Lee, C. C. (2012). A conceptual framework for culturally competent career counseling practice. *Career Planning and Adult Development Journal, 28*(1), 7–19.

Levi, A. (2018, February 28). *Exactly what to do when work stress messes with your relationship.* Health. https://www.health.com/relationships/work-stress-relationship-problems

Loft Resumes. (n.d.). *5 of the world's most creative video resumes.* https://loftresumes.com/blogs/news/6000724-5-of-the-worlds-most-creative-video-resumes

Lopez, J. (2018). 5 ways the job market will change in 2019. *Business News Daily.* https://www.businessnewsdaily.com/9633-job-market-predictions.html

Lorelle, S., Byrd, R., & Crockett, S. (2012). Globalization and counseling: professional issues for counselors. *The Professional Counselor, 2*(2), 115–123.

Mayo Clinic Staff. (2018). *Job burnout: How to spot it and take action.* https://www.mayoclinic.org/healthy-lifestyle/adult-health/in-depth/burnout/art-20046642

Meyers, L. (2015, December 22). *Worrying for a living.* Counseling Today. https://ct.counseling.org/2015/12/worrying-for-a-living/#

Mental Help Net. (2020). *Types of stressors (eustress vs. distress).* American Addiction Centers. https://www.mentalhelp.net/articles/types-of-stressors-eustress-vs-distress/

Moskowitz, M. J. (1977). Hugo Münsterberg: A study in the history of applied psychology. *American Psychologist, 32*(10), 824–842.

Münsterburg, H. (1912). *Vocation and learning.* Peoples University.

NAFSA, Association of International Educators. (2010). *Educating students for success in the global economy: A public opinion survey on the importance of international education.* Author.

National Career Development Association (NCDA). (n.d.). *NCDA history.* https://www.ncda.org/aws/NCDA/pt/sp/about_history

National Career Development Association (NCDA). (2015). *2015 NCDA Code of ethics.* https://www.ncda.org/aws/NCDA/asset_manager/get_file/3395

Occupational Information Network (O*NET). (2019). https://www.onetonline.org/

Pope, M. (2009). Jesse Buttrock Davis (1871–1955): Pioneer of vocational guidance in the schools. *Career Development Quarterly, 57*, 248–258.

Porfeli, E. J. (2009). Hugo Münsterberg and the origins of vocational guidance. *Career Development Quarterly, 57*, 225–236.

Richardson, T., & Johanningmeier, E. V. (1998). Intelligence testing: The legitimation of a meritocratic educational science. *International Journal of Educational Research, 27*(8), 699–714.

Savickas, M. L., Nota, L., Rossier, J., Dauwalder, J., Duarte, M. E., Guichard, J., Soresi, S., Van Esbroeck, R., & van Vianen, A. E. (2009). Life designing: A paradigm for career construction in the 21st century. *Journal of Vocational Behavior, 75*(3), 239–250. https://www.sciencedirect.com/science/article/pii/S000187910900058X

Savickas, M. L., & Porfeli, E. J. (2011). Revision of the Career Maturity Inventory: The adaptability form. *Journal of Career Assessment, 19*(4), 355–374.

Sokal, M. M. (1980). Science and James McKeen Cattell, 1894–1945. *Science, 209*(4452), 43–52.

Sokal, M. M. (2016). Launching a career in psychology with achievement and arrogance: James McKeen Cattell at the Johns Hopkins University, 1882–1883. *Journal of the History of Behavioral Sciences, 52*(1), 5–19. https://doi.org/10.1002/jhbs.21764

Spillman, J., & Spillman, L. (1993). The rise and fall of Hugo Münsterberg. *Journal of the History of the Behavioral Sciences, 29*(4), 322–338.

Smith, R. L., Engels, D. W., & Bonk, E. C. (1985). The past and future: The National Vocational Guidance Association. *Journal of Counseling & Development, 63*(7), 420–424.

Sue, D. W., Arredondo, P., & McDavis, R. J. (2012). Multicultural counseling competencies and standards: A call to the profession. *Journal of Counseling & Development, 70*(4), 477–486.

Super, D. E. (1980). A life-span, life-space approach to career development. *Journal of Vocational Behavior, 16*(3), 282–298.

The Muse. (2020.). *The ultimate interview guide: 30 prep tips for job interview success.* https://www.themuse.com/advice/the-ultimate-interview-guide-30-prep-tips-for-job-interview-success

U.S. Bureau of Labor Statistics. (2018). *Standard occupational classification and coding structure.* https://www.bls.gov/soc/2018/soc_2018_class_and_coding_structure.pdf

Whiston, S. C., & Blustein, D. L. (2013). *The impact of career interventions: Preparing our citizens for the 21st century jobs.* National Career Development Association & Society for Vocational Psychology.

Zytowski, D. G., & Swanson, J. L. (1994). Parson's contribution to career assessment. *Journal of Career Development, 20*(4), 305–310.

CHAPTER

Trait- and Decision-Based Theories in Career Counseling

Macy Waltz, Lynn Jennings, Stephen Jennings, and Janet Hicks

The only way to do great work is to love what you do. If you haven't found it yet, keep looking. Don't settle.
—Steve Jobs

When I first read this quote, I couldn't help but feel inspired and hopeful. It is exciting to know that, as career counselors, we have the opportunity to influence the lives of our clients in such positive ways. The idea that everyone has this opportunity to find happiness through a perfect job fit goes all the way back to the origins of counseling. As discussed in Chapter 1, counseling first evolved through a focus on matching client traits with job factors, thus assisting with vocational discernment. It isn't surprising, then, to learn that many of the basic career counseling ideas used today involve matching a person's characteristics with the factors needed in the job environment. Continue reading to learn information about the theorists who created these trait and factor theories, how they work, and how these theories can aid in the career decision-making process.

CHAPTER OVERVIEW

This chapter outlines the major trait and factor and decision-making vocational theories discussed in the career counseling literature. Basic premises, assessment, steps in the process, and limitations of the theorists' contentions are discussed in the sections that follow. Two case studies are included in the chapter to help you thoroughly understand how these theories are applicable with clients.

LEARNING OBJECTIVES

After reading this chapter you will be able to do the following:

- Know the origins, basic premises, and techniques used as part of the trait and factor and career decision-making theories
- Understand the limitations of trait and factor and career decision-making theories
- Recognize how assessment plays a role in trait and factor and career decision-making theories
- Apply concepts of trait and factor and decision-making theories when working with a fictional client

Frank Parsons and E.G. Williamson's Trait Theory: Premise of Theory

Frank Parsons's (1909) book entitled *Choosing A Vocation* begins by stating, "No step in life, unless it may be the choice of a husband or wife, is more important than the choice of vocation" (p. 21). Parsons was confident in the early 1900s that choosing a career path was life changing for an individual. In fact, Frank Parsons and E.G. Williamson's exploration on vocational guidance contributed greatly to career development and paved the way for future researchers. The concepts were developed into what we now know as the first career counseling theory, trait and factor theory. Let's break down this theory in order to acquire a clear grasp of its concepts.

Parsons's (1909) book described three steps an individual might take when selecting an occupation:

1. A clear understanding of yourself, your aptitudes, abilities, interests, ambitions, resources, limitations, and their causes
2. A knowledge of the requirements and conditions of success, advantages and disadvantages, compensation, opportunities, and prospects in different lines of work
3. True reasoning on the relationship between these two groups of facts

Several key terms offer further insight into Parsons's premises. For example, a *trait* can be defined as a distinguished characteristic or attribute (e.g., aptitudes, abilities, interests, ambitions, resources, limitations) of an individual that can be measured objectively, in this case through the use of psychological tests. The term *factor* examines characteristics of a job or line of work, including requirements and conditions, advantages and disadvantages, and compensation. The aptitude of a person is determining one's natural ability to perform a job. Aptitude is not as accurate as a person's interests when it comes to helping a client select an occupation.

Guided Practice Exercise 2.1 helps you better understand this connection between aptitude and interests. It encourages you to evaluate your own aptitudes, interests, abilities, and ambitions by creating a list. You will then spend time processing what you wrote down to determine if any connections exist.

Guided Practice Exercise 2.1 Introduction to Trait and Factor theory

After reading the steps listed by Frank Parsons related to trait and factor theory, what would your own personal assessment be for step 1? Create a brief list of your aptitudes, abilities, interests, and ambitions. Discuss your answers with a partner. In addition, share with your partner about a past job you believe did not fit your character traits. Was it difficult for you to feel motivated while working there? Did you feel like you were thriving?

The assessment involved in Parson's (1909) first two steps can provide significant assistance to a counselor helping a client with career choice. For example, trait and factor theory examines the person and job through the assessment of traits, interests, aptitudes, and job factors. The hope is for individuals to be connected to a job based off the relationship between their individual traits and the characteristics of the job.

Assessing individuals and the job market by using statistical measures and psychometric systems came years later. Researchers, including E.G. Williamson, used Parsons's original concepts to create new instruments and classification systems at the University of Minnesota. During World War II, trait and factor career assessments were further developed and utilized to assign recruits to suitable positions in the 1930s and 1940s. Federal funding was also provided toward these assessments in hopes of enhancing the war effort, which, in turn, positively impacted trait and factor theory. This continued focus and research on assessment during and after the war enhanced the reputation of the University of Minnesota and culminated in E.G. Williamson's directive and informative approach called the *Minnesota point of view*. Consequently, E.G. Williamson became known as a great contributor to trait and factor theory.

If you plan to pursue trait and factor theory and integrate it into your theoretical career counseling framework, it is important to know there are thousands of job descriptions, occupations, and, therefore, factors available today. Is trait and factor the best theory to use with clients? This is a good question. Determining which theory is best to use with a specific client may be difficult, and few studies report on the effectiveness therein (Atli, 2016). For this reason, counselors must spend time learning information about their client before providing any career assistance. Let's look at some assessments a trait and factor theorist might use to best understand their client's interests, aptitudes, and values in the next section.

Assessment

Trait and factory theory paved the way for the development of multiple assessments to be created. In the early stages, counselors relied on interviews and one-on-one discussions with clients to learn information.

This meant trait and factor theory's first step in the assessment process consisted of helping the client gain self-understanding by answering questions about his or her aptitudes, achievements, interests, values, personality, and assessments. This process morphed into a variety of assessments used to answer these questions today. Table 2.1 shows a list of assessment tools available for counselors to utilize in this process.

TABLE 2.1   **Trait and Factor Theory Assessments**

Scholastic Assessment Test (SAT)	Certification tests
American College Testing assessment (ACT)	Kuder Career Search
Differential Aptitude Test (DAT)	Strong Interest Inventory
Sixteen Personality Factor Questionnaire	O*Net Ability Profiler
Grades (academic achievement)	Thematic Apperception Test
Minnesota Multiphasic Personality Inventory	Super's Work Values-Revised
Work (feedback from employers or supervisors)	

Counselors will also want to be familiar with information about different occupations and their responsibilities (factors) to move clients through trait and factor theory's second step: being familiar with different lines of work. Luckily, several sources are available that categorize occupations. This means we do not have to sift through every single occupation available (over 12,000) to narrow it down to a short list for the client. Table 2.2 shows a list of systems counselors can utilize that categorize jobs and help clients learn about various occupations.

TABLE 2.2   **Systems**

Occupational Outlook Handbook (OOH)
U.S. Department of Labor
Dictionary of Occupational Titles (DOT)
O*Net classification system (replaced the DOT in the late 1990s)
Standard Occupational Classification System

Steps, Model, and Application

Williamson and Darley (1937) developed a six-step model to help counselors apply trait and factor theory. Following you will find the name of each step and a short paraphrase from Williamson and Darley's (1937) publication, *Student Personnel Work: An Outline of Clinical Procedures*.

The first step, *analysis*, focuses on gathering information through client interviews, assessments, questionnaires, and scaling questions. Some of the tests or questionnaires are given before the first session. The initial session will be an interview or intake comprised of closed and open-ended questions.

This provides the counselor an opportunity to develop a therapeutic relationship with the client while collecting, organizing, and evaluating information provided by the client.

The second step, *synthesis*, works toward assessing all the information from step one. Imagine opening a puzzle box and pouring out all of the pieces on a table. You must spend time figuring out the border of the puzzle and then separating pieces into piles that may go together. Diagnosing the client's issue takes time and effort; the counselor must find patterns in a client's behavior by organizing the puzzle pieces (client information, assessments, questionnaire, etc.) before completing the puzzle (making a diagnosis and projection). After synthesizing the information, a counselor will provide an explanation to the client about the information provided through each measure (interview, assessments, etc.). The counselor may ask more questions during this time if the client shared an interest in a specific field for clarification.

The counselor will identify the problem, causes, and a possible action plan in the third step, *diagnosis*. There may be outside stimuli influencing a client, for example to quit a job, earn a bigger salary, or even change their career path. Knowing this information helps the counselor discover what the client's main goals might be during counseling. The client's present issues can have a key impact on their next steps. The counselor may be pointing out multiple issues to the client during this step and will need confirmation from the client on the validity of each issue. After this discussion, the counselor and client will develop a plan together as to what changes need to be made.

Step four, *prognosis*, focuses on future decisions and possible career options. The client and counselor work together to create realistic goals and move the client in a positive direction. More education about potential outcomes is provided based on the client's goals. One question asked by the counselor might be, "If you choose to do this, then what might happen?" For instance, if a client is experiencing stress at home, how might this stress affect future grades if the client chooses to go back to school? This insight helps the client develop new solutions so they can achieve their goals.

During step five, general *counseling* is provided to the client by using various techniques. The purpose is to continue being supportive while also allowing the client to work toward personal goals set in previous sessions. Counselors have the opportunity to guide and educate clients through situations; clients learn how to apply problem-solving skills to current and future circumstances. This builds their self-esteem and equips clients to handle situations on their own.

Step six, follow-up, is the final step in Williamson's process: *reinforce, reevaluate, and check-in*. The counselor will continue encouraging the client toward their goals and helps them adjust as needed. The counselor provides further assistance if a problem occurs or if a new issue arises that the client doesn't feel equipped to navigate. This step also allows the counselor to evaluate personal counseling skills and determine if a different solution is available.

Many of the steps listed can be completed through computerized assessment, which has been helpful over the last 3 to 4 decades when conducted in conjunction with the client interview. Combining these measures provides a more holistic view for the client and counselor. Now that we understand how assessment is used and how we might combine assessment processes holistically when using trait and factor theory, let's turn our attention to the limitations when using this theory.

Limitations

Trait and factor theory is the first of its kind and, being an original, it has both advantages and disadvantages. We can agree that society has changed drastically since Frank Parsons developed the concept of vocational guidance. Since his time, we experienced new wars, social movements, and technological advancements. Although researchers continue to validate this theory (Atli, 2016), trait and factor theory does have its limitations. For example, trait-factor theory can be time consuming if the career counselor is not familiar with the client and job opportunities available. Also, the counselor is often viewed as the expert and may spend a great amount of time interpreting job factors in relation to client traits. Third, this theory originally overlooked multicultural influences, gender differences, family influences, medical history, sexual orientation, and non-Westernized viewpoints. Because of the importance of these issues, counselors should consider these facets when using trait and factor theory. Finally, critics state that the theory overemphasizes assessment and deemphasizes the therapeutic relationship.

John Holland's Interest Typology: Premise of Theory

It is often said that when a child likes to argue or is persuasive that the young person is going to grow up to be a politician or a lawyer. John Holland's interest typology builds on this premise of a person establishing interests and skills as they grow, and further that this development is believed to influence career choices. John Holland posits that an individual will typically be attracted to a career that will capitalize on their interests and personality. Little did anyone know 60 years ago that information in John L. Holland's (1959) article, "A Theory of Vocational Choice," would become widely used by vocational counselors.

Certain occupations, such as police officers and firefighters, might appeal to someone who has a strong sense of community and a desire to direct others in the middle of emergencies. These individuals might even like the adrenaline of saving lives, not to mention the emotional rewards accompanying the admiration often given by others. Holland's typologies would likely score this individual with a high social (S) score on the RIASEC. Other individuals, according to Holland, might be good at troubleshooting complex systems and even enjoy doing so as a hobby. According to Holland's theory, this individual might be drawn to a career as a computer technician, a mechanic, or an engineer (Holland, 1959). More information on typology and scores follows in the following sections.

The idea of matching skills, interests, and careers points to the idea that people are drawn to a particular career, so their emotional needs are met as well as their financial needs. This concept is often referred to as "*congruence* of one's view of self with occupational preference" (Holland, 1997, p. 35). Within this premise of congruent self and career, is the idea that there are environmental and hereditary influences that develop a person's self-identity. An individual's life history of reacting to environmental demands can influence their career interests as well (Holland, 1997). An individual who grows up raising cattle and farming might not be so quickly drawn to day trading in the city. They may have grown accustomed to quiet and solace in their work in the countryside. In this example, the environment set certain patterns the individual may have become used to such as planting and harvesting seasons. These factors could certainly influence an individual's interest and comfort in a career where they already feel a sense of contentment.

Holland's typologies are categorized into six modal personal style/orientations and matching occupational environments: realistic, investigative, artistic, social, enterprising, and conventional, commonly referred to by the acronym *RIASEC*. The underlying structure, or calculus, of the RIASEC types is represented by Holland's (1973, 1985a, 1985b, 1997) iconic hexagon (Nauta, 2010) as described in more detail in the next section.

Steps, Model, and Application

John Holland's theory of occupational personality fit (1966, 1973, 1985a, 1997) is often cited in research literature and, because of its ease of assessment and application, is still used today. Assessment instruments, as covered in the next section, are utilized to identify the dominant personality preferences from a list of six possibilities. The assumption is that there are six kinds of environments and that most people can be categorized into predominant modal personal orientations.

The six modal personal orientations are as follows:

- Realistic (R): Generally describes a person who likes to work with animals, tools, or machines. Avoids social activities like teaching and values practicality.
- Investigative (I): This person generally likes to study and solve math or science problems and would typically avoid leading others or work that involves selling or persuading others.
- Artistic (A): This personality type likes creative activities such as art, drama, and crafts and generally avoids tasks that are repetitive or highly ordered.
- Social (S): This person generally likes to help others as a teacher, nurse, police officer, or other vocation that involves giving instruction to others.
- Enterprising (E): This personality type likes to lead and persuade people. Selling things and ideas would fit this person's job description.
- Conventional (C): This personality type likes to work with records, machines, or numbers in a set, orderly manner.

Certain constructs such as *consistency and differentiation* are indicated on the hexagon by proximity of the codes the person identifies with. The construct of *identity* refers to how well an individual sees a "picture of one's goals, interests, and talents" (Holland, 1997, p. 5). Let's take a look at Guided Practice Exercise 2.2 where you will evaluate Holland's typology based on your own experiences.

Guided Practice Exercise 2.2 Exercise Holland Code Evaluation

Think about the jobs you held in the past. How do those jobs fit into the RIASEC for you? Was the job a good fit for you? Knowing what you now know about the RIASEC model, how will future jobs be different or similar to those in your past according to your personality type?

Assessment

John Holland's typological theory of persons and environments is regarded as the most influential in the field of career counseling (Brown, 2002). Given its popularity, it is the basis for many interest inventories, such as *Strong's Interest Inventory (SII)*, which will assess your three-letter Holland code. Dr. Holland also developed an interest inventory called the *Self-Directed Search (SDS)*, which has been updated several times and is still in use today. Many additional assessment tools have since been developed that utilize parts of the Holland codes. Table 2.3 shows a list of some of these more popular assessment tools that are readily available in paper form or are computer based.

TABLE 2.3   **Holland Assessments**

Assessment	Helpful Information
Self-Directed Search Form-R	This assessment takes about 25–35 minutes to administer and can be administered individually or in a group setting
Occupational Finder, Revised	Includes new/updated occupations with educational developmental level requirements
My Vocation Situation	Assesses for difficulties related to vocational decision making
Self-Directed Search Form E	This form will assist people with limited reading skills
SDS Career Explorer	Assessment and exploration that matches aspirations, activities, and talents to career choices and educational opportunities.
SDS Internet version	Internet version of assessment and exploration that matches aspirations, activities, and talents to career choices and educational opportunities
Position Classification Inventory	Helps employers use SDS results to apply the Holland codes to locate and explore matching current and future job openings
Environmental Identity Scale (EIS)	Assesses the connectedness of individual to nature (six environmental models)
Career Attitudes and Strategies Inventory (CASI)	Self-administered, self-scored, profiled, and interpreted. These scales provide a brief survey of attitudes, barriers, experiences, or strategies that may merit further exploration.
Vocational Preference Inventory (VPI)	This inventory has 4 uses. It can be used as a brief personality assessment with high school students through employed adults. It can also be used to complement to other vocational inventories. In addition, it can be used to assess vocational interests. And lastly, in the context of Holland's theory, it can be used to assess vocational interests and behavior.

Limitations

Spokane (1985) reports that research does not show the level of satisfaction Holland claims should be achieved through a correct match. For example, a career in computer programming might interest a person with a high RIASEC score in the area of *investigative or conventional,* yet this person might also have to utilize *social* activities in order to help others overcome computer problems. This situation would point to a lack of *congruence* (i.e., a mismatch between an individual's personality type and work environment), resulting in unacceptable levels of employment stress. As a result, the person might seek out new job opportunities in other departments or fields.

Some have criticized the contribution of Holland's theory and doubt its applicability with minorities and non-U.S. citizens (Brown, 2002). With the advent of the internet and the ability to do computer-based work from home, and on any given continent, some of Holland's typologies may be limited in describing these environments.

For additional guidance when applying Holland's theory to career counseling, refer to the following case study, which depicts an integration of trait and factor theory with John Holland's interest typology.

CASE STUDY

The following case demonstrates how trait and factor theory might be integrated with John Holland's interest typology while working with an adolescent. It utilizes a current online resource available through the U.S. Department of Labor. Feel free to look up this online resource along with its psychometric properties (Rounds et al., 2018).

John is a 15-year-old freshman who attends a small Texas high school. He must choose a direction of study before the first 6 weeks of school is finished. John's parents could tell he was anxious about making this decision, especially after visiting with his high school advisor. They thought it would be a good idea for John to go to a career counselor to help narrow down his options. The following script is from John and the counselor's second session. During the first session, the counselor interviewed John to learn about his aptitudes, abilities, achievements, interests, and values. She then introduced John to the O*Net website that we discussed in Chapter 1 of this text. At the end of the session, the counselor asked John to complete some homework by taking a free career assessment available through the U.S. Department of Labor (www.mynextmove.org/explore/ip). Since John had access to a computer, the counselor had him use the Internet version of the assessment.

Counselor: John, how did you feel after taking the free career test?
John: It was pretty easy. I'm not sure what the letters IER mean. I looked around on the website for a few minutes though.
Counselor: That's great! Let me start by explaining the letters to you.
(Counselor spends a few minutes explaining the meaning of his Holland code while modeling how to utilize the website).

Counselor: Do you have any questions about the results?

John: That makes sense. You know what I really do like to do is solve problems. Science is one of my favorite subjects because we do a lot of experiments.

Counselor: Well, let's see what kind of career options are available based on our talk last week and your test results. One thing to remember is test results are not all knowing. They simply offer insight. Ultimately, you are the best judge when it comes to choosing a career direction.

(The counselor allows John time to read through the directions in the Job Zone section).

Counselor: Do you have any questions so far?

John: Not yet!

Counselor: Okay, we've talked about what you like to do and the classes you enjoyed in middle school. When you think about your future, what comes to mind?

John: Well, my parents want me to go to college even though they didn't. I'm not sure what I want to do at this point.

Counselor: You have a lot of time to think about it and it is normal for your interests to change as you get older. One of our goals right now is to help you figure out which direction of study best fits what you want for high school. Learning this information can be helpful for when you make decisions after high school, too.

(The counselor allows John time to read about the job preparation slide).

Counselor: On the page, it gives you the option to decide how much time you'd like to spend preparing for a future job. For instance, how much preparation based off these options do you think it would take to become a lawyer?

John: Either high job or extensive job preparation.

Counselor: Great guess! Let's look at each option.

(The counselor allows time for John to explore the options he mentioned).

Counselor: It looks like you were right! It would take extensive preparation to become a lawyer. This means a person would have a lot of training, education, and experience to compete for that job.

John: That makes sense. My uncle is a lawyer and he talks about college and law school a lot.

Counselor: Exactly. Let's take a quick look at jobs requiring little to no preparation while we are here.

(The counselor allows time for John to explore this page).

Counselor: What differences do you see between this option and the one we looked at earlier?

John: This one seems like you need less education and training.

Counselor: That's right! Let's go back to the original page and click "Next" to learn about different career options. Which job zone do you want to look at first?

John: Let's try job zone three.

Counselor: It looks like this job section requires medium preparation. John, while we look through these jobs, think about your Holland code results and our discussion from last session.

John: Sounds good.

Counselor: On this page it provides a few examples of what jobs match your Holland code results best. You can click on each job and find out more information. Do any of these look interesting to you?

John: Maybe the police detectives.

(The counselor gives John a minute or two to click on the job title and read through the description).

Counselor: Tell me what you think about this position after reading through the information.

John: Well, it looks pretty interesting. I've always enjoyed watching shows about cops and the FBI.

Counselor: It sounds like this job matches well with what you like and your Holland code results. For homework I'd like you to explore this part of the site more. Read about different jobs and write down five that interest you the most. We can talk about this next week and it may help you decide on a direction of study.

John: Sounds good to me!

Person-Environment Fit Theory/Theory of Work Adjustment: Premise of Theory

One theory that emerged from trait and factor research was the theory of work adjustment (TWA), also known as the person-environment (P-E) fit or person-environment-correspondence (PEC) theory (Dawis & Lofquist, 1991). Researchers Rene Dawis and Lloyd Lofquist are the individuals most associated with this theory (Dawis & Lofquist, 1984). Many colleagues of Dawis and Lofquist also contributed over 3 decades of research to the development of TWA.

TWA was originally developed to meet the needs of vocational rehabilitation clients as researchers wanted to provide improved services to this population. Because of this, the focus of this theory is not on choosing a career but rather evaluating the relationship between an individual and their work environment and vice versa (i.e., vocational adjustment versus vocational development). Read on to learn more about the theory's development.

In the mid-1960s, psychologists Dawis and Lofquist, who worked at the University of Minnesota and were part of the Work Adjustment Project (Dawis et al., 1968), created the P-E model and collaborated with David Weiss on developing instruments to support the concepts of this theory. Research from the 1970's was elaborated on, such as connecting work needs and values and personality and work environment style. Focus was also placed on the relationship between individuals and the work environment.

The interaction between an individual and their work environment explains how one might adjust. For example, if it is a suitable match, he or she might experience job satisfaction, satisfactory job performance, and a healthy work adjustment. An unsuitable match might mean the individual worker experiences the opposite: dissatisfaction, poor job performance, and a higher chance of leaving the job. Two major components exist in this theory that predict work adjustment: satisfaction and satisfactoriness. *Satisfaction* means an individual feels just that, satisfied with the work he or she does. *Satisfactoriness* focuses on the employer's satisfaction with the employee's performance. Assessment is used to determine these levels.

Assessment

When the original P-E framework was developed, instruments to measure satisfactoriness, job importance, and worker aptitude were being created almost simultaneously. Dawis, Lofquist, and Weiss knew this would be necessary to "make it possible for vocational rehabilitation agencies and counselors to conduct follow-up studies of clients placed on jobs by using work adjustment measures and relating these to tenure on the job" (Dawis et al., 1968, p. 2). This high importance of assessment as placed on the theory overall and throughout each step make it nearly impossible to discuss the model apart from assessment. For this reason, assessment is embedded in the steps, model, and application discussion that follows.

Steps, Model, and Application

Three major steps are used within this theory to predict work adjustment: gain self-understanding, obtain knowledge about the world of work, and integrate information about self and the world of work (Dawis & Lofquist, 1984). The first step, gaining self-understanding, assesses an individual's abilities, values, personality, and interests. Counselors used the *General Aptitude Test Battery (GATB)* to learn the following: general learning, form perception (i.e., an individual's ability to perceive details in images, visuals), manual dexterity, spatial ability, finger dexterity, numerical ability, eye-hand coordination, verbal ability, and clerical ability. Abilities include aptitudes, one's natural ability, and learned skills. Values and needs, assessed in this step, can be measured by using the *Minnesota Importance Questionnaire (MIQ)*, whereas interests are usually obtained from one's values and abilities. Information about a client's values and needs are measured by evaluating information found in six key areas: achievement, status, safety, comfort, altruism, and autonomy. For example, comfort for an individual may be represented by the type of activity, security, or working conditions he or she experiences each day on the job. Check out the link under "Helpful Websites" at the end of this chapter if you would like to read more about some of the constructs listed (Winter, n.d.).

Step two, obtaining knowledge about the world of work, focuses on the specific job's ability and value patterns. Ability patterns are important within a certain job. For example, if the client wanted to be an accountant, the *GATB* scores may show a need for someone with high numerical ability. Remember, in step one, the focus was on the client's aptitudes, values, and needs. Step two wants to know what is important within an occupation and considers whether an individual meets those criteria. Ability patterns in this step include or expand on verbal ability, numerical ability, spatial ability, ability to form perception, clerical ability, eye-hand coordination, finger dexterity, and manual dexterity. Value patterns can be measured using the *Minnesota Job Questionnaire* (*MJQ*). This assessment measures the abilities and needs of many occupations by evaluating how much a job reinforces an individual's values.

The final step, integrating information about self and the world of work, uses information found from the *GATB* (abilities), *MIQ* (values), and one's personality. An individual's personality, or how they adjust to a job, is looked at through the following factors: flexibility, activeness, reactiveness, and perseverance. For example, if a client struggles to get to work at 8:00 a.m. and wants to increase correspondence with a job, she might ask her employer about flexible work hours. In this case, she is trying to change the work environment (activeness). The *Minnesota Occupational Classification System* matches the information found from each assessment to help a client gain more information on work adjustment. Several instruments, in addition to those listed in this section and as created by the Work Adjustment Project, devote themselves to assessment during these steps and are listed in Table 2.4.

TABLE 2.4   **Work Adjustment Project Instruments**

Minnesota Satisfaction Questionnaire (MSQ)
Minnesota Satisfactoriness Scales (MSS)
Minnesota Importance Questionnaire (MIQ)
Minnesota Job Description Questionnaire (MJDQ)
General Aptitude Test Battery (GATB)
Occupational Aptitude Patterns (OAPs)

Limitations

The TWA theory has been tested with many populations since its development. Although it covers many general, large group differences, it does not put major focus on small group differences (Dawis & Lofquist, 1984). Some differences potentially overlooked include gender, adjusting the needs assessment to include information about race and sex, sexual harassment, and socioeconomic status (Lyons et al., 2014). A second limitation regards the lack of focus on providing resources (coping mechanisms) for clients if a transition is on the horizon. When researching student athletes transitioning out of a sport, Leonard and Schimmel (2016) stated, "Literature on values and reinforcers is scarce, despite potentially being an important factor" (p. 64). Finally, a third limitation requires counselors using this theory to be well versed with the concepts and assessments if they are to utilize it with a client effectively.

Gelatt's Decision Theory: Premise of Theory

H.B. Gelatt developed decision theory in the early 1960's following his discovery of inadequacies in vocational guidance. This theory was developed during a time when "the past was known, the future was predictable, and the present was changing at a pace that was comprehendible" (Gelatt, 1989, p. 252).

Decision theory was based on rational objective frames of reference and required the individual to define purposes in a clear manner, collect and analyze relevant data, study possible alternatives, and evaluate possible outcomes. Though an appropriate approach during the 1960s, societal changes occurring over the next 20 years gave impetus to impending shifts in the theory's paradigm.

In 1989, Gelatt proposed a new decision-making theory entitled "Positive Uncertainty" (Gelatt, 1989). He justified this new theory and its shift in perspective by explaining individuals' needs and the ensuing ambiguity evident in the changing society. Although Gelatt shifted his focus in this way, he continued to maintain the prior validity of his ideas from the original theory he created in the 1960s.

By balancing the best parts of his 1960s theory and adding new insight based on societal changes, Gelatt was able to produce a theory that encouraged positive attitudes and a fresh outlook. With the emphasis on uncertainty, the new theory allowed for a new and different perspective to emerge, one that focused less on the scientific and rationale-based theories of the past. "Positive Uncertainty" allows a person to find balance between the old and new and allows an interactive framework to emerge. The theory helps a person consider and embrace change, ambiguity, and intuitive thinking (Herr & Cramer, 1996).

Assessment

Decision theory and positive uncertainty theory are both decision-making theories. The basic idea is for a person to decide how to maximize gains and minimize losses in their life, while looking at as much information regarding their choices as possible, and to make the most informed decision based on these premises. There is no formal assessment tool for this set of theories.

Steps, Model, and Application

Girshick (1954) stated, "You cannot solve your problems until you more clearly define your goal and the consequences of your decision" (p. 463). In Gelatt's decision theory, the sequential and cyclical decision-making process addresses this very idea. This theoretical framework requires that objectives are defined clearly, relevant data is collected and analyzed, possible alternatives are studied, and consequences or outcomes are evaluated. This process reveals coherent and heuristic guidance and counseling methods instead of primarily logical, scientific methods (Gelatt, 1962). Figure 2.1 depicts the decision theory model.

In this diagram of the decision theory model, one can see that decisions, no matter the subject, have the same basic characteristics and are approached in the same manner. Using this model, the process begins with an individual needing to decide (purpose/objective). Several actions can then be taken, and a decision, terminal or investigatory, is made on the basis of discovered information. Investigatory decisions are made due to more information being needed before making a terminal decision (cyclical). Once a terminal decision is made, if new information is presented, the cycle of gaining the new information can cause recycling in the process. In order to achieve a recommended course of action, one must access possible alternative actions, possible outcomes, and probabilities of outcomes and weigh the desirability of the outcomes prior to integrating and selecting an appropriate action. These concepts are also weighed by predictability and within the individual's value system until a specific criterion has been achieved and a decision made.

Positive Uncertainty

Three basic guidelines drive Gelatt's positive uncertainty theory in its definition and application: (a) information, (b) the process of arranging and rearranging, and (c) a choice of action (Gelatt, 1989). Due to the changes in information availability, much of the original theoretical definition developed in the 1960s changed over the next 2 decades.

The amount of information available to the public in the late 1980s was vastly different from that found in the 1960s. The process of arranging and rearranging data, a person's understandings in response to artificial intelligence, self-growth, research on the brain, and computer technology all impacted decision making. In the field of counseling, there was also a greater understanding as to how a person processes information. In fact, more knowledge was available on the multifaceted nature of decision making in general. The last part of the definition, choice, also changed. The concept of aiding someone in the decision-making process moved from

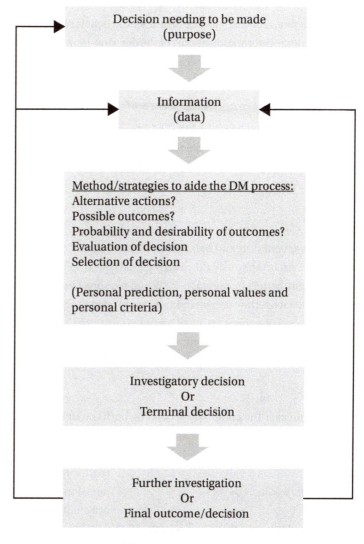

FIGURE 2.1 Gelatt's decision-making theory model.

"linear, rational, systematic strategies to recommending, teaching, intuitive, situational, and sometimes inconsistent methods for solving personal problems, or making decisions" (Gelatt, 1989, p. 254). Thus, in the 80s, we arrived at the model seen in Figure 2.1. Now let's read about Gelatt's guidelines when using the theory with clients.

Information Guideline

"Treat your facts with imagination but do not imagine your facts" (Gelatt, 1989, p. 254). Though vast amounts of information are easily attainable in today's electronic world, counselors must help clients validate facts and process this information so that it does not become overwhelming. We must also help clients see information in a light so that it isn't skewed through the client's personal bias. With positive uncertainty, we must, therefore, consider how the attitudes and beliefs of the client affect information processing and help them rearrange information as part of the decision-making process. Let's look at Guided Practice Exercise 2.3 where you are asked to consider how information processing affects your own decision making.

Guided Practice Exercise 2.3 Information Processing

The statement was made that all information is subjective. When reviewing information that you receive, is it possible for you to interpret something differently than another person? In what ways do you process information differently from others? How can this impact your decision-making process?

Process Guideline

"Know what you want and believe but do not be sure" (Gelatt, 1989, p. 254). Decision making is a compilation of simultaneously discovering goals, setting goals, and achieving goals (Gelatt, 1989). Gelatt (1989) likens beliefs to spectacles: "When persons change their beliefs, they change their spectacles; they change what they see, hear, know, want, and do. Beliefs determine how one behaves" (p. 254). The shift from decision theory to positive uncertainty, in the area of process, is the idea that you do not have to know what you want. Instead, there is a focus on encouraging the development of new wants and on a challenge to change or reexamine personal convictions.

Choice Guideline

Holistic choice is the compilation of using both the right and left brain; contemplation of past, present, and future; and flexibility across these concepts. Gelatt (1989) asserts that it is not possible to divide one's decision-making process from oneself, nor from truths, facts, and realities—these are all integral in the decision-making process. Positive uncertainty consists of a choice framework that includes "reflection, flexibility, rational and intuitive thinking" (Gelatt, 1989, p. 255).

Be rational unless there is a good reason not to be
—Gelatt (1989, p. 255)

Gelatt (1989) postulates that one cannot be inventive, creative, adaptable, and consistent. These ideas lead to uncertainty at some point, which calls for a need for flexibility. The future is unknown. One's choice calls for individuality, and therein lies the ability for imagination to lead to the invention of one's future. Case Exercise 2.1 asks you to consider the case of Briar and how the passage of time affects career development.

Case Exercise 2.1 Briar's Career Exploration

Briar is a 39-year-old recently divorced woman with one child who is a senior in high school. Briar has been a stay-at-home mother who has not worked since her early 20s. The last job she had was as a receptionist in a dental office prior to the birth of her child. She has an associate's degree in business administration. How has her life perspective changed in the past 19 years? How has the workforce changed in the past 19 years? How could these factors affect her decision-making process as she looks toward her future?

Limitations

This theory does not use formal assessments to make decisions. Rather, this theory uses a person's beliefs, uncertainties, attitudes, convictions, and intuitions to make career decisions. Where some may believe this to be a limitation, others believe this to be empowering, better encompassing a person's attitudes and beliefs. In positive uncertainty, attitudes and beliefs are integrated through the counseling relationship and into the decision-making process.

CASE STUDY

The following case demonstrates how the RIASEC modal and Gelatt's flexibility can be used with a client suffering from job dissatisfaction.

Barbara is a 45-year-old Caucasian female who has been employed as a receptionist for 15 years at a local doctor's office. She has recently become dissatisfied with her job and is looking to do something more fulfilling with her life. Barbara has always enjoyed working with others but is not fulfilled in her job as a receptionist. Barbara listed her dream job(s) as being a dental hygienist, a nurse, or a school counselor. In order to help Barbara, a self-directed search was administered, and Barbara's results came out with a code of SAI.

Counselor: Well, Barbara, looking at your score it seems that you have a pretty good idea of what may possibly fulfill you. The SAI you scored is right in line with being a dental hygienist.

Barbara: Okay. But that will mean I need to go back to school … at my age. Is that even possible?

Counselor: What do you think about that?

Barbara: Well, I don't know. I think it would be great to have a job where I feel fulfilled and happy, and this test I took confirmed that this is something that would accomplish that, but I feel like I am too old to go back to school.

Counselor: It sounds like you are considering doing this but feel afraid of failure. What is it that you are the most afraid of?

Barbara: I guess it would be that I leave a stable job, go to school, and then fail at this.

Counselor: It sounds like you are afraid of the unknown.

Barbara: Yes, and instability in the interim or switching jobs.

Counselor: Dental hygienist school is offered at the local community college at times that are designed for working adults. At this college it is a 2-year program.

Barbara: Seriously? I had no idea.

Counselor: How does that change your perspective of possibly doing this?

Barbara: If I could keep my day job while I am in school and be able to go to school at night, that's a game changer. I feel so much relief and hope that I may be able to make this change after all.

Counselor: So, on a scale of 1–10, how do you feel about possibly pursuing becoming a dental hygienist?

Barbara: I think an 8. I plan to call and inquire about it tomorrow. If everything works out, I hope to sign up for classes as soon as they will let me.

The client's fear of failure and middle age were originally seen as obstacles to her progress. Once she realized she could continue a stable life and achieve a dream job, she was able to envision making a life change that would leave her happy and fulfilled. By helping Barbara process her beliefs and values with rational facts, she was able to make a positive decision.

SUMMARY

Four theories were included in this chapter: trait and factor, Holland's interest typology, theory of work adjustment, and Gelatt's decision theory. Trait and factor theory assesses the characteristics of an individual and matches them with factors found in a particular job (Parsons, 1909). A good match between these traits and factors is believed to lead to positive job performance. The second theory covered in this chapter, Holland's interest typology, is one of the most prominent career theories used today. This theory focuses on six types (RIASEC) of work environments and matches them with an individual's interests and personality type (Holland, 1973, 1985a, 1985b, 1997). The third theory mentioned in the chapter, theory of work adjustment, focuses on individuals making career decisions regarding issues related to work adjustment. This theory believes satisfaction and satisfactoriness are both key indicators of work adjustment (Lofquist & Dawis, 1984). Gelatt's decision theory, the final theory discussed in the chapter, is comprised of four factors that could be used to guide an individual trying to make a career decision (Gelatt, 1962). Counselors who desire to use one of these theories should become familiar with the assessments and understand how to explain results effectively to a client. Above all, the best tool during a counseling session is you!

Keystones

- Trait and factor theory was the first career counseling theory and created the building blocks for every career theory used today.
- Work adjustment or PEC theory has been successfully applied to individuals facing job adjustments, different social issues, retirement, and gifted adolescents.
- Using the positive uncertainty model, one must gain necessary information, consider personal attitudes and beliefs about the information, and manage fear of uncertainty. When this is done, information can be arranged such that the client can come to a terminal decision.

- In Holland's typology, the assumption is that there are six kinds of environments and that most people can be categorized into three predominant modal personal orientations within the RIASEC modal.

Author Reflections

While writing and researching this chapter, it became increasingly clear to me that we engage in career counseling with all of our clients, no matter the presenting issue that brings them to counseling. In our practice, we work with children and families in crisis. Much of what brings people to counseling is poor decision making that leads to a crisis of some sort. Guiding a client through discovering what they want, setting goals to guide the process of change, planning for uncertainty, and unraveling the phobia of change into what the future holds is a glorious process to see. All this occurs while remaining realistic, optimistic, and intuitive despite witnessing a few failures along the way. Failures are evidence that we were attempting to change. John Gardner said, "Life is the art of drawing without an eraser." Every experience is an opportunity to learn, whether a positive one or one that takes us back to the drawing board, but nonetheless it is evidence of forward movement. —Lynn Jennings

Career counseling can provide a client with a sense of hope and direction for their future. When a client feels confused about what is next, the equipped career counselor can provide structure and guidance. Assessments can be a great tool during a session, but the experience is richer for the client if a counselor is competent in using the instrument. Some instruments confirm what a client might already know, while other times the counselor is providing new information. I believe helping an individual become more self-aware is powerful and can make an impact for years to come. How exciting that we get to be a part of that process with a client! —Macy Waltz

Additional Resources

The following resources provide additional information relating to the chapter topics.

Useful Websites

Winter, D. (n.d.). *Theory of work adjustment.* The Careers Group. https://careersintheory.files.wordpress.com/2009/10/theories_twa.pdf

This source discusses the theory of work adjustment and the P-E fit model in detail.

Books

Gelatt, H. B. & Gelatt, C. (2003). *Creative decision making: Using positive uncertainty.* Thomson Learning.

This source discusses Gelatt's decision making in greater detail.

Parsons, F. (1909). *Choosing a vocation.* Houghton Mifflin.

This source is the seminal and historical work created by Frank Parsons regarding trait/factor theory.

References

Atli, A. (2016). The effects of trait-factor theory-based career counseling sessions on the levels of career maturity and indecision of high school students. *Universal Journal of Educational Research, 4*(8), 1837–1847.

Brown, D. (2002). *Introduction to theories of career development and choice*. In D. Brown (Ed.), Career choice and development (4th ed.) (pp. 3–23). Jossey-Bass.

Dawis, R. V., & Lofquist, L. H. (1984). *A psychological theory of work adjustment: An individual-differences model and its applications*. University of Minnesota Press.

Dawis, R. V. & Lofquist, L. H. (1991). *Essentials of person-environment-correspondence counseling*. University of Minnesota Press.

Dawis, R. V., Lofquist, L. H., & Weiss, D. J. (1968). *A theory of work adjustment: A revision*. University of Minnesota Press.

Gelatt, H. B. (1962). Decision-making: A conceptual frame of reference for counseling. *Journal of Counseling Psychology, 9*(3), 240–245.

Gelatt, H. B. (1989). Positive uncertainty: A new decision-making framework for counseling. *Journal of Counseling Psychology, 36*(2), 252–256.

Girshick, M. A. (1954). Chapter VII: An elementary survey of statistical decision theory. *Review of Educational Research, 24*(5), 448–466.

Herr, E. L., & Cramer, S. H. (1996). *Career guidance and counseling through the lifespan: Systematic approaches* (5th ed.). Harper Collins.

Holland, J. L. (1959). A theory of vocational choice. *Journal of Counseling Psychology, 6*(1), 35–45.

Holland, J. L. (1966). *The psychology of vocational choice*. Waltham, MA: Blaisdell.

Holland, J. L. (1973). *Making vocational choices: A theory of vocational personalities and work environments*. Prentice-Hall.

Holland, J. L. (1985a). *Making vocational choices: A theory of vocational personalities and work environments* (2nd ed.). Prentice-Hall.

Holland, J. L. (1985b). *Manual for the vocational preference inventory*. Psychological Assessment Resources.

Holland J. L. (1997). *Making vocational choices: A theory of vocational personalities and work environments* (3rd ed.). Psychological Assessment Resources.

Leonard, J. M., & Schimmel, C. J. (2016). Theory of work adjustment and student-athletes transition out of sport. *Journal of Issues in Intercollegiate Athletics, 9*, 62–85.

Lyons, H. Z., Velez, B. L., Mehta, M., & Neill, N. (2014). Tests of the theory of work adjustment with economically distressed African Americans. *Journal of Counseling Psychology, 61*(3), 473–483.

Nauta, M. (2010). The development, evolution, and status of Holland's theory of vocational personalities: Reflections and future directions for counseling psychology. *Journal of Counseling Psychology, 57*(1), 11–22.

Parsons, F. (1909). *Choosing a vocation*. Houghton Mifflin.

Rounds, J., Hoff, K., Chu, C., Lewis, P., & Gregory, C. (2018). *O*Net Interest Profiler short form paper-and-pencil version: Evaluation of self-scoring and psychometric characteristics*. U.S. Department of Labor. https://www.onetcenter.org/dl_files/IPSF_PP.pdf

Spokane, A. R. (1985). A review of research on person-environment congruence in Holland's theory of careers. *Journal of Vocational Behaviour, 26*(3), 306–343.

Williamson, E. G., & Darley, J. G. (1937). *Student personnel work: An outline of clinical procedures*. McGraw-Hill.

CHAPTER

Cognitive, Social Cognitive, Happenstance, and Social Learning Career Theories

Janet Hicks, Eniye Aimienoho, Krystal Humphreys, Dara Brown,

and Elizabeth Ann Wardle

The greatest mistake you can make in life is to be continually fearing you will make one.
—Elbert Hubbard

Career choices can seem daunting and overwhelming due to the perceived permanence and impact of such a major decision. What if we make the wrong choice and it leads to future unhappiness? Will we be stuck in a job we hate because of a choice we make today? Fortunately, social cognitive and social learning theories, including happenstance, offer some relief from this fear. As you will read in the pages that follow, every experience can lead to learning that enhances and improves career development. Read on and discover how social cognitive theorists describe how we learn, how experiences improve job choices, and how both good and bad career decisions can be beneficial to our futures.

CHAPTER OVERVIEW

This chapter outlines the cognitive, social cognitive, happenstance, and social learning vocational theories discussed in the career counseling literature. You will learn the basic premises, assessments, steps in the process, and limitations of the cognitive, social cognitive, happenstance, and social learning vocational theorists' contentions. The end of this chapter offers an opportunity to apply what you learn via a case study.

LEARNING OBJECTIVES

After reading this chapter you will be able to do the following:

- Know the origins, basic premises, and techniques used as part of the cognitive, social cognitive, social learning, and happenstance theories
- Understand the limitations of cognitive, social cognitive, social learning, and happenstance theories
- Recognize how assessment plays a role in the theories discussed in this chapter
- Apply concepts of a cognitive approach (e.g., cognitive information processing) to aid in the career development of a fictional client

Krumboltz's Learning Theory

Krumboltz's learning theory was developed in 1979 by John Krumboltz as a social learning theory of career choices. Because Krumboltz based his learning theory on his own youthful career indecision experiences, he hypothesized, and later maintained, that career indecision was an effect or result of both adequate and insufficient learning experiences (Mitchell & Krumboltz, 1996). Over the next few decades, the theory was expanded on and reformulated so as to connect to other career counseling concepts (Krumboltz, 1994). Let's further examine some of the basic ideas of Krumboltz's theory in the passages that follow.

Premise

Krumboltz's theory revolves around his beliefs about learning. For example, he believed learning takes place through observation and experiences. He also coined the terms "instrumental" or "associative" to describe lifetime learning experiences that lead to career decisions. In order to best understand these learning experiences (e.g., instrumental or associative), we must first acknowledge that people have either positive or negative reactions to their learning experiences. The information that follows examines some of these potential reactions and types of learning based on these positive and negative experiences.

Instrumental learning occurs in direct response to consequences based on a person's own actions. For example, a person scoring low on a test or activity might base this consequence on a lack of study time. Suppose a student stays up all night playing video games and never studies for an exam that is the following day. It would come as no surprise to hear that the student received a failing grade. In this example, the failing grade serves as an instrumental learning experience because it was a consequence of the affected student's study habits and test preparation. The student's accompanying panic and disappointment serves as a negative reaction to this learning experience.

The second type of learning, *associative learning*, involves learning through observation. Observations might include responses witnessed in reaction to another's accomplishments. For example, suppose an individual receives praise and compliments upon graduating from law school. This praise then affects the aforementioned graduate's younger sibling, who suddenly wants to attend law school as well. Associative learning would imply that observations regarding the family and friend's responses and actions affected the sibling's decisions. Clearly, this example is a positive reaction to an observed experience.

As you can see from the examples given, learning takes place through observation and experiences and, according to Krumboltz, career selection and development is based on life events (Mitchell & Krumboltz, 1996). These life events are guided by four factors of career development: genetics, environment, learning, and tasks. *Genetic factors* constitute any inherited qualities or abilities that may limit or help an individual in career choices. These include the more obvious ones like sex, race, and disabilities, but also includes talents and intellectual abilities. For example, not everyone chooses athletics as their career choice, but for those who do, talent and genetic physique are most likely inherent within the person's characteristics. Also, consider the person who, when factoring out gravity, tends to have really good control over their body and its movements. This person might excel in those sports requiring good control such as track, dance, and martial arts. Now suppose this same person is of average height and has diminished eyesight. In this case, the person might never do well in sports like basketball or tennis due to lowered genetic abilities. Obviously, this person would most likely avoid a career in these types of sports.

The second uncontrollable factor that affects career development is environment. Events and outcomes that influence an individual's skill development, experiences, activities, and career preferences are known as *environmental factors* (Krumboltz et al., 1976). For example, government policies or laws that regulate or ban certain occupations can affect an individual's career development. Natural disasters or dangerous environments can affect economic conditions and physique. An individual who comes from a family of physicians and is enrolled in a math and science school for the majority of their education has experiences conductive to becoming a physician via home-based environmental learning. This is true despite their chosen career preference. In other words, we can't help but learn from those around us.

Task approach skills refer to those skills needed to get a job in a career field, develop the job, and maintain it. Krumboltz believes these tasks are developed over the lifespan. These skills include problem-solving skills, work habits, mental sets, and emotional and cognitive responses. We modify these skills as a result of positive or negative experiences. For example, the student mentioned before who failed the exam will, hopefully, modify their work habits to include better preparation and studying. The sibling of the law student who is considering law school as a career path may also be developing problem-solving skills and mental sets to better prepare for a law career.

When working from within the framework of Krumboltz's learning theory, individuals choose a career based on a sense of self and the inherent or learned ability to perform. This ability to perform is impacted by (a) lived and observed experiences and (b) skill sets established, in part, in response to genetics and environment. Once these strengths and weaknesses are considered, people may then blend their talents, interests, and skills to find appropriate and meaningful work. How does a person determine and blend these interests when using this theory? What other assessments might be helpful in this process? The sections that follow discuss some of the assessments that might aid counselors and clients when determining best career fit.

Assessment

Krumboltz (2009) states that assessments should be used to stimulate client learning rather than simply to match a person with certain traits or factors. Following are some assessments that may aid in client learning via conversations about outcomes. Additional information about these and other career assessments can also be found in Chapter 8.

The *Strong Interest Inventory* is a self-assessment tool used to figure out an individual's interests and, later, can be matched with genetic abilities, learned values, aptitudes, and skills to arrive at a potential career choice. The assessment was developed by E.K. Strong in the early part of the 20th century and was originally published in 1927 as the *Strong Vocational Interest Bank*. As an interest assessment, it measured people's likes and dislikes by comparing career satisfaction and common interests among those who were employed in the same career. The current *Strong Interest Inventory* contains about 291 items that pertain to subject areas, leisure activities, and characteristics (Donnay & Borgen, 1996). Because interests change over time, a person is not expected to commit to a job forever.

Katharine Briggs and her daughter, Isabel Myers, developed the *Myers–Briggs Type Indicator* after seeing Carl Jung's typology concepts. It was hoped the assessment, which utilized Jung's types, could help women's career success. This hope was based on the assessment's ability to uncover personality types and match them with careers and career preferences (Myers Briggs, n.d.).

The *MBTI* looks at a person's world perception and decision making. It assesses temperament, interests, needs, values, and motivation. Career counselors using this learning theory and personality assessment have the opportunity to have conversations in the session regarding career comfort and trait development. Guided Practice Exercise 3.1 asks you to consider ties between the MBTI and Krumboltz's theoretical premises.

Guided Practice Exercise 3.1 The MBTI and Social Learning Theory

As you read in the passage, the MBTI assessment looks at aspects of a person's personality. In fact, it assesses each person on a continuum regarding the following factors: introversion/extroversion, intuitive/sensory, thinking/feeling, and judging perceiving. Let's look at a couple of these facets, introversion/extroversion and judging/perceiving. For example, those whose test results indicate introversion recharge by spending time alone whereas extroverts energize through time spent in the company of others. Another type, the perceiving personalities, are spontaneous and see time as a renewable resource. Those testing in the judging category, however, adhere to and place importance on deadlines.

While considering these types, think about Krumboltz's premise that humans have inherent genetic abilities and also learn from their environment. Do you believe introversion, extroversion, judging, and perceiving are inherited or learned personality traits? Explain your response. How does knowing this fit with social learning?

The *Career Beliefs Inventory* was designed to discover factors that block an individual's career development. This instrument consists of 25 scales designed to find difficulties and examine beliefs regarding career paths. Factors examined include current career situations, conditions needed for happiness, decision factors, willingness to change, and motivation (Krumboltz, 1994. The assessment helps individuals recognize and understand how beliefs about self, learned behaviors, and life events may cause trouble and create career blocks that may need to be removed.

Because Krumboltz changed some of his contentions with the addition of his happenstance learning theory, his theory's steps, model, and application, as well as theoretical limitations, will be discussed in the following sections in this chapter.

Happenstance Learning Theory

Happenstance learning theory (HLT) was developed by John Krumboltz (2009) as a modification to his original social learning theory (as seen in the previous section of this chapter). Krumboltz originally contended that career counseling's purpose was to help clients make career decisions. This contention changed with the introduction of HLT, however. HLT touts the important goal of teaching clients to take career action so they know how to manage their own lifetime career issues. This lifetime learning stance occurs in lieu of simply assisting with one-time career decisions (Krumboltz, 2009). HLT does use career indecision in the learning process, however.

According to HLT, career indecision leads to opportunities and unplanned paths from which clients can potentially benefit (Krumboltz, 2009). The theory emphasizes that chance events can have positive or negative consequences over a client's life and also affect their career choice and path (Krumboltz et al., 1976). Guided Practice Exercise 3.2 asks you to examine your past experiences and determine potential future success based on your own past learning.

Guided Practice Exercise 3.2 Happenstance in Your Own Career

Take a moment and jot down jobs you have held over your lifetime. Think about things you learned in these jobs, whether you enjoyed the job or not. Next, compare the things you learned with skills you need in your future career (i.e., counseling). What skills will help you help others? What experiences will help you fit in this new career field? (Hint: Business experience might help those going into private practice or with record keeping.) How will your past experiences help you get hired in the future? Are there job or learning experiences from your past that you thought were wasted but you now see as beneficial? How might Krumboltz respond to your thought process?

Premise

HLT involves acting on unplanned events (Krumboltz et al., 1976). For example, unpredictable social factors, chance events, and environmental conditions are important influences and can be acted on to create new career choices and opportunities. Case Exercise 3.1 asks you to examine the issues of a client and frame the approach based on this HLT perspective. Be sure to remember that counselors operating from the HLT's framework focus on sets of attitudes and approaches in a client's career that would otherwise be overlooked. HLT assists clients as they respond to life events and conditions of life and helps them learn through their own experiences.

Case Exercise 3.1 Dayne's Frustration

Dayne comes to you, the career counselor, for help finding a job. Dayne majored in education and, after entering student teaching, realizes she does not like teaching at all. She begins to cry as she tells you she has wasted thousands of dollars and four years of her time getting a "wasted" degree. Considering that happenstance theory believes all learning and past experiences offer opportunities for success, what would you say to Dayne? How might her degree and past learning help her find a suitable career path?

Assessment

HLT uses assessment as a learning tool and does not focus only on links between personality traits and occupational characteristics (Krumboltz, 2009). During the assessment phase of career counseling, clients are assessing accomplishments and exploring actions based on unplanned life events. HLT also uses assessment to "stimulate client learning" (Krumboltz, 2009, p. 143). In this regard, a number of interest inventories; personality assessments; and belief, thought, and development inventories can be used to assist clients. A few examples follow.

Career Beliefs Inventory

This assessment is beneficial to the client in that it helps uncover personal beliefs regarding careers, decision making, fear of failure and other such aspects. By examining such things as current career situations, conditions needed for happiness, decision factors, willingness to change, and motivational factors, clients learn about themselves so they can create new approaches that lend themselves to career success. Counselors can use instrument results to confront client beliefs that impede success (Krumboltz, 2009).

Career Thoughts Inventory

Although this assessment might be confused with the *Career Beliefs Inventory*, it is quite different. This instrument measures dysfunctional and maladaptive thinking affecting career decision making (Sampson et al., 1999. The inventory has 48 scales that fall into three categories, including decision-making confusion, external conflict, and commitment anxiety. Instrument completion takes only 7 to 15 minutes and the final score represents overall thinking that might be considered dysfunctional. When a person presents as dysfunctional, they may be unaware of unplanned events and/or less likely to act on them. This inability to use actions to their advantage may become a springboard toward a negative outlook on current career choice.

Career Development Inventory

Inventories that assess an individual's career development and provide insight and goals for problems associated with career choice and planning skills are beneficial for use when working within HLT's contentions (Krumboltz, 2009). As such, the *Career Development Inventory* is used to judge and evaluate an individual's readiness for exploration, information and decision making, and planning orientation. The inventory also contains cognitive and attitudinal scales. The Career Development Inventory measures an individual's career maturity and determines steps the client might use to progress. All information is based on the client's appropriate developmental level as based on age and experience.

Steps, Model, and Application

Since happenstance theory emphasizes the need for career counselors to assist in "taking action" for career satisfaction, numerous career choices may emerge. Because unlimited options may be inevitable for some, counselors would do well to discover client expectations about career exploration and counseling. After this, they can work with the client on ways to respond positively to life conditions and events (Krumboltz et al., 1976).

A client goes from having the false belief that they have no control of their life and future to viewing unplanned events as opportunities. This new empowered mind-set can be achieved by working with clients in identifying times in the past where they achieved or handled events effectively. Clients can then be taught to reframe unplanned events as opportunities. For example, clients go from viewing life as something that is constantly throwing curveballs at them to a new mind-set where curveballs are viewed as an opportunity to hit the ball. However, the client must be taught to act, or hit the ball, or efforts are in vain.

As mentioned, happenstance theory requires the counselor and client to be action oriented. Success means clients must develop certain skills in career counseling and take certain steps that lead to appropriate action (Krumboltz et al., 2013). The first such skill is curiosity. This skill helps clients see opportunities as something to learn from and explore. The curious client is motivated to explore and act without hesitation. The second skill is persistence, a skill that deals with moving forward, beyond obstacles and setbacks. Those who persist do not give up or accept an outcome because they are determined to find a way to go around or past blockades.

The third skill, flexibility, teaches clients how to adapt. A client who is learning how to address different events and circumstances may become less rigid. An inflexible client might be one who reacts the same way and does the same thing regarding every single event or situation. These clients may become extremely frustrated and shut down when things don't go as planned. A career counselor working from this theoretical framework can help an inflexible client adapt to various events. Teaching the client to stay open and continue working toward the goal despite impediments can be crucial in this instance.

The next skill, optimism, is a critical skill for clients because it allows them to have a positive attitude when presented with new opportunities. Whereas pessimists view foreign and new things with negative attitudes and predict the worst outcomes, optimists view new events as opportunities and limit habitually negative attitudes. The final critical skill deals with risk taking. This skill helps prepare clients to face unplanned events without fear. Thus, clients may be less apt to avoid important decisions that might be life changing.

When making decisions, Krumboltz (2009; Krumboltz et al., 1976) uses the DECIDES acronym. Each letter stands for a step required for appropriate decision making in this theory. The steps, in order, are define the problem; establish a plan of action; clarify the values; identify what the alternatives are for the client; discover likely outcomes; eliminate alternatives; and start the action plan. Each step in the process imbeds the empowerment mind-set, action-taking premises, and skills mentioned previously in this section as part of its process.

Krumboltz (2009) makes the following suggestions for counselors working with clients from an HLT premise: Prepare clients for counseling, help clients see their issue as the first phase in a career process, use past successes to create future success, help clients recognize opportunities, and assist in changing dysfunctional beliefs that impede progress. Clients who change impeding thoughts and beliefs and take career action demonstrate counseling success. Finally, Krumboltz (2009) also contends that counseling is a lifelong process that doesn't abruptly end once the client makes a career decision.

Limitations

When working within Krumboltz's (2009; Krumboltz et al., 1976) theoretical frameworks, counselors must become adept at dealing with clients' uncontrollable issues. For example, counselors must be able to discuss the anxiety and disappointment some have regarding genetic inabilities. Consider the person who wants to be an airline pilot but has uncorrectable vision issues. Career counselors may have to help this person come to terms with the fact that this physical issue may block their career path. Let's turn our attention to Guided Practice Exercise 3.3 and think about genetic inabilities and their potential impediments.

Guided Practice Exercise 3.3 Genetic Inabilities

What genetic inabilities might affect certain careers? Make a list of jobs and the genetic characteristics these jobs may require. The first items on your list might be a basketball player, a horse jockey, an airline pilot, and a flight attendant. What genetic abilities might these jobs require? What other jobs and genetic ties can you think of?

Counselors must also be able to discuss environmental issues such as discrimination and help clients understand what can and cannot be done in response. While HLT focuses on capturing unplanned events and circumstances and creating consequential success, many in our society are given less opportunities than others. Consider the minority who, despite past skills, education, and training, are bypassed for a position because of her culture. Women also face advancement issues regarding what is termed the *glass ceiling* (i.e., the inability to move beyond a certain professional hierarchy due to gender) as do those in the LGBTQ community who face the *lavender ceiling*. It may be more difficult for clients with fewer advantages to stay optimistic and take risks, especially those who have been socialized to avoid taking such actions.

Another limitation evident in this theory involves research and validation. For example, it is difficult to validate a theory containing so many variables. As such, genetics, environments, learned versus associative experiences, and task approach skills create a situation where determining which factor has a significant effect, let along validating the effect, is difficult.

Finally, a lack of research involving this theory and its use with culturally diverse groups is an issue. Although the theory mentions genetics and environmental factors as influencing career decisions, this concept is difficult to apply to diverse groups given the theory's western male perspective. Chapter 7 will discuss these issues with regard to discrimination, advocacy, and career issues in greater detail. Now let's turn our attention to another theory involving a social cognitive approach, Lent, Brown, and Hackett's social cognitive career theory.

Lent, Brown, and Hackett's Social Cognitive Career Theory

Premise

The social cognitive career theory (SCCT), of Lent, Brown, and Hackett (1994) is somewhat of a newcomer to the repertoire of career theories but is grounded in Bandura's (1986) general social cognitive theory. It is a theory of cognitive and motivational processes and is utilized to study many areas of psychosocial functioning (e.g., educational, behavioral, medical, and organizational development).

The SCCT focuses on three cognitive-person variables, which are the underpinning of this model: one's self-efficacy beliefs, outcome expectations, and personal goals (Lent et al., 1994). The theory examines how these three variables interact with other aspects of a person and their environment, such as their ethnicity, gender, barriers and social support. Definitions of the three variables are as follows:

- Self-efficacy refers to how someone views their own capabilities, and this can change depending on one's environment, work, personal experience with success and failure, and task at hand.
- Outcome expectations refer to someone's beliefs about the consequences or outcomes of performing certain tasks or specific behaviors.
- Personal goals include both performance goals (which might refer to a grade in a class or to maintain a certain GPA) and choice goals (which might refer to someone's chosen major).

Lent, Brown, and Hackett (1994) analyzed these three variables to examine cognitive-person variables that enable someone to exercise agency, or personal control, regarding their own career development. Additionally, they analyzed variables, such as physical attributes (e.g., race and gender); environmental, extra-person, or contextual, and behavioral variables; and interactions that influence someone's career choice.

The researchers also studied career barriers of different types that influence someone's carrier choice. Barriers, according to Swanson and Woitke (1997), "are events or conditions that make career progress difficult" (p. 434). According to Crites (1969), barriers may be environmental barriers, such as workplace discrimination, or intrapersonal barriers, such as self-concept. While Bandura (1986) emphasized someone's perception about their ability to overcome barriers, Lent, Brown and Hackett (1994) further emphasized a strong belief regarding one's capabilities to overcome environmental obstacles, or coping efficacy, which could make someone more likely to persevere and accomplish their goals.

Assessment

When providing career counseling for someone who is just beginning to plan their career, a battery of tests can be utilized to help with career exploration and decision making. For example, a client might take a personality assessment, an interest assessment, or an aptitude test. Aptitude and skill tests might help strengthen client self-efficacy toward certain jobs when evidence is given toward success in certain areas. The next section will briefly discuss the application of this model.

Steps and Application

Lent et al. (1994) combined elements and created a comprehensive approach that offers an integrative system of concepts (e.g., interest development, decisions, and actions) that attempt to explain internal and external factors that impact career development. These approaches focus on three factors: (a) how academic and career interests develop, (b) how educational and career choices are made, and (c) how academic and career success is achieved. As you might expect when using a social cognitive model, Lent et al. (1994) posited that career development occurs as a result of self-efficacy, outcome expectation, and personal goals. Chapter 12 goes into greater detail regarding how this theory is applied in the career counseling setting. For this reason, we will not delve into more specifics in this chapter. Now let's turn our attention to another theory focusing on cognitions, Hackett and Betz's self-efficacy focused theory.

Hackett and Betz's Self-Efficacy Focused Theory

Premise

The concept of self-efficacy was first introduced by Bandura (1977) and is defined as one's belief about whether they believe they are capable of performing a task successfully. An individual's self-efficacy is thought to be determined by four sources of information: performance accomplishments, vicarious learning, emotional arousal, and social persuasion (Bandura, 1977). *Performance accomplishments* include how successful, or not, one is at mastering tasks that increase in difficulty. The more successful an individual is at completing tasks and using those skill sets to complete more difficult tasks, the more likely they are to believe they are able to be successful in achieving more challenging future tasks. *Vicarious learning* involves seeing the successes or failures of others believed to be similar and internalizing those experiences to define capabilities. *Emotional arousal* speaks to the physiological reactions that one experiences when faced with new tasks. The more uncomfortable and unpleasant the symptoms are, the more unlikely an individual is to attempt or be successful at accomplishing the task at hand. The final source of information, *social persuasion*, involves the amount of external support and encouragement an individual receives.

Hackett and Betz adapted Bandura's theory and applied it to career choice. Specifically, they looked at the significance of gender differences, educational requirements, and occupational duties. Hackett and Betz (1981) proposed that self-efficacy was a more significant factor in career choice than an individual's personal interests, values, and abilities. Hackett and Betz more specifically explored self-efficacy and the career choice and development of women.

Assessment

Because Hackett and Betz's theory focuses heavily on self-efficacy, assessment of this construct is helpful when working within the theory's premises. The *Career Decision-Making Self-Efficacy Scale* and

Occupational Self-Efficacy Scale are described next as two examples that might be utilized to measure client self-efficacy.

Career Decision-Making Self-Efficacy Scale

One of the most notable assessments used to measure self-efficacy in relation to career choice is the *Career Decision-Making Self-Efficacy Scale* (Taylor & Betz, 1983). This assessment looks at tasks that are essential to choosing a career path and attempts to measure how capable individuals believe they are in their ability to complete these tasks. The assessment measures five domains: accurate self-appraisal, gathering occupational information, goal setting, making plans for the future, and problem solving (Betz, 2000; Taylor & Betz, 1983). A 10-point Likert scale is used to assess whether an individual believes they have complete confidence (rated as a 9) or no confidence (rated as a 0). The *Career Decision-Making Self-Efficacy Scale* (Taylor & Betz, 1983) is available in its original 50-item version that assesses 10 items per each of the five domains or in a 25-item version that assesses five items per each of the five domains, entitled the Career Decision-Making Efficacy Scale, Short Form (Betz et al., 1996).

Occupational Self-Efficacy Scale

The *Occupational Self-Efficacy Scale* was developed by Hackett and Betz (1981) and is a 20-item scale that looks at 20 different occupations. The scale measures individuals' perceived self-efficacy related to the academic requirements and job duties necessary for success in the specific occupations mentioned on the scale (Hackett & Betz, 1981). It was originally intended to measure gender differences and representation among occupational fields, specifically looking at the underrepresentation of females employed in traditionally male-dominated occupations (Betz, 2000).

Specific to the career development of women, Betz and Hackett (1997) identify the importance of using both formal and informal assessment interviews with females in career counseling to accurately gauge their self-esteem and self-efficacy.

Steps and Model

Hackett and Betz (1981) tailored their self-efficacy focused theory to examine the significance of gender differences, educational requirements, and occupational duties during the process of choosing a career path. To explore the existence of potential gender differences represented in the workforce, Hackett and Betz tested men and women using the *Occupational Self-Efficacy Scale*. Results inferred differences between men and women regarding self-efficacy. Men scored similarly in both male- and female-dominated careers, and in contrast, women scored significantly higher than men in female-dominated careers and significantly lower in male-dominated careers (Betz, 2000; Hackett & Betz, 1981). These results suggest that while men feel confident in their ability to be successful in traditional male and female occupations, women demonstrate lower levels of self-efficacy in relation to traditional male-dominated professions and thus tend to eliminate such career options prematurely in their career searches.

When working with women, it is suggested that counselors reintroduce the options of traditionally male-dominated careers so that women understand that they do not have to limit themselves and their career choice based on gender roles, self-efficacy expectations, or cultural expectations or barriers (Betz &

Fitzgerald, 1987; Betz & Hackett, 1997). Essentially, the counselor's job is to encourage individuals to look at their personal interests, values, and abilities that may have been compromised due to low self-efficacy.

Utilizing an individual's support system in conjunction with career-specific counseling can also be beneficial. Research has shown there is a strong correlation between teacher and parental support and encouragement when it comes to increasing career decision making, self-efficacy, and career optimism (Garcia et al., 2015). This shows the need for counselors to work with schools and families within the support systems and social environments of children and to encourage career exploration. Counselors must also minimize potential limitations based on gender and gender roles.

Limitations

While Hackett and Betz's self-efficacy focused theory emphasizes female career decision making, it neglects male career decision making. Men also struggle with internalization of gender roles and cultural expectations, potentially causing them to eliminate traditionally female-dominated career options. True equality requires that men's issues also be examined and addressed. One additional gender-related consideration involves the dichotomous view this theory takes regarding gender. It is important for counselors to be culturally competent and sensitive to the LGBT population and how such gender and cultural influences affect them.

The self-efficacy focused theory (Hackett & Betz, 1981) also fails to look at how the impact of past failures impede individuals' development of self-efficacy and self-esteem. Lent and Hackett (1987) suggest that if people have few successful experiences of task or skill mastery or have limited contact with successful role models, they may be less likely to believe they are able to be successful in acquiring, learning, or mastering skills necessary for potential careers.

Although the theory acknowledges that gender roles and cultural influences lead people to eliminate possible career options on the basis of low self-efficacy, limited interventions exist for how to minimize or increase self-efficacy. More research is needed to further determine what interventions counselors in schools, universities, or vocational programs can utilize to help individuals build career decision-making self-efficacy.

As you read in this section, Hackett and Betz focused on beliefs and thoughts a person has about their own ability (i.e., self-efficacy). Now we turn our attention to another theory that focuses on changing cognitions, the cognitive information processing approach. Read on and learn how overcoming negative thoughts can impact career development in this model.

Cognitive Information Processing

Cognitive information processing (CIP) was developed by a group of researchers consisting of James Sampson, Gary Pearson, Robert Reardon, and Janet Lenz in 1991. The theory integrated Aaron Beck's cognitive theory, with career development and decision making to apply to both career decision making and reaching goals of obtaining employment (Sampson et al., 1999). Beck's theory was developed on the belief that irrational beliefs influence behavior and emotion (Beck, 1976). With CIP, these irrational thoughts or dysfunctional thought processes are used to affect career problem solving and decision making. Let's delve into more specific premises of the CIP theory.

Premise

Career decision making is a cognitive process that interacts with affective processes and is often accompanied by frustration and anxiety (Sampson et al., 1999). Thus, CIP helps clients grow by reinforcing information-processing skills that help develop self and occupational knowledge. This processing means the counselor must assist with two major tasks when utilizing the CIP theory: (a) identification of the client's needs and (b) necessary interventions to develop processing abilities and skills to meet those needs now and in the future (Sampson et al., 1999). As part of this, clients learn about themselves regarding personal work ethic, motivations, skills, and weaknesses. This knowledge is then applied to specific jobs. For example, some jobs require strong artistic backgrounds, certain skills, schooling, physical strength, and duration. For CIP theory, problems in these areas are considered chasms between what is occurring and what is desired or where people are employed and where they want to work (Sampson et al., 1999). For example, a client might say, "I just graduated college and I need to find a job." In this instance, a gap exists between today's status and the future job desired. The counselor's role is to find strategies to help overcome this divide.

As you can see from this example, some key issues to consider when working with CIP include problem solving, decision making, and communication. Sampson et al. (1999) discuss the *communication, analysis, synthesis, valuing, and execution (*CASVE*) cycle* and the *pyramid of information processing domains*. The pyramid of information processing domains encompasses the CASVE cycle and involves extensive knowledge of self. The process is described in more detail later in this chapter and entails a great deal of self-assessment.

Assessment

When working in the CIP framework, clients are first assessed on the nature of their career problem and readiness for career counseling. This career readiness assessment helps determine strategies and content of counseling sessions. For example, can the client be helped through self-directed interventions or do they need more targeted assistance (Sampson et al., 2000)?

Next, counselors assess the client's automatic thoughts, be they positive or negative cognitions, using an instrument such as the Career Thoughts Inventory. As mentioned when discussing happenstance theory earlier in this chapter, the *Career Thoughts Inventory (CTI)* was developed to assess dysfunctional career thoughts. Using this valid and reliable assessment in conjunction with cognitive information processing theory might aid in time management, assist in strategy development, and improve the dysfunctional career thoughts impeding job attainment (Sampson et al., 1996). Additional instruments might also be used to assess other constructs such as career beliefs, career maturity, or career identity (Sampson et al., 2000).

One major factor also assessed as part of CIP is self-knowledge. For example, the foundational level of the pyramid of information processing discussed previously includes the assessment of client values, interests, and skills. The client also learns about personal metacognitions such as self-talk, self-monitoring, self-control, and other aspects related to personal awareness. Informal assessments such as card sorts or tailored exercises can help clients determine whether job requirements clash with personal values, interests, and skills (Sampson et al., 1999). It is also important to assess the client's perceptions about these facets. Discussion with clients as they look at job options can help determine client self-efficacy and thoughts (Sampson et al., 1999). Case Exercise 3.2 discusses the case of Ben, an unhappy salesman. See if you can use assessment outcomes to determine issues affecting Ben's employment.

Case Exercise 3.2 Ben's Values

> Ben comes to career counseling and says his boss is driving him crazy. He says he is a salesman and his superiors are always upset with his sales numbers. The boss wants Ben to increase customer prices, yet Ben knows company prices have fallen. It is obvious Ben is very unhappy in his job. You decide to give Ben cards with values listed on them. Ben places them in order of importance according to his own values. The following cards show, in order, (a) honesty, (b) empathy for others, and (c) clarity. Do you think Ben's values might be in conflict with his current job requirements? How would you help Ben?

Let's now move into a greater discussion on the CIP approach's steps and strategies.

Steps, Model, and Application

A good understanding of the CIP approach begins with an examination of the pyramid of information processing domains. The bottom of the pyramid consists of self-knowledge (as detailed in the assessment section in this chapter) and knowledge about career options. The middle of the pyramid requires understanding of client current and typical problem-solving methods, and the top of the pyramid encompasses how thoughts intercede in solving employment issues (Sampson et al., 1999).

Once a client understands their personal interests and values and has knowledge of career options as encompassed in the pyramid's base, they must learn about their own decision making. This middle section of the pyramid encompasses what Sampson et al. (1999) refer to as the CASVE cycle. Table 3.1 shows each factor in the CASVE cycle, along with a short description of each factor, including communication (C), analysis (A), synthesis (S), valuing (V), and execution (E).

As the table illustrates, the CASVE cycle details a process for attaining employment and can be used several times throughout the job search. For example, a college student who has no idea what major to select might use the CASVE cycle to determine areas to study and, after graduation, could employ the process again to target specific jobs. This client might employ the strategies a third time when choosing a position from numerous job offers.

One particular issue noted in Table 3.1 involves what Sampson et al. (1999) refer to as closing the employment "gap" (p. 4). This gap describes the distance between where the client is today and where they wish to be in the future. For example, the a person indecision in choosing one position from several options creates a gap between indecision and career placement. Case Exercise 3.3 asks you to analyze a client's issue and determine the career gap experienced.

TABLE 3.1   **The CASVE Cycle**

Factor Response	Process	Possible Client Response	Effective Response
Communication	Create need for a career decision via internal cues	Procrastination or motivation	Respond to cues
Analysis	Understand connection between thoughts and employment decision making	Accepting incongruent jobs	Reflect on learning
Synthesis	Expand and narrow job options	Too many options	Narrow but keep options; apply learning; remove employment gap
Valuing	Finalize job options	Discouragement	Target specific job or positions; accept job offer
Execution	Act on priority list	Not closing the gap	Send resumes; prepare for job transition

(Information adapted from Sampson et al., 1999)

Case Exercise 3.3 The Retirement Gap

Shaniqua has been working as an accountant for the past 40 years. She wants to retire but is unsure how she will spend her time if she decides to do so. Shanique has thought about going back to school to become an artist but she is afraid she will fail. What employment gap is Shaniqua experiencing? How could the CASVE cycle be used to help Shaniqua?

The top of the pyramid describes a process for helping clients understand how personal cognitions affect employment issues. Self-talk, self-awareness, monitoring, and control are important factors during this stage (Sampson et al., 1999). *Positive self-talk* can be used to help motivate clients to stay focused, avoid discouragement, evaluate positions clearly, stay active in the job search, and follow through with decisions. *Cognitive restructuring* helps eliminate counterproductive thought processes while also boosting these positive cognitions. Once positive cognitions are in place, the client can see connections between thoughts, feelings, and actions, a phenomenon Sampson et al. (1999) refer to as *self-awareness*. *Monitoring* involves knowing when to gather information, when to ask for help, and when a step is completed. *Control* involves the ability to stop negative cognitions, solve problems, and make decisions.

The Counseling Process

With CIP, information is processed in specific steps beginning with screening, translating, encoding to short-term memory, storage in long-term memory, activating, retrieving, and transforming into working memory in order to arrive at a solution (Sampson et al., 2000). Counselors first asses their client's career decision-making readiness before beginning the counseling process (Sampson et al., 2000). Does the client even need this type of career counseling right now, and why or what is the underlying reason the client is now wanting career help? The level of development and need is paired with the correct levels of resources for the client. When a client is ready and developed enough to make complete career decisions, they can also choose and use career resources without full dependence on the counselor.

Next, the counselor identifies client needs. Are they needing a work environment to fit issues regarding relationship and family issues? What career choice best fits the current needs of the client? The counselor then works with the client to highlight career necessities and looks at how, why, and where to meet them. For example, a client wanting to be a professional ballerina is given training and skill requirements related to this career. The client might then be referred to a dance academy or another place specializing in the development of athleticism. Sampson et al. (1999) refer to this as problem solving in that it removes the "gap between their existing and desired state of affairs" (p. 5). Negative cognitions must be challenged and replaced with positive self-talk to improve client outcomes (Sampson et al., 1999, 2000).

Next, the counselor and client process other potential paths and options. Dance lessons at academies might be cost prohibitive, therefore other options can be suggested such as community studios, beginning dance classes, or other athletic skill–building events. Once presented with these alternatives, the counselor and client decide which choices are feasible, realistic, and attainable. For example, the client may have a knee injury resulting in occasional pain. Will taking up ballet cause further injury? Counselors might help clients consider forms of dance that are less exhaustive on the body's knees.

Applying the solution process to the client's decision is the final step. After strategies have been found, the client uses learning to move forward. For example, the client in the previous discussion involving dance might need new dance shoes and a dance-related wardrobe and may showcase their skill and become a dance choreographer instead of a performing ballerina.

Limitations

As with all models, a few limitations are evident. For example, altering cognitions, as suggested when using CIP, requires the ability to analyze, process, and think about our own thinking (*metacognition*). Needless to say, this process requires a certain level of intelligence and cognitive ability. Those with cognitive impairments may be unable to process at levels needed to understand, identify, and alter automatic thoughts when using this model.

Another limitation involves the assessment component. The readiness assessment suggested when using this model needs more research if it is to fully help clients (Sampson et al., 2000). Research might also bring about additional instruments or measures targeted toward specific and unmeasured career readiness constructs (Sampson et al., 2000). These measures would ensure counselors use strategies that target the client's specific issues and, thus, aid in client problem solving and decision making.

The case study that follows offers a glimpse at what implementation of the CIP approach might look like in a client session.

The following case demonstrates use of CIP with a fictional client named Lupe, a 40-year-old married woman who works at an engineering firm. As a single mother, she is the sole bread winner in her family. Her son, Ricky, is 10 years old and in the third grade. Lupe was told yesterday that her job was being eliminated as part of a company downsizing. Follow along as the counselor uses the CIP model to assist Lupe.

Counselor: What would you like to see happen as a result of our time together?

Lupe: I would like to find a job that I like as well as the one I am losing. I have been an electrical engineer at the same company for 10 years. I never thought I would be in this position.

Counselor: It seems you are facing what we call a gap.

Lupe: What is a gap?

Counselor: It just means you find yourself unemployed today and you really want a new position. The gap is the distance between where you are today and that new job. I think we can work on closing this gap. Would you like that?

Lupe: Yes, I really want to do that.

Counselor: The first thing I would like to do is learn a little about you, your interests, values, and beliefs. I have some assessments we can use to do that. Okay?

Lupe: Sure

Counselor: Great. I have some cards here that you can put in order by preference.

Lupe: You want me to arrange the cards by what I like most?

Counselor: Yes, let's spread them out on this table.

Lupe arranges the cards in order by interest. After conducting several screenings and a career readiness assessment, the counselor finds that Lupe is moderately placed on career readiness, problem solving, and career decision making. For this reason, the counselor believes she can be assisted using a self-directed strategy.

Next, the counselor goes over the pyramid and CASVE cycle with Lupe to ensure she understands the process. Once Maria has established goals for her career services, the counselor sends Maria to the library to search jobs that meet her interests, values, beliefs, and abilities. Lupe states she is familiar with the O*Net (as discussed in Chapter 1) and agrees to use this tool to begin this career exploration and decision-making process:

Counselor: Lupe, it seems you are ready to research some career options related to your interests, values, and beliefs. I think we can start working toward your goal of finding the right position by having you look up some options on the O*Net in the library. Does this sound okay?

Lupe: I can definitely start this.

Counselor: Bring the list of potential jobs you find during your research to next week's session. At that time, we will discuss them.

Lupe: I feel better now just having a plan.

Counselor: Before you go, let's look once again at the pyramid and CASVE hand-outs I gave you. We will be working toward the top of the pyramid throughout our time together. Today, we worked on your self-knowledge and, by next week, you will know more about career options discussed as part of the base of the pyramid.

During the next visit, Lupe and the counselor discuss her thoughts about various jobs and help her overcome defeating thoughts. This process is ongoing since Lupe's thoughts may change throughout the sessions.

SUMMARY

Several cognitive, social cognitive, happenstance, and social learning theories were discussed in this chapter. Krumboltz's social learning theory surmises that we learn from others through observation and reinforcement, whereas happenstance learning theory believes that all learning serves a purpose and every experience leads to potential career success. Hackett and Betz applied Bandura's social learning premises to career development and tout the development of client self-efficacy. The cognitive information processing approach uses career readiness assessment, cognitive alterations, and the CASVE cycle to help clients solve problems and find appropriate jobs. The keystones offer a glimpse at some of the major points made in this chapter.

Keystones

- Krumboltz's social learning theory touted that learning occurred through two forms: instrumental (learning through direct experiences) and associative (learning through observation).
- Happenstance learning theory emphasizes that chance events can have positive or negative consequences over a client's life and that these consequences also affect career choices and paths.
- Hackett and Betz and Lent, Brown, and Hackett adapted Bandura's theory and applied it to career choice. Hackett and Betz (1981) believed self-efficacy was more significant in one's career choice than individual values, interests, and abilities. Lent et al. (1994) posited that career development occurs as a result of self-efficacy, outcome expectation, and personal goals.
- The CIP model was developed not only to help with career exploration and problem solving, but also to help clients find appropriate work.

Author Reflections

Of all the chapters in this textbook, this one seems to offer such relief. I can't help but feel great serenity knowing that we can help clients who fear decision making to see the positive aspects within every career choice. Even bad decisions can lead to the best outcomes. My own career journey included many deviations from what I originally anticipated, yet every turn along the way helped lead to the career happiness I have today. I think clients who understand that career development is just that, a developmental process, understand every decision is but one brick in what will be a very long path. We learn from every decision and from every person we encounter. This learning is invaluable as we navigate our way toward career opportunities. I hope this chapter helped you, as a future counselor, understand your own career development and what will be a journey toward your own future success as well as that of your clients. —Janet Hicks

Additional Resources

The following resources provide additional information about the content provided in this chapter.

Articles

Krumboltz, J. D. (2009). The happenstance learning theory. *Journal of Career Assessment, 17*(2), 135–154.
> This article describes happenstance theory in greater detail for further study.

Sampson, J. P., Lenz, J. G., Reardon, R. C., & Peterson, G. W. (1999). A cognitive information processing approach to employment problem solving and decision making. *Career Development Quarterly, 48*(1), 3–18.
> This article describes the CIP approach in greater detail and offers additional examples for further study.

References

Bandura, A. (1977). *Social learning theory*. Prentice-Hall.

Bandura, A. (1986). *Social foundations of thought and action: A social cognitive theory*. National Institutes of Mental Health. Prentice-Hall, Inc.

Beck, A.T. (1976). Cognitive therapy and the emotional disorders. New York: International Universities Press.

Betz, N. E. (1981). Implications of the null hypothesis for women's career development and for counseling psychology. *The Counseling Psychologist, 17*(1), 136–144.

Betz, N. E. (2000). Self-efficacy theory as a basis for career assessment. *Journal of Career Assessment, 8*(3), 205–222.

Betz, N. E., & Fitzgerald, L. F. (1987). *The career psychology of women*. Academic Press.

Betz, N. E. & Hackett, G. (1986). Applications of self-efficacy theory to understanding career choice behavior. *Journal of Social and Clinical Psychology, 4*(4), 279–289.

Betz, N. E. & Hackett, G. (1997). Applications of self-efficacy theory to the career assessment of women. *Journal of Career Assessment, 5*(4), 383–402.

Crites, J. O. (1969). *Vocational psychology: The study of vocational behavior and its development*. New York: McGraw-Hill.

Donnay, D. A. C., & Borgen, F. H. (1996). Validity, structure, and content of the 1994 Strong Interest Inventory. *Journal of Counseling Psychology, 43*(3), 275–291.

Garcia, P. R. J. M., Restubog, S. L. D., Bordia, P., Bordia, S., & Roxas, R. E. O. (2015). Career optimism: The roles of contextual support and career decision-making self-efficacy. *Journal of Vocational Behavior, 88*, 10–18.

Hackett, G., & Betz, N. (1981). A self-efficacy approach to the career development of women. *Journal of Vocational Behavior, 18*(3), 326–339.

Krumboltz, J. D. (1994). The Career Beliefs Inventory. *Journal of Counseling & Development, 72*(4), 424–428.

Krumboltz, J. D. (2009). The happenstance learning theory. *Journal of Career Assessment, 17*(2), 135–154.

Krumboltz, J. D., Mitchell, A. M., & Jones, G. B. (1976). A social learning theory of career selection. *The Counseling Psychologist, 6*(1), 71–81. https://doi.org/10.1177/001100007600600117

Lent, R. W., & Hackett, G. (1987). Career self-efficacy: Empirical status and future directions. *Journal of Vocational Behavior, 30*(3), 347–382.

Lent, R. W., Brown, S. D., & Hackett, G. (1994). Toward a unifying social cognitive theory of career and academic interest, choice, and performance. *Journal of Vocational Behavior, 45*(1), 79–122.

Mitchell, L. K., & Krumboltz, J. (1996). Krumboltz's learning theory o career choice and development. In D. Brown, & L. Brooks (Ed.), Career choice and development (3rd editions). San Francisco: CA: Jossey-Bass.

Myers Briggs Company. (n.d.). The history of the Myers Briggs Type Inventory. Retrieved from https://eu.themyersbriggs.com/en/tools/MBTI/Myers-Briggs-history

Sampson, J. P., Lenz, J. G., Reardon, R. C., & Peterson, G. W. (1999). A cognitive information processing approach to employment problem solving and decision making. *Career Development Quarterly, 48*(1), 3–18.

Sampson, J. P., Peterson, G. W., Lenz, J. G., Reardon, R. C., & Saunders, D. E. (1996). *Career thoughts inventory*. Psychological Assessment Resources.

Sampson, J. P., Peterson, G. W., Reardon, R. C., & Lenz, J. G. (2000). Using readiness assessment to improve career services: A cognitive information processing approach. *Career Development Quarterly, 49*(2), 146–174.

Super, D. (1953). A theory of vocational development. *American Psychologist, 8*(5), 185–190.

Swanson, J. L., & Woitke, M. B. (1997). Theory into practice in career assessment for women: Assessments and interventions regarding perceived career barriers. *Journal of Career Assessment, 5*, 431–450. https://doi.org/10.1177/106907279700500405

Taylor, K. M. & Betz, N. E. (1983). Applications of self-efficacy theory to the understanding and treatment of career indecision. Journal of Vocational Behavior, 22(1), 63–81.

CHAPTER 4

Developmental Career Theories and Models

Elizabeth Ann Wardle, Janet Hicks, and Leslin Ossoff

An individual's self-concept is the core of his personality. It affects every aspect of human behavior; the ability to learn, the capacity to grow and change. A strong, positive self-image is the best preparation for success in life.
—Joyce Brothers

The self-concept, as stated by Joyce Brothers, is an important consideration in a person's personality and, consequently, their career development. It is an inherent component in the career search decision-making process and may factor into a person's ability to attain and maintain a position. As indicated by Donald Super (Herr, 1997), a popular developmental career theorist, our self-concept travels with us throughout our lifetime and is seen as a major component of career development. Read on to discover more about Donald Super and other theorists such as Ginzberg and colleagues, Tiedeman and O'Hara, and John Crites.

CHAPTER OVERVIEW

This chapter outlines the developmental vocational theories discussed in the career counseling literature. Students learn basic premises, assessment, steps in the process, and limitations of theorists' contentions. Students will apply this knowledge to a fictional client at the end of the chapter and again when integrating counseling theory in sessions later in the text.

LEARNING OBJECTIVES

After reading this chapter, you will be able to do the following:

- Understand developmental vocational theories and techniques
- Understand the concepts of Ginzberg et al.'s developmental theory, Donald Super's life span life space, Tiedemann and Ohara's developmental theory, and Crite's vocational developmental project
- Apply developmental vocational techniques with clients who are facing career counseling/vocational discernment issues.

Ginzberg, Ginsburg, Axelrad, and Herma's Developmental Theory

The following information will help you understand more about the developmental theories. Let's begin with the developmental approach by Ginzberg and Associates.

Premise

The basic premise of Ginzberg, Ginsburg, Axelrad, and Herma's developmental theory is that "career development is a life-long process" based on stages or phases of developmental patterns that are largely irreversible (Ginzberg, 1951, p.186). The original theory was derived from the work of Eli Ginzberg, an economist, who was working on a research grant from Columbia University. He was studying occupational choices of "upper middle-class young men because of their privilege to choose their careers" (Kilhefner, 2018, p. 1). Sol Ginsburg, Sidney Axelrad, and John Herma were part of the research team, and their role was to interview the subjects, analyze the data, and write results. The group developed research conclusions and published them in 1951 in a work entitled "Occupational Choice: An Approach to a General Theory." This work was important because its contentions led the way for other theories (Voliva, 2014). Let's delve further into the basic concepts of this theory by examining the steps, model, and application touted as part of the basic premises.

In a nutshell, the major role of assessment in career counseling is self/career exploration—a complementary process
—Prediger (1995, p. 1)

Assessment

When looking at career development from a developmental perspective, assessment does not end at any particular point in time. Rather, it is an ongoing process throughout a person's lifetime. As a developmental theory, then,

Ginzberg et al.'s process can be aided through use of assessments that help clients explore and arrive at career decisions. This exploration and decision making are referred to as *crystallization* and *specialization*. Table 4.1 describes these crystallization and specialization stages.

TABLE 4.1 Ginzberg et al.'s Realistic Stages

Stage	Stage Title	Stage Characteristics
Stage 1	Exploration	The person chooses a career path but remains open to consider other opportunities.
Stage 2	Crystallization	The person commits to a particular career choice and begins to focus on that pathway more than any other to an extent not demonstrated before. A career pattern becomes clear.
Stage 3	Specification	The individual now focuses on a particular job. A compromise is made between desires and opportunities.

Assessments such as personality instruments, interest inventories, and values tests might aid clients as they move through these crystallization and specialization stages. For example, personality assessments might help the person have enough insight to narrow down career options and compromise on possibilities. Interest inventories can be used to match careers with a person's likes and dislikes. Values assessments can help clients determine whether personal beliefs align or conflict with specific jobs. Personality, interest, and values instruments combine to yield responses that further career exploration and, as discussed in Chapter 1, the O*Net can be used to target job possibilities. In short, assessment offers knowledge that lends itself to the lifelong planning, preparation, and training required for chosen careers (McKay, 2019).

Steps, Model, and Application

Ginzberg's developmental theory originally began with play in childhood and ended during the stages of adolescence and early adulthood. Ginsberg's career choice theory has three periods of career development: fantasy, tentative, and realistic. Let's look at each of these periods in greater detail.

> *The roots of intrinsic work satisfaction can probably be found in the play activities of children. Although we have little knowledge of the linkage between play and work, it surely exists*
> **(Ginzberg, 1951, p. 223).**

- The first phase is called the *fantasy period.* This period occurs before the age of 11 at a time when children tend to believe in endless career possibilities. At the same time, they have little understanding of what is required for job preparation, such as training, education, economic factors, or specific skills. They typically say, "When I grow up, I'm going to be a … " Once they approach the age of 11, their activities and interests more accurately relate with career choices rather than simply play.

- The second phase is called the *tentative period*. This period falls between the ages of 11 and 17 and consists of four stages. During this time, adolescents recognize and become able to identify and focus on career requirements. Table 4.2 shows the stages and descriptions for children operating in the tentative period.

TABLE 4.2   **Ginsberg et al.'s Tentative Stages**

Stage	Stage Title	Stage Characteristics
Stage 1	Interests	Children/adolescents are able to identify their likes and dislikes.
Stage 2	Capacity	A child/adolescent begins to learn how their abilities match up with their interests.
Stage 3	Values	At age 15, a child/adolescent becomes aware of how work can fulfill their values.
Stage 4	Transition	This stage begins when a child/adolescent accepts responsibility for their actions and demonstrates independence and freedom of choice.

- Ginzberg et al.'s final phase is called the *realistic period*. This period occurs beginning at age 17 and continues through young adulthood (Ginzberg, 1951). Three stages are evident during this time and are depicted in Table 4.1.

Ginsberg has since revised this theory to reflect a lifelong occupational decision-making process. The theory now accounts for occupational changes occurring in midlife as well as during post-retirement. Revisions were created to describe job changes occurring well beyond adolescence and into early adulthood, thus overcoming the previous theoretical limitation associated with the shortened adult career span (Kilhefner, 2018).

The revised theory now also touts the reversibility of early career choices. For example, while early choices are thought to impact career development throughout the life span, the revised theory touts that these choices can be changed over time as a person's needs and internal characteristics change (Ginzberg et al., 1972). Guided Practice Exercise 4.1 asks you to consider your own career development based on Ginzberg et al.'s theory.

Guided Practice Exercise 4.1 A Lifespan of Songs

Take a sheet of paper and write the three periods discussed by Ginzberg et al. (fantasy, tentative, and realistic) across the top of the page. Under each time period, create a list of songs you remember that describe your own career development during this time in your life. Share your list with a partner and discuss how these songs tie to Ginzberg's stages and how they relate to the theory. Discuss issues in your life as related to the songs.

Limitations

Despite the theoretical revisions mentioned previously in this chapter, Ginzberg et al.'s theory has been criticized for not taking sociological issues into consideration (Goodluck et al., 2018). For example, educational and career guidance inequities exist and create differing opportunities for clients, depending on worldwide location. Unclear links between universities and specific careers may further exacerbate these inconsistencies and affect choices made in the tentative and realistic periods.

Despite these limitations, Eli Ginzberg's career choice theory deserves credit as being the first of the developmental career theories. In fact, it has been called the foundation on which the newer career development theories were created (Kilhefner, 2018). Another theory, Donald Super's life span, life space career development theory, built on Ginzberg's work and will be discussed in the next section.

Donald Super's Life Span, Life Space Developmental Theory

Premise

Donald Super, a psychologist, was a colleague and consultant of Eli Ginsberg at Columbia University and helped with his work and theories. Concerned that Ginsberg's work had limitations, Super extended Ginzberg's original stages from three to five and also made changes to the theory's substages (Zytowski, 1994; New Zealand Government,

In choosing an occupation, one is, in effect, choosing a means of implementing a self-concept.
—Donald Super

2019). The result was Super's *life span, life space theory*, a theory surmising that career choice was not an entry-level event, but a lifelong process (Herr, 1997).

Super's work helped to shape and define career counseling for over 50 years (Herr, 1997). According to Nevill (1997), Super's career was unique in that "he spanned the three realms of theory, research, and application" and "he wanted his ideas and discoveries to be useful and accessible to other individuals" (p. 1). Super not only provided theories and data, but he also contributed tools to be utilized in research, assessment, and counseling. He spent his career revisiting, revising, and expanding his previous work and was always responsive to the need for change.

Part of this responsiveness included looking into many aspects within a person's development. For example, Super's research and publications addressed the importance of work as being a part of the human identity. Identity was seen through developmental stages and career development was viewed as occurring across the life span. Work self-concept occurred through physical and mental growth, observations of work, modeling, environment, and life experiences.

According to Zytowski (2017), Super is considered to have played a pivotal role in the synthesis of work values and today's career development theory. While Ginzberg focused on work satisfaction, Super was more interested in work values. This interest and accompanying research led to the development of the Work Values Inventory (Zytowski, 1994). Further, work with Nevill led to a Value Scale (VS), as published in 1985. The Value Scale is available in several translations and was intended for use in cross-cultural studies of vocational behavior.

Results from Super's research for the Work Importance Study, for which the Values Scale was created, were included in a book published with Branimir Sverko, a colleague from Yugoslavia, titled *Life Roles, Values, and Careers in International Perspective* (1995). This multinational study examined work values in traditional capitalistic and socialistic societies and included research from 10 countries: Australia, Belgium, Canada, Croatia, Italy, Poland, Portugal, the United States, Japan, and South Africa. This study provided results that support the universality and stability of values. These values demonstrate the fulfillment of personal potential as a life goal, regardless of the boundaries of culture, status, and gender.

According to Prediger (1995), Super's focus on understanding of the self-brought about "Super's dictum," which has its roots in the ancient Greek thought/teaching, "know thyself." According to Super's dictum, "an occupation gives one the chance to be the kind of person one wants to be; hence, career choices are based on self-concepts projected into career options" (Prediger, 1995, p. 1). Career counseling helps the client to better understand their career options by organizing information and data from various assessments to formulate a plausible career plan. Let's further examine how assessment is an important component as part of the life span, life space theory in the next section.

Assessment

For Super, career development was a lifelong work that lasted 50 years. His contribution to the field of career assessment and development counseling included multiple assessments, publications, and research. Following is information on several of his assessments.

First, Super's *Work Values Inventory* measures the importance of someone's core values, work activities, work interactions, and work environment. This values assessment offers help when considering personal morals, ethos, and beliefs that are part of the career decision-making process. Super's *Career Concern Inventory* assists career counselors as they work with clients who may be changing jobs, planning retirement, or changing jobs too frequently. A third assessment, Super's *Career Development Inventory,* is used to help high school and college students make career plans. The *Values Scale,* another assessment, is used to measure the importance of 21 individual values that are relevant to career choice and the workplace (Kapes & Whitfield, 2002). Finally, the *Salience Inventory* is used to measures someone's commitment and participation in five life roles (student, worker, citizen, home and family, and leisure) and will be mentioned later in this chapter when we discuss the assessment of Super's life career rainbow (Career Research, n.d.).

An additional assessment, the *FOCUS-2,* evolved as the most recent version of the Education and Career Exploration System's education exploration assessments. It was developed in 2000 to assist high school and college students with career exploration and followed seven other assessment programs that began in 1967 (FOCUS 2, n.d.). As one of the first computer-assisted career planning systems ever developed, it offered a new assessment medium and involved several developers. For example, the project team included Frank Minor, PhD, psychologist with IBM; Donald Super, Columbia University Teachers College; and David Tiedeman, career theorist. Continue reading to learn more about the specifics of Super's life span, life space theory including interesting items such as Super's life career rainbow, his stages, roles, cycles, and mini cycles.

Steps, Model, and Application

Super viewed career development as occurring via cycles and mini cycles. Throughout a person's life span, individuals were believed to venture through a number of stages and to hold many life roles. Each role encompassed a certain amount of a person's space at any given time (Super, 1957).

Super also believed a person could recycle through the stages and, over time, roles could change. These changes might result in the person recycling through the stages or experiencing a series of mini cycles. As a result, the client's age might not necessarily coincide with the ages and stages listed in Super's life span. To help better clarify this premise, Super's life spans and roles can be seen in Tables 4.3 and 4.4.

TABLE 4.3 **Super's Life Span**

Stage	Stage Title	Age	Stage Characteristics
Stage 1	Growth	0–14	Development of self-concept, attitudes, needs, and general world of work
Stage 2	Exploration	15–24	"Trying out" through classes, work experience, and hobbies. Tentative choice and skill development
Stage 3	Establishment	25–44	Entry-level skill building and stabilization through work experience
Stage 4	Maintenance	45–64	Continual adjustment process to improve position
Stage 5	Decline	65	Characteristics: Reduced output; preparation for retirement

TABLE 4.4 **Super's Life Roles**

Role, Timeframe, and Characteristics
Child: From birth to school age, and then, in the 50s–60s, when parents are aging and need assistance from their children
Student: School age, depending on country of origin, usually begins at 3–4 years and may last until the age of 16, or, depending on higher education and college, into one's 20s. At the present, many people are attaining continued education throughout their lifetime.
Leisurite: A term, coined by Super, which refers to how people spend their leisure time. This may be time spent in adolescence or time spent after retirement.
Citizen: Refers to the time spent in community service, usually unpaid. Many people participate in community service when their children are getting older, as they typically have more free time.
Worker: The time someone spends in employment.
Parent: The time spent on raising children. This usually ends when children are in their mid to late teens. However, it may also include time spent in higher education and sometimes when children return home.
Spouse: The time spent in a committed relationship, including the activities to maintain the relationship role.
Homemaker: Typically begins when someone leaves the home of their parents and sets up homemaking in a home of their own. Includes time spent on cooking, decorating, cleaning, shopping, maintenance, and so on. (Mulder, 2018).

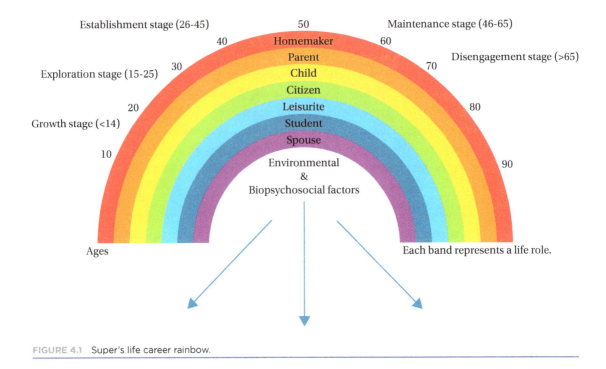

FIGURE 4.1   Super's life career rainbow.

Life Career Rainbow

In 1957, Super wrote what is considered his defining book, *The Psychology of Careers*, and modified his concepts in 1980. The life career rainbow is the result of that modification. It depicts the various roles (as seen in Table 4.4) that one plays at different times in one's life. The life stages are depicted around the edges of the rainbow, and the life roles are placed within each of the rainbow's bands. Along each of the bands, there are different sizes of dots, and the sizes depict the amount of time that someone spends on that role (Mulder, 2018). Figure 4.1 depicts Super's life career rainbow.

Super's Archway Model of Career Determinants

Super (1963) created a second model he called the archway of career determinants. It was intended to make more explicit these environmental and intrapersonal determinants of career that are the developmental tasks of the career rainbow model. The basic tenets in Super's developmental tasks are the ideas that (a) individuals differ in abilities, interests, values, and so on; (b) intrapersonal characteristics make individuals more or less suited to certain careers; and (c) these differences and the careers available to an individual at any given time are influenced by situational factors (Psychology, n.d.c). Super created a graphic to describe how personal and sociological factors form a foundation and culminate in the career self-concept.

The archway model of career determinants in Figure 4.2 looks like an arch. The left pillar of the arch consists of the needs, values, and interests that make up the personality. Intelligence, aptitude, and special abilities also integrate into the personality spectrum. Above the personality, on this same pillar,

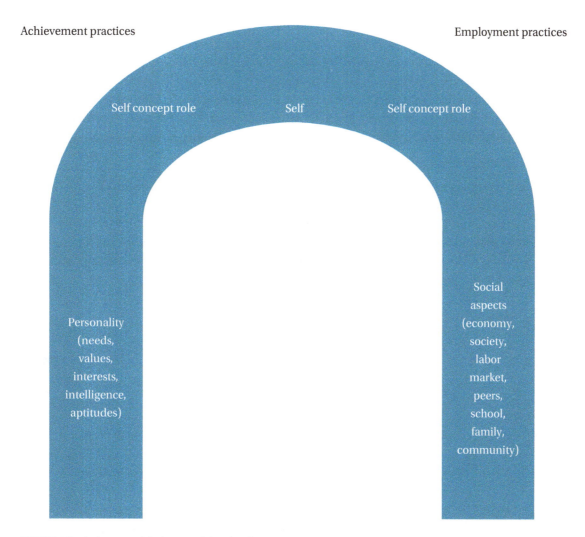

Achievement practices   Employment practices

Self concept role   Self   Self concept role

Personality
(needs,
values,
interests,
intelligence,
aptitudes)

Social
aspects
(economy,
society,
labor
market,
peers,
school,
family,
community)

FIGURE 4.2   Archway model of career determinants.

are developmental stages and roles. The self-concept sits at the top and in the center of the archway, indicating its reliance on the factors on which it sits.

The right side of the model consists of sociological factors such as the labor market, society, and economy. As part of this sociological foundation, the community, school, family, and peers integrate. Above the sociological components lie developmental stages and roles. The right side of the graph curves to the right, forming the right side of the arch. Again, the self sits in the center, illustrating how personal and situational determinants result in a unique career self-concept.

Limitations

As with all theories, some limitations are evident. Some feel the theory overemphasizes the role of the individual and underestimates the role that the environment and culture play in career choice

(Psychology, n.d.c). While Super's theory recognizes that situational determinants play a role in career choice, some believe it does not recognize the impact of discrimination against people of color. Additionally, some expand on this cultural aspect and believe that the emphasis on individual choice does not consider the role that family plays in certain cultures (Psychology, n.d.c). Guided Practice Exercise 4.2 asks you to look at your own life span and determine your roles and how they fit within Super's stages.

Guided Practice Exercise 4.2 Your Life Span and Roles

Take a moment and look over Super's contended life roles. Which of these roles have you held in your life? Which are you managing now? Draw a rainbow and label each band with a role you have held. List ages from birth to age 80 on the circumference of the rainbow. Color in each band to illustrate how much time each role took at each stage of life. Do you think this would be a good activity to have a client complete? How would you modify it for a variety of clients and concerns?

Tiedeman and O'Hara's Choice and Adjustment Ego Development Theory

Premise of Theory

David Tiedeman's ego development theory was introduced in 1963 (Tiedeman & O'Hara, 1963). This theory, choice and adjustment, was considered ground breaking, as it emphasized the role of ego development in the career development process, and in particular career decision making (Hershenson, 2016). Healthy ego development was a result of the mastery of crisis, as defined by the psychosocial theory of Erikson, which allowed an individual to develop a positive view of the work environment.

Each man owns his own life. I only hope that he is the architect of his future as he lives it.
—Tiedeman

Career decision-making skills and career development was also considered when the individual sought identification and acceptance of their evolving self through the process of differentiation and integration. It also separated differentiation and integration of decision making into two distinct processes: preoccupation, or anticipation, and accommodation, or implementation.

Tiedeman's theory was considered one of the first constructivist-based theories in career development (Tiedeman & Miller-Tiedeman, 1984). Constructivism concludes that the individual creates their own meaning, and constructivist theories are, therefore, based on individual autonomy and meaning. Chapters 9 and 10 will integrate two constructivist counseling theories, narrative therapy and solution-focused brief therapy, with career theory.

The most enduring contributions of Tiedeman and O'Hara's theory were the role of ego identity development in career development, the significance of differentiation and integration as a part of an evolution of career decision making, and the role of purposeful action when dealing with a lack of coherence.

Tiedeman worked with multiple collaborative partners, including Anna Miller, Gordon Dudley, and John Peatling. These researchers considered multiple revisions and adaptations of the original theory before arriving at the final theory. Continue reading to see premises and steps described in these final revisions.

Steps, Model, and Application

Influenced by the developmental theory of Ginzberg et al. (1951), the Tiedeman and O'Hara model has two stages. The first, *anticipation*, is comprised of the substages of *exploration, crystallization, choice,* and *clarification*. During this period, the individual goes from having somewhat disorganized career choice thinking to increased clarification. The person then moves to the *implementation and adjustment* period, which is comprised of the substages of *induction, reformation*, and *integration* and involves the development of a sense of self and vocational identity (Oliver, 1977). As the individual goes through the previously mentioned stages, *differentiation* and *integration* occurs in sync with Erikson's ego-identity developmental stages. At the same time, the relationship between personality and career must be balanced and the person must navigate biological, sociological, and psychological issues (Grande, 1964).

The person-to-situation, person-to-world, and orientation-to-work factors gradually evolve from within a personal reality perspective. To emphasize this personal reality and individuality in career decision making, Tiedeman and O'Hara (1963) coined the term *I-power*. The individual may arrive at a career impasse based on external factors (e.g., war, job loss, financial crises) or psychological drives (e.g., unmet needs) but, ultimately, each person chooses their own behaviors. When career impasses occur, the person goes through the previously mentioned stages, beginning with exploration and ending with integration. Should integration not occur, the person may choose to adapt or withdraw and start over. As the person becomes more familiar with the evolving nature of the career development process, they experience growth and are more apt to refine or adapt to a decision (Tiedeman & O'Hara, 1963). Throughout the process, assessment can be used to guide decision making. Case Exercise 4.1 asks you to consider Tiedeman and O'Hara's steps when reviewing the case of Tara, a high school graduate with few career skills who needs to make a career decision.

Case Exercise 4.1 Tara's Indecision

Tara is an 18-year-old female who has just graduated high school. She feels very down on herself because she wants to go to college but feels she must enter the job market to support her family. How does Erikson's ego development play a role in Tara's issue? Which of Tiedeman and O'Hara's stages would Tara be functioning in? What guidance would you give Tara? How could you teach Tara about the career development process using Erikson and Tiedeman and O'Hara's stages?

Assessment

Tiedeman's assessment process focused heavily on decision making. A few pertinent assessment tools used as part of Tiedeman's theory include the *Information System for Vocational Decisions* (*ISVD*), one of the earliest computer-based career guidance programs. The *Assessment of Career Decision Making (ACDM)*, as developed by Vincent Harren, was also useful in that it was specifically designed to measure career decision-making skills and, to date, has been revised seven times (Psychology, n.d.b.). In 1967, Tiedeman was also a collaborative partner of Minor, Super, and Myers in the development of the Education and Career Exploration System (ECES) (FOCUS 2, n.d.).

Limitations

According to Psychology (n.d.b), Tiedeman's theory has been criticized for being somewhat complicated and for using unclear terminology. A question has also risen regarding its related assessments. For example, some questions have risen as to whether the Information System for Vocational Decisions even relates to the theory. Numerous assessment revisions may invite outside influences or constraints, making assessment validity difficult to measure (Psychology, n.d.b.).

Another limitation of the theory concerns the efficacy of the research guiding the theory's development. The original sample was small and homogenous, leading to concerns when applying premises to diverse groups (Psychology, n.d.b). Now, let's turn our attention to an interesting concept that affects persons over time, John Crites's career maturity.

Crites's Vocational Development Project

The information that follows will introduce you to Crites's Vocational Development Project. Read along and discover how the concept of maturity affects career development.

Premise

The developmental theory of John Crites and his conceptualization of maturity is based on the developmental model of Donald Super. Super (1953) suggested that, in addition to systematic changes occurring within an individual (e.g., aptitudes and achievement, physical changes, goals, interests and values, interpersonal relationships, motives and personality, health, physique and strength), persons should look at work life (Pressey & Kuhlen, 1957). Crites (1969) contended that *work life* (i.e., occupational choice and job-adjustment behavior during the years of adolescence and adulthood) be recognized independently while still existing in relationship with the systematic changes Super suggested.

Theoretical Development and Application

In order to study the developmental phenomenon of adjustment, educational achievement, and vocational maturity as dimensions of development in adolescence, John Crites developed a cross-sectional and longitudinal study to collect data on the interrelationships of the systematic variables mentioned. His subjects were 483 fifth graders who would participate in current assessments and follow-up measurements 7 years later. These meant students would be followed from grades 5 to 12. The outcome of the research demonstrated that early adjustment was related to later adjustment, in addition to educational achievement and vocational maturity. These scores correlated with ratings for each student that were provided by their teacher and school counselor (Crites, 1982).

This assessment tool and process is still useful to determine the maturity of students and their ability to make career decisions. Career development interventions can be implemented as necessary. Read on to learn more about specific assessments and how they help in the career maturity process.

Assessment

Crites created the *Career Maturity Inventory* in 1960 to determine students' career attitudes regarding the creation of vocational planning. In 1973, career planning competencies including world of work and self were added to the original assessment. Two additional revisions were subsequently made, with the most recent changes made in 1995 (Crites & Savickas, 1996). Over these two revisions the Career Maturity Inventory was improved to make it more user friendly and to ensure appropriate use with high school students and adults. The most recent version assesses career competence, attitudes, and maturity through a 50-item standardized instrument. It is one of the leading instruments for the assessment of career maturity (Crites & Savickas, 1996).

Crites also developed the *Career Adjustment and Development Inventory* to measure issues related to current employment (Crites, 1982). For example, potential and current work integration, work/peer relationships, and career advancement issues were assessed using this instrument. When using the instrument, 110 items are scored, with results ranging from integrative (removes negative issues), adjustive (reduces negatives issues), and non-adjustive levels (doesn't remove or reduce negative issues).

Limitations

Several limitations have been mentioned regarding Crites's career maturity approach (Kapes & Whitfield, 2002; van't Wout & van Dyk, 2016). For example, it has been recommended that additional research is needed to address reliability, construct, and criterion-related validity in the *Career Maturity Inventory* (Kapes & Whitfield, 2002). Numerous research inferences based on instrument validity would go a long way in ensuring assessment meaning and the efficacy of consequential interventions.

Some researchers argue about the operational definition of Crites's career maturity. The limitation of the variables (adjustment, educational achievement, and vocational maturity) has been challenged by a study of young members of the African Defense Force who found the factors influencing career maturity to be self-efficacy, occupational information, self-appraisal, commitment, challenge, emotional intelligence, and continuous improvement (van't Wout, & van Dyk, 2016). More research may be needed to uncover aspects contributing to the construct of career maturity.

CASE STUDY

The following case illustrates how Ginzberg et al. and Super's premises might be used to assist a fictional client in his career development. Excerpts tying information to specific theories are included to help you better understand some of the information in this chapter.

John is a 17-year-old high school junior. He is the oldest of three children. John's parents are both college graduates. His father is a production engineer for a local refinery and his mother is a registered nurse and works for a home health care provider. He is contemplating his attendance at the college of his choice and also his major. *Ginzberg et al. would say John is transitioning into the realistic period and Super might focus on the various roles John is functioning within in addition to targeting John's stage of career development.*

John's mother has always hoped that he would become a doctor, but John states that while it is a well-paying career, he doesn't want to deal with sick people. His father has stated that he just wants John to choose wisely and hopes that he doesn't extend his college attendance by changing his major. So, he has encouraged John to talk to a career counselor at the local community college, because he says that if John doesn't have a good idea about a major, he's worried that he "will take too many courses that won't count and end up with a five-year degree, or worse, drop out and not finish." Tiedeman and O'Hara might focus on John's I-power in that he ultimately makes his own choice.

John was always small for his age. While he loves sports, he did not have the height for basketball or the size for football. He did play Little League baseball but states that he doesn't want to be a kinesiology major and feels like the competition for any career in baseball is unrealistic for him. Super would consider these aspects crucial in that they contribute to the development of John's career self-concept.

Neither of his parents is insisting that he follow in their footsteps or attend their previous schools. John's parents started a college fund for each of their children when they were small, and most of their college is already paid for, but changing majors and adding extra courses means added tuition costs. He understands why his father doesn't want him to change majors, lose credits for courses that won't count, and end up running out of money that was set aside for his education.

John has been a good student, with a B or better grade average. He knows that it is important to study, and he has good study habits. He states that he knows that when he has decided on a major, he will apply himself and be a serious student. However, he is very unsure about what he wants to study. *Crites might consider John's work life, or the adjustments he is facing as he transitions from being an adolescent to entering adulthood. Tiedeman and O'Hara might focus on John's ego development. Some of this may be his transition from identity versus role confusion, as mentioned by Erik Erikson (1980), in conjunction with career-related decision making.*

Counselor: Hello John, I am Mrs. Jackson, and as a career counselor here at Ridge View College I can help you to explore career options and to decide on your college major.

John: Thank you, Mrs. Jackson, right now, I don't have a clue.

Counselor: Why don't you tell me a little about what your parents do and also about your friends' parents? What are some of the careers that they have that might sound like something you would want to consider?

John: Well, Mrs. Jackson, my mother is a nurse and she thinks I ought to be a doctor, but I don't like being around sick people. My father is a process engineer for Black Water Refinery. But I don't think that I want to go into engineering. That's means I would have to take lots of math classes, and … well … I'm not a bad student, but math just isn't my favorite subject."

Counselor: Tell me about the classes that you do like better than math.

John: Well … I like the science classes. I have taken biology, chemistry and physics and made A's in all of them. I like history, and English is okay. Computer science was a breeze.

Counselor: Well, John, I have just the assignment that I think will make your decision about a college major a little bit easier. Will you be able to spend some time in our computer lab, about 2 to 3 hours? There are three career assessments that I would like for you to complete, and I think that will help you learn more about yourself and, hopefully, make your choices a great deal easier.

John: I can stay here today and do that.

Counselor: Great! Let me walk you around to the computer lab and introduce you to the person who runs it. Is that okay with you?

John: Okay.

Counselor: Mrs. Brown, this is John, and he needs to complete a *Myers-Briggs Type Inventory* (a personality assessment), a *DISCOVER* (a skills and abilities assessment), and a *Strong Interest Inventory* (an interest instrument), please.

Mrs. Brown: No problem. We have an available computer and enough time for him to finish.

Counselor: Great! Just send him back to my office when he has his printed reports.

Mrs. Brown: He should be finished in approximately 2 hours.

Counselor: John, when you have finished here in the computer lab and have your reports, just come back to my office, and you and I will discuss what that information says about some career choices that just might be for you.

When John returns, the counselor and John look over his assessments and use the O*Net to search for information. Once John narrows his list of potential majors and career fields, he is asked to complete a values checklist to ensure no values conflicts exist regarding career paths. Because John seemed somewhat unmotivated even after selecting his major, the career counselor asks John to draw a rainbow showing how his roles today differ from his preferred future roles. John discusses meaningful efforts that will move him to his desired state.

SUMMARY

Many theorists, such as Ginzberg et al., Donald Super, David Tiedeman, and John Crites understood the importance of viewing career issues as longitudinal rather than cross-sectional. These theorists' developmental theories made great strides in studying the way someone makes a career choice, whether they are happy with their choices, and what career counselors can do to help someone with their career concerns. From basic premises to assessment of constructs, developmental level has become an important career facet.

From the early days of Ginzberg to Super, and to Tiedeman and to Crites, the importance of assessments to study a person's career choice, their motivation, their values, and how their personality affected their job, has been evident. Each of the developmental theorists we studied in this chapter made important contributions, and most created assessment tools we continue to use today. Despite the limitations of assessments and theoretical premises, these items can become catalysts for additional research that, hopefully, helps us to better understand paths to successful and satisfying careers.

Keystones

- From the early days of developmental theory, the importance of assessment was evident.
- Super's dictum of "know thyself," makes sense in career counseling when we are helping someone figure out their career choices
- Studying the career theorists and the amount of knowledge they have provided is extensive.

Author Reflections

Preparing to write this chapter gave me a great opportunity to learn more about the theorists I didn't study when I took career counseling. There is so much knowledge and information in the developmental theories about personal understanding that can be applied to daily living, not just a career! It has been well worth the review! This gives a whole, new meaning to growing up and getting a job! —Ann Wardle

Additional Resources

The following resources provide additional information about the content provided in this chapter.

Organizations

American Counseling Association

https://www.counseling.org/

   The American Counseling Association is the national organization for counselors.

National Career Development Association (NCDA) (Division of American Counseling Association)

   http://www.ncda.org.

Originally the National Vocational Guidance Association, NCDA was one of the founding associations of ACA in 1952. NCDA provides professional development, connection, publications, standards, and advocacy to career development professionals who inspire and empower individuals to achieve their career and life goals.

Books

Wood, C., & Hayes, D. (2013). *A counselor's guide to career assessment instruments*, 6th ed., Broken Arrow: National Career Development Association.

References

Bandura, A. (1997). *Self-efficacy: The exercise of control*. Freeman.

Career Research (n.d.). *Career salience*. Career Research. http://career.iresearchnet.com/career-development/career-salience/

Crites, J. O. (1969). *Vocational psychology*. McGraw-Hill.

Crites, J. O. (1982). Testing for career adjustment and development. *Training and Development Journal, 36*(2), 20–28.

Crites, J. O., & Savickas, M. (1996). Revision of the Career Maturity Inventory. *Journal of Career Assessment, 19*(4), 131–138.

Erikson, E. (1980). *Identity and the lifecycle*. Norton.

FOCUS 2. (n.d.). *FOCUS 2 history*. https://www.focus2career.com/History.cfm

Goodluck, K., Odike, E. L., & Anake, P. (2018). An appraisal of Eli Ginzberg and associates' theory of career development. University of Calabar. https://www.researchgate.net/publication/324954575_AN_APPRAISAL_OF_ELI_GINZBERG_AND_ASSOCIATES_THEORY_OF_CAREER_DEVELOPMENT_By_GOODLUCK_KINGDOM_UMEGBEWE_DEPARTMENT_OF_EDUCATIONAL_FOUNDATIONS_GUIDANCE_AND_COUNSELLING_UNIVERSITY_OF_CALABAR_CALABAR_NIGER

Ginzberg, E. (1972). Towards a theory of occupational choice: A restatement. *Vocational Guidance Quarterly, 20*(3), 169–175.

Ginzberg, E., Ginzburg, S., Axelrad, S., & Herma, J. (1951). *Occupational choice: An approach to a good theory*. Columbia University Press.

Grande, P. (1964). Tiedeman and O'Hara on career development: Choice and adjustment. *Counseling and Values, 8*(3), 103–105.

Herr, E. (1997). Super's life-span, life-space approach and its outlook for refinement. *Career Development Quarterly, 45*(3), 238–246.

Hershenson, D. B., (2016). Historical perspectives of career development theory. In M. A. Stebnicki (Ed.), *The professional counselor's desk reference* (pp. 411–420). Springer.

Kapes, J., & Whitfield, E. (2002). *A counselor's guide to career assessment instruments* (4th ed.). National Career Development Association.

Kilhefner, J. (2018). *Career advice: The career theories of Eli Ginzberg*. The Nest. https://woman.thenest.com/career-theories-eli-ginzberg-15464.html

McKay, D. (2019, October 21). *Using an interest inventory: How your likes and dislikes are a clue to the right career*. The Balance Careers. https://www.thebalancecareers.com/interest-inventories-526168

Mulder, P. (2018). *Super's life career rainbow*. Toolshero. https://www.toolshero.com/psychology/personal-happiness/life-career-rainbow/

Nevill, D. (1997). The development of career development theory. *Career Development Quarterly, 45*(3), 288–292.

New Zealand Government. (2019, December 6). *Super's theory*. https://www.careers.govt.nz/resources/career-practice/career-theory-models/supers-theory/

Oliver, L. (1977, September). *An overview of career development theory*. U.S Army Research Institute for the Behavioral and Social Sciences. https://apps.dtic.mil/dtic/tr/fulltext/u2/a077932.pdf

Prediger, D. (1995). Assessment in career counseling. *ERIC Digests*. https://www.counseling.org/resources/library/ERIC%20 Digests/95-18.pdf

Pressey, S. L., & Kuhlen, R. G. (1957). Psychological development through the life span. New York: Harper & Row.

Psychology. (n.d.a.). *Crites' career theory*. https://psychology.iresearchnet.com/counseling-psychology/career-assessment/ career-maturity-inventory/

Psychology. (n.d.b.). *Tiedeman's theory*. https://psychology.iresearchnet.com/counseling-psychology/.../tiedemans-theory/

Psychology (n.d.c.). *Super's theory*. https://psychology.iresearchnet.com/counseling-psychology/counseling-theories/ supers-theory/

Super, D.E. (1953). Career patterns as a basis for vocational counseling. *Journal of Counseling Psychology, 1*, 12-20.

Super, D.E. (1957). *The psychology of careers*. New York: Harper.

Super, D. E. (1963). Self-concepts in vocational development. In D. E. Super, R. Starishevsky, N. Matlin & J. P. Jordaan (Eds.), *Career development: Self-concept theory* (pp. 1–16). College Entrance Examination Board.

Super, D., & Sverko, B. (1995). *Life roles, values, and careers: International findings of the work importance study*. Jossey-Bass.

Tiedeman, D. V., & Miller-Tiedeman, A. L. (1984). Career decision making: An individualistic perspective. In D. Brown & L. Brooks, (Eds.), *Career choice and development: Applying contemporary theories to practice* (pp. 281–310). Jossey-Bass.

Tiedeman, D. V., & O'Hara, R. P. (1963). *Career development: Choice and adjustment*. College Entrance Examination Board.

Tiedeman, D., Roe, A., Super, D, Holland, J. (1972). *Perspectives on vocational development*. American Personnel and Guidance Association.

van't Wout, C, & van Dyk, G., (2016). Factors influencing career maturity in the South African National Defense Force: A diagnostic approach. *Journal of Psychology in Africa, 26*(1), 29–34.

Voliva, J. (2014). *Ginzberg, Ginsburg, Axelrad, & Herma's developmental model*. Prezi. https://prezi.com/frasucmitczc/ ginzberg-ginsburg-axelrad-hermas-developmental model/

Zytowski, D. (1994). A Super contribution to vocational theory: Work values. *Career Development Quarterly, 43*(1), 25–31.

Figure Credits

CHAPTER

Psychological, Sociological, Gender, and Diversity-Based Career Theories

Krystal Humphreys, Dara Brown, and Janet Hicks

Dreams are extremely important. You can't do it unless you imagine it.
—George Lucas

George Lucas is one of the most imaginative minds in the film industry. Most of us would not guess that his lifelong dreams of being a race car driver were shattered by a debilitating fear that resulted from a tragic car accident. This struggle forced him to imagine a new dream, a dream that would later grace the silver screen. Career counseling theorists have taken many different approaches to helping individuals facing similar struggles find their strengths, imagine dreams, set goals, and even alter plans when life takes a different turn.

CHAPTER OVERVIEW

Often, we find clients who are searching for direction and purpose in life. These inner desires to create life meaning are connected by many aspects of an individual to include current and future career choice. Many career theories, as mentioned in this textbook, have focused on a person's development, personality, self-concept, and diversity, among other areas. Career counseling theories are meant to help counselors navigate the various factors affecting their client's career choice. Helping clients understand their individual factors aids in the process of goal setting and ultimately allows them to reach or even change their imagined dreams as life demands.

For these reasons, we must look at the unique influences each individual brings to the career counseling setting. As a result, this chapter will outline the psychodynamic, psychological, sociological, and gender- or diversity-focused vocational theories discussed in the career counseling literature. Basic premises, assessment, steps in the process, and limitations of theorists' contentions are included with each theory. Knowledge of each theory will be applied to case studies at the end of the chapter and again when integrating counseling theory in sessions later in the text.

LEARNING OBJECTIVES

After reading this chapter, you will be able to do the following:

- Identify the basic premise of each theory
- Apply assessments associated with each theory
- Integrate steps of each theoretical process when working with diverse clients
- Analyze the limitations of theorists' contention
- Apply knowledge to clients through fictional case studies

Brill's Psychoanalytic Theory

Premise

Brill's psychoanalytic theory of vocation is rooted in the traditional concepts of psychoanalysis. Brill was a true believer in psychoanalysis and worked with Freud until his death. He greatly influenced society by translating much of the writings of Sigmund Freud and Carl Jung into English.

In Brill's (1921) *Fundamental Concepts of Psychoanalysis,* he applies the fundamentals of psychoanalysis to vocational choice. He believes that we begin counseling with a symptom and, after analysis, we uncover a hidden wish that the client holds for their future or vocation (Brill, 1921). The central tenant of an individual's career choice is based on past experiences and influences. However, the main concept of Brill's theory is *sublimation*. Freud (1896) first introduced sublimation as a defense mechanism and defined it as being a method for satisfying unconscious impulses in a socially acceptable manner. For example, an individual who, as a child, desires aggressive behaviors may grow up to play sports in an attempt to satisfy his or her aggressive desires.

Brill (1921) attributes vocational choice to other areas within the unconscious mind. Psychoanalysts believe that individuals strive to replicate experiences in childhood and satisfy unfulfilled, unconscious desires. Childhood experiences have great influence on career development and are expressed through latent content within dreams (Brill, 1921). Brill's work is based on several of his clients. One client, a lawyer, had a childhood experience where he told a significant lie to his parents. After many years, he began having dreams of being judged before God. As a result, he grew up and became a lawyer. Brill (1921) was quick to separate dreams from fairy tales. He believed that imagined fairy tales were the result of "archaic" thinking and often represented repressed and sublimated needs. These repressions occurred so the person might fit in with society and its standards. Case Exercise 5.1 discusses the case of John the butcher. See if you can determine how Brill's theory is evident in John's case.

Case Exercise 5.1 John the Butcher

John is a 29-year-old butcher who says he was in legal trouble in his teens. Once he became gainfully employed as a butcher, however, he stopped his involvement in criminal behavior. John discloses that, at one time, he had fantasies of killing animals and, later, people. He is happy to report that since becoming a butcher, these fantasies have disappeared. How might Freud's defense mechanism of sublimation be at work in John's case?

Brill's psychoanalytic approach to career choice assumes that individuals who are in a profession satisfying conscious and unconscious desires will not suffer from career burnout or failure (Brill, 1921). Instead, symptoms of work-related burnout are attributed to mental illness. Failure, on the other hand, occurs when a person works in an unfit vocation.

People enter into unfit work-related circumstances when attempting to please others. Brill (1921) suggests that parents can easily hinder their child's vocational experiences by choosing or suggesting their vocation. Parents observe children's characteristics in an attempt to find their child's ideal vocation. In an effort to provide success for their children, parents place pressure on youth to enter vocations that do not sublimate for unconscious desires. In addition, other figures in a person's life make work-related suggestions that do not satisfy the driving forces within the individual.

Brill (1921) gives an example of this premise using a client from within his own practice. He describes a female schoolteacher who came to him with much anxiety. After completion of analysis, she did not desire to return to teaching. He suggested that she take philanthropy classes at Columbia University, which she continued, even after her symptoms of anxiety reappeared. Brill asked her why she continued with the course and her response was "because you told me to take it" (Brill, 1921). This is a clear example of how people tend to choose or change occupations based on relationships with key people in their life.

Assessment

Assessment in this theory appears to share the same therapeutic functions as traditional psychoanalysis but with a focus on career choice. Assessment involves uncovering motives or drives that have pushed an individual toward a particular career choice (Brill, 1921). Unlike the trait and factor theorists mentioned in Chapter 2, Brill (1921) suggests that career counseling should not provide advice for an individual or assume that each person has qualifying attributes for a particular vocation. Instead, Brill believes one should use psychoanalysis to investigate psychic activity and that clients should follow childhood paths. Further, one must assess the unconscious motives that drive the sublimation process.

Steps, Model, and Application

The concepts of this theory follow the traditional steps associated with psychoanalysis. In all reality, it is psychoanalysis applied to vocational choice. Psychoanalysis serves to reduce symptoms, such as anxiety, and create more adaptive functioning (Brill, 1921). One does this by focusing on two specific goals. Traditionally, these goals are (a) to bring unconscious motives into consciousness and (b) to foster behavior that is founded on realistic ideals rather than unconscious desires (Brill, 1921). The therapist accomplishes these two goals by providing an environment conducive to self-awareness as needed for change. By identifying feelings associated with memories and uncovering meaning through dream work, this level of self-awareness becomes a reality.

The first concept in the psychoanalysis approach is the *blank screen*. This approach is the therapists' way of maintaining a relationship with their client that is nonjudgmental and avoids knowledge of the therapist's personal life (Brill, 1921). It allows the client the opportunity to project onto the therapist and express feelings that originally occurred in an earlier relationship.

Free association begins after the client has seen the therapist on several occasions. While lying on a couch without the ability to view their therapist, the client will discuss any memories, feelings, thoughts, or fantasies (Brill, 1921). This allows the client to express any desires or thoughts without judgment from the therapist. The same can be applied to career development. For example, a client might discuss memories and internal desires associated with vocation.

Interpretation of things revealed during free association is essential to the process. During this time, the therapist offers meanings of behavior, dreams, resistance, defense mechanisms, and the therapeutic relationship (Brill, 1921). In addition, interpretations are founded on thoughts and feelings presented by the client. Often, reactions from interpretations are used for further analysis.

Dream work is a central concept associated with this theory. As discussed earlier, client hidden wishes and desires are expressed in the latent content of dreams (Brill, 1921). *Latent content* is the unknown, symbolic content of dreams. A client may discuss a memory during free association that is related to a dream. During analysis, the therapist will make these connections and find the underlying meaning for the client. The unconscious desires are brought into consciousness and help the client find self-awareness. Often, these hidden desires are the driving force in career choice (Brill, 1921).

Limitations

Brill's theory does not take diversity issues into consideration. First, most of his research is based on men in the work force. He attributes much of men's' unconscious vocational desires on an ultimate desire to compete with other men in their mother's life (Brill, 1921). He feels these men ultimately have an unconscious motivation to outdo their fathers or other men whom their mother admires, even their family doctor. Since access to psychoanalysis was mostly available to wealthy men, this theory of career choice can be seen as having limitations with women or those who are not a part of a higher socioeconomic status.

Bordin's Psychodynamic Theory

Premise

When discussing Bordin's psychodynamic approach to career choice, we must first consider the basis of psychodynamic theory. Psychodynamic theory looks much like psychoanalysis; however, it is not solely based on Freud's theory. Rather, it takes into consideration the theories from his followers such as Carl Jung and Alfred Adler, among others. In addition, the duration of psychodynamic theory tends to be shorter than psychoanalysis. Still, the foundation of the theory is the internal driving forces and unconscious desires associated with the individual person.

Bordin stays true to the inner motives of the individual while describing his theory in terms of *work* and *play*. Bordin (1994) believes that other career theories focused too much on tests and assessments because they attempted to be "realistic" and avoid the wishes, dreams, and inner desires of a person. He also contended that self-expression and play be considered luxuries and used only after meeting basic needs. Bordin (1994) believed that people would sacrifice safety and choose a dangerous life in order to fulfill their desire for self-expression. For example, he believed that the inner desires and workings of the *self* and self-expression are more powerful than the need for basic survival.

As an alternative to investing in interest inventories and assessments focused on learning and the history of the individual, Bordin (1994) proposes gaining a full understanding of human action by fixating on the ideas of work and play. He believes that inner motives for work and play interact in a complex fashion. For example, is a professional ballet dancer working or playing? What about an athlete or a musician? Work and play are also approached differently by diverse persons. For example, some individuals take time off from work to do things such as play golf. Some will work during times when they are able to be off from work (Bordin, 1994). In either example, basic needs are not necessarily being met. Another example might be the "starving artist" or those in the fine arts industry attempting to succeed as professional musicians, dancers, artists, and actors/actresses. These artists will often give up basic needs for their craft. Examples such as these attempt to examine how people fuse work and play into a meaningful experience.

Assessment

As previously stated, Bordin believed that interest inventories and other assessments placed too much emphasis on conforming to societal pressures and left out the inner dreams of the individual. Bordin (1994) felt the counselor should assess clients on several key elements pertaining to the inner-outer quality in work and play. The elements he associated with work and play were spontaneity, effort, compulsion, intrinsic and extrinsic rewards, satisfactions, and motives (Bordin, 1994).

Spontaneity

Bordin (1994) describes spontaneity as being the individual's motivation to express oneself and reach the places of inner and outer joy. These natural impulses to express oneself are ingrained in who we are and lack effort or preplanning. Each person has a desire to express themselves in a way that is reflective of their inner wishes and dreams. These are individualistic and make each of us unique. Our spontaneity can be described as the inner motivation for work and play.

Effort

Effort makes play a complex notion and requires energy (Bordin, 1994). It is the physical, psychological, emotional, and intellectual exertion needed to accomplish the end result of a spontaneous action. The reason that it complicates *play* in our lives is because this *work* adds the needed time for rest.

Compulsion

The continued effort required for play that began with spontaneity begins to feel more like compulsion. In mental health, we often use the term "compulsion" to describe an act that cannot be controlled, yet is not desired by the individual (Bordin, 1994). Compulsion occurs when issues arise in fusing the efforts of work and play. For example, a professional ballet dancer feeling pressure to perfect an art may morph from spontaneous desires of artful expression to perfectionistic compulsions.

Intrinsic and Extrinsic Reward, Satisfaction, and Motive

The internal struggle between work and play is also affected by internal and external forces (Bordin, 1994). *External motivations* are attained through rewards such as awards, money, and praise. *Internal motivation*, on the other hand, consists of rewards based on the internal satisfaction of the experience. For example, an externally motivated advertising agent may work long hours to achieve success and receive a promotion in their company. An internally motivated advertising agent would work long hours because they enjoy the actual act of brainstorming ideas and feeling creative.

Steps, Model, and Application

Career choice is often expressed by personality and can be determined by how well a person has been able to fuse work and play. Instead of using assessments to determine career choice, Bordin (1994) prefers to evaluate personality, lifestyle, and intrinsic motives. He begins his model with what is described as *mapping*. Mapping is used to determine the intrinsic motives within each person and ways these motivations are met in various occupations.

In the process of mapping, a career counselor analyzes several intrinsic motives. These include *precision, nurturance, curiosity, power, aesthetic,* and *ethics and concerns with right and wrong*. These motives are used to find a way to fuse work and play, which ultimately determine career choice. As we look at each intrinsic motive, we can see similarities with Brill's thoughts on sublimation, meaning that they both determine career choice as established by the inner, unconscious desires of an individual. Table 5.1 describes each factor used in mapping.

Limitations

Several limitations are associated with Bordin's theory. First, while Bordin believes that cultural issues, socioeconomic factors, gender, and other issues are career factors, they are not imbedded as part of his theory. He does not discuss how one's culture may affect the internal motivations that are examined in his career analysis. Second, Bordin assumes that occupations can be molded to fit intrinsic motivations. There are circumstances, however, where an occupation may not conform to a person's inner desires. Bordin also assumes that these intrinsic motivations are more powerful than one's circumstances. This

TABLE 5.1   **Factors Found in Mapping**

Factor	Description	Examples
Precision	Motivation and satisfaction, which comes from organized thoughts and actions	Lawyers, mathematicians, surgeons, administrative assistants
Nurturance	Motivation to devote oneself to the growth and change of living things	Farmers, social workers, psychotherapists
Curiosity	Inner desire to know more about complexities and inner workings of what we view in our daily life	Scientists, engineers
Power	Physical, psychological, social, or legal power over another	Judges, politicians, machine operator, professional athletes
Aesthetic	Motivation to have sensory or rhythmic satisfaction	Artistic professions or any in-born talent
Ethics and concerns with right and wrong	Part of being human and separating ourselves from others. It is the definition, justification, and enforcement of the spirit of the law.	Military, law enforcement, religious leaders

may be true for some individuals, but for others, cultural and personality aspects may affect whether some pursue their inner motivations. For example, those in a collectivist society may make choices for the good of their group rather than to please their own individual desires.

Roe's Psychologically Focused Theory

Premise

Although research gives little credence to many of Anne Roe's contentions (Brown et al., 1997), her contributions continue to be seen as influential in career development. She won several awards for her vocational research after spending years working in various roles. Her recognition did not come easy. Harvard initially rejected her for a faculty position because she was a woman (Wrenn, 1985). Even after she became a full professor at Harvard, men in the department were outraged by her presence.

Contrary to Bordin's theory suggesting career choices are based on intrinsic motivation, Roe believed career choice was based on needs. As such, her theory was largely founded on Maslow's (1943) hierarchy of needs in relation to parent-child relationship patterns. A description of this concept follows.

Despite research invalidating the concept (Brown et al., 1997), Roe believed primary caregivers and early childhood experiences to be indirect influencers on career choice (Roe, 1956, 1957). She proposed several parent-child relationship patterns that affected needs and, later, behavior to satisfy needs (Roe, 1957).

These seven basic needs included psychological needs; safety, belonging and love; importance, respect, and self-esteem; information acquisition; beauty; and self-actualization. Roe went even further and touted that these early parent-child interactions determined personality and resulted in occupation-seeking behaviors geared *toward people* or *not toward* people (Roe, 1957). For example, a child who receives a warm and accepting relationship from their parents will seek out careers that foster the same type of environments. Empirical evidence does tout that people who have a more human orientation, or, in Roe's terms "toward people," are likely to be found in occupations demanding social interaction (Brown et al., 1997; Levine, 1963).

Assessment

Several assessments are based on Roe's theory. The first assessment, the *Parent-Child Relations Questionnaire,* was developed in response to Roe's theory of parent-child interaction (Roe & Siegelman, 1963). The assessment measures parent behavior toward their children. It consists of 10 subtests that measure characteristics such as love, protection, demand, rejection, neglect, cause, symbolic-love reward, direct-object reward, symbolic-love punishment, and direct-object punishment (Roe & Siegelman, 1963).

Other inventories measure similar traits such as the *Career Occupational Preference System Inventory (COPS).* This inventory measures levels of interest in 14 career cluster categories (Knapp et al., 1984). Roe and Lunneborg (1990) proposed that Maslow's needs be assessed via individuals' need satisfactions as found in different occupations. That being said, the *Minnesota Importance Questionnaire* (*MIQ*) can also be used to evaluate several levels of needs in a client (Brown et al., 1997).

Steps, Model, and Application

In order to fully understand Roe's contentions and application of the theory, Table 5.2 depicts parenting styles and Table 5.3 shows Roe's eight occupational *fields* of interest. Application of Roe's theory involved tying these parenting styles to six occupational *levels* that mimicked early childhood home environment. Table 5.4 shows a depiction of Anne Roe's six occupational levels by level of responsibility.

TABLE 5.2 **Parenting Styles**

Style	Description
Overprotecting	Attends to all childhood needs
Overdemanding	Makes many demands on child
Loving acceptance	Parenting based on concern, love, acceptance, and child's worth
Casual accepting	Parenting based on concern for child when it is considered feasible
Neglecting	General lack of love or concern. Characterized by rejection and abandonment

TABLE 5.3 **Eight Occupational Fields**

Field	Description	Examples
Service	Concerned with the needs of others	Firemen, police, military, counselors
Business	Concerned with face-to-face commodities or investment	Salesmen, buyers, public relation workers
Organization	Concerned with efficient functioning of an organization	Bankers, legal clerks, government workers
Technology	Concerned with production, maintenance, and transportation	Mechanics, engineers
Outdoor	Concerned with cultivation and preservation of resources	Farmers, those in forestry, miners, landscapers
Science	Concerned with theory and application of theory	Academics, pharmacists, scientists
General culture	Concerned with the preservation of cultural heritage	Journalists, ministry, linguistics, educators
Arts and entertainment	Artistic/special skills in the creative arts	Artists, actors, dancers, musicians

TABLE 5.4 **Roe's Six Occupational Levels**

Level	Occupation Type	Skill Description
1	Professional/management	Independent, full responsibility
2	Professional/management	Semi-independent responsibility
3	Entry-level management	Moderate responsibility
4	Skilled labor	Training required
5	Semi-skilled labor	On-the-job training
6	Unskilled labor	Little to no training needed

Limitations

Several limitations are associated with Roe's theory. Theorists such as Brill and Bordin might say Anne Roe's theory does not consider the internal forces or desires within a person. As stated previously in this chapter, Bordin (1994) believed that these intrinsic motivators were far more powerful than any other basic need.

Roe's theory has also not shown promise when researched. Although, Brown et al. (1997) attribute lack of empirical evidence to the misconceptions of her theory, many feel her contentions are non-evidence based. Further research is needed in a manner that associates parenting to career choice in an indirect way if Roe's theory is to be taken seriously (Brown et al., 1997).

Another possible limitation is the fact that parents may have different parenting styles. The assessment she created does have a male version. However, this does not account for aspects of two different parenting styles interacting with one another. Guided Practice Exercise 5.1 asks you to consider your own parents, how you were parented, and accompanying thoughts about your own childhood with regard to career counseling.

Guided Practice Exercise 5.1 Childhood Experiences and Career Choice

How did your childhood experiences affect your career choice? Look at Anne Roe's theory and identify your parent–child interactions. See if these interactions played a role in your desire to work "toward" or "away" from people. Discuss these ideas with a partner and its implications on your career development.

Circumscription and Compromise Theory

Premise

Linda Gottfredson's circumscription and compromise theory was developed in 1981. The theory primarily looks at how counselors working with school-aged children can help guide them toward career choice. Gottfredson looked at how individuals are attracted to and dissuaded from certain career paths as they grow and develop. This process begins in childhood and continues through adolescence and beyond, depending on one's individual needs and perspectives of the world.

With the introduction and continuing advances of technology, as well as societal strides toward equal opportunity employment, individuals are tasked with career selection from an early age (Gottfredson, 1981, 2005). When presented with an overwhelming number of career options as well as societal pressure to choose an academic or career track, even young children can experience anxiety. Gottfredson (1981, 2005) believed this anxiety could lead children to make incompatible career choices, thus increasing the need for counselor guidance and assistance.

Although much of the research surrounding the circumscription and compromise theory involved school-aged children, it is also applicable for adults considering career changes or workforce reentry (Gottfredson, 1981, 2005). Adults inherently stereotype jobs as being male or female oriented and understand job prestige. Gottfredson believed adults made choices based on these premises (Gottfredson, 1981).

Gottfredson's theory relied heavily on the cognitive domain, as demonstrated in Bloom's taxonomy of educational objectives (Anderson et al., 2001; Bloom et al., 1956). This model purports that individuals learn in a hierarchical manner. For example, people first learn isolated facts by remembering, identifying similarities and differences (understanding), making educated guesses by using previously learned information (applying), assessing various options and opportunities (analyzing), determining that some choices are more appropriate than others (evaluating), and developing a plan to achieve a goal (Anderson et al., 2001; Bloom et al., 1956).

Assessment

The phenomenological and experiential nature of self-development evident in Gottfredson's theory incurs an absence of links to formal assessments. Gottfredson (2005) offers that traditional vocational interest inventories only capture broad groupings of traits and interests and do not explain the impact of gender roles and social constructs such as socioeconomic status, income, race, and ethnicity.

Steps and Model

The processes of circumscription are broken down into four stages: orientation to size and power, orientation to sex roles, orientation to social valuation, and orientation to internal, unique self. Table 5.5 illustrates these important stages in Gottfredson's model.

TABLE 5.5 **Stages of Circumscription**

Dimension	Stage	Age Range	What Children Acknowledge
	Orientation to size and power	3–5 years old	Adults have roles and responsibilities
Gender	Orientation to sex roles	6–8 years old	Gender roles
Prestige	Orientation to social valuation	9–13 years old	Education level Income Lifestyle Socioeconomic status Race Ethnicity Religion
Field of Work	Orientation to internal, unique self	14+ years old	Personal interests Core values Personality Abilities

According to Gottfredson (1981, 2005) and Blanchard and Lichtenberg (2003), individuals are more likely to first compromise the field of work dimension, then their social level dimension, and lastly their sex-type dimensional beliefs. This makes sense since, chronologically and developmentally speaking, individuals are more likely to hold onto their earlier, more engrained beliefs (gender roles) than they are the ones that they learn later in life (field of work, personal interest).

In summary, the process of circumscription involves individuals eliminating various careers based on a series of dimensions, as depicted in Table 5.5. The process of compromise occurs when individuals are left with career options they consider acceptable and favorable. They then begin to eliminate some of the more favorable careers based on accessibility (Gottfredson, 2005).

The question, then, surfaces as to what exactly leads people to eliminate some desirable careers and not others. Gottfredson (1981, 2005) suggests three reasons people may compromise their highly preferred careers for less favorable but more accessible ones: truncated search and limited knowledge (obtaining quick but limited information from friends or family), bigger investment and better accessibility (investing in education, skills, volunteer work), and the good enough or not-too-bad career (settling for an easier to attain job within the person's comfort zone).

Limitations

Two major limitations are evident in the circumscription and compromise theory. First, the theory's heavy emphasis on childhood development treats adolescent experiences as being equal to adult issues (Swanson & Fouad, 2010). Other theories, such as the developmental self-concept theory developed by Super (1957) or the eight stages of psychosocial development developed by Erikson (1959), acknowledge the various life struggles, changes, and crises that may occur throughout the life span. The second limitation of the circumscription and compromise theory involves the lack of assessment needed to measure the phenomena of development (Swanson & Fouad, 2010). This lack of assessment and accompanying research leaves Gottfredson's theory up for debate.

Astin's Sociopsychological Model

Premise

Helen Astin's (1984) sociopsychological model of career choice stemmed from her own personal experiences. Astin grew up in Greece and, as a child, desired to pursue a career in architecture. Gender and cultural norms prevented her from pursuing her dreams, however, and her family encouraged her to choose something more practical and realistic. In response she chose elementary education training. Astin's father was an engineer, and her family quickly pointed out that the field of engineering and architecture offered minimal opportunity for women. She later pursued a degree in psychology and focused her thesis on the topic of career development for women.

Based on her own life experiences, Astin's sociopsychological model looks at how an individual's needs as well as their social interactions in early childhood impact their interests, both positively and negatively (Astin, 1984). Astin's theory mimics Roe (1956) and Bandura (1977) in that it identifies the importance of childhood experiences and learning from others' career behaviors and decision making. This sociopsychological model looks at both sociological influences in a person's life, such as interactions with others and cultural influence, as well as psychological influences (e.g., personal needs, expectations, and motivations) (Astin, 1984; Gothard, 2001).

Despite her interest in career choice and opportunity for women, the sociopsychological theory can be used with both men and women. Specifically, it explores how men and women are both motivated in similar ways to enter into the workforce and perform job duties (Astin, 1984; Gothard, 2001). The model is based on four principles, which include (a) that work motivation satisfies three basic needs, including survival, pleasure, and contribution; (b) that career choices are based on expectations regarding how accessible work is for an individual and how much work satisfies the needs of survival, pleasure, and contribution; (c) that career expectations and opportunities are based on interactions with family, peers, early work experiences, and cultural implications; and (d) that career expectations are changed by job opportunity, which can also lead to changes in career choice and job performance (Astin, 1984). One of the strengths of the sociopsychological model is that it is sensitive to cultural limitations. Looking at the varying degrees of opportunity, or limits thereof, allows the sociopsychological model to be applied to both advantaged populations as well as disadvantaged populations, cultural minorities, and women.

Assessment

Just as Astin's theory considers interactions between personal learning and experiences, so does the *Career Beliefs Inventory* (Krumboltz, 1991, 1994). This inventory's psychosocial approach attempts to measure the beliefs and generalizations people hold about themselves and work. It is thought that these beliefs and generalizations may prevent people from achieving their career goals (Krumboltz, 1991). For this reason, counselors might use these assessment results to work with people to change distorted beliefs.

The Career Beliefs Inventory can be used to help individuals match their career aspirations with various academic or work environments as well as to explore new learning experiences and the development of new interests (Krumboltz & Jackson, 1993). When counselors use this assessment to suggest new learning experiences or interests, they may be engaging in a proactive intervention. People have the tendency to focus on skill sets they currently possess, failing to take into consideration their ability to change, learn, and adopt new skills that could open the door for many more career options (Krumboltz & Jackson, 1993).

The Career Beliefs Inventory (Krumboltz, 1991, 1994) consists of 95 items that are grouped into 25 different scales. The scales measured in this assessment include employment status, career plans, acceptance of uncertainty, openness, achievement, college education, intrinsic satisfaction, peer equality, structured work environment, control, responsibility, approval of others, self-other comparisons, occupation/college variation, career path flexibility, post-training transition, job experimentation, relocation, improving self, persisting while uncertain, taking risks, learning job skills, negotiating/searching, overcoming obstacles, and working hard. These 25 scales are also broken down to measure an individual's current career situation, what they deem necessary to be happy, things that influence decision making, changes they are willing to make, and efforts they are willing to demonstrate.

Steps and Model

As previously mentioned, the sociopsychological model is based on four basic principles: work motivation, sex-role socialization, structure of opportunity, and expectations (Astin, 1984). Work motivation shows the reasons people enter into the workforce and why they continue to work. Sex-role socialization demonstrates what environments people are introduced to and have contact with early on in their lives. It further shows how they learn traditional gender roles. The internalization of such gender roles has a significant impact on what careers people deem appropriate for them, what work they are capable of, and what they like and/or are good at doing. Structure of opportunity explores the various cultural implications that make certain careers more or less available, accessible, or practical for an individual. These three principles work together to develop the expectations people have of themselves and of employers.

Work Motivation

People are thought to be motivated to work for three reasons; *survival, pleasure, and contribution. Survival* speaks to one's ability to provide for basic needs such as food, water, clothing, heat, shelter, and paying bills. *Pleasure* involves people's ability to enjoy their work and feel good about what they do. *Contribution* refers to one's ability to serve others and give back to the community in a positive way.

Sex-Role Socialization

Gender is thought to be a significant factor in the life domains of *play, family, school*, and *work.* Play refers to social interaction with peers, emotional expression, and learning social norms. *Family* includes observing and learning gender roles and responsibilities from parents and extended family, including communication and career choices. *School* involves interaction with peers, modeling by adult mentors, introduction to careers, and guidance for courses and educational programs. *Work* speaks to one's success and failure with job performance, differentiating between job expectation and realistic job experience and performance, learning what jobs duties one is able to perform and/or prefers, job availability on the basis of gender, and societal reactions to career or career interest.

Structure of Opportunity

Whether it be by gender, culture, ability, access, or knowledge, individuals are thought to have differing experiences regarding career availability based on the following criteria: *distribution of jobs, sex-typing of jobs, discrimination, job requirements, economy,* and *family structure. Distribution of jobs* refers to job availability (job industry and type of work) in certain geographic locations. *Sex-typing of jobs* involves the traditional gender assignment of various careers. *Discrimination* includes the lack of opportunity for job availability or hiring on the basis of cultural factors such as gender, age, or race. *Job requirements* speak to the limitations of employment based on education requirements, physical ability, or training. *Economy* details the dynamic availability and demand for certain jobs based on funding, demand, or sociopolitical trends. *Family structure* describes the career knowledge and opportunities, parental modeling, single parenthood, caregiving demands, time limitations, income need, or medical benefits needed to provide for family.

Expectations

Personal and career expectations are thought to develop from a combination of one's work motivation and the internalization of sex-role socialization and structure of opportunity experiences. This may impact an individual's career self-efficacy, self-esteem, work ethic, or the personal value they have as an employee.

Limitations

One of the main limitations of the sociopsychological model is that it has not been well supported by research since its development by Astin in 1984. It is suggested this lack of research may be a result of the lack of operational definitions of the model's basic principles and domains (Betz & Fitzgerald, 1987; Brooks, 1990; Harmon, 1984; Hoi & Hiebert, 2005). If independent researchers and different studies are operationally defining constructs differently, the reliability of such research remains weak.

Another possible limitation of this model is that it fails to emphasize a full array of biological factors that may impact a person's life and career opportunities or choice. It does emphasize gender as well as cultural factors such as race and ethnicity in the opportunity domain, but it does not explicitly address additional biological factors such as physical health, genetic vulnerabilities, and disabilities. The use of biopsychosocial interviews and assessments are common in the field of counseling. It is important to look at the biological, psychological, and social aspects of a person, both independently as well as how they overlap and work together to define each unique individual in a holistic way. Guided Practice Exercise 5.2 asks you to consider the biopsychosocial aspects of career development and ways to assess these factors in order to implement them into the career theories presented in the chapter.

Guided Practice 5.2 Biopsychosocial Aspects and Career Development

How do biopsychosocial aspects affect career development? Many of these theories address internal motivations, societal, and cultural factors yet lack biological factors. Discuss how a person's biological, psychological, and social aspects affect career development. Identify ways to assess these factors and how you could implement them into the theories presented in this chapter.

CASE STUDY

This chapter offers several theoretical stances a counselor might use to assist a client. The following potential client scenario offers potential responses based on Anne Roe's psychologically focused theory. These responses are suggestions and should not be regarded as the only possibility when working with this fictional character.

Kara is a 37-year-old mom of two. She is recently divorced and is now attempting to reenter the work force. Prior to having children, Kara was in the finance industry and made more money than her husband. She enters counseling because of the stress of going back to work. Kara does not believe she wants to work in finance again but finds it difficult to start over in a new career and is not sure what career she would enjoy. Kara loves being a caregiver and has always enjoyed being with others.

Following an assessment on parent-child interaction and a needs-based assessment, the session begins as follows:

Therapist: Kara, I can see that you are very concerned about entering the work force after taking care of your young children and are thinking of changing your career. You took a *Parent-Child Interaction Inventory.* Can you tell me a little more about your experiences with your parents?

Kara: My parents were really supportive of me growing up. They were always willing to help when needed but let me explore things I enjoyed. I always pressured myself to appear to be successful. That's why I chose finance. I used to look at money and think "success."

Therapist: It sounds like they tried to help you find out what you wanted to do when you grew up, but some of the pressure that you put on yourself made you make a choice that fit only an idea of success. Tell me more about how your needs have changed since having children.

Kara: As I have gotten older, I don't need "things" as much. What I really need is some adult interaction and something that I enjoy, something that makes me feel like I'm making a difference in the world. I have always liked taking care of people and used to think I wanted to be a teacher, doctor, nurse, or something like that growing up.

Therapist: What I heard you say is that you enjoy helping people and that you need some adult time, maybe even some friendship. Tell me a little more about things that you feel would give you adult interaction and the satisfaction of helping others, like being a teacher or nurse.

Kara: I think that going into the teaching profession might be interesting. I like the idea of making a difference with kids and being able to share those commonalities with other teachers. I think I could build some friendships and have summers off with my kids.

Therapist: It sounds like teaching is something that can meet all of the things you are looking for in a new profession. You would be helping others, meeting new adults, and would still have time with your children. We can talk through ways to make your goal a reality in our next session.

During this session, Kara and her therapist identified the interactions she had with her parents. Her interactions were supportive and nurturing, which makes her desire a profession that is "toward people." In addition, the therapist helped Kara identify her needs. They discussed professions that would meet Kara's needs while also including her natural desire to work in a profession that is "toward people." In this situation, it would be important to work through Kara's anxieties about changing professions and help her find resources to achieve her ultimate goal of teaching.

SUMMARY

We live in a world that is in a constant state of change. As our environment changes, the economy, people, circumstances, and careers available also morph. As career counselors, we must continue to pursue the most beneficial ways to help our clients in an ever-changing world. When selecting theories for practice, we should consider theories that take diverse populations into account.

We discussed several theories in this chapter. Brill's psychoanalytic theory offered a look at vocations from the perspective of an individual's hidden desires. These desires, when appropriate for career development, were analyzed and expressed positively in society (Brill, 1921). Expanding on the ideas of psychoanalysis, Bordin offered a theory focusing on unconscious desires and their effect on the self-expressions of work and play. He believed the ability of an individual to fuse work and play determined whether meaningful experiences would occur (Bordin, 1994). Roe's psychologically focused theory was largely based on the ideas presented in Maslow's hierarchy of needs. She believed vocation was indirectly related to our early childhood experience with caregivers, but was also directly influenced by psychology, sociology, and biology (Roe, 1956). Parent-child relationship patterns were thought to affect a person's needs. The person would then try to fulfill the need through career choice. Gottfredson (1981) based her developmental theory on school-aged children and how they developed to understand themselves and the world around them. Lastly, Helen Astin's theory was based on her own experience and the inability to pursue her desired career choice due to gender and cultural norms. As a result, she looked at career development for women and how individual needs, as well as social interaction, impacted career both positively and negatively (Astin, 1984). Overall, these theories offer a wide range of ways to approach diverse clients in career counseling.

Keystones

Several issues arise when applying career theories in a counseling session. Following are suggestions to help therapists overcome obstacles to using the theories and techniques discussed in this chapter:

- Sometimes, when beginning career counseling with a new client, your role may change in response to client needs. Therapists will often ask, "What if my client starts to focus on issues in their life that are causing depression and anxiety?" First, we must remember that we are counselors, and regardless of what our client initially identifies as their desire for work in the counseling relationship, we must often refer or change roles to assist with career-related life situations. If the client is overwhelmed by anxiety or other issues, then we first shift our focus so that our client's needs are met. When this happens, we must ensure client understanding regarding our role, offer informed consent, and give referrals to address these needs.
- A question that is often asked is, "What if my client still lacks motivation after identifying needs, experiences, desires, and careers that seem to be a perfect fit?" Remember, individual client personalities will also affect career choice and may be key when assessing motivation. Giving an assessment, such as the *Meyer–Brigg's Typology Indicator*, can offer insight into personality traits and careers that align with those traits.

Author Reflections

In every environment where I have worked, I have used career counseling. Almost every client I have worked with, ranging from those in a school, partial hospitalization facilities, safe houses for sex trafficking survivors, and academic institutions, has career needs. Career counseling is a powerful tool to create meaning and a future for your client regardless of setting.

When I was working in a safe house for sex trafficking survivors, most of our discussions were based on their career and future. Many of these women lacked a support system and personal goals from a young age. Their desire to talk about what they wanted and could be in life was the main focus of counseling. Their trauma often took a back seat as they sorted through unfulfilled dreams and goals. One of the women was around 25 years old and had been lured into the sex industry through her need to obtain drugs. We quickly discovered that she always had difficulty in school and that she felt "stupid." After several sessions, I suggested the facility have her tested for dyslexia. She did, in fact, have undiagnosed dyslexia. We often assume that schools will catch these issues in our kids. However, there are times when they go unnoticed. Her dyslexia had caused many issues in school, where she often had poor behavior and lacked motivation and a support system. I gave this sex trafficking survivor the *Meyer's Brigg Typology Indicator*. After giving her these results, there was a joy in her face that I had not seen before. She said she felt "normal." That assessment, along with the diagnosis of dyslexia, validated her identity, a major issue while she was growing up. Our counseling session quickly shifted from her discussion of feeling "worthless" to setting goals and achieving a new desire to become a nurse. Unlike many sex trafficking survivors, she completed her year-long recovery, got a job at a coffee shop, and signed up for classes to finish her GED. Her road to becoming a nurse was long but outlined clear goal-oriented steps. As you can see from this example, the power of using career theory in our counseling practice is unmeasurable. We have the ability to facilitate an environment that fosters acceptance and an inner motivation to create a life of purpose for our clients. —Krystal Humphreys

Additional Resources

The following resources provide additional information about the content provided in this chapter.

Video

Geiger, M. (2015). Career theory: Anne Roe, needs theory [Video file]. https://www.youtube.com/watch?v=8JzGHQGQx1c
   This video explains Roe's needs theory in greater detail.

Website

Workforce Central Career Center. (2019). *Resources for career counselors*. https://workforce-central.org/
   This site offers a variety of career resources for counselors working in career development.

References

Anderson, L. W., Krathwohl, D. R., Airasian, P. W., Cruikshank, K. A., Mayer, R. E., Pintrich, P. R., Raths, J., & Wittrock, M. C. (2001). *A taxonomy for learning, teaching, and assessing: A revision of Bloom's Taxonomy of Educational Objectives* (Complete edition). Longman.

Astin, H. S. (1984). The meaning of work in women's lives: A sociopsychological model of career choice and work behavior. *The Counseling Psychologist, 12*(4), 117–126.

Bandura, A. (1977). *Social learning theory*. Prentice-Hall.

Betz, N., & Fitzgerald, L. (1987). *The career psychology of women*. Academic Press, Inc.

Blanchard, C. A., & Lichtenberg, J. W. (2003). Compromise in career decision-making: A test of Gottfredson's theory. *Journal of Vocational Behavior, 62*(2), 250–271.

Bloom, B. S., Engelhart, M. D., Furst, E. J., Hill, W. H., & Krathwohl, D. R. (1956). *Taxonomy of educational objectives: The classification of educational goals. Handbook 1: Cognitive domain*. David McKay.

Bordin, E. (1990). Psychodynamic model of career choice and satisfaction. In D. Brown & L.Brooks, *Career Choice and Development* (pp. 102-144). San Francisco, CA: Jossey-Bass.

Bordin, E. (1994). Intrinsic motivation and the active self: Convergence from a psychodynamic perspective. *Convergence in Career Development Theories: Implications for Science and Practice.* Consulting Psychologists Press.

Brill, A. A. (1921). *Fundamental conceptions of psychoanalysis.* Harcourt, Brace, and Company.

Brooks, L. (1990). Recent developments in theory building. In D. Brown & L. Brooks (Eds.), *Career choice and development* (2nd ed.) (pp. 364-394). Jossey- Bass

Brown, A. (2016, October 6). *Key findings about the American workforce and the changing job market.* Pew Research Center. http://www.pewresearch.org/fact-tank/2016/10/06/key-findings-about-the-american-workforce-and-the-changing-job-market/

Brown, M., Lum, J., & Voyle, K. (1997). Roe revisited: A call for the reappraisal of the theory of personality development and career choice. *Journal of Vocational Behavior, 51*(2), 283-294.

Erikson, E. (1959). *Identity and the life cycle.* International Universities Press.

Freud, S. (1896). The aetiology of hysteria. *Standard Addition, 3,* 191-221.

Gothard, B. (2001). Career development theory. In B. Gothard, P. Mignot, M. Offer & M. Ruff (Eds.), *Career guidance in context* (pp. 10-37). SAGE.

Gottfredson, L. S. (1981). Circumscription and compromise: A developmental theory of occupational aspirations. *Journal of Counseling Psychology Monograph, 28*(6), 545-579.

Gottfredson, L. S. (2005). Using Gottfredson's theory of circumscription and compromise in career guidance and counseling. In S. D. Brown & R. W. Lent (Eds.), *Career development and counseling: Putting theory and research to work* (pp. 71-100). Wiley.

Harmon, L. W. (1984). What's new? A response to Astin. *The Counseling Psychologist, 12*(3-4), 127-128.

Hoi, M. M., & Heibert, B. (2005). Career development of first-year university students: A test of Astin's career development model. *Canadian Journal of Career Development, 4*(2), 22-31.

Knapp, R., Knapp, R., & Knapp-Lee, L. (1985). Occupational interest measurement and subsequent career decisions: A predictive follow-up study of the COP System Interest Inventory. *Journal of Counseling Psychology, 32*(3), 348-354.

Krumboltz, J. D. (1991). *Career Beliefs Inventory.* Consulting Psychologists Press.

Krumboltz, J. D. (1994). The career beliefs inventory. *Journal of Counseling & Development, 72*(4), 424-428.

Krumboltz, J. D., & Jackson, M. A. (1993). Career assessment as a learning tool. *Journal of Career Assessment, 1*(4), 393-409.

Levine, S. (1963). Occupation and personality: Relationship between the social factors of the job and human orientation. *Personality and Guidance Journal, 41,* 602-605.

Maslow, A. H. (1943). A theory of human motivation. *Psychological Review, 50*(4), 370-396.

Meir, E. (1968). Structural elaboration of Roe's classification of occupations. *Israel Program for Scientific Translations, 19,* 1-115.

Roe, A. (1956). *The psychology of occupations.* Wiley.

Roe, A. (1957). Early determinates of vocational choice. *Journal of Counseling Psychology, 4*(3), 212-217.

Roe, A., & Lunneborg, P. W. (1990). Personality development and career choice. In D. Brown & L. Brooks, *Career Choice and Development* (pp. 68-101). San Francisco, CA: Jossey-Bass.

Roe, A., & Siegelman, M. (1964). The origin of interests. *The APGA inquiry series.* American Personnel and Guidance Association.

Super, D. E. (1957). *The psychology of careers.* Harper & Row.

Swanson, J. L., & Fouad, N. A. (2010). *Career theory and practice: Learning through case studies.* SAGE.

Wrenn, R. (1985). The evolution of Anne Roe. *Journal of Counseling and Development, 63*(5), 267-275.

PART TWO

Career Counseling With Diverse Populations

CHAPTER

Career Counseling Across the Lifespan

Janet Hicks and Cody Dickson

> *The key to human development is building on who you already are.*
> —Tom Rath

So far in this text, you read about theorists and their premises regarding career development, decision making, and trends. This chapter begins the second section of the book and shifts the focus to issues and premises related to client diversity in career counseling. One aspect of diversity focused on in career counseling involves aging and its relationship to career development, inherent stages in the process, counselor attitudes, knowledge, skills, and appropriate counselor advocacy. As inferred in the quote, as we move through our lives, we can either grieve the loss of our past or learn from each moment and use it to advance toward future success. Read on and discover how career development changes over a person's lifetime and how the counselor plays a role in helping clients through this process.

CHAPTER OVERVIEW

This chapter discusses age-related career issues and best practices when working with diverse clients of all ages. The following sections discuss particular issues, theories, and methods for helping clients overcome age-related oppression and unequal opportunities and stresses particular interventions depending on client age. Strategies for helping youth establish career goals in elementary, middle, and high school are discussed and followed by specific interventions for working adults and retirees. The case study at the end of the chapter demonstrates how life span issues and theorists' contentions merge with counseling methods to assist a fictional, but realistic, client.

LEARNING OBJECTIVES

After reading this chapter you will be able to do the following:

- Understand career development at different ages and stages of life
- Be familiar with needs of clients throughout the life span
- Distinguish between the career development needs of school-aged children, college-level adults, those in the workforce, clients in job transitions, and those facing or managing retirement
- Apply knowledge of client needs by examining a case study
- Understand job issues faced by those in the workforce including sexual harassment and work/life balance
- Integrate several career theories from previous chapters as they relate to age and developmental aspects of career (e.g., Donald Super's life span, life space theory, Linda Gottfredson's circumscription and compromise theory, and Ginzberg et al.'s developmental theory)
- Understand the challenges and issues clients face based on age-related oppression

Relevant Theorists

To fully understand how developmental levels affect career counseling, counselors must grasp the foundations therein. In this light, we now turn our attention to theorists who impact our perspectives of development.

Developmental Theorists

Kegan's Constructive Developmental Theory

It goes without saying that a client's developmental level affects how we respond to career needs. A young child and a retiree obviously have different needs and levels of understanding and require different responses. Let us discuss some of the developmental theorists and how they tie to career processes.

Kegan's (1982, 1994) constructive developmental theory describes several orders (stages) that describe development of young children through adulthood. These consist of order 0, incorporate balance; order

1, impulsive; order 2, imperial or enduring; order 3, interpersonal or social; order 4, institutional or self-authoring; and order 5, interindividual or self-transforming.

Stage 0, or the *incorporate balance stage*, describes young infants up to 18 months or 2 years of age (Kegan, 1982). Life revolves around reflexes, impulses, and the primary caregiver. Although our career counseling clients are rarely this age, parent counseling is often helpful to serve the future needs of these babies. For example, parents can establish a college fund for their new child.

Stage 1, the *impulsive stage*, reminds us that young children may not have the ability to see perspectives beyond their own. The impulsive stage refers to children around ages 2 to 7 who make impulsive and ego-centric decisions based on their own needs (Kegan, 1982). Children in this stage may begin to understand that jobs exist but do not have the ability to consider others' perspectives.

The second stage, or order, is the *imperial stage*. Preadolescent students, teens, and adults functioning in this stage are primarily focused on their own wants and needs but do have the ability to see others' viewpoints. In this stage, decisions are made based on social perceptions, perceptions of others, or impulses. Jahn (2018) thinks adults can move from order 2 to order 3 more effectively if career counselors utilize abstract thinking during career sessions, including the consideration of several viewpoints, when making career decisions.

After a couple of years at the imperial level, some college-aged students begin to function within order 3 or, the *interpersonal level*. Those functioning at this level begin to exhibit personal values but are still heavily influenced by peers and significant others in their life (Kegan, 1994). Decisions may be made based on how they affect others. Because of this, career counselors might help those functioning in this level to make more authentic career choices based on their own, rather than their parents' desires (Jahn, 2018).

Only 20 to 40% of adults will reach order 4, the *institutional stage* during adulthood (Erikson, 2006; Jahn, 2018). Decisions, at this stage, are based on how they fit theoretical knowledge. Those who reach this stage can be recognized by their ability to reflect on and adjust behaviors in response. Because these adults are able to see themselves both uniquely and distinctly from others and make abstract decisions, they have the ability discuss their career desires with others, such as parents, significant others, or friends who hold different opinions (Jahn, 2018). Although these adults are prepared to control their own lives and career paths, career counselors can help them understand and reflect on their own values, thus leading to these purposeful career choices (Jahn, 2018).

Very few adults will reach order 5, the *inter-individual level*. Those who do reach this stage are primarily over the age of 40 (Erikson, 2006). Persons at this level author, regulate, and create their own lives through effective abstract decisions. Contradictions are welcomed and desired, thus creating a stance of not knowing in these individuals. These people see their work environment as part of a greater community or cause and can be encouraged to continue learning should a job transition occur.

Case Exercise 6.1 ties Kegan's theory to career decision making. In this case, a student named Richard seems to be in the wrong college major. Read this exercise and determine how you might help Richard. See if you can determine which order he seems to be functioning in.

Case Exercise 6.1 The Case of Richard

Richard is a 19-year-old college-aged student who approaches you, the career counselor in the university career center. Richard says he wants to be an engineer. After talking to Richard for about an hour and giving him some career assessments, it is clear Richard's interests are not a fit for engineering. Plus, Richard says he hates math. What would you do to help Richard? Which of Kegan's orders is Richard most likely functioning within? Does the order he is functioning within help determine the career counselor's plan of action?

Erikson's Psychosocial Developmental Stages

Erik Erikson's theory provides an agentic view of human development as he focuses on developmental successes and human potential (Erikson, 1950, 1968, 1975). The following quote by Erikson encompasses much of his theoretical angle:

> *In the social jungle of human existence, there is no feeling of being alive without a sense of identity.*
> –Erik H. Erikson

As the quote implies, In Erikson's (1950, 1968, 1975) view, humans continue to develop their identity throughout their lifetime and, in fact, cannot exist without it. With regard to career development, Erikson believes people become more aware of themselves while participating in their particular sociohistorical contexts.

Our careers comprise one of these primary contexts. Erikson was keenly aware that our psychosocial development relies on social interactions in all areas of our life and that these interactions make us feel alive. Further, these social interactions with family members, intimate partners, peers, colleagues, coworkers, and other significant individuals convey important messages to us about who we are and what we do. Because these messages contain societal and cultural ideals, mores, and practices that the individual internalizes in response, they can sometimes be mixed, unpredictable, or simply accepted without thought.

Throughout life, including our career life, the formation of identity results from slowly becoming aware of oneself, one's individual characteristics, and one's place in the world. It is the result of an individual's decisions and choices regarding what they will believe, who they will be, and what values they will hold.

Identity is impacted by and seen in all cultures. For example, religious beliefs and experiences, political orientation, personal societal values, marrying into another culture, and accepting a particular family occupation are but a few examples that can affect identity. These experiences may culminate in career self-efficacy or lack thereof, career opportunities based on these learnings (Krumboltz, 2004), or compromise and circumscription (Gottfredson, 1981, 2005).

This discussion of psychosocial development is, therefore, important to consider when engaging individuals of all ages and personal backgrounds in career counseling. Counselor awareness of the challenges and changes in the career landscape for diverse clients, particularly age-related issues, is vital. Career fulfillment provides clients with a sense of self and a sense of being alive, as Erikson notes. Now that we understand Erikson's premises regarding identity, let's delve into his stages.

Erikson's (1950, 1968) stages consist of *trust versus mistrust* between (ages 0–2); *autonomy versus shame and doubt* (toddler); *initiative versus guilt* (preschool age into elementary school); *industry versus inferiority* (elementary school age*); identity versus role confusion* (adolescence); *intimacy versus isolation* (young adulthood); *generativity versus stagnation* (middle adulthood); and *integrity versus despair* (late adulthood). We will begin our discussion on each stage beginning at the preschool age since this is the point where career counselors begin working with children in school and community settings.

The *initiative versus guilt* stage comes into play around preschool and continues until around the time children enter school. Children at this stage are beginning to take initiative, make judgments, and take risks. Children often show frustration when their initiative does not result in the desired or expected response. Because children at this stage are beginning to make judgments, career counselors working with children at this stage might benefit them by introducing a variety of job types including field trips to various places of employment or by having guest speakers.

Around the ages of 9 to12, children are functioning in the *industry versus inferiority* stage. Children in this stage may begin to doubt their future as they experience failures, often for the first time. Fortunately, they also begin to recognize their talents and gifts during this stage. Because children in this stage need to see success, job shadowing might be helpful through programs such as "take your child to work" days. It helps youth at this stage to see that their parents have both successes and failures and that no job is perfect.

Around the time children enter middle school, they have transitioned into the *identity versus role confusion* stage, where they remain throughout high school (ages 13–19). During this stage, youth experience mixed feelings and ideas about how they will fit into the adult world. Youth at this stage may question adult ideas and participate in risk-taking behaviors to fit in. Mentoring programs as well as job shadowing programs might be helpful for youth at this stage. Mentors who are not parents can offer advice and encouragement without having to serve in an authoritarian role.

Intimacy versus isolation occurs during young adulthood. These individuals seek out careers in order to find and sustain partnerships. These young adults are just beginning their careers and may need help deciding on a career path or figuring out how to obtain or use the educational levels they desire.

Generativity versus stagnation occurs during middle adulthood. Adults functioning in this stage want to leave their mark on life. For this reason, they may seek career counseling to attain promotions or seek enough status to support a family. Career counseling can help these individuals use the skills they have to maintain career status while also assisting with the confidence to ask for promotions or pay increases. Often, people at this level lose jobs and need assistance finding suitable positions at a desired level.

Integrity versus despair occurs during late adulthood. People functioning in this level must come to terms with previous successes or unmet goals. Career counselors can help these retiring individuals appreciate the contributions they once made to the workforce and even encourage them to volunteer or pursue other career goals.

Career Theorists and Age-Related Development

Several career theories tie in with age-related development. In this section, we focus on a handful of theories that seem particularly conducive to either life development or issues regarding age. For a more in-depth discussion on these and additional developmental career theorists, you may wish to review

Chapter 4. Following is a quick review of three of those theorists: Ginzberg and colleagues, Gottfredson, and Super. Because Tiedeman and O'Hara's theory, as discussed in Chapter 4, is an obvious tie with Erikson's ego development, we will not be redundant and cover this here. This chapter intends to help explain ties between three developmental career theories and human development that might not be as obvious.

Ginzberg and Colleagues

Ginzberg et al. (1951) suggest that career choice is a process that includes some level of compromise. As discussed in detail in Chapter 4, this process of choice is threefold from fantasy and tentative through realistic choices. The fantasy stage from birth to 10 years old emphasizes play in career development whereas later stages transition to career selection (Ginzberg et al., 1951).

Gottfredson

Gottfredson's theory of circumscription and compromise, as discussed in Chapter 5, says people form their career objectives through a selection and elimination process (Edwin & Prescod, 2018; Gottfredson, 1981, 2005). Gottfredson postulates that individuals eliminate potential careers based on perceived academic ability, prestige, gender identity, personal interest, and their personal belief of career attainability. Furthermore, this practice usually corresponds approximately with the preschool, elementary, middle, and high school years but continues throughout life.

Super

As discussed in Chapter 4, Donald Super viewed career development as a cyclical process revealing itself over an individual's lifespan (Super, 1980). According to Super (1980), the growth phase of career development occurs during elementary school. The growth phase is characterized by students' development across career dimensions such as informational desire, exploration about the world and the self, obtaining and retrieving career information, and awareness of the students' likes and dislikes. This successful career exploration is associated with career decision self-efficacy and information attainment (Cheung & Arnold, 2014) and may help youth develop a secure base for further career development. According to Super, career development continues throughout adulthood, and stages can cycle and recycle as needed. The developmental nature of Super's theories make them especially helpful in understanding how career development begins in preschool, or before, and extends into retirement and beyond. Let's consider Guided Practice Exercise 6.1, where you are asked to ponder connections between these theorists and age-related career development.

Guided Practice Exercise 6.1 Career Theory and Age

This chapter and prior chapters in the text discuss several career theorists. How might client age correspond or disagree each career theorist's contentions. For example, how might a retired person be affected by Ginzberg et al.'s theory? Or, how might a child fit into Gottfredson's contentions? Look back at Chapters 1–5, select two or three theorists, and ask yourself, "Are all ages represented by this theory? Who is left out? Who is represented best by the theory?"

All of these theorists have one major premise in common: Career development and/or learning begins early in life. For this reason, a discussion on the developmental aspects of career development would be remiss without discussing issues that begin in childhood. The next section starts a discussion on preschool career development; continues with information regarding elementary and secondary school career counseling, college counseling, and workforce counseling; and ends with career development information regarding those facing retirement.

Career Counseling in Preschool

Let us begin our discussion of career development across the lifespan with an axiom "Career development is a lifelong process that begins in childhood" (as cited in Edwin & Prescod, 2018, p. 3). Many career, developmental, and psychosocial theorists would assert that childhood play is the first demonstration of children exploring careers (Edwin & Prescod, 2018; Ginzberg et al., 1951; Super, 1953, 1978). It is said that Frank Lloyd Wright, the gifted architect, claims his love for building began in his childhood while playing with blocks. Watch any group of children play alone or with others and you will often observe them mimicking adult career tasks (e.g., playing with tools to build or working on a play computer or phone). For young children, play is both symbolic and practical. Over time, this career-related play can work to develop social and emotional skills as well as being informative and narrative (Bierman & Motamedi, 2015).

Many career theorists tout the importance of continuing career development through play in the elementary years (Edwin & Prescod, 2018). For example, Ginzberg et al. (1951) stress a focus on career development activities for elementary school–aged children through adult ages (Edwin & Proscod, 2018). Let's looks at some of the standards and guidelines that have been developed to guide career counseling in elementary and secondary schools.

Counseling in Elementary and Secondary Schools

The *American School Counseling Association's (ASCA, 2012) national model* states that school counselors assist students with social/emotional, academic, and career development. Fortunately, this means school counselors are trained to help youth begin focusing on career development and on future success at an early age. Even elementary school counselors "assist students in evaluating interests, abilities, skills, and achievement" and advise them so they can set goals toward future career success (ASCA, 2017, p. 1). Secondary counselors continue this career-related assistance throughout both middle and high school (ASCA, 2017a, 2017b). Many of the standards guiding students via the *ASCA national model* coincide with other entities such as the federal interagency committee entitled the National Occupational Information Coordinating Committee (NOICC).

The National Occupational Information Coordinating Committee (2010) published career development guidelines to guide children through appropriate career development. The guidelines encompass elementary, middle, and high school levels and cover topics such as self-knowledge, educational and occupational exploration, and career planning. In elementary school, children are tasked with things such as understanding links between learning and future work, learning interaction skills, and awareness of different occupations. Once the child begins middle school, goals shift to learning skills to locate jobs and understanding skills needed to become employed in a variety of occupations. Once the student enters high school, they begin focusing on maintaining interpersonal behaviors, understanding skills to enter higher education, and using skills to locate and apply for jobs (NOICC, 2010). Guided Practice Exercise 6.2 asks you to discern differences you might see when working with these guidelines to assist youth from different educational levels.

Guided Practice Exercise 6.2 Developmental Differences

As stated in the passage, elementary school children are asked to become aware of occupations, and middle school children must learn skills to locate jobs and understand skills required within a variety of occupations. High school youth must know skills for entering higher education as well as skills to locate and apply for jobs. Assume you are working with a child from each of these developmental areas. How would you accomplish these tasks while staying within the child's ability and developmental levels? What specific activities might you and the child both engage in?

The National Career Development Association's (NCDA, n.d.) website lists several of its own standards and guidelines. While the NCDA guidelines are not age specific, they do cover three domains (personal/social, educational achievement, and career management) and describe goals (e.g., knowledge acquisition, application and reflection) that include processes at youth developmental levels (NCDA, n.d.). For example, the NCDA's (n.d.) knowledge acquisition goal states, "Youth and adults at the knowledge acquisition stage expand knowledge awareness and build comprehension. They can recall, recognize, describe, identify, clarify, discuss, explain, summarize, query, investigate and compile new information about the knowledge" (p. 1). At the application level students must "seek out ways to use knowledge" (p. 1) and, in compliance with the reflection goal, youth and adults integrate career knowledge into situations and behaviors. These goals can, obviously, be tailored to the child's developmental level and incorporated into school-based career programs. For an additional glimpse into these NCDA guidelines and programs using them, check out the link listed under the Additional Resources section at the end of this chapter as well as information on specific career programs in Chapter 15.

Now that we have discussed standards and guidelines used with school-aged children, let's see if you can use this to help an actual client. Case Exercise 6.2 asks you to consider how you might help Maria, a middle school student who is undecided as to her career path.

Case Exercise 6.2 The Case of Maria

Maria is a 14-year-old middle school student who says she is confused about her career path. She always wanted to be a veterinarian but says, now that she is an eighth grader, science is not fun anymore and she is feeling lost without her dream. Considering that Maria is in Erikson's identity versus role confusion stage and within Kegan's second stage, what career activities might help Maria? How does knowledge of these developmental stages help determine a plan of action for Maria's career counselor? What career theorists might agree with your premises?

College Counseling

Once youth enter college, they are faced with choosing college majors and may feel uncertain about their specific career path. The NOICC (2010) standards, as mentioned in the section on elementary and secondary counseling, state that adults should have the ability to function in educational learning, locate and understand employment information, and have the ability to find, apply for, and maintain jobs. This means college-aged persons must, for the first time, travel down a specific career path via their college major or upon entry into the job market.

This first-time decision making means college career counselors are greatly needed if college-aged adults are to use their talents, skills, and interests to find meaningful employment. Several challenges do exist for this population, however. First, let's discuss a few statistics. In 2014, 47% of the campus study body, on average, sought help through their campus career center (National Association for Colleges and Employers, 2014). At the same time, Gallagher (2015) surveyed college counseling centers and found ratios averaging only one counselor to 2,081 students. This is especially challenging for campuses who do not have a specific career center. College counseling centers stated they only spent 5% of their time working with students on career issues (Gallagher, 2015). This means career centers are especially needed and must work efficiently if they are to be able to help students.

If college career counselors are to best assist students' career decision making, they must consider students' specific developmental levels. For example, college-aged students may begin their education working within Kegan's (1994) order 2 imperial stage. During this stage, decisions are made based on social perceptions, perceptions of others, or on impulses. This means that while college students may not truly internalize their parent's wishes, they will often choose jobs others like or reject them simply because they want to establish their own identity. Some students move from Kegan's (1982, 1994) order 3 interpersonal level to the order 4 institutional level by the time they graduate. Career counseling might offer the support, encouragement, and safety to seek new opportunities as they effectively move through these stages (Jahn, 2017). Chapter 15 will discuss specific program and opportunities available through college counseling or career centers.

Counseling in the Workforce

Despite being gainfully employed, many in the workforce face issues requiring career counseling (Allan et al., 2016; Whiston & Cinabon, 2015). Several issues occurring in the workforce and addressed regularly include family issues, sexual harassment, decision making when pondering promotions, discrimination, finding work-life balance, and even workplace bullying (Allan et al., 2016; Einarsen et al., 2016; McLaughlin et al., 2017; Whiston & Cinabon, 2015).

Although it is illegal to sexually harass a person at work, these issues do occur. *Sexual harassment* is defined as "unwelcome sexual advances, requests for sexual favors, and other verbal or physical harassment of a sexual nature" (U.S. Equal Employment Opportunity Commission (EEOC), n.d.a.). Sexual harassment can also include "offensive remarks about a person's sex" (U.S. EEOC, n.d.b.). Career counselors can not only help victims cope and find new job opportunities when needed; they can also refer clients to reputable attorneys for legal assistance. The same can be true for those facing discrimination or bullying in the workplace. Chapter 7 will discuss these issues of oppression as faced by diverse populations in greater detail.

Technology has made it impossible for workers to escape work-related tasks and find down time; 94% of workers surveyed stated they worked over 50 hours per week with around half of workers stating they put in over 65 hours per week (Dominus, 2016). These numbers explain high numbers of workers reporting work-related stress and burn out. Career counselors can help workers learn to balance work and personal lives and rid themselves of perfectionism so that they are not only happier but more productive. Dominus (2016) discusses several strategies for improving *work-life balance* and happiness. She touts the importance of reducing perfectionism, turning off technology, exercising and meditating, focusing on priorities, and minimizing stressful habits. All of these are topics counselors can address.

Job Transitions

Before we begin this section, consider your own personal career development and how you arrived where you are today. Guided Practice Exercise 6.3 asks you to complete a career lifeline and discuss your findings.

Guided Practice Exercise 6.3 Career Lifeline

Take a moment and reflect on your career experiences since birth. Draw a career lifeline depicting events that occurred leading you to your study today. For example, did your parents save for your college education before birth? Did you take particular classes in middle or high school that charted a particular path? Did you make decisions that affected your options? Did unplanned events change your career direction? After drawing your lifeline, look over the events and discuss at what stages career counseling might have been beneficial for you.

The career lifeline exercise illustrates that career counseling issues do not always begin or end once adults enter the workforce. Unplanned events for which you had no control and prior decisions all affect our present and future. Events such as *underemployment* (below full-time or year-round employment often resulting in worker poverty), *overemployment* (working an excessive number of hours), and job losses and transitions spillover into family and personal issues and regularly affect those in the workforce. Chapter 14 discusses family issues related to career counseling in more detail. Let's looks at some statistics describing a few common job transitions.

A longitudinal study conducted between 1957 and 1964 found that the average person changed jobs over 11 times and experienced 5.6 periods of unemployment between the ages of 18 and 48 (U.S. Bureau of Labor Statistics, 2020). These statistics were especially prevalent for low-skilled workers since, as educational levels decreased, periods of unemployment increased. These periods of job loss and transition can be especially stressful and depressing for those affected, as well as for their families. Because job transitions may cause feelings of loss of control, and due to realizations that more career knowledge and skill are needed to successfully navigate the transition, people often seek counseling at this time (Minta & Kargul, 2016).Consequently, career counselors can be invaluable resources while helping these workers find suitable employment. Guided Practice Exercise 6.4 asks you to consider your own past jobs and consider connections between transitions and current opportunities.

Guided Practice Exercise 6.4 Past Jobs

Create a list of the jobs you have held throughout your lifetime. Have you held more or less jobs than those in the study who average over 11 changes between ages 18 to 48? What did you like or dislike about these jobs? How did you manage to cope during your job transitions? If you had been your own career counseling client, what help would you have wanted? How did these transitions affect the career path you are on today?

Other, less stressful job transitions include voluntary job changes or promotions. Even during these controllable changes, workers may feel anxiety and need assistance. Just because someone has the job skills to enter a new job or field doesn't mean they have the career knowledge to make the change. Again, career counselors can help with assessments, career exploration, and decision making.

Retirement Issues

Before discussing specific retirement issues as part of career development, let's consider Erikson's (1950, 1968) last stage of psychosocial development as mentioned at the beginning of this chapter. You will recall that, during this stage, integrity versus despair, late adults look back at their lives and either feel accomplished or experience despair regarding unmet goals. Consequently, it is important when helping clients facing this stage to recognize that many options are still available. For example, they can continue working and/or participate in hobbies or educational endeavors. Work-related accomplishments are still possible regardless of age, and each person's situation is unique. For this reason, career counseling can be beneficial and may help offset depression that often results in later life (Aziz & Steffens, 2013). A one-size-fits-all approach isn't feasible or helpful when working with this population, however, as each retiree has a different story and needs. A few statistics and initiatives are prevalent regarding work and retirement.

Today's older adults typically work beyond the age of retirement (Meyers, 2017). For some, this means working additional years at the same job, whereas others take on completely different jobs or cut back to part-time work. Much of this decision is determined by the health or desires of the retiree. For those wishing to continue in the work force, career counselors can offer counseling to help manage anxiety related to career change, assessments, career exploration, and decision-making assistance.

The American Association of Retired Persons (AARP, n.d.) created an initiative entitled, "Reimagine Your Life" to help retirees adjust post retirement. This initiative offers strategies and suggestions for retired persons to help them feel productive and happy in their remaining years. Following is a synopsis of this process.

Six steps exist in the *"Reimagine Your Life" philosophy* (AARP, n.d.). The first strategy suggests reflecting on the person's life story and recreating meanings. The first strategy involves altering personal narratives that lead to disturbances. Reframing life events and meanings has the potential to change negative mind-sets. The second strategy involves building connections. Since many support systems have disappeared over time, seniors might create their own group of supporters and mentors. The third strategy discusses exploration and learning. Retirees are encouraged to travel, take courses, or learn things they once had no time to discover. The fourth strategy discusses narrowing options. Once the previous step involving exploration has been implemented, opportunities can be narrowed to include only those considered most advantageous. The fifth strategy is called repack and requires the person to eliminate obstacles or impediments that are blocking future goals. The final strategy requires making a move or acting regarding the selected goals. Career counselors can definitely help seniors through this process via cognitive, narrative, decision-making, and assertiveness techniques. Clearly, these steps guide late adults through Erikson's final stage of psychosocial development. Retirees can empower themselves to work as much or as little as they like, learn new things, and take actions they desire.

Age-Related Oppression and Advocacy

The Age Discrimination in Employment Act (ADEA) forbids age discrimination in "hiring, firing, pay, job assignments, promotions, layoff, training, benefits, and any other term or condition of employment" against workers over the age of 40 (U.S. EEOC, n.d.a). Despite this, older adults often face employment discrimination in hiring and promotion, and such acts can be difficult to prove (Meyers, 2017). Employers may silently discriminate because job training can be costly in terms of time and resources and because many wonder if the benefits of hiring an older person outweigh the costs (Meyers, 2017). Career counselors can help older adults through advocacy, validating concerns, and helping them find available positions accepting of senior workers. Guided Practice Exercise 6.5 asks you to discuss oppressions that older workers might face and ways counselors can help.

Guided Practice Exercise 6.5 Advocacy and Oppression of Older Workers

Take a moment and think about ways older workers might be discriminated against. Be specific. For example, an older worker is asked to work fewer hours because they earn more than junior workers and cost the company more money. Is this discrimination? What other specific examples can you imagine? How would you help these older workers?

Emerging Job Trends for Upcoming Generations

According to Selingo (2016), career development training must change if we are to keep up in the 21st century. Technology and automation are changing job opportunities, and globalization makes competition for these opportunities more difficult. Katz and Krueger's (2016) study on employment growth found that freelancing positions have been greatly impacting job opportunities since 2005. This trend is important because it brings to light the changing job market. This means that while our knowledge of particular jobs is important, these jobs can disappear at any time. Consequently, we must emphasize lifelong learning to clients so that they have the ability to stay current and transition as the career market changes (Selingo, 2016). As Krumboltz's happenstance learning theory contended in Chapter 3, Selingo (2016) believes every learning experience can be compiled into new opportunities and college students, and those within other stages can be taught to use past experiences to create new opportunities. These past experiences can be constantly supplemented with additional learning. Career counselors must morph with these changes and infuse them throughout clients' lives or face stagnation. Guided Practice Exercise 6.6 Asks you to contemplate changes affecting the career development of clients from all age groups.

Guided Practice Exercise 6.6 Changes

Consider how careers and job openings have changed in your lifetime. How do these changes affect how we help those in each age group? Discuss things career counselors must learn or do differently as a result of these changes.

CASE STUDY

The following case demonstrates the importance of developmental concepts when working with a fictional client named Fran. Fran is a 70-year-old woman who comes to your counseling office and asks for help finding a way to spend her extra time. She recently retired and says she is lonely because all her friends are at work. The counselor offers assessments to Fran and notices that she does not seem to fit criteria for depression or other mental health issues. The following case illustrates what a career counseling session might look like for Fran.

Fran: I am just so lonely, and I feel lost after working all these years. I need to feel productive again.

Counselor: It sounds like you would like to get involved in something you find fulfilling that also offers social connections.

Fran: Yes, exactly. Can you help me figure out what to do with my time? I am still in great health and I have a reasonable income, but it just seems like I could be doing something helpful outside of the house. Going back to work just makes me stressed out though.

Counselor: Tell me what you mean by "stressed out."

Fran: I guess it just scares me. Here I am 70 years old and I know no one will want an old person around. I am not sure what to do. I am not sure I want a regular job. I just want to be doing something.

Counselor: I think anyone in your shoes would be a little afraid of entering a new environment (normalizing). You seem to have many skills and you have learned much that can be helpful to others over your career lifetime (complimenting). Tell me things you always wanted to do but never had time because you were busy working.

Fran: I always wanted to work with children, but I was so busy in my job as an accountant that I was busy. I feel like I should know what I want to do. Sitting around all day isn't making me happy.

Counselor: It sounds like you feel pressured to jump into something quickly, but you are sad and lonely just sitting at home all day (paraphrasing). I think it is perfectly normal to take as much time as you need to make this decision (normalizing). Tell me how you would feel about exploring a few community options. You can research this week, narrow those options down over the next couple of weeks, and, eventually, create a plan to get involved in an activity involving other people, including children, a few hours a week.

Fran: I like that. We can just take it one step at a time.

Counselor: Yes, we have plenty of time to figure this out.

Fran: How can I deal with my sadness while we work on this?

Counselor: First, let me tell you how much I admire your willingness to come to career counseling for help. You have many skills and interests that are going to help you move past this (*complimenting*). I agree with you that you should not be sad all the time (*bridge in solution-focused feedback as discussed in Chapter 10*). Since you are in good physical health, I think it might be beneficial to see your physician and start walking outside the house or exercising regularly (*task*).

Fran: Well, I guess that would be good for me and it certainly won't hurt anything.

It seems Fran is experiencing what Erikson termed despair. During this stage, Fran should be encouraged to avoid comparing herself with others and should be allowed to move at her own pace. She can explore her options, narrow down her choices, and get involved in work or leisure activities a little at a time. Pacing is important because retirees who jump into too many activities at once may experience stress or depression (Meyers, 2017). For this reason, the counselor did not pressure Fran to immediately apply for jobs or suggest a number of immediate activities.

SUMMARY

This chapter covered some of the major career milestones experienced in a person's life. Career development begins with birth and ends with death. Every experience between the two events affects career opportunities and learning. Some of the major issues discussed in this chapter include career development in elementary, middle, high school, college, the workforce, job transitions, and before and after retirement. Career and developmental theorists detail stages that guide career counselors as they work with clients of varying ages. The keystones capture some of the major ideas covered in this chapter.

Keystones

- Career counseling occurs at all ages and stages of life.
- Theorists such as Kegan (1994) and Erikson (1950, 1968) as well as standards and guidelines from NCDA and NOICC assist and guide counselors working with all ages.
- Retirement is now occurring later in life and many are returning to work after retirement.
- Advocacy and strategies are needed to help older workers who face oppression.
- Career counselors must help clients actively direct their own learning if they are to succeed in today's competitive market.
- Those in the workforce need assistance handling issues such as sexual harassment, job losses, discrimination, and work-life balance leading to stress and burnout.

Author Reflections

I am very fortunate to have had the opportunity to work on career development issues with a variety of clients throughout a number of ages and stages. From my time working as a school counselor in a middle school to my work helping those in a homeless shelter, career development has been the one counseling aspect that I enjoyed most. From helping elementary children transition into middle school, and later into high school, I found myself intrigued as to the speed at which career growth can occur. It is quite exciting to watch. I had the opportunity to visit with children at all three developmental levels and see how their career development transitioned over time. I learned that children who focused on future planning and had parents who emphasized long-term career-based goals were more apt to value school and continuous learning. I can't tell you how great it feels to watch youth transition into successful working adults. Watching them move through the life span from childhood to adulthood and become happy and productive has been one of the greatest blessings of my life.

I know you are reading this because you have set personal career goals for yourself. My advice to you is this: Don't be mediocre if you are going to work with people. They deserve your best! They are counting on your help. I wish you great success as you move forward in your own career development. —Janet Hicks

Additional Resources

The following resources provide additional information about the content provided in this chapter.

Useful Websites

Equal Employment Opportunity Commission: https://eeoc.gov

This website offers current legal information and definitions for a variety of workplace issues.

National Career Development Association (n.d.): https://www.ncda.org/aws/NCDA/pt/sp/guidelines

This site is the official website of the National Career Development Association. Links on this page cover ethical standards, career guidelines, and numerous other interesting documents.

National Occupational Information Coordinating Committee: http://www.jencius.net/Handouts/NOICCStandards.pdf

This site links to the NOICC standards where specific standards can be perused.

Journals

Adultspan

This journal contains articles devoted to human growth and development and is the flagship journal for the Association for Adult Development and Aging, a division of the American Counseling Association.

Books

Arulmani, G., Bakshi, A. J., Leong, F. T. L., & Watts, T. (2014). *Handbook of career development: International perspectives.* Springer.

This book discusses lifespan development as it integrates with diversity in career development.

References

Allan, B. A., Dexter, C., Kinsey, R., & Parker, S. (2016). Meaningful work and mental health: Job satisfaction as a moderator. *Journal of Mental Health, 27(1),* 38–44. https://doi.org/10.1080/09638237.2016.1244718

American Association of Retired Persons (AARP). (n.d.). *Reimagine your life.* https://www.aarp.org/work/working-after-retirement/info-10-2013/reimagine-your-life.html

American School Counseling Association. (2012). *ASCA National Model: A framework for school counseling programs.* Author.

American School Counseling Association (ASCA). (2019a). *The essential role of elementary school counselors.* https://www.school-counselor.org/asca/media/asca/Careers-Roles/WhyElem.pdf

American School Counseling Association (ASCA). (2019b). *The essential role of middle school counselors.* https://www.schoolcoun-selor.org/asca/media/asca/Careers-Roles/WhyMiddle.pdf

American School Counseling Association (ASCA). (2019c). *The essential role of high school counselors.* https://www.schoolcounselor.org/asca/media/asca/Careers-Roles/WhyHighSchool.pdf

Aziz, R., & Steffens, D. (2013). What are the causes of late life depression? *Psychiatric Clinicians of North America, 36(4),* 497–516.

Bierman, K. L., & Motamedi, M. (2015). Social emotional learning programs for preschool children. In J. Durlak, C. Domitrovich, R. P. Weissberg, and T. Gullotta (Eds.), *The handbook of social and emotional learning: Research and practice (pp. 135–150).* Guilford.

Cheung, R., & Arnold, A. (2014). The impact of career exploration on career development among Chinese university students. *Journal of College Student Development, 55(7)*, 732–748.

Dominus, S. (2016, February 25). Rethinking the work life equation. *New York Times*. https://www.nytimes.com/2016/02/28/magazine/rethinking-the-work-life-equation.html

Edwin, M., & Prescod, D. (2018). Fostering elementary career exploration with an interactive, technology-based career development unit. *Journal of School Counseling, 16*(13).

Einarsen, S., Skogstad, A., Rørvik, E., Lande, Å., &Nielsen, M. B. (2016). Climate for conflict management, exposure to workplace bullying and work engagement: A moderated mediation analysis. *International Journal of Human Resource Management, 29(3), 549–570*. http://doi.org/10.1080/09585192.2016.1164216

Erikson, E. H. (1950). *Childhood and society*. Norton.

Erikson E. H. (1968). *Identity: Youth and crisis*. Norton.

Erikson, E. H. (1975). *Life history and the historical moment*. Norton.

Erikson, K. (2006). The constructive developmental theory of Robert Kegan. *The Family Journal, 14(3)*, 290–298.

Gallagher, R. P. (2015). *National survey of college counseling centers*. University of Pittsburgh. http://d-scholarship.pitt.edu/28178/1/survey_2014.pdf

Ginzberg, E., Ginsberg, S., Axelrad, S., & Herma, J. (1951). Occupational choice: An approach to a general theory. *The Educational Forum, 16(1)*, 122–123. https://doi.org/10.1080/00131725109341444

Gottfredson, L. S. (1981). Circumscription and compromise: A developmental theory of occupational aspirations. *Journal of Counseling Psychology (Monograph), 28*(6), 545–579.

Gottfredson, L. S. (2005). Using Gottfredson's theory of circumscription and compromise in career guidance and counseling. In S. D. Brown & R. W. Lent (Eds.), *Career development and counseling: Putting theory and research to work* (pp. 71–100). Wiley.

Jahn, S. (2018). Using collage to examine values in college career counseling. *Journal of College Counseling, 21(2)*, 180–192. https://doi.org/10.1002/jocc.12096

Katz, L. F., & Krueger, A. B. (2016). The rise and nature of alternative work arrangements in the United States, 1995–2015. Princeton University and NBER. https://scholar.harvard.edu/files/lkatz/files/katz_krueger_cws_resubmit_clean.pdf

Kegan, R. (1982). *The evolving self: Problem and process in human development (2nd ed.)*. Harvard University Press.

Kegan, R. (1994). *In over our heads: The mental demands of modern life*. Harvard University Press.

Krumboltz, J. D., & Levin, A. S. (2004). *Luck is no accident: Making the most of happenstance in your life and career*. Impact Publishers.

McLaughlin, H., Uggin, C., & Blackstone, A. (2017). The economic and career effects of sexual harassment on women. *Gender and Society, 31(3)*, 333–358.

Meyers, L. (2017, November 29). *Preparing for retirement goes beyond a good 401(k)*. Counseling Today. https://ct.counseling.org/2017/11/preparing-retirement-goes-beyond-good-401k/#

Minta, J., & Kargul, J. (2016). Significance of educational and vocational counselling in low-skilled people's narratives. *British Journal of Counseling & Development, 44(2)*, 210–220.

National Association for Colleges and Employers. (2014). *The college class of 2014* [Survey report].

National Career Development Association (NCDA). (2004). *National Career Development guidelines framework*. https://www.ncda.org/aws/NCDA/asset_manager/get_file/3384?ver=16587

National Occupational Information Coordinating Committee (2010, June 29). *NOICC standards*. http://www.jencius.net/Handouts/NOICCStandards.pdf

Selingo, J. (2016, October). Colleges must reinvent career counseling. *Chronicle of Higher Education, 28*, B16–20.

Super, D. E. (1953). A theory of vocational development. *American Psychologist, 8(5)*, 185–190.

Super, D. E., & Hal, D. T. (1978). Career development: Exploration and planning. *Annual Review of Psychology, 29*, 333–372.

U.S. Bureau of Labor Statistics. (2020, January 16). *National longitudinal surveys*. https://www.bls.gov/nls/nlsfaqs.htm#anch4

U.S. Equal Employment Opportunity Commission (EEOC). (n.d.a.). *Age discrimination*. https://www.eeoc.gov/laws/types/age.cfm

U.S. Equal Employment Opportunity Commission (EEOC). (n.d.b.). *Sexual harassment*. https://www.eeoc.gov/laws/types/sexual_harassment.cfm

Whiston, S., & Cinabon, R. G. (2015). The work-family interface: Integrating research and career counseling practice. *Career Development Quarterly, 63(1)*, 44–56. https://doi.org/10.1002/j.2161-0045.2015.00094.x

CHAPTER

Career Counseling for Diverse Populations

Dara Brown and Krystal Humphreys

It is time for parents to teach young people that in diversity there is beauty and there is strength.
–Maya Angelou

You can do what I cannot do. I can do what you cannot do. Together we can do great things.
–Mother Teresa

Diversity surfaces in our society in countless forms. Human beings have the tendency to categorize people in an attempt to organize and understand them. In doing so, populations with similar characteristics, interests, or situations have the tendency to build closer relationships with one another and shy away from other populations. In doing this, we fail to acknowledge the limitations of our own population and how others may help strengthen us, achieve our goals, and grow one another.

Each diverse population faces unique barriers to life fulfillment. On an individual level, people have the need to explore and seek out life's personal meaning and purpose. It is common for people to satisfy this meaning and purpose in life through employment. Despite career aspirations, however, individuals may come up against barriers because of membership in certain cultural groups. Because of this, career counselors are tasked with assisting people as they attempt to navigate these barriers and obtain meaningful employment.

CHAPTER OVERVIEW

This chapter discusses career issues faced by those coming from diverse populations. Sections discuss particular issues, theories, and methods for helping clients overcome oppression and unequal opportunities and stresses particular interventions. Strategies for helping minorities, women, LGBTQ persons, individuals with disabilities, displaced workers, the economically disadvantaged, military veterans, and ex-offenders are discussed, and strategies are given to help with career-related and advocacy issues.

LEARNING OBJECTIVES

After reading this chapter, you will be able to do the following:

- Identify current issues and barriers for each of the diverse populations reviewed
- Apply specific career counseling interventions with diverse populations
- Utilize the American Counseling Association (ACA) Code of Ethics (2014) and the American School Counselor Association (ASCA) national model (2012) to navigate ethical issues
- Apply knowledge to clients by using case studies

Multicultural Issues and Workforce Populations

This section raises awareness as to what populations within the workforce are considered minorities and in need of assistance. This knowledge intends to help counselors advocate for clients so they avoid further or continued oppression. Read on as we learn about these populations.

Workforce Populations

Diversity in the workforce is continuing to increase within both the private sector, military, and government. Perhaps this is partially because strategies have been put in place over the last few years to purposefully recruit this more diverse workforce (Chrobot-Mason, 2012). Changes in demographics affect this applicant pool and are usually attributed to immigration policies, shifts in economic growth, and wartime status, among other variables (Lowenstein & Glanville, 1995). During and after periods of wartime, an influx of refugees enter the workforce (Lowenstein & Glanville, 1995). Traditionally, California and Texas have the largest immigrant populations, and those increases continue to grow (Migration Policy Institute, 2018). However, after the 2007–2009 Great Recession, significant increases were also seen in foreign-born populations in states such as

North Dakota, West Virginia, South Dakota, Minnesota, Indiana, Delaware, Florida, and Nevada (Migration Policy Institute, 2018).

Statistics show interesting trends in the workforce. For example, in the United States, one-third of the labor force is comprised of minorities (Burns et al., 2012). Of these minorities in the workforce, 58% of Hispanics are male and 42% are female. African Americans in the workforce consist of 47% males and 53% females (Burns et al., 2012). Since the 1950s, the number of women in the labor force has increased. Women now account for 47% of the workforce, a change, since they only represented 29.6% in 1950 (Burns et al., 2012). Other interesting statistics show 6.28% workers in the United States identify with the LGBT community and 11% of workers tout having a disability.

The medical profession is seeing many changes in the workforce. For example, minority populations have grown since the 1990s (Lowenstein & Glanville, 1995). While minorities in the medical industry have increased, most are employed in technical positions and are not employed in more highly respected positions such as physicians and surgeons. According to French, O'Rourke, and Walsh (2014), about 72% of physicians in the United States are White and 50.8% are female. About the same is true for surgeons.

The U.S. military has long used recruiting tactics to increase diversity. Their primary goal is to employ a workforce resembling the cultural demographics seen in the United States (Reynold & Shendruk, 2018). Historically, the Marine Corps recruits more Hispanics than any other branch of military service. Meanwhile, the Army has more Blacks than any other service, boasting an equal number of Black and White female employees (Reynold & Shendruk, 2018). To date, the Navy recruits more Asian troops and the Airforce employs the largest number of women.

Multicultural Issues in the Workforce

This section will focus on multicultural topics and concerns that counselors commonly face when working with clients in a variety of settings. It will provide you with information and theories to consider in order to assist and meet the individual needs of each client.

Multicultural Competence in the Workforce

Over the past few years, organizations and companies developed strategies for recruiting diverse populations. Despite these advances employers failed to instill the multicultural competence needed to promote a supportive workplace environment (Chrobot-Mason, 2012). Chrobot-Mason (2012), states that the fields of counseling and psychology developed and implemented multicultural competencies shortly after Sue et al. (1982) defined multicultural competencies for counselors. Other professions, such as business, however, failed to begin developing multicultural competencies until much later (Chrobot-Mason, 2012). As a result, many companies are struggling to quickly implement multicultural competence and change the cultural environment so that they can meet the needs of their new workforce.

Language Barriers

Language barriers often affect organizations and businesses in a negative manner. For example, issues with language in the workplace can result in discrimination, particularly for those employees from the immigrant population. Organizations comprised of numerous nationalities may find slowed communications due to unfamiliar vocabulary, accents, grammatical errors, and slang terms associated with unfamiliar languages (Lauring & Klitmoller, 2017). Lauring and Klitmoller's (2017) study on workplace environment found that openness to language diversity in the workplace had a strong relationship with employees' creativity and performance. Employers who require employees to conform to the dominant language may perpetuate feelings of workplace exclusion and affect employees' personal identities (Lauring & Klitmoller, 2017).

Imagine being in an environment that is unaccepting of your native language. Your language (both verbal and nonverbal) is an intricate and unique part of your personal culture and identity. For this reason, the vast majority of professions have now begun researching multicultural competence, verbal, and nonverbal communication barriers so they can best foster multicultural growth in their working environment. Guided Practice Exercise 7.1 asks you to consider personal implications of language restrictions in the workplace.

Guided Practice Exercise 7.1 Language Barriers

Suppose you have been asked to work in a counseling agency where most employees speak a language other than your native language. Now, suppose you have been told you cannot speak your native language at work but must complete all tasks in the dominant language of this workplace environment. How would this affect your identity? How might your work performance suffer?

Conflict in the Workplace

Workplace training often excludes those from outside the dominant culture, resulting in increased need for conflict resolution. For this reason, culture-based conflicts can be difficult to resolve. Behaviors related to conflict in the workplace may foster feelings of tension, distrust, anger, and alienation (Lowenstein & Glanville, 1995). Managers or others in authority must know which cultures traditionally emphasize confrontation and those that avoid confrontation (Lowenstein & Glanville, 1995). Fostering an environment that is accepting of diversity and considers cultural aspects when using conflict resolution is essential to our changing workforce.

Stress in the Workplace

Work environments that do not support multicultural competencies may exacerbate employee stress. For example, immigrants who experience discrimination and lack of support in the workplace will have higher rates of anger, psychological distress, loneliness, poor coping skills, and low self-esteem (Pasca & Wagner, 2011). On the contrary, work environments that are supportive of cultural differences have increased job satisfaction, self-worth, job security, health, and reduced uncertainty among workers (Pasca & Wagner, 2011).

Spirituality in the Workplace

In recent years the counseling profession has emphasized spirituality and religion as a part of multicultural competence (Rupert et al., 2018). Traditionally, training in spirituality has been neglected in most professions, even counseling. Resulting from a wave of research in the behavioral healthcare industry that linked spirituality/religion to better health outcomes, the fields of counseling and counseling psychology have adjusted training (Hage, Hopson, Siegel, Payton, & DeFanti, 2006). Even so, religious and spiritual training tends to be scattered throughout multicultural training without a clear idea as to how much training is received or sufficient. The same holds true in the workplace environment. As a part of multicultural competency training, businesses might consider incorporating aspects of religion and spirituality into practice. Practices greatly vary among religions, and the needs of each individual in the workplace should be considered (Kamri et al., 2017; Krahnke & Hoffman, 2002).

Career Counseling for Disabled Persons

Issues surrounding the employment of individuals with disabilities is a long-standing topic of discussion for career counselors (Hernandez et al., 2000; Lindsay et al., 2018; Snyder et al., 2010). Individuals with disabilities are met with many barriers and concerns when entering the work arena. Some of these issues include discrimination, issues related to physical and/or psychiatric disabilities, and the utilization of relevant advocacy competencies. Counselors also need to be aware of the programs and interventions necessary to assist in the success of disabled persons in the workforce. They can advocate for better practices and educate the community and potential employers. Only 18.7% of individuals with a disability were employed in the United States in 2017 as opposed to 65.7% of individuals without a disability (U.S. Bureau of Labor Statistics, 2020).

Discrimination

Individuals with disabilities face discrimination on many levels in society. Not only does discrimination prevent people with disabilities from being employed, but it continues to remain a barrier to success for those who obtain employment. Specific to the workplace, research shows that people with disabilities perceive that they receive lower salaries and less opportunity for career advancement and are employed in jobs with lower prestige than the population at large. Further exacerbating the problem, jobs found by disabled persons are often not compatible with their capabilities, education, or training (Villanueva-Flores et al., 2017). This speaks to the low value employers often assign to disabled employees and may also affect the way disabled employees internalize their own value in the workforce.

When comparing the previously presented statistic (18.7% of employed disabled individuals versus 65.7% of employed nondisabled individuals), assumptions can be made regarding how employer and societal discrimination may influence these numbers (U.S. Bureau of Labor Statistics, 2020). For example, employers may wrongfully believe that employing a disabled person is not a worthy investment, that they lack the ability to perform the same duties as nondisabled employees, or that they do not possess the ability to learn new skills or apply adaptations that lead to success. Because society may hold these beliefs about disabled persons, disabled individuals may also begin to believe much myths. For this reason, career counselors are tasked with engaging in advocacy efforts for and with disabled persons.

Physical disabilities come in a variety of forms, including but not limited to restrictions related to sight, hearing, and mobility. Technological advances have provided never before seen employment opportunities for these individuals (Cawthon et al., 2016). Even with these new opportunities, employment rates of individuals with physical disabilities was only 12.8% in the United States in 2016 (Kraus, Lauer, Coleman, & Houtenville, 2018).

A notable income disparity exists between individuals with physical disabilities and those without physical disabilities. For example, the average income for an individual with a physical disability is approximately $25,000 a year (Cawthon et al., 2016). This is approximately $10,000 less than employed individuals who do not present with physical disabilities (Kraus, Lauer, Coleman, & Houtenville, 2018).

Fortunately, many government-assisted programs are available to assist persons with physical disabilities. These programs often allow persons to receive medical treatments and interventions that increase their likelihood for successful employment (Dutta et al., 2008; Smith et al., 2017). Competent career counselors must become educated and informed about these community sources so they can best help clients.

When discussing clients with psychiatric disabilities, we include those presenting with mental, behavioral, and emotional disorders that impact their ability to function in various major life areas, including the workforce (Henry et al., 2016). A common myth surrounding the employment of individuals with a psychiatric disability is that work responsibility causes individuals to experience distress, leading to increased psychiatric symptoms. On the contrary, responsibility and routine can provide these individuals with a sense of purpose. Research shows employment often results in positive self-esteem, interpersonal skills, decreased psychiatric symptoms, and greater overall satisfaction with life (Bond, et al., 2001; Burns, et al., 2009; Kukla et al., 2012).

Community mental health agencies working with this population understand both the employment limitations placed on them as well as the import role employment plays in their mental health and positive recovery. Because of this, many mental health agencies have begun hiring individuals with psychiatric disabilities as peer providers, a job that involves them working with other individuals who have mental health diagnoses (Chapman, Blash, Mayer, & Spetz, 2018). These peers help clients with life management and symptom coping. They also serve as positive role models for opportunity and success. In such positions, individuals with psychiatric disabilities transition from consumers to experts.

Gender Issues in Counseling

Gender is an important consideration when working with clients in career counseling. Some of today's gender-based issues involve the aging workforce, pay gap, lack of women in fields of science and math, and the restructuring of traditional gender roles. Let us examine some of these issues more closely in the sections that follow.

Age and Gender

Many developed countries have an almost equal number of men and women in the workforce, with numbers of employed women continuing to rise. One particularly interesting gender issue concerns the number of older women in the workforce. For example, employers report larger numbers of women over the age of 65 in their employ than men from within the same generation (Austen, 2016). This is largely because the life expectancy of women is longer than that of men.

Despite these trends, women may not earn as much as their male counterparts in later life. For example, in Australia, women account for only half of the retirement income dispensed in the country yet comprise over 50% of the population (Austen, 2016). These disturbing statistics seem to imply that women in developed societies must work into their later years if they are to achieve income parity with men. Thus, career counselors may see more women reentering the workforce at a variety of ages and stages of life.

Because numbers of women entering the workforce have increased (Cowan, 1976; Ruggles, 2016) and women now make up almost half of those employed (Toosi & Morisi, 2017), a large part of the workforce could be pregnant or giving birth at any time. Unfortunately, policy uniformity does not exist for women returning to work after giving birth. While the Family and Medical Leave Act of 1993 (2006) does require that most women receive time off, it is not necessarily paid, putting financial burden on families (Spiteri & Xuereb, 2012). Some workplace environments, however, such as those with under 50 employees, are not required to give women needed time off to recover from childbirth and care for their newborn (Vahratian & Johnson, 2009).

Nonetheless, discrimination against pregnant women in work environments such as academia is common (Walters & McNeely, 2010) and stressors are felt long after giving birth. Many women report feeling overwhelmed in trying to meet the requirements of both roles (mother and worker) in the first year of giving birth (Spiteri & Xuereb, 2012). Even women who attempt to enter the workforce after their children have been in school full time or have left home and report stress while trying to compete for jobs and perform among younger workers.

Gender gaps have long been evident in the professions of science, technology, engineering, and math (STEM). Specifically, the gender gap is even more evident among those in academic levels of STEM (Walters & McNeely, 2010). Because recruiting from a mandatory quota system is considered unconstitutional, Title IX does not allow companies to discriminate based on gender (Education Amendments Act of 1972, 2018). This makes it difficult to ensure that more women are considered when hiring positions in STEM.

Changes in Gender Roles

Past traditions whereby women held primary responsibility for household duties are slowly eroding as new generations create new gender roles (Kolpashnikova, 2016). For example, more women are entering the workforce and more men are choosing to stay at home. A growing body of literature and media attention is, therefore, devoted to investigating the stay-at-home dad and how society is or is not accepting these new gender roles (Kolpashnikova, 2016). Some suggest that both genders are facing discrimination, women in the work place and men who are staying at home (Chesley, 2011; Rochlen et al., 2010). Since few resources are available for stay-at-home dads, counselors must become familiar with community resources to help these men as well as their female counterparts. Guided Practice Exercise 7.2 asks you to consider how gender affects personal career development.

Guided Practice 7.2 Gender Roles

Take a moment and think about your own gender and the ways in which your own career choices may have been impacted by gender roles. Have you experienced any discrimination or privilege because of your gender? Discuss these experiences with a partner or in a small group. In what ways are your experiences similar to or different from others? Have you learned anything new about how gender has impacted the career choice or development of others? As a career counselor, identify ways that you might attempt to mitigate negative experiences or career choices of future clients.

Career Counseling Issues for LGBTQ Persons

Lesbian, gay, bisexual, and transgendered persons, as well as those questioning sexuality (LGBTQ), experience barriers in the community that may be enhanced in the workplace. Career counselors need to be aware of the following issues specific to the LGBTQ population: identity in the workplace, the lavender ceiling, salary disparities, social interactions in the workplace, and existing laws, policies, and procedures related to LGBTQ employment.

LGBTQ Identity in the Workplace

LGBTQ individuals are more likely to suffer from mental health issues than their heterosexual counterparts (Mongelli et al., 2019). When compared to heterosexual individuals, LGBTQ persons are 2.5 times more likely to experience symptoms of depression, anxiety, and substance use issues and are four times more likely to attempt suicide (American Psychiatric Association, 2017). Perhaps this is because in addition to stressors faced by others in society, this group must also decide whether they wish to have their sexual orientation or gender identity revealed in the workplace. This decision may lead to increased feelings of stress, anxiety, or incongruence. For example, those who choose to remain silent must carry this burden while those who openly express themselves may risk potential discrimination, unemployment, and underemployment and lack of career opportunity (Benozzo et al., 2015; Norman et al., 2017).

Lavender Ceiling

Many people are familiar with the concept of a *glass ceiling* or lack of career advancement opportunity for women and minority populations in the workplace (Cotter et al., 2001). The *lavender ceiling* refers to the same limitations regarding promotional opportunities for LGBTQ individuals (Gerdo, 2010). Despite hard work, LGBTQ individuals may be overlooked for promotions or may refrain from drawing attention to themselves for fear of discrimination or mistreatment (McNulty et al., 2017). Career counselors must

TABLE 7.1   Salary Comparisons by Gender and Sexual Orientation

Sexual Orientation and Gender	Average Salary
Bisexual men	$85,084.43
Heterosexual men	$83,469.48
Gay men	$56,936.46
Heterosexual women	$51,461.45
Lesbian women	$45,606.42
Bisexual women	$35,980.36

Source: Prudential Financial (2017)

become multiculturally competent if they are to be able to help this group achieve their full potential, attain deserved promotions, and achieve earnings parity.

LGBTQ individuals tend to have lower family incomes when compared to their heterosexual counter-parts (Pew Research Center, 2013). Research shows that the income disparity for LGBT individuals may be an overlap of multiple factors including sexual orientation, age, and gender. Career counselors might, therefore, assist LGBTQ persons by helping them achieve the confidence and skills needed to negotiate higher-paying salaries. Table 7.1 shows salary comparisons based on sexual orientations, salary, and average age.

Employment Laws, Policies, and Procedures

In addition to salary disparities, LGBTQ populations experience other forms of oppression and discrimi-nation fairly frequently in the workplace. The United States does not currently have any existing laws that protect LGBTQ employees from workplace discrimination on the basis of sexual orientation or gender identity (Human Rights Campaign Foundation, 2017). In addition, only 21 U.S. states and the District of Columbia have laws that prohibit employment discrimination based on both sexual orientation and gender identity (Human Rights Campaign Foundation, 2019). This means that LGBTQ persons in the United States are being denied jobs, fired, overlooked for promotions, experience workplace harassment, and have no legal basis from which they can advocate for themselves. Despite the lack of legal advocacy available, career counselors are tasked with implementing therapeutic interventions and advocating for LGBTQ clients so they might attain vocational success.

Career Counseling Issues for Military Veterans

Despite the overwhelming verbal gratitude extended to military veterans for their service, they often face multiple employment barriers after their service has ended (Stern, 2017). Competent career counselors can become aware of specific issues related to military veteran employment, such as the impact of mental health in the workplace, disabilities and the effect on military veterans, and ways to help veterans transfer skills from the military to civilian setting. We will examine some of these issues in the sections that follow.

Mental Health and the Workplace

In today's society, military service is often associated with mental health concerns (Bagalman, 2011). A study of over 4.4 million veterans stated that 1.5 million of these veterans were diagnosed with one or more of the following mental health issues: depression (13.5%), post-traumatic stress disorder (9.3%), substance use disorder (8.3%), anxiety disorder (4.8%), and serious mental illness (3.7%) (Trivedi et al., 2015). In addition, veterans of the Iraqi and Afghanistan conflicts returned home with higher rates of traumatic brain injury than those returning from previous wars (Bagalman, 2011). Supportive work environments must be able to address these veterans' needs. A few suggestions for achieving this include identifying and minimizing potential triggers, recognizing warning signs of distress while at the same time being careful not to patronize veteran employees for having needs, allowing veterans to develop and utilize coping skills, being knowledgeable about existing employee assistance programs, allowing participation in community programming such as support groups, and incorporating flexibility in paid time off (PTO) utilization.

Disabilities and Stereotypes

Although the previous portion of this chapter entitled "Career Counseling with Disabled Persons" is applicable and worth revisiting when discussing disabled military veterans, several issues are specific to military service and deserve focus. As an unfortunate result of combat, military veterans may present with medical conditions ranging from chronic pain to limb amputation. Stone and Stone (2015) modified Stone and Colella's (1996) social cognitive model and used it to examine stereotypes employers hold about the career reentry of disabled veterans. The model looks at how employers categorize military veterans by their war enlistment (Vietnam, post–September 11, etc.), generates stereotypes about veterans based on their service dates (physical limitations, mental health concerns, substance abuse issues, overly aggressive, etc.), and makes a determination about potential job performance abilities and employee-employer compatibility based on the stereotypes (Stone & Stone, 2015). The hiring manager then determines perceived veteran job performance based on pre-existing stereotypes. This determination may be completely different from the veteran's actual job performance capabilities. As a result, this model demonstrates how overgeneralization, stereotypes, and negative stigmas inhibit employers' abilities to view veterans as unique individuals separate from their veteran status.

Limited Transferable Job Skills

Many branches of the military offer appealing benefits such as education and on-the-job career training. In addition to these skills, veterans also acquire helpful career-enhancement characteristics such as discipline, leadership, and teamwork skills as part of their military experience (Stone & Stone, 2015). Despite these positive work qualities, skill sets, and their on-the-job training, veterans continue to have difficulty obtaining and maintaining employment (Davis & Minnis, 2017; Stone & Stone, 2015). Some suggest this might be due to their inability to transfer military job skills to civilian employment (Davis & Minnis, 2017; Stone & Stone, 2015). Research suggests that military veterans have the tendency to focus on previous military technical skills when searching for civilian employment and fail to recognize or emphasize their teamwork, communication, leadership, and conflict-resolution skills (Davis & Minnis, 2017). Career counselors can work with military veterans to develop civilian employment–focused resumes and identify potential job opportunities that match their skill sets as well as career interests.

Career Counseling Issues for Ex-Offenders

Incarceration is often viewed as a method for "paying off one's debt to society." While paying off a monetary debt involves creating a blank slate and removing future barriers, this is often not the case for ex-offenders, who experience multiple societal barriers when attempting to reintegrate back into society. Some of the issues career counselors should be aware of when working with ex-offenders include the *ban-the-box movement*, limitations of supervision that impact employment, and methods for reframing antisocial qualities so they become prosocial employable strengths. Each of these issues is discussed in the sections that follow.

Limited Educational and Vocational Skills

Prior to incarceration, many ex-offenders' career lifestyles were misaligned. Many jobs, including minimum-wage jobs, require a high school diploma. Research infers that approximately 70% of offenders and ex-offenders dropped out of high school (Travis et al., 2001). Career counselors might encourage offender and ex-offender populations to obtain high school equivalency diplomas (i.e., GEDs) so that they are prepared for future employment opportunities.

Many ex-offenders are immediately denied employment because of their former criminal status. For example, ex-offenders are often asked to report criminal conduct on job applications via an application question or "box" that requires a yes or no response regarding past criminal behaviors. In many cases, this box, then, immediately eliminates any possibility of future employment for those trying to better their futures and stay out of trouble. The idea behind the ban-the-box movement is that employers get to know the person for who they are and the qualities they possess before refusing to see them based only on their criminal history. To accomplish this, 23 states passed legislation to remove questions surrounding the topic of past criminal behavior on initial job applications (Rodriguez & Avery, 2016). Despite this movement, a majority of U.S. states and providences continue to judge ex-offenders by their past choices (Flake, 2015). If people are capable of change, ex-offenders deserve opportunities and access to career options so as to improve their plight in life.

Advocacy Competencies

Counselors are called to advocate for their clients (American Counseling Association, 2014; Lewis et al., 2003). This standard of practice is essential when working with oppressed and minority populations. The advocacy competency domains exist on six levels, including working with a client and on behalf of a client, each of which exists in three different arenas: client, community, and public (Lewis et al., 2003).

Client Arena

This advocacy domain involves a counselor working with a client on an individual level (Lewis et al., 2003). A counselor can either empower the client or advocate on their behalf. Examples of client empowerment may include identifying and enhancing the client's career-compatible skill sets, role-playing job interview questions, and/or assisting with identifying and changing the client's internalized self-defeating beliefs and career self-efficacy. Specifically, career counselors might help clients identify access to potential job opportunities, connect with community resources to assist with job training, encourage client involvement with support groups, and/or suggest utilization of agencies offering medical, financial, or interpersonal assistance.

Community Arena

This domain involves client advocacy at the community level (Lewis et al., 2003). Examples of this type of community level advocacy may include developing alliances with community groups working to make positive changes for oppressed or minority populations or bringing awareness to schools, employers, or the community regarding employment barriers. Examples of working on behalf of a client may include working with community agencies and implementing a plan for change and/or introducing research to the local community as evidence of a need for programming and employment-seeking interventions.

Public Arena

This advocacy domain involves counselors working with or on behalf of a client at the larger macro level (Lewis et al., 2003). Examples of working with a client at this level might include distributing information and bringing awareness to the general and counseling communities about employment changes needed for oppressed or minority populations and/or by helping clients recognize and overcome barriers of oppression and discrimination they are experiencing in the workplace. Counselors might work with oppressed or minority clients by lobbying for political changes impacting career opportunities and/or by introducing effective interventions for oppressed or minority clients through presentations, research, and publications. Guided Practice Exercise 7.3 asks you to reflect on barriers some clients may experience in the workforce.

Guided Practice 7.3 Minority Barriers

Think about a personal situation where you have worked with a person who experienced a barrier (or barriers) to employment based on their membership to a diverse minority population. What were the specific barriers to employment? Using the ACA advocacy competencies, in what ways could a career counselor help someone in this situation by working both with the client and on behalf of the client?

Ethical Issues

Counselors are called to practice in ethical ways and are governed by various legislative bodies to ensure that they are upholding state and national standards. This section covers pertinent ethical guidelines that review multicultural standards.

American Counseling Association Code of Ethics

The American Counseling Association (ACA, 2014) ethical code is the primary resource for counselor standards of practice. This set of ethical standards serves as a guide for therapeutic intervention and decision making. Because multicultural competence plays a major role in counselor competence, it is not surprising that many of the ACA ethical standards overlap with themes of diversity and career development.

Standard C.2.f focuses on the continual need for counselors to obtain continuing education and training so that they are well informed about current research and trends. It is essential that career counselors stay up to date on the newest information and most efficacious interventions for working with diverse populations. This knowledge can provide career counselors with the tools they need to best help their clients.

Standard E.1.a stresses the importance of using educational, mental health, psychological, and career assessments to assist clients with decision making and treatment planning. Assessment is essential to the therapeutic process because it provides a way to measure counseling outcomes. This is especially important when working with diverse clients because many counseling therapies are based on Western philosophies and may prove unhelpful in some cultures (Arredondo & Tovar-Blank, 2014; Bedi, 2018).

Counselors must also consider bias inherent in assessments, especially when working with diverse clients. This bias is one of many reasons ethical career counselors interpret assessment results, utilize testing manuals, and explain the purpose and limitations of assessment as part of the career development process. Chapter 8 will discuss bias and its implications in assessment in greater detail. Guided Practice Exercise 7.4 asks you to peruse the ACA (2014) Code of Ethics regarding multicultural counseling.

Guided Practice Exercise 7.4 Ethical Considerations

Peruse a copy of the American Counseling Association's Code of Ethics. As you are reading each code, ask yourself, "How does this standard relate to multicultural counseling or diverse clients?" Pick out two or three codes that, in your opinion, highly impact counseling diverse populations and explain your choices in a small group.

CASE STUDY

This chapter discusses diverse groups and populations and many issues they face when entering the workforce. The following fictitious client scenario demonstrates the utilization of the American Counseling Association advocacy competencies and provides potential responses a career counselor might use when working with diverse clients.

Dan is a 34-year-old male who was recently fired from his job after 4 years of employment. His employer justified the termination stating that Dan was no longer seen as a "good fit" for the company. Dan suspects this is actually because his coworkers learned he is gay, and he recently moved in with his partner. Dan is angry the company fired him because of his sexual orientation and feels this is a discriminatory act. No laws in Dan's state protect his employment rights. Dan has been applying for new jobs but fears the same thing might happen to him again in several years even if he starts over in a new company.

First, the career counselor conducts an intake and a needs-based assessment. After this, the session begins as follows.

Counselor: Dan, it sounds like you are struggling with managing quite a few things. You have strong feelings related to your recent job loss and you are worried about your future career. Tell me more about what an ideal job and work environment might look like for you.

Dan: After everything that happened at my last job, I just want to be happy and accepted. It makes me so mad that after years of hard work, they learn more about who I am as a person and suddenly I am not good enough. I want my boss to know who I am and accept me and my lifestyle without it impacting my career.

Counselor: You want to be accepted and valued at a company for your work and not for your sexual orientation. I heard you mention about not being good enough. Describe some examples where you are good enough at work.

Dan: I always got my work done and put so much effort into my assignments. I was there for 4 years! That was longer than most of the other people who worked there. That is how I became a supervisor there. I was training people and then, all of a sudden, I'm told I am not a good fit for the company? That doesn't even make sense.

Counselor: It sounds like you have a good work ethic, are committed to your job, have good leadership skills, and were thorough with your assignments. Those are great qualities that you should be proud of and that any employer would find desirable. How do you plan to make those qualities known to these employers that you are submitting applications to?

Dan: Well, I guess I can highlight them more in my resume. But even if I get hired, I still have to deal with figuring out whether they are going to accept me being gay. I don't want to have to go through this again. I mean, it's not like I can interview them and ask if they hate gay people.

Counselor: So, how do you think you might be able to figure out which companies are supportive of LGBTQ individuals?

Dan: Well, my friends gave me a few numbers of other people they know who experienced similar things. Even telling people I barely know about my situation, they've mentioned some group that meets and talks about LGBTQ issues. Apparently, a lot of the people there have been through this kind of thing before. Maybe some of them know more about which companies to stay away from and which are going to be more accepting of my sexuality.

Counselor: So, it sounds like you have some information and community resources to help you prepare a more focused job-search.

Dan: Yeah. It would sure help to not waste my time. That really might be helpful. I blew it off before as something people say just to make you feel better, but it might actually help me learn from others' experiences.

Counselor: It does sound like a hopeful option. So, let me review what we've discussed. Despite your company saying you were no longer a good fit, we identified things about you and your work employment skills that are actually quite desirable. These qualities and skills show that you are indeed good enough. You are going to use the things we identified to update your resume. Also, you plan to attend one of the weekly LGBTQ groups you were given information about. During this group meeting, you plan to talk to others who have been discriminated against and gain information about potential employers who might be more accepting of your sexual orientation. Hopefully, these new employers can alleviate your fear of being fired for the same reason in the future.

Dan: Yeah. I think that I can do both of those things this week.

Counselor: Okay. So why don't we end our session here for the day and we can check back in next week to see how these goals went for you.

In this session, Dan and the counselor discussed two advocacy activities, and Dan agreed to implement them over the next week. The first advocacy activity involved advocacy with the client on an individual level. For example, the counselor encouraged Dan to identify his employment strengths and recreate his resume, thus advocating for himself via distribution of his own employable skills. The second advocacy attempt consisted of advocacy with the client on the community level. As part of this, Dan agreed to make connections with already existing groups in his community. The goal was for Dan to gain information and resources that might help focus his employment search.

SUMMARY

Diversity is often discussed as a positive aspect that enhances learning and growth in the classroom and workplace. In reality, however; each diverse population experiences a degree of oppression, discrimination, and barriers to success. As this chapter pointed out, these experiences commonly have a negative impact on career opportunity and advancement. Career counseling can help people break down these barriers and change client lives.

Keystones

Career counselors may be presented with the following issues while working with clients who belong to diverse populations:

- Diversity is a dynamic in that population identifiers change with time. Along with this, the barriers populations face and the assistance programs available also change. In response, new research surfaces and guides effective interventions. With so many changes and over-lapping population identifiers in existence, counselors may feel overwhelmed and have difficulty identifying career counseling goals. It is important to remember that just because clients belong to a particular population does not mean that all barriers or issues apply to them. Active listening skills are necessary to determine what the client wishes to achieve from their participation in career counseling.

- The field of counseling affords therapists the opportunity to work with people from all walks of life. Career counselors may not feel comfortable or equipped for meeting the needs of clients who belong to diverse populations or come from cultures significantly different from their own. Although unfamiliar, uncomfortable, or intimidating at times, career counselors can assist clients if they become multiculturally competent. Career counselors must continue to work on their own attitudes, knowledge, and skills by seeking consultation, supervision, and education. They must also stay up to date with social, political, and therapeutic trends so they can best advocate for and with clients.

Author Reflections

It was never my intent to seek employment as a career counselor. Nonetheless, career issues were a common topic found in every one of my counseling-related work settings. For example, college students in institutions were always attempting to find their identity and direction in life. In other counseling settings, individuals with pervasive mental illness were seeking belonging and community acceptance. And finally, as a sex offender treatment provider, offenders were attempting to reinvent themselves and do things "the right way."

I have always known that I wanted to be a counselor and had a decent understanding of what this meant for my future. In working with offender populations, it still amazes me that the resilient, creative, and intelligent individuals I work with meet societal resistance on a daily basis. These individuals are simply trying to obtain employment that fits well below their capability and value, simply because they are tasked with proving themselves. They are often barely able to provide for themselves and, unlike myself, have no idea what their future holds. Being their counselor is much like stepping onto a rollercoaster of continual ups, downs, and loops. By the end, I can only hope for the best outcome of joy and happiness instead of trauma. When working with offenders and focusing on career and life fulfillment, I hope that the roller coaster stays on track. It can run off track when clients give up hope due to endless barriers they must face. Despite the long ride, I have seen countless ex-offenders become successful and obtain careers that they love. It is these successes that motivate me to continue working with offenders and ex-offenders. —Dara Brown

Additional Resources

The following resources provide additional information about the content provided in this chapter.

Organization

Association for Multicultural Counseling and Development:

https://www.counseling.org/about-us/governance-bylaws/candidate-profiles/divisions-and-regions/
association-for-multicultural-counseling-and-development

This group is a division of the American Counseling Association and is the national organization focusing on diversity, multicultural, and social justice activities.

References

American Counseling Association. (2014). *ACA code of ethics.* Author.

American Psychiatric Association. (2017). *Mental health disparities: LGBTQ.* file:///Users/justin/Downloads/Mental-Health-Facts-for-LGBTQ.pdf

Arredondo, P., & Tovar-Blank, Z. G. (2014). Multicultural competencies: A dynamic paradigm for the 21st century. In F. T. L. Leong, L. Comas-Díaz, G. C. Nagayama Hall, V. C. McLoyd, & J. E. Trimble (Eds.), *APA handbooks in psychology. APA handbook of multicultural psychology, Vol. 2. Applications and training* (pp. 19-34). American Psychological Association.

Austen, S. (2016). Gender issues in an ageing society. *Australian Economic Review, 49*(4), 494-502.

Bagalman, E. (2011, May 5). *Traumatic brain injury among veterans. Congressional Research Service Report.* http://www.nashia.org/pdf/tbi_among_veterans_may_2011.pdf

Bedi, R. P. (2018). Racial, ethnic, cultural, and national disparities in counseling and psychotherapy outcome are inevitable but eliminating global mental health disparities with indigenous healing is not. *Archives of Scientific Psychology, 6(1),* 96-104.

Benozzo, A., Pizzorno, M., Bell, H., & Koro-Ljungberg, M. (2015). Coming out, but into what? Problematizing discursive variations of revealing the gay self in the workplace. *Gender, Work and Organization, 22(3),* 292-306. https://doi.org/10.1111/gwao.12081

Bond, G. R., Resnick, S. G., Drake, R. E., Xio, H., McHugo, G. J., & Bebout, R. R. (2001). Does competitive employment improve non-vocational outcomes for people with severe mental illness? *Journal of Consulting and Clinical Psychology, 69(3),* 489-501.

Burns, C., Barton, K., & Kerby, S. (2012, July 12). *The state of diversity in today's workforce.* Center for American Progress. https://www.americanprogress.org/issues/economy/reports/2012/07/12/11938/the-state-of-diversity-in-todays-workforce/

Burns, T., Catty, J., White, S., Becker, T., Koletsi, M., Fioritti, A. & Lauber, C. (2009). The impact of supported employment and working on clinical and social functioning: Results of an international study of individual placement and support. *Schizophrenia Bulletin, 35(5),* 949-958. https://doi.org/10.1093/schbul/sbn024

Cawthon, S. W., Leppo, R., Dickson, D., Schoffstall, S., & Wendel, E. (2016). The art of managing expectations: Vocational rehabilitation counselors as mediators of expectations between clients who are deaf and potential employers. *JADARA, 50*(1). Retrieved from https://repository.wcsu.edu/jadara/vol50/iss1/2

Chapman, S. A., Blash, L. K., Mayer, K., & Spetz, J. (2018). Emerging roles for peer providers in mental health and substance use disorders. *American Journal of Preventive Medicine, 54*(6), 267-274.

Chesley, N. (2011). Stay-at-home fathers and breadwinning mothers: Gender, couple dynamics, and social change. *Gender & Society, 25(5),* 642-664.

Chrobot-Mason, D. (2012). Developing multicultural competence to improve cross-race work relationships. *Psychologist-Manager Journal, 15(4)*, 199–218. https://doi.org/10.1080/10887156.2012.730440

Cotter, D. A., Hermsen, J. M., Ovadia, S., & Vanneman, R. (2001). The glass ceiling effect. *Social Forces, 80*(2), 655–682.

Cowan, R. S. (1976). The "Industrial Revolution" in the home: Household technology and social change in the 20th century. *Technology and Culture, 17*(1), 1–23.

Davis, V. E., & Minnis, S. E. (2017). Military veterans' transferrable skills: An HRD practitioner dilemma. *Advances in Developing Human Resources, 19*(1), 6–13.

Dutta, A., Gervey, R., Chan, F., Chou, C., & Ditchman, N. (2008). Vocational rehabilitation services and employment outcomes for people with disabilities: A United States study. *Journal of Occupational Rehabilitation, 18*(4), 326–334.

Education Amendments Act of 1972, 20 U.S.C. §§1681–1688 (2018).

Family and Medical Leave Act of 1993, 29 U.S.C. §§ 2601–2654 (2006).

Flake, D. F. (2015). When any sentence is a life sentence: Employment discrimination against ex-offenders. *Washington University Law Review, 93*(1), 45–102.

French, J., O'Rourke, C., & Walsh, R. (2014). A current assessment of diversity characteristics and perceptions of their importance in the surgical workforce. *Journal of Gastrointestinal Surgery, 18*(11), 1936–1943.

Gedro, J. (2010). The Lavender Ceiling atop the Global Closet: Human Resource Development and Lesbian Expatriates. *Human Resource Development Review*, 9(4), 385–404.

Hage, S., Hopson, A., Siegel, M., Payton, G., & DeFanti, E. (2006). Multicultural training in spirituality: An interdisciplinary review. *Counseling and Values, 50(3)*, 217–236.

Henry, A. D., Barkoff, A., Mathias, J., Lilly, B. J. & Fishman, J. (2016). Policy opportunities for promoting employment for people with psychiatric disabilities. *Commonwealth Medicine Publications, 140*, 1–14.

Hernandez, B., Keys, C., & Balcazar, F. (2000). Employer attitudes towards workers with disabilities and their ADA employment rights: A literature review. *Journal of Rehabilitation, 66*(4), 4–16.

Human Rights Campaign Foundation. (2017). *Corporate equality index 2018: Rating workplaces on lesbian, gay, bisexual, transgender, and queer equality*. https://www.hrc.org/campaigns/corporate-equality-index

Human Rights Campaign Foundation. (2019, June 27). *Employment: State maps of laws & policies*. https://www.hrc.org/state-maps/employment

Kamri, N. A., Basir, S. A., & Ramlan, S. F. (2017). Implementing ethical codes at workplace: A discussion on the factors of the enforcement, employee awareness and understanding. *Pertanika Journal of Social Sciences & Humanities, 25*(2), 761–782.

Kolpashnikova, K. (2018). American househusbands: New time use evidence of gender display. *Social Indicators Research, 140*, 1259–1277. https://doi.org/10.1007/s11205-017-1813-z

Krahnke, K., & Hoffman, L. (2002). The rise of religions and spirituality in the workplace: Employees' rights and employers' accommodations. *Journal of Applied and Behavioral Management, 3*(3), 277–284.

Kraus, L., Lauer, E., Coleman, R., & Houtenville, A. (2018). *2017 disability statistics annual report*. Institute on Disability. https://disabilitycompendium.org/sites/default/files/user-uploads/2017_AnnualReport_2017_FINAL.pdf

Kukla, M., Bond, G., & Xie, H. (2012). A prospective investigation of work and nonvocational outcomes in adults with severe mental illness. *Journal of Nervous and Mental Disease, 200*(3), 214–222.

Lauring, J., & Klitmoller, A. (2017). Inclusive language use in multicultural business organizations: The effect on creativity and performance. *International Journal of Business Communication, 54*(3), 306–324.

Lewis, J. A., Arnold, M. S., House, R., & Toporek, R. L. (2003). *American Counseling Association advocacy competencies*. https://www. counseling.org/docs/default-source/competencies/aca-2018-advocacy-competencies.pdf?sfvrsn=1dca552c_6

Lindsay, S., Cagliostro, E., Albarico, M., Mortaji, N., & Karon, L. (2018). A systematic review of the benefits of hiring people with disabilities. *Journal of Occupational Rehabilitation, 28*(4), 634–655.

Lowenstein, A., & Glanville, C. (1995). Cultural diversity and conflict in the health care workplace. *Nursing Economics, 13*(4), 203–212.

McNulty, Y., McPhail, R., Inversi, C., Dundon, T., & Nechanska, E. (2017). Employee voice mechanisms for lesbian, gay, bisexual and transgender expatriation: The role of employee resource groups (ERGs) and allies. *International Journal of Human Resource Management, 29*(5), 829–856.

Migration Policy Institute. (2018, July 10). *Immigrants in the U.S. states with the fasted growing foreign-born populations*. https:// www.migrationpolicy.org/article/immigrants-us-states-fastest-growing-foreign-born-populations

Mongelli, F., Perrone, D., Balducci, J., Sacchetti, A., Ferrari, S., Mattei, G., & Galeazzi, G. M. (2019). Minority stress and mental health among LGBT populations: An update on the evidence. *Minerva Psichiatrica, 60*(1), 27–50.

Norman, D., Hunter, Q., & O'Hara, M. (2017). Career development. In C. B. Roland & L. D. Burlew (Eds.), *Counseling LGBTQ adults throughout the lifespan (pp. 6–9.* American Counseling Association.

Pasca, R., & Wagner, S. (2011). Occupational stress in the multicultural workplace. *Journal of Immigrant Minority Health, 13*, 697–705. https://doi.org/10.1007/s10903-011-9457-6

Pew Research Center. (2013, June 13). *A survey of LGBT Americans*. http://www.pewsocialtrends. org/2013/06/13/a-survey-of-lgbt-americans/

Prudential Financial. (2017). *The LGBT financial experience, 2016–2017*. http://corporate.prudential.com/media/managed/ PrudentialLGBT2016-2017.pdf

Prudential Financial. (2018). *The cut: Exploring financial wellness within diverse populations*. http://news. prudential.com/content/1209/files/PrudentialTheCutExploringFinancialWellnessWithinDiversePopulations. pdf?utm_source=newsroom&utm_medium=landingpage&utm_campaign=thecut

Reynolds, G., & Shendruk, A. (2018, April 24). *Demographics of the U.S. Military*. Council on Foreign Relations. https://www.cfr. org/article/demographics-us-military

Rochlen, A. B., McKelley, R. A., & Whittaker, T. A. (2010). Stay-at-home fathers' reasons for entering the role and stigma experiences: A preliminary report. *Psychology of Men & Masculinity, 11*(4), 279–285.

Rodriguez, M., & Avery, B. (2016). *Ban the box: U.S. cities, counties, and states adopt fair-chance policies to advance employment opportunities for people with past convictions*. https://www.nelp.org/publication/ban-the-box-fair-chance-hiring-state-and-local-guide/

Ruggles, S. (2016). Marriage, family systems, and economic opportunity in the USA since 1850. In S. M. McHale, J. Van Hook, V. King & A. Booth (Eds.), *Gender and couple relationships* (pp. 3–41). Springer.

Rupert, D., Moon, S. H., & Sandage, S. S. (2018). Clinical training groups for spirituality and religion in psychotherapy. *Journal of Spirituality in Mental Health, 21*(3), 163–177. https://doi.org/10.1080/19349637.2018.1465879

Smith, D. L., Atmatzidis, K., Capogreco, M., Lloyd-Randolfi, D., & Seman, V. (2017). Evidence-based interventions for work participation for persons with various disabilities: A systematic review. *OTJR: Occupation, Participation and Health, 37*(25), 3S–13S.

Snyder, L. A., Carmichael J. S., Blackwell, L. V., Cleveland, J. N., & Thornton, G. C. (2010). Perceptions of discrimination and justice among employees with disabilities. *Employee Responsibilities and Rights Journal, 22*(1), 5–19.

Spiteri, G., & Xuereb, R. (2012). Going back to work after childbirth: Women's lived experiences. *Journal of Reproductive and Infant Psychology, 30*(2), 201–216.

Stern, L. (2017). Post 9/11 veterans with service-connected disabilities and their transition to the civilian workforce: A review of the literature. *Advances in Developing Human Resources, 19*(1), 66–77.

Stone, D. L., & Colella, A. (1996). A model of factors affecting the treatment of disabled individuals in organizations. *Academy of Management Review, 21*(2), 352–401.

Stone, C., & Stone, D. L. (2015). Factors affecting hiring decisions about veterans. *Human Management Review, 25(1)*, 68–79.

Sue, D. W., Bernier, J. E., Durran, A., Feinberg, L., Pedersen, P., Smith, E. J., et al. (1982). Position paper: Cross-cultural counseling competencies. Counseling Psychologist, 10, 45–52.

Toosi, M., & Morisi, T. L. (2017, July). *Women in the workforce before, during, and after the Great Recession.* U.S. Bureau of Labor Statistics. https://www.bls.gov/spotlight/2017/women-in-the-workforce-before-during-and-after-the-great-recession/pdf/women-in-the-workforce-before-during-and-after-the-great-recession.pdf

Travis, J., Solomon, A., & Waul, M. (2001). *From prison to home: The dimensions and consequences of prisoner reentry.* Urban Institute.

Trivedi, R. B., Post, E. P., Sun, H., Pomerantz, A., Saxon, J. A., Piette, J. D., Maynard, C., Arnow, B., Curtis, I., Fihn, S. D., & Nelson, K. (2015). Prevalence, comorbidity, and prognosis of mental health among US veterans. *American Journal of Public Health, 105*(12), 2564–2569.

U.S. Bureau of Labor Statistics (2020, February 26). *Persons with a disability: Labor force characteristics – 2017.* https://www.bls.gov/news.release/pdf/disabl.pdf

Vahratian, A., & Johnson, T. R. B. (2009). Maternity leave benefits in the United States: Today's economic climate underlines deficiencies. *Birth Issues in Perinatal Care, 36*(3), 177–179.

Villanueva-Flores, M., Valle, R., & Bornay-Barrachina, M. (2017). Perceptions of discrimination and distributive injustice among people with physical disabilities: In jobs, compensation and career development. *Personal Review, 46*(3), 680–698.

Walters, J., & McNeely, C. (2010). Recasting Title IX: Addressing gender equity in the science, technology, engineering, and mathematics professoriate. *Review of Policy Research, 27*(3), 317–324.

PART THREE

Practical Aspects for Working With Clients: Assessment and Theoretical Integration

CHAPTER 8

Assessment in Career Counseling

Brandon Awbrey

Knowing yourself is the beginning of all wisdom.
–Aristotle

I've spent the better part of my career helping people discover themselves. In my experience, a solid grasp on the facts and an honest examination of those facts is the difference between effective decision making and wasting effort pursuing fruitless paths. I've always been in awe of the responsibility we have as counselors to uphold high standards, especially when providing information. Clients value our conclusions, and it is in the spirit of accuracy and truth that we approach the topic of assessment.

CHAPTER OVERVIEW

Vocation is one of the prime sources impacting an individual's identity (Super, 1990). What one is going to spend their lives trying to accomplish, how they will make their living, and how much that process will define who they are is central to many life decisions. Due to the ever-developing body of knowledge and product offerings in the marketplace, you will not find a review of specific products in this chapter. Any mention of specific items is not meant to endorse, rather to use as an example. The purpose of this chapter is to discuss the general principles underlying assessment in career counseling so that counselors can evaluate findings and wisely choose assessment processes.

LEARNING OBJECTIVES

After reading this chapter, you will be able to do the following:

- Develop an understanding of career assessment types and methods
- Understand the factors involved in selecting and using standardized measures
- Learn how to help clients become informed consumers of assessment results and corresponding market research

Purpose and Goals of Assessment

Since Frank Parsons's (1909) pioneering work in vocational guidance, much of career assessment has been focused on matching the level and importance of individuals' various traits to the environmental factors of a vocation. As you learned in Chapter 2, this trait and factor approach is used to find a fit between the consistent aspects of an individual and the aspects of different types of professions (Holland, 1997). Because of the fluid nature of the world of work, research into satisfactory trait and factor matches is ongoing.

The purpose of individual assessment is to obtain accurate and useful knowledge clients can apply to steer the course of their lives. It is reasonable to assume that a client has given their career and job-related ventures a great deal of time and consideration and has ideas that impact the exploration and decision-making process. Counselors are not simply facilitators of various instruments; rather, they use information gleaned from various measures to add to the counseling process.

Understanding the Underlying Constructs

All measurement is relative to defining constructs, and results are derived from comparisons within the constraints of these conceptual definitions (Flake, Pek, & Hehman, 2017). For example, in some personality measures such as the *MBTI (Myers–Briggs Personality Indicator)*, a trait is measured on a continuum between two opposing values such as introversion and extroversion (Myers, 1962). The assumption is that an individual who possesses more of one trait will possess less of the opposite. Other personality instruments such as those that measure *the Big Five* (the constructs of openness, conscientiousness, extraversion, agreeableness, and neuroticism; Costa & McCrae, 1985), measure the intensity of each trait. Extroversion is also measured in the Big Five, but without the assumption or measurement of an opposite trait. The defining theoretical constructs are just as important to understand as the measure.

Selecting the best methods of assessment to use with a client can be a daunting task. Some will take the standardized battery approach, giving a range of instruments and offering to interpret results. Others will use an individualized and less methodical approach. No single "best way" exists to approach assessment.

Types of Assessment

Each type of assessment provides a single piece within a larger context. Only by assessing multiple aspects can one be reasonably confident in drawing conclusions. A single instrument is only as good as the relevance of the construct to the overall problem. For example, if a client values providing for their family over their own personal satisfaction, an interest inventory may not be as relevant to the decision. Of course, it can provide valuable factor information once personal priorities are considered.

Some of these traits remain stable throughout the life span, while others will change with time and experience (Schultz et al., 2017). For this reason, we would not reuse old assessment results if we want them to be useful and current. As you recall from Chapter 6, helping clients understand career in the larger context of human development can be a worthwhile conversation, especially for those investing significant amounts of time and money while training for their career.

Intakes

A thorough intake can make a great deal of difference in how a counselor interprets data collected from other assessment measures and sources. Demographic information can provide a valuable context regarding a client's life roles, personal values, economic concerns, ethnic identity, or life factors that might alter the standard interpretation of results from other measures. For example, as discussed in Chapter 7, clients with a past felony conviction may find it difficult to find employment in certain jobs or industries.

An intake can also help identify those areas in the decision-making process where the client is already comfortable and where they may be stuck. This allows the counselor to focus time and energy in areas where the client needs the most guidance. The interview is limited to the self-awareness and extent of the client's knowledge while also depending on the subjective reasoning of the counselor for interpretation. Figure 8.1 illustrates this concept via a sample intake questionnaire.

> Beyond demographic data that you feel is relevant here are some questions that may help guide the interview. You can create other questions that address any patterns or concerns you see. The main purpose is to help the client discover motivation and insight within themselves as well as clarify barriers or problems that can interfere with career development and choice.
>
> 1. **"Without factoring in education, time, what others want for you, or any other limitation; if I could wave a wand and make you qualified for any job on the planet and it would pay you what you needed, what would you want to go do tomorrow morning?"** Assessing *interests* with a version of "the miracle question" from SFBT allows the client to set aside barriers and focus on pure desirability for a moment. Follow up questions can help clarify the client's thinking about the idea including motivations, perceived limitations, and other negative or positive aspects. Examples:
>   - **"What is the best thing you can think of about that job?"**
>   - **"What do you see is the biggest barrier to that?"**

(Continued)

2. "Has anyone ever told you that they saw you in a particular career or role? Do you have things that you are naturally gifted with?" This can help assess *personality or skills* that the client may possess as well as other's impression of the client.

3. "When you reach the end of your life, what is it that you will want to have accomplished the most? What else is on your life's 'bucket list'?" Assessing priorities and goals can also grant insight into values.

4. "What defines your success today, this year, this decade, over a lifetime?" Assessing the standards of measure the client applies to themselves may reveal limits or cognitive distortions to be addressed.

5. Who are the people you can count on to cheer for you or help you succeed?

FIGURE 8.1   Sample intake questionnaire.

Interest Inventories

Interest Inventories typically are based on the idea that the attractiveness of certain tasks corresponds with inherent preferences for work tasks. They are typically based on a trait and factor theory such as John Holland's RIASEC model (as discussed in Chapter 2; Holland, 1997). Often, interest inventory results conflict with the client's perceptions of "interest" and may even result in surprise as to some of the potential job matches presented. Tests like these identify traits and, often, list typical jobs for people presenting with those traits. In this case, trait measurement may not necessarily coincide with interest levels or present a good fit for listed occupations. For example, a respondent may have indicated a preference for the outdoors and a strong preference for the building trades. Jobs such as forestry service ranger or field biologist may come up as matching, but the client may have no interest in the life or lifestyle of either of those professions.

The demands of the labor market, open job positions, and emerging new occupations can be a moving target; therefore, predicting an exact match throughout a person's career lifetime is difficult at best. We must help the client understand that assessment results are categorical while also ensuring that proper definitions are given for each category's characteristic. These facets are essential if we are to maximize client benefit based on assessment results (Lyons et al., 2015).

Values Assessments

Human motivation is complex and not easily assessed, yet it has been the topic of much study in the social sciences. Intrinsic values, or deeply held ideas of what is important or meaningful in life, seem to be a discerning factor in performance (Ryan & Deci, 2000). Values instruments are harder to define because the idea of important values can differ from one theoretical model to the next. One such example illustrating values constructs that might be assessed is the theory of work adjustment from Chapter 2 and shown in Table 8.1.

TABLE 8.1 **Theory of Work Adjustment**

How well does the client's work personality match what the working environment provides?
Twenty needs in six underlying values (Rounds et al., 1981)
Achievement value: Ability utilization, achievement
Comfort value: Activity, independence, variety, compensation, security, working conditions
Status value: Advancement, recognition, authority, social status
Altruism value: Coworkers, social service, moral values
Safety value: Company policies and practices, Human Resources, technical supervision
Autonomy value: Creativity, responsibility

(Dawis & Lofquist, 1968, 1984)

Most values instruments only assess theoretically relevant values, granting a view of the client through that lens. What provides key meaning and motivation for an individual may not be adequately measured with a single instrument. Combining values instruments with a clinical interview can help provide valuable context and a more holistic assessment. Vocational values are often inextricably tied to culture, often to the level of being part of one's core identity. These core values can be hard to operationalize in a formal assessment. Case Exercise 8.1 asks you to consider how inventories might be used to assist a fictional client.

Case Exercise 8.1 The Case of Adam

Adam took the *Myers–Briggs Type Inventory (MBTI)* to understand why he does better with certain jobs than others. Adam has always been great with technology but was struggling as a programmer. After seeing the *MBTI* results inferring strong extroversion levels, Adam was able to look back at the job and understand his behaviors. For example, he would go days without speaking to others while writing code. He was at his best and most satisfied when attending meetings and working on team projects with others. Armed with this information, he was able to choose a software development role that required frequent interaction with others. Can you think of other assessments that might benefit Adam? How might intakes, values assessments, aptitude tests, and other such inventories also benefit Adam?

Personality Inventories

The term "personality" encompasses the enduring traits and preferences of a person and that make that person unique. This unique personality occurs regardless of the person's environment. An encompassing and meaningful definition of personality eluded theorists for decades (Allport, 1961; Mischel & Shoda, 1999; Fiest & Feist, 2009). Theoretically, by maximizing congruency between these persistent characteristics and the demands of certain professional environments, one will find greater satisfaction (Holland, 1997).

Much like the trait and factor matching that occurs when using interest inventories, one can categorize jobs by demands: social interaction versus isolation, creativity versus conventionality, individual versus

TABLE 8.2   Commonly Used Interest, Personality, and Values Assessments

Interest Inventories	Personality Instruments	Values Assessments
Strong Interest Inventory	Myers–Briggs Type Inventory	MSQ/MIQ
Self-Directed Search	NEO-PI	MSS
O*Net Interests Profiler	Clifton Strengths Finder	SIGI 3
MAPP*	Big Five	MyPlan
COPS (COPS system)	Riso–Hudson Enneagram Keirsey Temperament Sorter	COPES (COPS system)

Measures multiple aspects (interest, personality, and/or values)

collective responsibility, detailed organization versus flexibility, and by dozens of other traits. Matching the results of a personality instrument to these job demands allows a client to predict job fit based on personality traits. The key difference between personality and interest instruments is that one does not have to be interested in something for it to match personality factors. For example, someone with an aptitude for systematic and organized work may do well in computer programming or accounting. They may, however, have absolutely no interest in sitting at a computer for hours every day. Perhaps they wish to ply those traits toward an interest in a craft such as automotive refinishing, a vocation that requires well-practiced techniques and procedures. Guided Practice Exercise 8.1 examines this type of job fit as based in interest and personality assessments. Table 8.2 shows commonly used interest, personality, and values inventories.

Guided Practice Exercise 8.1 Finding an Internship Match

Suppose you are working in a college career center and asked a client to complete a battery of assessments. These assessments were aimed at helping the client choose an internship from an array of opportunities. The client is in his third year of computer science study and, by all accounts, is very gifted in his work. The interest inventory is based on John Holland's theory and returns an RIA (realistic, investigative, artistic) result. His personality type, according to the *Myers–Briggs Type Inventory (MBTI)*, presents as an ESTJ (extroverted, sensing, thinking, judging type). Based on the results of these two measures, what personal traits could factor into the decision as to the type of internship the client may lean toward? What environments would be the best fit for this client? It may be helpful to review information covered on Holland and his RIASEC code from Chapter 2.

Achievement, Skill, and Aptitude Tests

This category encompasses a range of instruments designed to determine how much a person knows (*achievement tests*), how effective they are in performing certain tasks (*skill assessment*), or whether they have the ability to learn the material or task at hand (*aptitude tests*). Standardized national tests such as

TABLE 8.3 **Commonly Used Achievement, Aptitude, and Skills Tests**

Achievement Tests	Aptitude Tests	Skills Assessments
California Achievement Test	Graduate Records Exam	CAPS (COPS system)
ACT/SAT	TOEFL	StrengthsQuest
Peabody Individual Achievement	Woodcock-Johnson III (IQ)	Miller Analogies Test
Weschler (WIAT-III)	DAS-II (IQ)	CareerOneStop

the *ACT, SAT, Graduate Records Examination (GRE), Medical College Admission Test (MCAT), Law School Admission Test (LSAT),* to name a few, are used to assess requisite base knowledge and skills for entry into further study. These measures have long been studied for the predictive value on future academic performance with inconclusive results (Dabaliz et al., 2017; Hiss & Franks, 2014). While the tests may not demonstrate a high degree of predictive validity in learning ability, they do have value in determining what a person knows about a range of topics at one point in time.

Other instruments, such as the *Wechsler Individual Achievement Test (WIAT-III)* (Wechsler, 2008b), or the *Woodcock-Johnson IV* (Schrank et al., 2014) are commonly used as scholastic diagnostic tools to measure academic performance or achievement. The *WIAT* can be compared with *Wechsler Adult Intelligence Scale (WAIS)* IQ score to identify discrepancies in a client's performance and latent ability (IQ). These comparisons can help identify problem areas in a client's life such as an undiagnosed learning disability (Stano, 2004). Table 8.3 shows a listing of common instruments used and distinguishes achievement instruments from aptitude and skills tests.

Career counselors may not spend a great deal of time measuring achievement or current skill since that is the one aspect discussed in this chapter that is most malleable through education or training. These inventories provide valuable insight into planning future education and training needs or matching a current skill set to available jobs. This is one of the more practical assessments as it can have a great deal of impact on immediate planning and intervention. Case Exercise 8.2 asks you to ponder how you might realistically interpret achievement and aptitude results to a client with low scores.

Case Exercise 8.2 The Case of Doug

Doug came in to the counseling office at the small community college wanting help with his career.

Counselor: What is your major?

Doug: Well I want to do engineering, but my advisor said it wasn't a good idea. He said my test scores weren't good enough for it.

The counselor looks at the academic information on file and sees that the client's ACT mathematics score was in the bottom quartile when compared to other test takers. The placement tests administered at the beginning of Doug's college career rate his mathematics level as being lower than the remedial course. He is currently enrolled in, and failing, his remedial mathematics course.

Diagnostic and performance indicators show the client does not have the requisite aptitude for mathematics needed to become an engineer. Doug would have to complete a minimum of three semesters of remedial work, three semesters of college-level mathematics, and three Calculus classes to be ready for engineering coursework. If he was successful in every course, he would spend eight or nine academic terms just getting prepared to begin the degree program (up to 8 years of college to earn a baccalaureate degree).

How do you respond therapeutically while at the same time providing realistic and honest information to the client?

Informal Assessment

Not all assessment data is gleaned through direct questioning or paper-and-pencil testing. For example, one method of assessment, informal assessment, has been recognized as part of the history of vocational guidance and often utilizes client experiences, perceptions, and observations in lieu of assessment scores. This history discusses not only the application of these informal assessments but also details their development based on client experiences and perceptions. Most informal assessment practices are considered unproven because they do not have objective data to support their use. That does not mean that information obtained from these measures is baseless or cannot be extremely valuable to the client. Many of these assessment techniques are grounded in theories that have passed tests of intellectual rigor (Chen, 2003; Savickas, 1993; Super, Brown, & Brooks 1990). As opposed to standardized assessments that are structured and normed using population comparisons, informal assessments are more subjective. One of the advantages to the nonstructured and informal assessment approach is that it allows counselors and clients to examine the process as well as results (Brott, 2001). Thus, most informal assessment methods, including those described in the next sections, can be customized to meet specific client needs.

Card Sorts

Card sorts are typically used as a values clarification and prioritization tool. When using this informal assessment tool, clients are given cards listing various values with or without descriptions. These cards are then categorized by the client into general categories using descriptors such as must have, like, and indifferent. The number of cards per category should be limited so the client must engage in prioritizing and decision making. Once categories depict values priorities, the activity can be used to process the thinking and meaning behind each selection. Processing this activity can help the client identify and clarify the most important values or aspects desired and found with certain careers. Several card sort activities are available and can be used as activity guides, but counselors can also cocreate and personalize cards with clients to make them especially relevant. Guided Practice Exercise 8.2 asks you to create and categorize cards to determine your own values.

Take a moment and write down some values you consider important. Examples might include honesty, flexible working hours, high pay, prestige, and other such factors. Once you have your list of values, categorize them using the categories mentioned in the passage. Next, look at your list of most important values. Will your future career encompass these values?

Checklists

Checklists are designed to encourage a thorough and methodical thought process. What good would it do for a client to find the perfect career fit only to discover it is not compatible with the desired lifestyle or geographic location? Professional organizations, universities, private companies, and human resource firms are a good source to find prepared checklists specific to those entities. Custom checklists relevant to the client, especially those constructed with the client, not only provide the benefits of the checklist but teach the thinking skills required to create one.

Preprepared checklists can also be used to enlighten clients. For example, the client who says, "I don't think I have any skills" can complete a skills checklist listing numerous skills previously undertaken such as organized events, balanced checkbook, washed dishes, washed the car, created an inventory of items, drove a car, and numerous other activities. The client "checks" those items previously undertaken and may be surprised as to the number of skills possessed.

Genograms

Genograms are commonly used in structural family theory and offer a way to visually organize a wealth of information (Minuchin, 1974). The use of genograms to identify value patterns that persist across generations, especially important cultural values and contexts, is a function useful to career professionals. For example, genograms that list not only family members and relationships but also occupations are invaluable in showing occupational themes across generations. Clients can then examine these patterns and discuss whether they choose occupations due to their own interests, simply because of family expectations, or due to ease of occupational access. Also, because genograms are personalized by family and culture, clients may place higher importance on them than they do other standardized assessments. Case Exercise 8.3 asks you to consider a case where a genogram offers career insight.

Case Exercise 8.3 The Case of Ashley

Ashley (24) recently separated from active duty in the military and is looking into civilian careers. While in the military, Ashley was an accountant, but she is not sure she wants to continue with that type of work. Traditional assessments indicate she has an interest in accounting, management, and other business areas. Her personality and values assessments dovetail with the results of the other assessments. She is still unsure and, despite strong indications from the assessments, she is having difficulty making a career decision. Family is important to her, and her family is offering ideas about what she should do next. Her counselor suggests a career genogram to see if patterns are evident in generational family occupations. As part of the genogram, descriptions are given for each family member's job, what hobbies or passions they maintained, and how long that person spent doing each job.

Ashley takes the next few days to gather the information and returns to see the counselor. They go over the results together. It is found that her mother's family were immigrants. Meanwhile, her grandfather worked in a restaurant kitchen for years before starting his own business, which her uncle still owns. Her maternal grandmother took care of the family while her grandfather spent upward of 70 hours per week working. Further, her mother worked as a critical care nurse and her father managed a manufacturing business started by his grandfather.

After discussing the genogram with the counselor, Ashley begins to realize that her family has been focusing their own interests and values rather than considering Ashley's talent and experience. Ashley took another look at her results and decided to follow what the results were inferring. As Ashley's counselor, how would you help her reach her new career goals? How would you help her discuss her choices with her family?

Lifelines

Lifeline activities are used to identify defining events and their impact on a person's life. Clients choose a number of events between birth and the present, both positive and negative, and chart those moments on a scale, similar to the one in Figure 8.2.

Discussing these events and the meaning they provide in the client's life may offer insight regarding helpful or negative patterns. The client can then identify strengths and/or places to strengthen. This informal assessment may help clients view the course of their lives, what they lost or gained from experiences, and how events shaped their attitudes and beliefs.

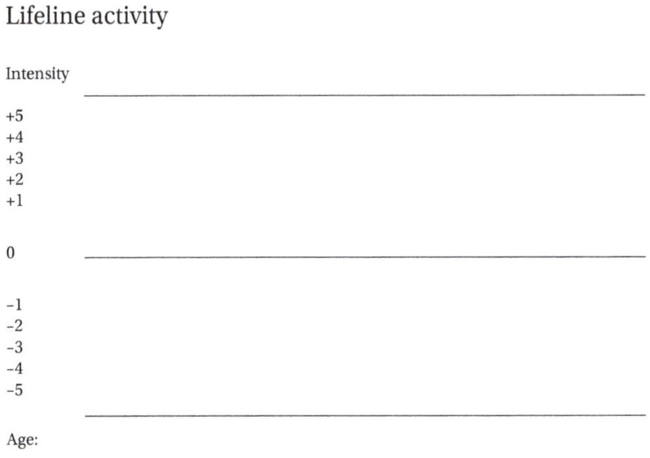

Lifeline activity

Intensity

+5
+4
+3
+2
+1

0

−1
−2
−3
−4
−5

Age:

FIGURE 8.2   Lifeline activity.

Fantasy and Other Activities

Counselors have used *fantasy and imagination-based activities* such as role-playing for decades. (May, 1994; Moreno, 1946; Perls et al., 1951). Whether the fantasy activity is based on Gestalt ideas or another theoretical premise, talented career professionals can design new interventions to reach diverse clients.

Finding and using these techniques comes with a certain amount of professional diligence. Some questions to ask when engaging something new include the following:

1. **What is the intended purpose of the activity (assessment, client insight and reflection)?**
2. **What is the logical/theoretical basis used?**
3. **What are the potential risks involved to the client or therapeutic relationship?**

One common fantasy activity that might be useful in vocational discernment is sand tray. *Sand tray* has been used in play therapy and other contexts and can have relevant applications in career counseling. Clients can form connections from unconscious choices or see patterns that were not apparent using more straightforward means (Sangganjanavanich & Magnuson, 2011). Chapter 13 goes into more detail regarding creative techniques such as sand tray and how it can be useful for clients in career counseling.

Computer-Based Assessments

The development and increasing accessibility of technology allows for most instruments to be administered via computer, tablet, or other device. Some of the advantages include instant and more reliable scoring. Without the possibility of human error, and near instantaneous tabulation, clients can begin working with results immediately, rather than having to wait for subsequent sessions. Another advantage is remote access to materials and direct purchase of measures. Clients can be directed to resources and can choose whether to engage. They can also choose the depth of engagement and the degree of financial investment they wish to undertake. Results can be delivered securely, along with pre-written individualized measurement interpretations. Clients are also not limited by geography or transportation issues when taking assessments via computer.

Despite the advantages, however, technology-delivered assessments do have limitations. While pre-written responses work for specific measures, they do a poor job of individualizing client results. Another danger inherent in computer assessment is that clients or counselors may select instruments that look like legitimate assessments but are poor reproductions. Even worse, these assessments may be solicited simply so that businesses can obtain marketing information. Needless to say, selecting appropriate instruments is crucial if we are to offer assessments with therapeutic value. The next section discusses this issue in more detail.

Selecting Instruments

Understanding basic information about how measures are created and professionally vetted is requisite knowledge for any career counselor. Unless counselors are informed consumers of professional and non-professional diagnostic products, a client cannot hope to truly understand the process and give informed consent. The primary danger is that the client or counselor will rely on results that have no more scientific basis than what might be found in a fashion magazine self-quiz. Social media and the daily exponential rise in internet-based assessment makes it important that all consumers know how to evaluate content.

Reliability and Validity

Every instrument creator wants to know that what they have created serves the designed purpose. Science demands evidence, and to that end the creators must demonstrate that evidence through public peer review. Most instruments have published studies where description of methodology is available. Learning to look at a set of results, especially where an instrument was used in multiple studies, and discerning how well it would work for a client is not terribly complex. While it is important to learn the finer nuances of assessment, a fundamental understanding should serve these primary concerns: (a) How well does the instrument measure the concept or construct? and (b) How applicable to my client are the results?

To that end, social scientists use methods to determine the reliability and validity of an instrument. Imagine an archery target with a bull's eye in the center and concentric circles extending outward. Now pretend that every administration of the instrument is a single shot at the target. *Reliability* concerns the instrument's ability to get consistent results, that is, free of random error (Zedeck, 2014). In target shooting, they call it a "grouping," or how tightly the shots cluster around one another.

Validity is the ability of the instrument to measure the construct it was intended to measure (Zedeck, 2014). How close to the center are the shots? Using the archery example, you can have a tight grouping in the corner of the target, completely missing the desired place. While this consistency indicates a reliable result, the outcome is not measuring what the instrument intended to measure. Therefore, an instrument can be highly reliable (consistent) and completely invalid (testing the wrong thing).

You can also have shots all over the target with the occasional hit in the center. This would be an unreliable result and also invalid. From this example, you can see that an instrument must have reliability (consistency) to be valid (testing what is intended). Also, accidental or occasional validity is not validity: "Even a broken clock is right twice a day." The following are a few of the more common methods of determining reliability and validity respectively:

Test-retest reliability: "*Test-Retest reliability* (or test-retest correlation) involves giving the same individuals a given measure on two different occasions; the scores are then statistically correlated to measure the consistency of responses between the first and second administration" (Zedeck, 2014, p. 375).

Internal consistency: "Many instruments are designed with multiple items that measure the same construct, including reverse-scored items. A participant should respond consistently to similar items in the same manner if an instrument is to be described as having *internal consistency*" (Zedeck, 2014, p. 179).

Content validity: "*Content validity* is the extent that the instrument measures the construct" (Zedeck, 2014, p. 61). A personality assessment with 10 items intending to assess the Big Five would have a low content validity for the simple reason any variation in a single item on the instrument would produce profound differences in the resulting measure of that construct. Not only are there too few items to demonstrate a pattern of response for each theoretical construct measured, but also not enough content exists to provide various ways to present the material. This can also result in testing bias.

Criterion validity: "*Criterion validity* exists when statistical correlations infer common results when comparing measures designed to test the same construct" (Zedeck, 2014, p. 70). Does the measure vary in the same direction and roughly to the same degree as the criterion (i.e., *concurrent validity*), or does it predict the direction and degree of an outcome measured at a later time (*predictive validity*) (Zedeck, 2014)?

Discriminant validity: "Testing the correlation of criterion that should differ based on constructs tested and finding lack of correlation infers *discriminant validity*" (Zedeck, 2014, p. 99). For example, if the questions are measuring the fun factor of a job and that fun and task complexity has not been previously correlated in other studies you would expect them not to be correlated in the results from this instrument. Further, if comparing intelligence tests with personality tests, you would expect discriminant validity since the constructs being tested differ. Guided Practice Exercise 8.3 asks you to look up information and discern use of an instrument.

Guided Practice Exercise 8.3 Instrument Selection

> Before class, visit www.16personalities.com/ and evaluate this instrument for use with a client. Assume your client is a young adult of at least average intelligence. Find the published information to answer the following questions: (a) What theoretical constructs is this assessment based on? (b) What have the creators used to verify the reliability and validity of the instrument? (c) Based on the published information on the website, would you recommend the instrument to a client? If so, are there any circumstances that would contraindicate use?

Norming

To be able to compare the results of an instrument against the general population, test creators typically administer the instrument to various groups to establish parameters on the scales in the instrument. Researchers use detailed descriptions of the target populations to contextualize the results for later comparison with others. Once these studies establish comparison data, individuals can compare their own scores to these *norms* and draw conclusions (Zedeck, 2014). Sometimes you see these referred to as *standardized tests*.

Meaningful comparisons can be drawn provided similar populations are used as the norming or comparison group. Using the instrument with populations that differ significantly from those it was normed on, however, can produce invalid results. One such example might include using an instrument normed on adults with middle school children. It is generally up to the practitioner or researcher to determine if the instrument would be appropriate or if results would be reliable unless explicitly stated by test documentation. For this reason, the American Counseling Association (2014) Code of Ethics states that practitioners have access to the instrument's manual when interpreting test results.

Cost

As professionals, counselors want to be responsible stewards of the resources for which they are entrusted, whether those resources are fees charged to clients or agency funds. Selecting a measure on cost alone is unethical as there are hundreds of free products on the market that are not scientifically vetted (ACA, 2014; National Career Development Association (NCDA), 2015). Even some proven instruments have a free version that has not met the same standards and was meant to be used as a product demonstration, not a diagnostic tool. Many legitimate testing companies allow participants to take the full instrument free or for minimal fees yet limit interpreted results to simple replies. In doing this, they hope to encourage clients to compensate them for the full version of the test and for more specific results. In short, these testing procedures offer your client access to the full validated instrument, but access to full results, norm comparisons, and other valuable data could be restricted.

Cost consideration is client centered, but economic reasons are not the only reason to select/deselect an instrument. One has to strike a balance between providing affordable service and quality service. Are the instruments necessary for the task at hand? Is the instrument the counselor selects a valid measure for the questions the client wants addressed? Is it cost effective for the product provided? Is the counselor competent to administer and interpret the instrument?

Common Ethical Issues in Career Assessment

The National Career Development Association (NCDA, 2015) and the American Counseling Association (ACA, 2014) each publish a code of ethics with an entire section dedicated to the ethical use of assessment. Not every conceivable ethical dilemma is covered in any code of ethics. Rather than provide a comprehensive review and evaluation of all of the ethical standards involved in assessment, this section provides a targeted view of assessment via the moral principles the code was founded on. Additional information on these codes can be found in the codes of ethics listed in the Additional References section of this chapter.

The Six Moral Principles

Autonomy: Clients remain informed enough about the assessments and assessment process to provide consent for any and all portions of the relationship. In ethical practice, clients understand what measurements counselors are using and why they are being assessed. Clients are also given the option to refuse participation in assessment at any time.

Nonmaleficence: Making sure no harm can come to a client from any part of the counseling process is the counselor's greatest responsibility. It takes diligence to evaluate even the benign aspects of counseling for potential harm and ensure client safety at all times.

Beneficence: While harm may be easy to avoid in most cases of career counseling, mediocrity is not. It may be tempting to use new techniques, interventions, or entertain new ways of reaching clients. A counselor must make sure that what they offer clients provides a benefit.

Justice: Treating clients equitably is the foundation of this principle, but that does not apply exclusively to boundaries, fees, and so on. An element of justice in assessment is to ensure the instruments utilized appropriately measure the construct as based on the client's culture, education, ability, and so on. An instrument that is culture bound in Western culture may not equally apply to a client who is a new immigrant and unfamiliar with cultural constructs. Informal assessment measures rely on counselor judgement to weigh data appropriately, so understanding context is even more important to justly assess and interpret.

Fidelity: Determining setting, communicating, and fulfilling expectations are all facets established by the counselor. Regarding assessment, especially where there is third-party interest, counselors should be completely transparent and offer required disclosures to third parties and fulfill stated promises to the client. If the assessments will be used for research purposes, the client should give consent (autonomy) and know how the data will be used (fidelity).

Veracity: The moral principles in this section are strongly interwoven. Veracity is dealing truthfully with others. It is a requisite principle to the other principles listed in this section, as clients cannot have true autonomy if given false information.

Beyond the Codes

Beyond the moral principles are a few concerns not expressly addressed in the code of ethics. Despite this lack of listing in the codes, however, counselors should be aware of the following issues. While non-standardized or informal instruments are not prohibited by the code of ethics, counselors must still ensure the assessment provides a benefit to the client (E.1.b, E.2, E.6; NCDA, 2015). The instrument or assessment technique needs, at minimum, to have some theoretical reasoning behind it.

When offering commercially printed and copyrighted instruments, professionals should be aware of any restrictions regarding administration (ACA, 2014; NCDA 2015). Counselors must know under what circumstances, if any, clients are allowed to take printed assessments off site. This is because test security is a major concern for many standardized measures. Aptitude tests in particular, because of the weight placed on the validity of the scores by college admissions and other decision makers, are held to the highest measures of security. Testing facilities and personnel facilitating these tests must be approved in advance. Although not as secure as aptitude tests, many psychometric tests also require that only trained individuals purchase and have responsibility for materials. Clients are to be properly informed of assessment results and educated on terminology and significance so that they may fully understand the results. Guided Practice Exercise 8.4 asks you to consider ethical considerations for administering assessments in career counseling.

Guided Practice Exercise 8.4 Ethical Use of Assessments

An assessment is given to a client to discover his values. The counselor found the assessment online and knows little about it except it is free. After giving the assessment, the counselor and client discuss the results. When asked what the results mean, the counselor tells the client, "We can figure this out together." What ethical considerations are violated in this scenario? What would you do differently to ensure no ethical violations occur?

The following case illustrates how an interpretation of assessment results might appear in an actual career counseling session.

Counselor: I am looking at your test results from your *Self-Directed Search*. You will notice the three-letter summary code listed on this score report. All of the letters have numbers beside them, and the three-letter code indicates your top three. These infer the three vocational personality traits you resonate with the most. The number indicates the strength of that preference.

Client: My strongest one is realistic? What does that mean?

Counselor: Let's look at the description of the realistic type. (*The counselor reads the description with the client.*) Does that sound like what you think of yourself?

Client: Mostly, yeah. So I have to pick one of these occupations listed (*as she thumbs through the papers*)?

Counselor: Oh, not at all! These are sample occupations that may fit with your interests and personality, but that doesn't mean you have to pick from these. The important thing to remember here is that these are typical examples, not a short list of choices for your life. Look at the list and tell me if any of these might be something you want to consider.

SUMMARY

Assessment is designed to provide valuable information to clients and counselors and helps in the career decision-making process. A major consideration when deciding whether or how to assess relates to client needs. In fact, client benefit is the standard on which all other standards are judged. It does not matter if the instrument used is one of the most scientifically validated assessments in existence if the underlying construct is not relevant to the client's current concerns. For this reason, career professionals would be well served to learn as much as possible about assessment types, tools, and techniques so as to have a large base from which to draw upon. The keystones capture some of the major premises of this chapter.

Keystones

- Assessment is holistic and involves looking at all aspects of a client's life and may involve a number of measurements, observations, and sources.
- Instruments often measure constructs on a scale from low to high.
- Several categories of assessments are available, ranging from standardized instruments to informal assessments (e.g., card sorts, genograms, and fantasy activities).

- Reliability and validity are important considerations in test selection.
- An instrument must be reliable to be valid.
- Norming an instrument helps the client in that they can then make comparisons of their performance to others.
- Counselors should not use instruments they are not trained to use.
- Counselors should not use instruments with clients for whom the instrument is not normed.
- Counselors must know and consider ethical codes when using assessment.

Author Reflections

Working as a college counselor for over a decade, then as a counselor educator, I have had the privilege of walking alongside some incredible people as they made major life choices. You never know what the catalyst for change in direction or momentum will be. Sometimes it was an observation or a bit of insight that they had. It was worth taking the time to understand the assessments because many clients had the wrong idea about how to use the results. The assessments help clients understand themselves, but there is a danger in relying too heavily on the results. A client may begin to think of themselves in those terms, to accept labels, and to some extent, accept the limits of those labels. "It says I'm an introvert, but I have plenty of friends ..."

One of the reasons I do not fully endorse self-assessments, even those designed for self-scoring, is that I see the contribution a knowledgeable professional can make toward deeper understanding as to how those results uniquely apply. The diversity of human existence cannot possibly be encompassed by the description of a resulting "type." There is more to a person than the results of a single instrument. Counselors are well trained in nuances that no instrument can measure and, therefore, the services you provide are invaluable to the process.

—Brandon Awbrey

Additional Resources

The following resources provide additional information about the content provided in this chapter.

Codes of Ethics

American Counseling Association. (2014). ACA code of ethics. Author.

This code has a section devoted entirely to assessment.

National Career Development Association. (2015). *NCDA code of ethics*. https://ncda.org/aws/NCDA/asset_manager/ get_file/3395/ncda_code_of_ethics_for_web.Pdf

These codes offer insight into ethical practices in career counseling and assessment.

Websites

The O*Net Career Exploration Tools: https://www.onetcenter.org/tools.html

This site offers profilers to accompany the O*Net job search site discussed in Chapter 1 of this text.

References

American Counseling Association. (2014). *ACA code of ethics*. Author.

Allport, G. W. (1961). *Pattern and growth in personality*. Holt, Reinhart, & Winston.

Brott, P. E. (2001). The storied approach: A postmodern perspective for career counseling. *T Career Development Quarterly, 49*(4), 304–313.

Chen, C. P. (2003). Integrating perspectives in career development theory and practice. The Career Development Quarterly, 51(3), 203–216.

Costa, P. T., & McCrae, R. R. (1985). *The NEO personality inventory manual*. Psychological Assessment Resources.

Dabaliz, A. A., Kaadan, S., Dabbagh, M. M., Barakat, A., Shareef, M. A., Al-Tannir, M., Obeidat, A., & Mohamed, A. (2017). Predictive validity of pre-admission assessments on medical student performance. *International Journal of Medical Education, 8*, 408–413.

Dawis, R. V., Lofquist, L. H., & Weiss, D. J. (1968). A theory of work adjustment: A revision. *Minnesota Studies in Vocational Rehabilitation, 23, 15*.

Dawis, R. V., & Lofquist, L. H. (1984). *A psychological theory of work adjustment: An individual-differences model and its applications*. University of Minnesota Press.

Ryan, R. M., & Deci, E. L. (2000). Self-determination theory and the facilitation of intrinsic motivation, social development, and well-being. American psychologist, 55(1), 68.

Fiest, J., & Fiest, G. (2009). *Theories of personality*. McGraw-Hill.

Flake, J. K., Pek, J., & Hehman, E. (2017). Construct validation in social and personality research: Current practices and recommendations. *Social Psychological and Personality Science, 8*(4), 370–378. https://doi.org/10.1177/1948550617693063

Hiss, W. C., & Franks, V. W. (2014, May 2). *Defining promise: Optional standardized testing policies in American college and university admissions*. Paper presented at the *National Association for College Admission Counseling, Itasca, IL*.

Holland, J. L. (1997). *Making vocational choices: A theory of vocational personalities and work environments (3rd ed.)*. Psychological Assessment Resources.

Lyons, S. T., Schweitzer, L., & Ng, E. S. (2015). How have careers changed? An investigation of changing career patterns across four generations. *Journal of Managerial Psychology, 30*(1), 8–21.

May, R. (1994). *The courage to create*. Norton.

Minuchin, S. (1974). *Families and family therapy*. Harvard University Press.

Mischel, W., & Shoda, Y. (1999). Integrating dispositions and processing dynamics within a unified theory of personality: The cognitive-affective personality system. In L. A. Pervin (Ed.), *Handbook of personality: Theory and research* (2nd ed.) (pp. 197–218). Guilford.

Moreno, J. L. (1946). *Psychodrama, Vol. 1*. Beacon House.

Myers, I. B. (1962). *The Myers–Briggs Type Indicator: Manual (1962)*. Consulting Psychologists Press. http://dx.doi.org/10.1037/14404-000

National Career Development Association. (2015). *NCDA code of ethics*. Author.

Parsons, F. (1909). *Choosing a vocation*. Houghton-Mifflin.

Perls, F., Hefferline, G., & Goodman, P. (1951). *Gestalt therapy*. Julian Press.

Rounds, J. B., Henley, G. A., Dawis, R. V., Lofquist, L. H., & Weiss, D. J. (1981). *Manual for the Minnesota Importance Questionnaire: A measure of vocational needs and values*. University of Minnesota Press.

Sangganjanavanich, V. F., & Magnuson, S. (2011). Using sand trays and miniature figures to facilitate career decision making. *e Career Development Quarterly, 59*(3), 264–273.

Savickas, M. L. (1993). Career counseling in the postmodern era. Journal of Cognitive Psychotherapy, 7(3), 205–215.

Schultz, L. H., Connolly, J. J., Garrison, S. M., Leveille, M. M., & Jackson, J. J. (2017). Vocational interests across 20 years of adulthood: Stability, change, and the role of work experiences. *Journal of Research in Personality*, 71, 46–56.

Schrank, F. A., McGrew, K. S., Mather, N., Wendling, B. J., & LaForte, E. M. (2014). *Woodcock–Johnson IV tests of cognitive abilities*. Houghton-Mifflin Harcourt - Riverside.

Stano, J. F. (2004). Wechsler abbreviated scale of intelligence. *Rehabilitation Counseling Bulletin, 48*(1), 56–57.

Super, D. E., Brown, D., & Brooks, L. (1990). Career choice and development: Applying contemporary theories to practice.. Jossey-Bass

Wechsler, D. (2008). *Wechsler Adult Intelligence Scale: Technical and interpretive manual (4th edition)*. Pearson.

Zedeck, S. (Ed.). (2014). *APA dictionary of statistics and research methods*. American Psychological Association.

CHAPTER

Using Narrative Therapy in Career Counseling

Janet Hicks and Cassandra Riedy Rush

There is no greater agony than bearing an untold story inside of you.
–Maya Angelou

This powerful quote by Maya Angelou is a reminder that each of us has a story that unveils who we are and what we enjoy and that divulges our secret desires. It also reminds us just how important it is to discover our potential through personal narratives. According to this quote, ignoring these narratives can be detrimental to the development of a person's potential and happiness. This chapter draws on these premises and describes an important theoretical tool, narrative therapy, that integrates with career theories to uncover personal stories and inherent career motives, desires, and passions. This chapter discusses narrative therapy and its specific techniques and how it integrates with a number of specific career theories described earlier in this text.

CHAPTER OVERVIEW

This chapter explores the theoretical underpinnings and practical implementation of narrative therapy in light of its application in career counseling. Its aim is to provide its reader with background knowledge regarding narrative therapy, to synthesize narrative therapy with effective career counseling methodology, and to challenge its reader to envision the application of narrative therapy in career counseling, including ethical ramifications and limitations. The case study illuminates how narrative therapy could infuse the career counseling process in a way beneficial to clients. The chapter concludes with additional resources for those interested in further researching narrative therapy.

LEARNING OBJECTIVES

After reading this chapter you will be able to do the following:

- Understand the basics and background of narrative therapy and specific techniques therein
- Know how narrative therapy integrates with a number of career theories described in the first half of this textbook
- Recognize the limitations and ethical issues that are evident when using narrative therapy as part of the career decision process
- Envision and apply narrative therapy with fictional clients

Narrative Therapy: Theoretical Background and Premises

The practice of narrative therapy is underpinned by the beliefs that we live into the stories we craft for ourselves and that we can find change, growth, and healing by altering our story (Sween, 1998). Narrative therapy originated through the family therapy practice of social workers Michael White and David Epston during the 1980s (White, 2009). White and Epston infused narrative therapy with academic and social trends of the time, such as feminism and the impact of broader social climates on families, as well as the writings of past thinkers, such as Foucault's focus on power asymmetries (Denborough, 2009). They published the first narrative therapy textbook, *Narrative Means to Therapeutic Ends*, in 1990, enabling the spread and flourishing of the practice (White & Epston, 1990). Today, counselors employ narrative therapy in countries around the world. Narrative therapy centers operate in a wide array of nations such as India, Australia, Chile, Canada, Mexico, and France (Narrative Practices Adelaide, 2020).

Narrative therapy is predicated on post-structuralism, constructivism, multicultural awareness, and collaboration. Michael White refers to narrative therapy as post-structuralist (White, 2004). Counselors practicing with a post-structuralist orientation maintain that presenting problems are not indicative of deep-seated or underlying structural issues (Tarragona, 2008). Instead of searching for a client's inner self, post-structuralist thought suggests that the counselor listen to and accept the client's story in his or her own words (Tarragona, 2008). *Constructivism* and multicultural awareness are tightly intertwined in narrative therapy. The application of a constructivist lens begs the counselor to recognize that societies and cultures construct dominant narratives that can greatly impact or even suppress a client's personal narrative (Doan, 1997; Madigan, 2011). The narrative therapist works closely with a client to identify the dominant discourses of society and culture and to empower the client to reauthor his or her narrative in his or her voice, free from external pressures (Combs & Freedman, 2012). The narrative therapist is continually conscious of power dynamics and does not envision his or herself as an expert, rather a collaborator in the client's process of gaining distance from problematic discourses and reauthoring his or her narrative (Combs & Freedman, 2012; Semmler & Williams, 2000).

The process of narrative therapy operates on a few key theoretical tenets:

- "The person is not the problem. The problem is the problem" (White, as cited in Corey, 2005, p. 261).
- "Thick" descriptions enable individuals to approach life with adaptive resilience.
- Individuals have the ability to choose what they allow to become a part of their identity.

"The person is not the problem. The problem is the problem" (White, as cited in Corey, 2005, p. 261). An important aspect of narrative therapy is the non-pathologizing approach that enables individuals to gain distance from their presenting problems (Tarragona, 2008; White, 2007). A counselor utilizing this approach will conceptualize his or her clients' cases in a way that envisions any presenting problem as an obstacle that is not inherently a part of clients' identities, and his or her treatment plans will include the process of externalizing the presenting problems from clients' identities through a series of questions. The counselor will carefully word these questions to indicate the separation of the client and the presenting problem. The nature of this line of questioning will be described in more detail in the "externalizing the problem" section of this chapter. This non-pathologizing approach of seeing the problem external from individuals can serve to support individuals struggling with finding themselves outside of dominant societal discourses that are causing them harm (Semmler & Williams, 2000). Consider, for example, the case of a young Black man named George who feels a societal pressure to act without sensitivity or emotion despite his inclination to emote. A counselor could reframe language the client may use about himself like "weak" or "soft" and instead refer to "the external pressure to not express oneself."

"Thick" descriptions enable individuals to approach life with adaptive resilience. In narrative therapy, it is the client's description of a problem that constitutes the reality of the problem. Therefore, a counselor will pay close attention to the way in which a client describes his or her presenting problems. Commonly, these descriptions of problems are "thin," (Morgan, 2000). "Thin" descriptions are often the internalization of simplistic, generalizing statements that other people have made, which minimize the client's ability to creatively make meaning and determine personal strengths to leverage in response to problems (Morgan, 2000). "Thick" descriptions, on the other hand, provide clients with the creative freedom to make new, wellness-oriented meanings in response to challenges and to harness already present personal strengths. Continuing with the aforementioned case, the label of "weak" or "soft" would be a thin description of George, whereas a thick description would be that George recognizes his emotions when feeling them and at times desires to express those emotions and could include examples of times when George has expressed his feelings with other individuals to the benefit of himself and the individuals.

Individuals have the ability to choose what they allow to become a part of their identity. Narrative therapy empowers clients with the role of author. In the process of authorship, clients actively write their identity by connecting the events of their lives in a particular way and making meaning of their experiences. A counselor helps to facilitate clients' freedom in this process by enabling clients to separate themselves from disenfranchising self-conceptualizations and external voices as well as to take ownership of desired elements of their identity. Recognizing dominant discourses, externalizing the problem, and thickening descriptions are aforementioned ways in which the counselor facilitates clients' separation from undesired identity elements. Another intervention used by narrative therapist to maximize clients' freedom in their personal identity is a re-membering conversation (Russell & Carey, 2002). A re-membering conversation asks a client to consider and decide which individuals are given the privilege of membership in his or her identity (Russell & Carey, 2002). For example, in the case of George, George may decide in a re-membering conversation to omit individuals who have called him "weak" or "soft" from membership in his identity and to privilege the voices of individuals who have supported his emotional expression and intelligence.

Specific Techniques

The counselor's role in narrative therapy is to help facilitate the deconstruction of the presenting problematic narrative and the authoring of a new, positive, strengths-focused narrative. Throughout the collaborative process, the counselor invites the client to be the expert of his or her life. There are various interventions and techniques available to the narrative therapist supporting a client in career counseling. These interventions and techniques are designed to inspire creativity and the identification of nuances while empowering the client to weave together a new personal story from the discovery of new meaning in past experiences. A select few of these therapeutic tools are discussed in the subsequent sections.

Externalizing the Problem

"If the person is the problem there is very little that can be done outside of taking action that is self-destructive" (White, 2007, p. 26. The technique of externalizing the problem facilitates the client's ability to separate the problem from his or her identity, shifting the problem's nature from pathological or inherent to external. Narrative therapy founder Michael White (2007) suggests that the counselor take an "investigative" approach to the externalizing conversation in which the aim is to bring to light the problem's character, activities, and impact. The externalizing conversation generally follows a loose, four-part structure: defining the problem, understanding the problem's impact, evaluating the problem's impact, and explaining and exploring the evaluation (Tarragona, 2008; White, 2007). Usually, to begin the externalizing process, a counselor will ask a client to define the problem in his or her own words. Many times, the counselor will ask the client to give the problem a name and use other questions that elicit a detail-rich description of the problem. Some counselors invite clients to personify the problem by describing its physical characteristics and personality traits (White, 2007). After the client has defined and described the problem, the counselor asks questions to elicit a thorough account of the effects and influence of the problem (Tarragona, 2008; White, 2007). Often, the counselor will invite the client to use metaphors to depict his or her relationship with the problem. For example, a client may develop the metaphor of a toxic friendship with a particular problem (White, 2007). The counselor strives for as "thick" a description of the problem as possible in order to invite the most opportunities for meaning making and identifying personal resources that help the client to address the problem. Ways that a counselor can "thicken" the description of a problem include asking about its impact on relationships with particular individuals, such as supervisors or colleagues, and its impact on relationships in particular settings, such as the office or an academic institution (Tarragona, 2008). In order to, next, invite the client's evaluation of the impact of the problem on his or her life, the counselor may ask questions such as "How do you feel about these developments?" or "If this were served up to you as a fate in life, would you have any questions about it?" (White, 2007). Finally, a counselor might ask questions such as "Why do you feel this way about this development?" or "Would you tell me a story about your life that would help me to understand why you would take this position on this development?" in order to facilitate the client's exploration and explanation of his or her evaluation of the problem's impact (White, 2007). During the process of exploration and explanation of the problem's impact, the counselor has the opportunity to help the client recognize the broader context and implications of the problem, such as the potential dominant societal discourses substantiating or maintaining the problem's influence (Tarragona, 2008). The counselor also has the opportunity to help the client situate the problem into a positive personal narrative of resiliency and strength (White, 2007).

A career counselor can use externalization to help the client deconstruct his or her narrative, gaining distance from problems or dominant discourses that impede his or her professional progression. For example, picture a client who has been laid off and carries self-esteem issues even though the layoff was not performance based. Externalization can help the client to depersonalize the layoff as well as recognize the impact the layoff has had on his or her self-esteem. As well, the layoff can be placed in the broader context of the economic climate through the use of externalization.

Definitional Ceremony and Outsider Witnesses

The process of externalizing the problem includes the element of placing the problem into the broader context (Meehan & Farquharson, 2012). The definitional ceremony also invites the broader context into the therapeutic process. Born out of the post-structuralist view on which narrative therapy is based, the definitional ceremony is an opportunity to harness the power of community in identity formation and maintenance by inviting outsiders to engage in the therapeutic practice (White, 2005). A counselor will work closely with a client to decide on who will be the outsider witnesses for this ritual. Those chosen should be individuals who are trusted to witness the client's narrative without sharing judgment, affirming or applauding, or opining in response. They will be asked to retell and engage in conversation what they have heard with as minimal personal introjection as possible (White, 2005). The client can choose family, friends, colleagues, supervisors, neighbors, or any other community members he or she deems appropriate to be outsider witnesses (Walther & Fox, 2012).

The definitional ceremony is a four-part ritual that involves the telling and retelling of aspects of the client's story (Leahy et al., 2012). The client shares an aspect of his or her narrative with varying degrees of counselor involvement, ranging from facilitating the entire telling to being present without participation. The counselor then initiates the outsider witnesses' retelling of the client's story through questions regarding what aspects of the story were striking and what insight they gained from witnessing the telling (Leahy et al., 2012). The third step is the client's retelling of the outsider witnesses' retelling (White, 2005). Finally, the counselor facilitates reflections by the client and the outsider witnesses on the telling and retellings shared in the first three parts of the ceremony (Morgan, 2002).

As a career counselor, the definitional ceremony can serve to help a client establish his or her desired professional identity. For example, picture a client who has decided to make a shift in career tracks due to life experiences, perhaps leaving a full-time job to enter an academic degree program, and is ready to openly share the formative narrative that constitutes the identity development. A definitional ceremony would provide this client therapeutic space to share with the support of his or her counselor's facilitative skills and guidance. Through the ceremony, the client may thicken his or her narrative, gaining insight from hearing his or her narrative retold and deepening his or her motivation to shift career paths.

Guided Practice Exercise 9.1 Performance Anxiety and the Definitional Ceremony

The definitional ceremony can be an effective therapeutic tool that helps a client to establish a desired identity within his or her community. However, clients may experience fear of sharing their story with others, some form of performance anxiety. How would you work with a client to address his or her fears? Would you still suggest he or she participates in a definitional ceremony? How could you, in the facilitator role, tailor a definitional ceremony to the unique needs of each client? What other ways are there for the client to express their narrative besides telling it?

Unique Outcomes

As a client shares his or her problem-saturated narrative in therapy sessions, his or her counselor will look for aspects, unique outcomes, of the client's story that contradict or indicate a reality other than the problem (Draucker et al., 2006; Morgan, 2002. The counselor can use multiple lenses to look for these unique outcomes, including looking for emotional, cognitive, and behavioral aspects of the client's narrative that stand apart from the problem (Payne, 2011). As well, the counselor can investigate various tenses, asking the client about the past, present, and future, increasing opportunities to illuminate unique outcomes. As the counselor identifies these unique outcomes throughout the therapeutic process, the counselor will facilitate the client's development of the ability to recognize them his- or herself. Unique outcomes provide the foundation upon which a client can build an alternative narrative, separate and apart from the problem narrative. The counselor will also facilitate the client's development of the ability to expand on unique outcomes, thickening the plot of the narrative and, therefore, enabling many opportunities to harness personal strengths and resilience while addressing future problems. The process of thickening the plot of a narrative is discussed as the next specific narrative therapy technique.

As a career counselor, unique outcomes begin the process of helping the client to substantiate the career identity, trajectory, or change that he or she ultimately desires. Consider, for example, a counselor working with a client who lacks a sense of self-efficacy regarding interactions with supervisors. This counselor could ask "Is there a time in the past that you felt adequately heard or understood by your supervisor?" or "What response from a supervisor would indicate that you had communicated well?" The counselor could then expand on the unique outcome by drawing out a theme, such as the emotion, cognition, or behavior the client has associated with the experience.

Thickening the Plot

As discussed previously in this chapter, one goal of narrative therapy is to thicken the plot of the client's narrative in order to create more opportunities for leveraging already present strengths and talents. A counselor has creative freedom to explore how he or she can best serve the client in thickening the plot. The most basic requirement in doing so is to elicit further details about unique outcomes. Narrative therapy founder Michael White detailed the use of a particular line of questioning that expands on unique outcomes utilizing narrative "landscapes" (White, 2007). The two landscapes that White draws on to elicit details about unique outcomes are the landscape of action and the landscape of consciousness (Draucker et al., 2016). The landscape of action focuses on the who, what, when, and where of events in a client's life (Draucker et al., 2016). For example, a counselor orienting to the landscape of action may ask, "Have you ever been able to escape the problem, even for a few minutes?" (Freedman & Combs, 1996). The landscape of consciousness focuses on making meaning of the events in the landscape of action. A counselor orienting to the landscape of consciousness will ask questions regarding motivations, insights, and emotions, such as "What do your wishes tell you about what is important to you?" (Draucker et al., 2016).

A career counselor may use the landscapes of action and consciousness to thicken the plot of a client's narrative and provide room for creativity regarding professional identity and future career decisions. Thickening the plot may be particularly useful for a client who is unsure of what direction to take in his or her career path. A counselor serving a client in the process of discernment can use the landscapes of action and consciousness to illuminate potential career paths. For example, he or she could ask the client "As a child, what did you want to be when you grew up?" and then expand on the themes that emerge around the client's childhood aspirations by asking "What does this childhood dream say about what matters to you in life?" This question addresses the landscape of consciousness. The next question could address the landscape of action by asking "Is there another time that you can think of where [previous answer] mattered to you?" The counselor can continue to alternate between the landscapes to thicken the plot of the client's motivational narrative.

Therapeutic Letters

Counselors practicing narrative therapy strive to facilitate a lasting shift toward resilience and wellness in the client's personal narrative. Many counselors employ the technique of writing therapeutic letters in order to underline narrative shifts in a way that clients can carry with them in a more permanent medium than dialogue (Speedy, 2005). Counselors' letters highlight various aspects of therapeutic conversations, such as ways a client has discovered to be more compassionate to his- or herself, unique outcomes, or questions the counselor has suggested a client continue to ponder (Pilkington, 2018). Letters also, more implicitly, reveal to a client that his or her counselor has sincerely listened to and considered his or her narrative (Douglas et al., 2016). Hugh Fox (2003), narrative therapist, writes that using clients' quotes verbatim, questions, the subjunctive mood, reflexive verbs and puns, and humor are effective techniques in letter writing.

A career counselor can utilize letters to highlight aspects of the therapeutic process and help put to paper the narrative developments that unfold during sessions. Consider a client who is trying to find balance between time spent at work and time spent with family. A counselor could write this client a letter after a session spent discussing the pros and cons of taking a lower-paying job that enables more family time due to a shorter commute and less business trips. This letter may include sentences like, "You take seriously your responsibility to your children, both as a caregiver and a financial provider," as well as verbatim quotes like, "You told me, 'Getting home one hour earlier means mealtime with my family.'"

The Integration of Narrative Therapy With Career Counseling Theories and Models

Now that you understand the background and foundations of Narrative Therapy, let's shift gears and focus on how this integrates with career counseling theory. We begin by discussing how Donald Super's career premises merge with Narrative Therapy. By understanding the synthesis of counseling and career theory, we can merge the approaches for use with clients.

Donald Super's Career Theories

As discussed in Chapter 4, Donald Super contended that the best form of career counseling involves an integration of psychological components, life situations, and knowledge of the client's world insight (Maree & Di Fabio, 2018). These situational and personal factors can be illustrated through personal stories and memories, thus leading to client insight on career fit as well as therapeutic factors (Super, 1990). Thus, narrative therapy integrates well with Super's theoretical premises and helps the client understand his or her own self-concept. The following example illustrates how the client's personal story (e.g., narrative therapy) offers this career-oriented insight.

Consider the client, Fred, who was recently released from prison on parole. Fred feels the world is unfair and he is consistently being turned down for jobs. The career counselor might respond as follows:

Counselor: Fred, tell me about your last interview.

Fred: I went in and they asked if I had been convicted of a crime. So, I got mad and told them that I wouldn't waste any more of their time because they wouldn't hire me anyway.

Counselor: Fred, tell me a story when you were a child that you still remember.

Fred: I remember when I was about 5 and my dad came home and started yelling at me for smearing toothpaste all over the bathroom. I told him I didn't do it, but he just kept yelling.

Counselor: What did you do?

Fred: I just walked out of the room. I guess that is what I am still doing. Hmmm!

In this case, Fred seemed to instantly see connections between his past and current behaviors by simply telling his own story. This falls in line with contentions by Maree and Di Fabio (2018), who state that narrative therapy has the ability to help clients understand connections between life situations and the self, thus offering better examinations of the world of work. This may also help the client understand and facilitate what Super (1990) called the self-concept. It seems Fred was better able to understand his own self-concept and could be taught better responses to interviewee questions by examining additional narratives about past experiences. Narrative therapy can be the link between past narratives that drive current career issues (Cardoso et al., 2014).

Super's career theory might also be an integral premise when using narrative theory as a medium for career decision making. Clients might be asked to recall stories from their childhood, characters from stories with whom they identify, and to create other constructivist narrations that tie to a career theme. For example, career counselors might have a client describe memorable events from childhood, discuss role models throughout their lifetime, relay book or movie events and characters, and discuss scenes they feel strongly about. Clients might also create themes that depict careers that match these values. Doing these things allow the person's career self-concept to evolve as part of the client's life theme and inherent personal values. Super (1990) states that career issues are best supported when "psychological insights" are integrated with "an understanding of the interaction between individuals and their life-situations and knowledge of the real-world" (p. 134). We will look in more detail at how this process occurs and how clients are led toward action in the case study at the end of this chapter.

Guided Practice Exercise 9.2 Narrative Career Timeline

Narrative therapy can be the link between past behaviors that drive current career issues. On a sheet of paper, draw a horizontal line from the left-hand side to the right-hand side. Along the line, create a career timeline by chronologically plotting each academic and professional institution you have studied or worked. Under each institution write some common behaviors of yours at that place. Do you see any themes? Any changes over time? How might this activity facilitate the therapeutic process? How would using narrative therapy help to incorporate this activity into the therapeutic process?

Gottfredson's Circumscription and Compromise

Donald Super's (1990) career theory and Gottfredson's (1981) circumscription and compromise theory share an important concept: the importance of the self-concept. It comes as no surprise, then, that just as narrative therapy's techniques help promote the self-concept as discussed by Super, it also integrates with Gottfredson's core belief in the importance of the self-concept that was mentioned in Chapter 4. Gottfredson's further contention that we eliminate rather than choose career options is also especially conducive to narrative therapy's techniques. Let's explore this concept in the information that follows.

Gottfredson believed that clients eliminate positions that do not fit the person's self-concept. For example, she stated that we rule out jobs that do not fit society or our culture's standard of prestige or gender fit (Gottfredson, 1981). This blends well when using narrative therapy since it allows the client to tell a story that describes real-world perceptions that illustrate these biases. As the client tells stories from their childhood or current situation, lists heroes, and discusses other cultural experiences, the career counselor listens for themes that might elicit career gender or prestige bias. The following example highlights what prestige bias might look in a session with 17-year-old Henry. Henry seems concerned that he can't find a job he enjoys and that is prestigious enough to please his mother.

Henry: (while looking at a list of job opportunities) I don't like any of these jobs you are showing me.

Counselor: Okay, maybe we can shift gears and you can tell me a little more about yourself. That might help us find some additional ideas. Tell me about a time when you were a child that you did something with your family that you enjoyed.

Henry: I remember cooking dinner together on my birthday when I was 7 years old. My aunt taught me to bake and cut out cookies. We had flour all over the kitchen, but it was a memory I will never forget.

Counselor: Tell me another memorable story when you were a little older and doing something.

Henry: I remember coming home with a group of friends when I was about 12 years old and my mother had made an ice cream cake for us to eat. It was a beautiful cake and I was so proud that my mother was able to do this. My friends were impressed also. I remember being so intrigued by how she got ice cream inside a cake that I cut it in pieces to figure it out.

Counselor: It sounds like you like to cook and are intrigued by food creation.

Henry: Yes, I like to cook but my family will not approve of just a cooking job. I promised my mother I would get a college degree.

Counselor: Maybe we could look at some college majors that work in food services.

Henry: There are college degrees that deal with food and cooking?

Counselor: Yes, would you like to look at some of these possibilities?

Henry: Yes, for the first time I am thinking maybe I can find something to major in that will please my mother and me.

The counselor noted that Henry ranked cooking as a low-status job and a college degree as more prestigious and socially acceptable. Once the counselor gained insight into this type of potential bias via Henry's stories, possibilities could be discussed that merged his interests with his need for prestige through a college degree.

It would be remiss not to also consider cultural issues that might be affecting Henry's career issues when determining the presence of prestige bias. For example, the career counselor must also consider other cultural factors found within Henry's family to ensure this is truly prestige bias and not a cultural issue. Duarte (2017) states this focus on "cultural factors and their implications for counseling reinforces the importance of having a sound understanding and evaluation of individual life themes and the contexts in which they manifest (p. 1). For this reason, the career counselor in Henry's case would ask for additional narratives that offer better insight into Henry's cultural beliefs and background before automatically assuming the issue is one of prestige bias. Case Exercise 9.1 asks you to consider a client whose gender and culture is impeding career success and to assess how narrative therapy might be especially helpful in this instance.

Case Exercise 9.1 Hidden Gender and Cultural Issues

Xi is a 35-year-old Chinese male who recently immigrated to the United States. While helping Xi select potential job options, he seems only to gravitate toward jobs in technology, mathematics, or engineering despite having no interest in these fields. How might narrative therapy help uncover hidden cultural or gender issues? Suppose you ask Xi to tell stories from his childhood and he shares that the only jobs his family supported were technology, mathematics, or engineering, but he loves cooking. How would you help Xi? How might Gottfredson's theory fit with this client's issue?

Krumboltz's Happenstance Theory

Mitchell, Levin, and Krumboltz's (1999) stance that past job experiences create stepping-stones toward future career success blends beautifully with White's (2007) narrative therapy. For example, Shefer (2018) describes narrative tools for changing a client's "problem-saturated story" into a "preferred story" (p. 101). This focus on future success through past experiences blends Krumboltz's happenstance theory and these narrative tools and offers a method for helping clients find future success. To best understand this process, however, you must first understand the difference between a problem and preferred story.

The *problem-saturated story* consists of shared client narratives focusing on the past as if it consists of completely truthful failures. Over time, these failures are reframed so they may be viewed differently and seen from another perspective. In contrast, the *preferred story* consists of past experiences redefined as catalysts for positive change and creates understanding that can eventually coincide with the preferred career. Clients must observe and analyze personal criticisms related to the problem-saturated story and take a vocational preference questionnaire assessment and a *career genogram* (a technique whereby a family diagram is used to plot family ties and vocations) to fully understand their career story.

A unique method used to understand the career story is picture-related narrative therapy. During *picture-related narrative therapy*, clients draw pictures depicting early problematic memories (problem-saturated stories) and illustrations of preferred career desires (preferred stories; Taylor & Savickas, 2016). Pictures are analyzed and new meanings are assigned to memories. Clients are able to use past memories as a springboard to help see how current values can be put into their preferred world of work. Clients focus on their success story by drawing pictures that slowly move them into the preferred story.

Mitchell, Levin, and Krumboltz's (1999) career theory embeds itself into this style of narrative therapy in that both view past experiences as tools that can help improve one's future career. In conjunction with narrative therapy, career happenstance or chance can combine with future planning to create the best career options for clients. Clients looking at open positions can optimize their past experiences, both personally and professionally, with the preferred narrative to arrive at the best job fit in the present moment.

Mitchell, Levin, & Krumboltz's (1999) learning theory is also evident when using narrative therapy. Krumboltz (1999) believed we learn from our own experiences as we tell and analyze unique stories. By reframing our experiences, we are reevaluating the positive and negative reinforcements upon which we base our successes, risks, and self-evaluations. Fred, in the previous case, illustrates this point since he is reacting to job interviews by walking out as based on his past experiences. Just as he learned through positive and negative reinforcements initially, however, he can relearn his responses in a self-written preferred story. After Fred creates this preferred story where he obtains a job, the career counselor could help Fred think from success backward, thus helping him create steps where he applies new strategies that lead to career success. Discussions could also ensue on the types of reinforcements Fred received and what might be done differently to ensure future positive reinforcements. Case Exercise 9.2 asks you to apply some of these strategies based on learning theory and narrative therapy to help a client facing low career self-concept.

Case Exercise 9.2 Ricardo's Self-Concept

Ricardo has taken some career assessments and was given the assignment of researching some potential jobs over the past week. When Ricardo enters your office on the second week of career counseling, you ask, "What did you think of the jobs you researched over the past week?" Ricardo says, "These are some great jobs, but I am just not qualified for any of them. As an immigrant, they will not hire me for these jobs. I have never been able to get jobs that pay this well." Assuming Ricardo has the qualifications needed for several of the jobs on the list that he is interested in, how would you help him gain the self-efficacy needed to apply for these positions? How might social learning theory and past reinforcers be affecting Ricardo's self-concept? How could you help Ricardo move toward a preferred story?

Holland's RIASEC Codes

As seen in Chapter 2, John Holland developed a typology consisting of six categories. Each separate category, when combined with a second and third choice category, creates a three-letter Holland code that can be used to search careers that may fit client interests (Holland, 1959). Table 9.1 illustrates these typologies.

TABLE 9.1   **Holland's Typologies**

Category	Sample Job Aspects Enjoyed
Realistic (R)	Outdoors, working with machines
Investigative (I)	Solving/investigating/researching
Artistic (A)	Writing, dancing, painting, art
Social (S)	Working with/helping others
Enterprising (E)	Leading, developing
Conventional (C)	Organizing, filing, sorting

Narrative therapy can be used as a supplemental assessment to determine whether client job prospects "fit" the client's interests. For example, a client who seems uninterested in every job prospect might have motives beyond interest impacting the decision. These motives might involve psychological issues, low self-efficacy, low self-concept, cultural or gender issues, hidden disabilities, or any number of other issues not yet considered in career counseling sessions. Therefore, Holland's typology and narrative therapy, when used together, have the ability to ensure reliability of interest (e.g., compare Holland codes with narratives) or, in contrast, to point out discrepancies that require psychological, emotional, or other interventions that may be impeding career selection and success.

Consider the client who shows disinterest in every job prospect despite showing interest on several assessments. Once asked to share personal narratives, past experiences, heroes, favorite books, television programs, and other such stories, the client reinforces previous interests but indicates previous failures that impede progress. This now offers insight into what is actually occurring and leads to accurate interventions. The case study at the end of the chapter offers an example as to what this process might look like with an actual client. Consider Case Exercise 9.3 where a client shows no interest in any jobs that might tie to their Holland code.

Case Exercise 9.3 Holland Mismatch

Over the past couple of weeks, Carrie has just taken the Strong Interest Inventory, Self-Directed Search, and several other unstructured assessments and has a consistent Holland code across each assessment. Carrie hates every job option she has looked at based on this code. What might be causing this mismatch? What would you do to help her? How might narrative therapy be helpful in this process?

Savickas's Career Construction Theory

"Clients seek assistance from employment counselors to overcome the writer's block or narrative confusion that they experience as they move into the next chapter of their career story" (Savickas, 2011, p. 179). Through his work with career stories, Mark Savickas created the *Career Construction Theory (CCT)*. CCT holds, in the vein of constructivism, that individuals create personal construct of reality by making meaning of interactions with their environment through stories (Brown, 2014). Careers are constructed as individuals make meaning of professional experiences and vocational behavior (Brown, 2014; Savickas, 2011). Vocational behavior is determined by motivations, life themes, and adaptations (Del Corso & Rehfuss, 2011). Individuals find growth, change, and healing in their careers as they lean into the process of meaning making and understand themselves as protagonist and author of their career stories (Del Corso & Rehfuss, 2011).

Savickas (2011) envisions each individual as holding three roles: actor, agent, and author. His vision of personal roles and career stories integrates smoothly with narrative therapy. According to CCT, individuals are actors within a social context. This conceptualization recognizes the "cultural discourses" shaping career stories (Savickas, 2011). Integrating narrative therapy with CCT enables a counselor to facilitate the externalization of any of the "cultural discourses" that are problematic or detrimental to the client's career development. CCT views individuals as agents, goal setters who are capable of self-regulation (Savickas, 2011). Integrating narrative therapy techniques into CCT enables a counselor to help a client recognize his or her strengths, motivations, and capabilities as an agent through the process of identifying and thickening unique outcomes. CCT views individuals as authors, making meaning of their personal goals and their interactions with their social environment in the context of stories (Savickas, 2011). Narrative therapy provides a counselor the theoretical orientation and tools to empower a client to step into the creative role of author and to facilitate the authorship process.

Savickas's Career Construction Interview is a CCT intervention that could be enhanced through the use of narrative therapy techniques. The *Career Construction Interview* consists of four questions designed to invite aspects of the client's career story, such as his or her current script through exploring the story in his or her favorite book or movie and his or her typical role through exploring role models (Savickas, 2011). In order to expand on the client's answers, a career counselor could ask questions designed to investigate the landscape of action and the landscape of consciousness. The following example highlights the integration of the Career Construction Interview and narrative therapy in a session with 28-year-old Eugene. Eugene is at a career crossroads, trying to decide between entering a pre-law program or continuing to work as a consultant.

Counselor: Who were your mentors when you were growing up? Tell me about each of them.

Christina: I admired my teacher. She was super busy but always found time to make everyone in class feel good about themselves.

Counselor: Can you tell me about a specific time you remember about your teacher?

Christina: Sure. I remember a time when my friend got in trouble and blamed me for it. My teacher just talked to both of us in the hall and was really nice. Even though she had so much to do, she took time to show us she cared.

Counselor: What was so special about your teacher?

Christina: She was kind to everyone even when they didn't deserve it.

Counselor: What does this memory tell you about yourself?

Christina: I guess I want to be cared for and I don't want to be overlooked or blamed falsely.

Counselor: Have there been times this has come up in your job?

Christina: I guess it has. I get a lot of respect as a consultant and I am treated like I matter. I expect if I became a lawyer I would get demeaned by judges at times.

Through the question in the Career Construction Interview, the career counselor opens the door for a life theme of Eugene's to emerge. The counselor then expands on the theme by using questions as designed to expand the landscapes of action and consciousness. By processing Eugene's narrative regarding his role model, Eugene and his career counselor began to illuminate his desired role and the discrepancy between his current role and his potentially desired role. Both CCT and narrative therapy can help the two of them collaborate to identify strengths and motivations that will help Eugene fulfill his desired role.

Guided Practice Exercise 9.3 Your Own Career Construction Interview

Mark Savickas crafted the Career Construction Interview in order to illuminate micronarratives in a client's career story. He picked four micronarratives he deemed important. What micro-narratives do you think are important in a career story? Craft your own Career Construction Interview by writing down four questions you can ask a client that draw out micronarratives. Would you use this during a career counseling session?

Limitations and Ethical Issues

Counselors practicing narrative therapy and career counselors are all beholden to the American Counseling Association's (ACA, 2014) Code of Ethics. With its focus on dominant discourses, narrative therapy is likely to uncover social injustices, eliciting a counselor's ethical obligation under the ACA Code of Ethics to advocate for his or her client. According to the ethical code, counselors advocate on behalf of their clients as inhibitive injustices become apparent (American Counseling Association, 2014). Consider the example of a counselor practicing narrative career counseling with a client who is Latino, and it becomes apparent as the client shares his story that a dominant discourse in his narrative is one of experiencing systemic racism. Currently, he is facing what he believes to be biased promotion practices that have held him back from promotions and raises that less qualified Caucasian employees are being offered. His counselor faces the ethical obligation to discern if and where appropriate advocating on his behalf should take place. The ACA advocacy competencies detail the multiple levels, micro to macro, at which advocacy can take place (Ratts et al., 2010). The counselor must discuss with the client which advocacy level the client desires and is comfortable with before his counselor takes any action. The client may decide that he wants to act with his counselor on both a micro level, participating in empowerment practices, and a macro level, sharing information with the public (Ratts et al., 2010). He may also decide that he wants his counselor to act on his behalf by, on an individual level, helping him find legal representation to address his employer's promoting practices or, on a systemic level, participating in political advocacy on behalf of Latinos and other races who commonly experience racism in the workplace. An ethical counselor recognizes the needs for advocacy and competently explains the multiple levels of advocacy to his or her client, giving the client the choice of how advocacy takes place.

An ethical counselor also recognizes the limitations of counseling practices. Narrative career counseling, as with any counseling practice, has limitations. One limitation of narrative career counseling is the length of time the process generally takes. Narrative therapy tends to not be a "brief" therapy. However, there are ways to work with a client's story within a limited amount of time. Savickas's Career Construction Interview can provide a client with insight into important professional "micro narratives" in one session (Savickas, 2011). Finally, as with any therapy, it is the counselor's ethical obligation to ensure that they are competent in the practice of narrative career counseling before serving clients with this therapy.

The following case demonstrates the use of narrative therapy when helping a client, Shaquila, find a career path. Shaquila, a 30-year-old female client, states she has no idea what job she should consider. After building rapport, the counselor and Shaquila decide to focus sessions on learning more about different jobs so she can make a career decision, Shaquila also decides to take some career assessments, including the *Self-Directed Search (SDS)* mentioned in Chapter 8. Shaquila's *SDS* results come out with a typology of RIA, as based on John Holland's typology (see Chapter 8). After searching the O*Net and seeing a number of jobs on the list, Shaquila is disappointed and says none of them are a fit at first glance. Because many of the jobs appear to be male oriented in nature, the career counselor wonders if Shaquila is eliminating job prospects because she isn't interested or if it might be because she fears entering a job that might be perceived as a gender mismatch. For this reason, the career counselor decides to use narrative therapy techniques with Holland's typology and Gottfredson and Super's premises to learn more about Shaquila's self-concept and life themes.

Counselor: Since none of the job titles on the assessment profiles seem to stand out as interesting, perhaps we could try a different type of information gathering.

Shaquila: Sure. What did you have in mind?

Counselor: Maybe we could think back in time to when you were a child, before age 6 or 7, and you can tell me some stories from your childhood that you remember. What memories stand out from that age?

Shaquila: I remember I would spend time at my grandmother's house. She wanted me to learn to sew but I spent all my time taking her sewing machine apart and putting it back together. She would get upset because I removed the light bulbs and the needles. (*Shaquila laughs*)

The career counselor notes that this this might tie to the R (realistic) code in Shaquila's Holland code.

Counselor: (*laughing*) It sounds like you definitely did your own thing. What other stories do you remember?

Shaquila: Hmm . . . I remember playing outside with the animals. We lived on a farm and had horses. I loved the horses and went outside and followed them around. My mom was always yelling, "Get away from those horses heels. They will kick you!" I would just walk to their heads and pet them.

Again, interest in the outdoors with animals may fit with the R (realistic) Holland code.

Counselor: It sounds like you accommodated your mom's fears without giving up your animals. What were your favorite movies when you were an adolescent?

Shaquila: I loved Princess Leia in *Star Wars*. She had it going.

Counselor: What did you like about Leia?

Shaquila: She was a fighter, but she was also still feminine, elegant, and beautiful.

Counselor: What other characters did you like as an adolescent?

Shaquila: I like Moana in that movie because she does what she wants to do. It is one of the first movies I have seen where she isn't considered weak for being a girl.

The career counselor and Shaquila analyze themes found in the narratives. For example, it seems Shaquila remembers strong female characters who take charge and, even as a young child, she finds ways to take charge rather than passively following traditional female roles. This might lend itself to Gottfredson's premise that Shaquila is eliminating job prospects because of gender bias.

SUMMARY

Narrative therapy can be a therapy of empowerment. Counselors practicing from this theoretical orientation empower clients to recognize themselves separate and apart from presenting problems. They empower clients to distance themselves from dominant discourses, if contradictory to personal goals and motivations, and seek advocacy opportunities on a micro and macro level. They empower clients to take ownership of the role of actor, agent, and author and recognize their personal power as they interact with their environment. Those serving clients in narrative career counseling can enjoy a level of freedom, including inviting clients to incorporate any visual arts or performance arts or developing themes around anything that rings true to the client. Regarding career counseling, narrative therapy brings a holistic approach. Counselors using narrative therapy to practice career counseling will take a non-pathologizing, collaborative stance.

This chapter provided a brief history of the origins of narrative therapy as well as a basic overview of the theoretical underpinnings. Counselors who, like Michael White and David Epston, place predominant importance on collaboration, constructivism, and social justice may also agree with the key premises of narrative therapy. These premises are the externality of problems, the view that a detail-rich, reauthored narrative is a vehicle for change and wellness and the efficacy of individuals in crafting their own identity. Specific techniques of narrative therapy include externalization of the problem, unique outcomes, thickening the plot, definitional ceremonies and outsider witnesses, and therapeutic letters. Narrative therapy can be integrated into many standard career counseling theories such as those of Donald Super, Gottfredson's circumscription and compromise, Krumboltz's happenstance theory, Holland's RIASEC codes, and Savickas's career construction theory. An example of a smoothly integrated intervention is Savickas's career construction interview, which can be used to thicken the plot of a client's story and can be expanded on using narrative therapy in lines of questioning.

Keystones

- Narrative therapy presents a non-pathologizing approach to career counseling.
- Narrative therapy integrates with career counseling to provide a holistic therapeutic approach, which offers many opportunities for creativity.
- Narrative therapy may be instrumental in helping to empower clients who have been subject to racism or other forms of cultural bias in the workplace.

Author Reflections

While writing this chapter, four things kept entering my mind. First, I couldn't help but see how practically every career theory is imbedded into narrative therapy's premises. Because personal narratives are indicative of psychological, cultural, emotional, and career issues, it would be hard to find a career theory that did not integrate well with narrative therapy. Second, I must say I like thinking of myself as my own life and career actor, agent, and author. Narrative therapy and its premises are freeing! Third, narrative therapy left me feeling hopeful for everyone who can't seem to find their passion since it posits that the story can change as circumstances and desires change. Finally, I also find the inherent assessment potential of narrative therapy intriguing. Regardless of how much change a person experiences, their narratives seem to offer perspectives that, when used with other instruments, creates what, in my opinion, is a highly accurate holistic assessment.

I salute everyone reading this chapter who has decided that their next story involves some form of career counseling. Here's to the creation of a successful life narrative that leads you and your future clients where you all wish to go! —Janet Hicks

Additional Resources

The following resources provide additional information about the content provided in this chapter.

Books

Ratts, M. J., Toporek, R., & Lewis, J. A. (2010). *ACA advocacy competencies: A social justice framework for counselors*. American Counseling Association.

This book provides an in-depth exploration of the ACA advocacy competencies. It includes a survey assessing competency in advocacy. The topics include advocating on behalf of particular clients, such as LGBTQ and older adults, as well as in various settings, such as academic campuses.

Useful Websites

Dulwich Center: https://dulwichcentre.com.au/

Narrative therapy founder Michael White collaborated with other professionals to establish the Dulwich Centre in the 1980s, and he served as a director of the center until his death in 2008. The center provides counseling services, explores community health projects, trains therapists in narrative practice, and provides professionals with educational resources, including publishing *the International Journal of Narrative Therapy and Community Work* and hosting international conferences. The website provides a free online course on the basics of narrative therapy.

Re-Authoring Teaching: https://reauthoringteaching.com/

The mission of Re-Authoring Teaching is to create an online community of narrative therapy practitioners and students where they can share ideas and process resources. The site provides online courses and workshops as well as opportunities to consult with faculty.

Narrative Approaches: http://www.narrativeapproaches.com/

This website includes an archive of publications and papers on narrative therapy.

The Taos Institute: https://www.taosinstitute.net/

Founded on social constructionist theory, the Taos Institute is a nonprofit organization that provides educational resources and programs geared toward mental health, community health, and other healthcare professional subjects.

References

American Counseling Association. (2014). *ACA code of ethics*. Author.

Brown, S. D. (2014). *Career development and counseling: Putting theory and research to work*. Wiley.

Combs, G., & Freedman, J. (2012). Narrative, poststructuralism, and social justice. *The Counseling Psychologist, 40*(7), 1033–1060. https://doi.org/10.1177/0011000012460662

Del Corso, J., & Rehfuss, M. C. (2011). The role of narrative in career construction theory. *Journal of Vocational Behavior, 79*(2), 334–339. https://doi.org/10.1016/j.jvb.2011.04.003

Denborough, D. (2009). Some reflections on the legacies of Michael White: An Australian perspective. *Australian and New Zealand Journal of Family Therapy (ANZJFT), 30*(2), 92–108. https://doi.org/10.1375/anft.30.2.92

Doan, R. E. (1997). Narrative therapy, postmodernism, social constructionism, and constructivism: Discussion and distinctions. *Transactional Analysis Journal, 27*(2), 128–133. https://doi.org/10.1177/036215379702700208

Douglas, B., Woolfe, R., Strawbridge, S., Kasket, E., & Galbraith, V. (2016). *The handbook of counselling psychology*. SAGE.

Draucker, C. B., Smith, C., Mazurczyk, J., Thomas, D., Ramirez, P., McNealy, K., Thomas, J., & Martsolf, D. S. (2016). Unique outcomes in the narratives of young adults who experienced dating violence as adolescents. *Journal of the American Psychiatric Nurses Association, 22*(2), 112–121. https://doi.org/10.1177/1078390315621062

Duarte, M. E. (2017). Career counseling research-practice disparities: What we know and what we need to know. *South African Journal of Education, 37*(4), 1–7. https://doi.org/10.15700/saje.v37n4a1486

Fox, H. (2003). Using therapeutic documents: A review. *International Journal of Narrative Therapy and Community Work, 4*, 26–36.

Freedman, J., & Combs, G. (1996). *Narrative therapy: The social construction of preferred realities*. Norton.

Cardoso, P., Silva, J., Goncalves, M. & Duarte, M. (2014). Innovative moments and change in career construction counseling. *Journal of Vocational Behavior, 84(1)*, 11–20.

Gottfredson, L. S. (1981). Circumscription and compromise: A developmental theory of occupational aspirations. *Journal of Counseling Psychology Monograph, 28*(6), 545–579.

Holland, J. L. (1959). A theory of vocational choice. *Journal of Counseling Psychology, 6(1)*, 35–45.

Leahy, M. M., O'Dwyer, M., & Ryan, F. (2012). Witnessing stories: Definitional ceremonies in narrative therapy with adults who stutter. *Journal of Fluency Disorders, 37*(4), 234–241. https://doi.org/10.1016/j.jfludis.2012.03.001

Madigan, S. (2011). *Narrative therapy*. American Psychological Association.

Maree, J. G., & Di Fabio, A. (2018). Integrating personal and career counseling to promote sustainable development and change. *Sustainability, 10(11)*, 4176. https://doi.org/10.3390/su10114176

Meehan, T., & Farquharson, K. (2012). Community as outsider witness: Utilizing community members in the reconstitution of problem-saturated identities. *Journal of Psychology in Africa, 22*(4), 567–572. https://doi.org/10.1080/14330237.2012.10820569

Mitchell, K. E., Levin, A. S., & Krumboltz, J. D. (1999). Planned happenstance: Constructing unexpected career opportunities. *Journal of Counseling & Development, 77(2)*, 115–124.

Morgan, A. (2002). *What is narrative therapy?: An easy-to-read introduction*. Dulwich Center Publications.

Narrative Practices Adelaide. (2020). Teaching Connections. Retrieved March 17, 2020, from https://narrativepractices.com.au/connections/teaching-connections

Payne, M. (2011). *Narrative therapy an introduction for counsellors*. SAGE.

Pilkington, S. M. (2018). Writing narrative therapeutic letters: Gathering, recording and performing lost stories. *Journal of Narrative Family Therapy*, 20–48.

Ratts, M. J., Toporek, R., & Lewis, J. A. (2010). *ACA advocacy competencies: A social justice framework for counselors*. American Counseling Association.

Russell, S., & Carey, M. (2002). Remembering: Responding to commonly asked questions. *International Journal of Narrative Therapy and Community Work, 3*, 23–32.

Savickas, M. L. (2011). Constructing careers: Actor, agent, and author. *Journal of Employment Counseling, 48(4)*, 179–181.

Savickas, M. L., & Hartung, P. J. (2012). *Career Construction Interview*. http://www.vocopher.com/CSI/CCI.pdf

Semmler, P. L., & Williams, C. B. (2000). Narrative therapy: A storied context for multicultural counseling. *Journal of Multicultural Counseling & Development, 28*(1), 51–62.

Shefer, T. (2018). Narrative career therapy: From the problem-saturated story to the preferred story and career path. *Australian Journal of Career Development, 27(2)*, 99–107.

Super, D. E. (1990). A life-span, life-space approach to career development. In D. Brown & L. Brooks (Eds.), *Career choice and development: Applying contemporary theories to practice (2nd ed.)* (pp. 197–261). Jossey-Bass.

Sween, E. (1998). The one-minute question: What is narrative therapy? *Gecko, 2*, 3–6.

Tarragona, M. (2008). Postmodern/poststructuralist therapy. In J. L. Lebow (Ed.), *Twenty-first-century psychotherapies: Contemporary approaches to theory and practice (pp. 167–204)*. Wiley.

Taylor, J. M., & Savickas, S. (2016). Narrative career counseling: My career story and pictorial narratives. *Journal of Vocational Behavior, 97*, 68–77.

Walther, S., & Fox, H. (2012). Narrative therapy and outsider witness practice: Teachers as a community of acknowledgement. *Educational & Child Psychology, 29*(2), 10–19.

White, C. (2009, October). Where did it all begin? Reflecting on the collaborative work of Michael White and David Epston. *Context,* 59–60.

White, M. (2004). *Narrative practice and exotic lives: Resurrecting diversity in everyday life*. Dulwich Center.

White, M. (2005, September 21). *Michael White workshop notes*. https://dulwichcentre.com.au/wp-content/uploads/2014/01/michael-white-workshop-notes.pdf

White, M. (2007). *Maps of narrative practice*. Norton.

White, M., & Epston, D. (1990). *Narrative means to therapeutic ends*. Norton.

CHAPTER 10

Using Solution-Focused Brief Therapy in Career Counseling

Michael Moyer, Janet Hicks, and Brande Flamez

I have not failed. I've just found 10,000 ways that won't work.
Thomas A. Edison

T homas Edison understood that success requires perseverance and the ability to view failure as part of the process. This is important when assisting clients with career development since life offers constant change and challenges. Solution-focused brief therapy (SFBT) takes Edison's notion a step further through its premises that small changes can lead to bigger changes and that individuals possess the strengths and resources needed to resolve their own issues. In other words, those 10,000 ways that won't work have potential to lead into the one needed success. These notions can be quite empowering for clients facing career transitions, and, when combined with solution-focused techniques, success can even be found in what others might view as failure. Career counselors using SFBT harness past events, find positive exceptions, and channel these events into positive career development. Let us read more about SFBT, how it integrates well with career theory, and how it may be practically used in career counseling sessions. The chapter overview that follows will precede details on SFBT and is followed by explanations on career theory integration. Follow along as we navigate through career counseling from a solution-focused lens.

CHAPTER OVERVIEW

This chapter discusses the use of SFBT as an approach for conducting career counselling sessions with clients. SFBT is discussed along with its inherent techniques and how they apply to vocational discernment, career development, career maturity, and decision making. A case study gives a practical example as to how a career counseling session might look using this theory. A discussion on the syntheses of the theory with career counseling and theories is also infused into the chapter.

LEARNING OBJECTIVES

After reading this chapter, you will be able to do the following:

- Understand SFBT and its techniques
- Understand how SFBT integrates with several career theories you read about in the first part of this text (e.g., Donald Super's life span, life space theory, Linda Gottfredson's circumscription and compromise theory, Krumboltz's happenstance and learning theory, Ginzberg et al.'s developmental theory, and Dawis and Lofquist's theory of work adjustment/person-environment-correspondence theory)
- Apply SFBT with clients facing career counseling/vocational discernment issues

Solution-Focused Brief Therapy: Theoretical Background and Premises

SFBT was first developed and used in the early 1980s by Steve de Shazer, Insoo Kim Berg, and their team at the Brief Family Therapy Center in Milwaukee, Wisconsin (de Shazer, 1985). While Berg and de Shazer are most often associated with the origination of SFBT, the development of SFBT was also influenced by many theories, including brief psychodynamic therapy, cognitive behavioral theory, and systems theory (Seligman & Reichenberg, 2010). Over the past several decades, SFBT has moved from being an unknown and underused theoretical approach to one of the most widely used by counselors (Gingerich & Eisengart, 2000).

SFBT touts a few basic principles and beliefs. For example, mental health professionals using a solution-focused approach focus on building solutions rather than concentrating on problem solving. SFBT also emphasizes mental health instead of pathology. For this reason, the theory is widely accepted as being one of optimism in which words and beliefs can become reality (de Shazer et al., 1986).

Those gravitating toward this theory also believe change is constant. In fact, they believe a person cannot not change. As part of this change, solution-focused brief therapists believe that if you look for and emphasize what is going right, you will find even more of it. On the contrary, if you focus on what is going wrong, it is likely you will find more of what is going wrong in life (De Jong & Berg, 2013).

Key concepts related to SFBT include the following:

- Small changes can lead to bigger changes.
- Individuals possess the strengths and resources needed to resolve their own issues.
- You don't need to know a lot about a problem to resolve it.

Let us delve more into these concepts in the material that follows.

Small changes can lead to bigger changes is applying the "snowball effect" to change in career or personal counseling. By identifying small changes and the related behaviors/activities that may have led to those small changes, clients and counselors can use that knowledge to affect larger change. Simply stated, the collection of many small changes leads to bigger change (De Jong & Berg, 2013). Consider a client presenting with career concerns related to feeling tired much of the time, low energy, and decreased motivation. A counselor using the small changes can lead to bigger changes viewpoint may be interested in knowing if/when there have been days when the client experienced even the slightest bit of increased energy or motivation. If these energy or motivational increases are evident, what was happening on those days (e.g., Did the client go to bed or wake up at different times? Did they spend more/less time outside the office? Were they around specific coworkers, friends, or family members? etc.) By focusing on any small changes (client went to bed earlier, client was involved in career-related social interactions, client spent time outside the office, etc.), the counselor and client may be able to expand on those small changes to increase the likelihood of larger changes to the client's overall mood and career performance.

Individuals possess the strengths and resources needed to resolve their own issues is the belief that people have it within themselves to bring about the change they want to see happen (De Jong & Berg, 2013). Even though we all possess these strengths and resources, it is sometimes difficult to see their presence. The solution-focused career counselor's primary responsibility is to help the client identify those strengths, bring them to the surface, and use them to help the client set career-related goals. Highlighting and amplifying strengths will, in turn, help the client identify a solution to their career development concerns. Let us look at a sample client's career issue and try to identify some strengths they might use to help them find a job.

Case Exercise 10.1 Adelle's Career Esteem

Adelle is a 38-year-old woman who visits you for help in finding a job. She walks in with poor posture and her body language tells you she lacks the self-confidence to perform well at an interview. She tells you she hasn't worked in 15 years since her daughter was born. She stayed home and raised her daughter and now her marriage has dissolved. She tells you she has no skills and is afraid her soon-to-be ex-husband will take her daughter if she doesn't find a job. Do you believe Adelle has no skills? What did you learn about Adelle in this case that you might amplify to help boost her self-confidence and belief in her abilities? What has Adelle done that might be deemed as success?

You don't need to know a lot about a problem to resolve it. Solution-focused career counselors typically only see a benefit to understanding a limited amount of information about the problem. They have little interest in understanding the root cause of the complaint. Solution-focused career counselors also spend a limited amount of time trying to understand why a solution to the problem has yet to be found. Instead, career counselors using a solution-focused approach spend most of their time developing optimism that change will occur (Winbolt, 2011).

Specific Techniques

SFBT is a highly interactive therapeutic model in which the career counselor and the client collaborate to amplify positive change. Similar to many other theoretical models, the client-counselor relationship is a critical component to clients' achieving their goals. SFBT career counselors must be highly skilled in basic attending skills such as empathetic listening, posing open-ended questions, reflecting feelings, and active listening. Other, more specific techniques associated with SFBT are listed in Table 10.1 and discussed in the sections that follow.

Each technique listed in the table is discussed in greater detail and with regard to client interactions in career counseling.

Complimenting

Because clients seeking career assistance may present with low self-confidence, complimenting can be extremely helpful. Let us discuss what complimenting is within the realm of SFBT. Complimenting is a technique where career counselors recognize and point out strengths in clients so that they are later able to use these strengths to set goals and follow through with them (De Jong & Berg, 2013). Career counselors using this technique listen for positive client traits, talents, and characteristics and even reframe traits that might once have been deemed as negative. For example, a client in a sales position whose former boss berated him for spending too much time on paperwork and collections rather than sales might be complimented for his overly focused attention to details. What was once deemed as negative might be used to not only enhance the client's confidence but to help him recognize the need to find this factor in

TABLE 10.1   **Solution-Focused Techniques**

Technique	Purpose
Complimenting	Points out client strengths
Miracle question	Focuses on the true goal
Exceptions question	Finds past successes
Coping questions	Acknowledges client effort/strength
Scaling	Points out client motivation/stance
Normalizing	Creates feelings of universality

his future job prospects. Guided Practice Exercise 10.1 asks you to consider the role of complimenting as part of John Holland's typology in career sessions.

Guided Practice Exercise 10.1 Complimenting and the Holland Codes

As you recall from Chapter 2, John Holland created a typology often referred to as the RIASEC code. How might complimenting offer insight into a client's Holland code? Do you think complimenting can boost a person's self-confidence? If so, how would this new self-confidence impact their career development?

Miracle Question

Suppose you woke up in the morning and a miracle has happened: The problem is gone! What would be different? What would be the first indicator that the problem was gone? The *miracle question* is typically used as a way for solution-focused career counselors to help clients develop goals (De Jong & Berg, 2013). Many times, clients come to counseling not knowing the specifics about what they want to be different let alone how to make career improvements. A client may only know they want things to be "better." Using the miracle question, or a form of it, may help the client arrive at a better understanding of what constitutes "better" for them. In career counseling, the miracle question may focus on finding the perfect job, or it may open the door to discuss other impediments in the career process.

Exception Questions

When was the presenting concern not present? A career counselor may ask a client who reports becoming overly nervous during job interviews about times when they have been calm or times when they notice less anxiety. By asking such questions, the career counselor is asking the client to find an exception to the presenting concern. Clients are being asked to focus on what is going right instead of what is going wrong. Following one of the primary tenants of SFBT, the *exception question* encourages clients to look for successes rather than focusing on areas of concern (De Jong & Berg, 2013).

Coping Questions

"What has worked? How did you make that change? How were you successful during that time?" Coping questions encourage clients to verbalize and acknowledge the efforts they have put forward to realize change in their life (De Jong & Berg, 2013). By asking coping questions, career counselors ask clients to recognize their own strengths and ability to find successes. Coping questions fall in line with the basic tenants of SFBT in that *individuals possess the strengths and resources needed to solve their own concerns and that small changes can bring about larger changes*. Many clients may fail to recognize the small actions they have taken to bring about change. When a career counselor highlights those changes and asks specific questions about the small actions that went into the change, clients are better able to understand their own personal strengths. Case Exercise 10.2 asks you to identify changes a client has already taken to bring about positive career change.

Case Exercise 10.2 Manuel's Decision

Manuel is a 20-year-old college junior who says, "I have wasted the last 2 years of school because I know I just don't want to study engineering. I thought I would really like it, but after the few classes I have taken, I know I can't spend the rest of my life doing this." What has Manuel done to show he is not a failure? What would you ask him that would point out the small steps he has taken that are moving in the right direction?

Scaling

"On a scale of 1-10, where would you say your anxiety about finding a new career path is right now? On, that scale, 1 would mean you have no hope at all and believe it will never happen and a 10 would be that you are extremely confident a new career path will come up quite quickly." Scaling helps the counselor understand the intensity or level of concern from the client's perspective. For example, the author would argue everyone understands what it means to "struggle"; however, when a client describes struggling it is imperative the career counselor understands to what degree the client is struggling. By using *scaling questions*, the counselor is better able to step out of their own understanding of what it means to struggle and take the perspective of the client (De Jong & Berg, 2013).

Scaling questions provide an anchor and define the movement of the client. This movement can take place during one session or over the course of several sessions. A client might originally describe their anxiety as a 4 and then, after some time, report their anxiety has moved to a 3 or 2. Scaling helps define that movement has occurred, even if the movement is minimal. When there is movement, counselors can then use other techniques such as *coping questions* to amplify the small movement into larger success.

Normalizing

"You are not alone in facing this concern. You are not the problem; the problem is the problem." Clients may feel as though they are the only one going through a certain difficulty. Believing one is alone or somehow unique in their struggles may exacerbate the concern and make it more difficult for clients to see success. Career counselors following a SFBT approach can significantly aid clients by normalizing their concerns. Normalizing the concerns helps clients understand they are not the only ones facing difficulties and can make it easier for them to begin identifying solutions (De Jong & Berg, 2013).

Now that we have an understanding of solution-focused brief therapy and how its techniques can be used as part of career counseling sessions, let us look in depth at how these techniques work in conjunction with career counseling. We will begin by discussing stages in the career counseling process and follow this with a discussion on the integration with some of the career theories touted earlier in this text.

Stages in the Solution-Focused Career Counseling Process

Miller (2004) proposed a three-stage model when using solution-focused brief therapy in career counseling sessions. The first stage involves clarifying the problem, setting goals, and determining the purpose for the career counseling session. During this stage, clients are asked questions such as, "What do you hope to accomplish from our session today?" This type of question allows clients the ability to determine the outcomes they wish to accomplish. The second stage in Miller's model is called creating client self-helpfulness. During this stage, career counselors use exception questions and scaling to establish client-generated solutions. Miller's final stage involves helping the client move toward personal career goals, a process she calls constructing a meaningful message. During this stage, clients are given feedback and homework assignments. We will see how SFBT, career theory, and these stages are used when working with an actual client in the case study at the end of this chapter. Before moving on to the case study, however, let's see how SFBT integrates well with Super, Gottfredson, Krumboltz, Ginzberg et al., and Dawis and Lofquist's theoretical premises.

The Integration of SFBT With Career Counseling Theories and Models

Donald Super's Life Span, Life Space Career Theory

As you learned in Chapter 4, Donald Super created a popular and developmentally oriented career theory focused on life roles and self-concept (Super, 1953). Fortunately, Super's developmental career theory offered freedom from the idea that each person fits with only one specific job or job type throughout their lifetime. We use the word "freedom" because the idea that we are only suited to one job may cause anxiety later in life when job satisfaction is missing or in times of unemployment and job loss. These losses often result in lack of client self-esteem, self-worth, and job self-efficacy (Nica et al., 2016). During these life events, solution-focused brief therapy might be a productive theoretical medium for helping clients recycle through Super's stages. Let us discuss the integration of solution-focused brief therapy when working with this type of client.

Super contended that career development consisted of five stages (growth, exploration, establishment, maintenance, and disengagement) through which people could cycle and recycle without regard to numerical age (Super, 1953, 1978). This cycling and recycling meant that psychological rather than age-based tenets predicted successful stage completion. Thus, clients could experience stage success and experience feelings of hope at any age. Needless to say, this premise has the potential to eliminate feelings of failure during later life job losses or transitions and might create a more positive developmental path for these clients.

SFBT has the potential to further amplify this positive focus through specific techniques such as complimenting, exception questions, miracle questions, and coping questions. For example, solution-focused complimenting allows counselors the ability to point out the client's personal achievements, remove anxiety that may accompany the tendency to focus on age-stage progress, and has the potential to instill a sense of self-efficacy (De Jong & Berg, 2013). Solution-focused complimenting, along with additional techniques discussed next, then, may be used as an effective tool for moving self-defeated clients through Super's non-age–based developmental stages. This is especially important since self-defeated clients are better able to make decisions and follow up with productive actions once their self-worth is more intact (Brown, 2014).

So, how does a counselor use solution-focused techniques such as complimenting, exception questions, coping questions, and the miracle question to guide career development among clients? Following are some examples to help answer this question. Consider a middle-aged client who states she is experiencing anxiety because she thinks she "should know what career to pursue by this age." The solution-focused career counselor will help empower the client, reframe issues the client might see as negatives, and turn her negative thoughts and beliefs into a positive and helpful discussion. For example, the client may see her age as a detriment but, in reality, her age could be a tremendous strength. Because the client is not young, there are many past experiences and successes to draw on.

One of the best ways to channel the client's past experiences into catalysts for change is through exception questions (De Jong & Berg, 2013). The middle-aged client mentioned might first be asked exception questions such as, "What other major life decisions have you made? How did you handle those decisions? Have there been times when you outperformed younger colleagues because you had more experience? Tell me about these times." Responses to these questions can be used to reframe age as a positive attribute and to use effective past strategies to help with the current job issues.

These exception questions might then be followed up with solution-focused complimenting, thus pointing out the client's inherent strengths. Recognition of these strengths can empower the client so that she can more confidently approach a career decision. At this point, it may also be helpful to remind the client of Super's (1953, 1978) developmental stages (exceptions) she previously mastered in her last job or career (growth, exploration, establishment, maintenance, and disengagement). The client might benefit by knowing that these stages are normal as is going through them again when recycling into a new career. The integration of Super's theory with solution-focused brief therapy, in this instance, allows the client to accept herself where she is at this point in the process, use success from the past to help with future career development, and focus on personal strengths that will enhance her future success.

Coping questions might also help the client who feels completely hopeless following job loss. For example, the client who just lost his job might state he is "a complete failure." In this instance, the client might be asked a coping question such as, "How did you manage to pick up the phone and make this appointment?" A follow-up to this coping statement might be complimenting this client for having the tenacity to move forward in his career search despite these feelings. This compliment might be the catalyst for a cognitive change from defeat and inaction to self-worth and career action.

The miracle question can also be adapted to help the self-defeated client move forward in his career pursuit. Super's theory contended that the first stage, growth, focused on developing a self-concept based on abilities, roles, and relationships (Super, 1953, 1978). Because the self-concept can be altered through job loss, the miracle question can help clients rediscover early attitudes and uncover hidden information about how they relate to others. For example, a client, Maria, who states, "I just have no idea what I want to do," might be asked, "If you had the perfect job, what would it look like? How would you find this job?" The answers to the questions can uncover hidden attitudes and interests, help clients learn more about themselves, and compare their self-concept to potential jobs. These techniques may, therefore, help the client move through the growth to the exploration stage where they are ready to explore and even select career options. Guided Practice Exercise 10.2 asks you to consider how additional solution-focused techniques might help career counseling clients.

Guided Practice Exercise 10.2 Using SFBT Techniques With Super's Theory

Go back and review Donald Super's theory from Chapter 2. Next, take a few minutes and read the solution-focused techniques detailed in this chapter. What solution-focused techniques were not mentioned with regard to integration with Super's theory in this chapter? How might those techniques be applied? For example, how might scaling be used to help Maria (the client mentioned in this passage) determine where she is in the career development process?

The case study at the end of this chapter details a client session integrating SFBT with Super's premises and developmental career counseling model. This session offers additional insight into how an actual career counseling session might look using Super's premises in conjunction with solution-focused techniques.

Gottfredson's Circumscription and Compromise

As you read in Chapter 5, Linda Gottfredson believed we select jobs through a process she called circumscription and compromise (Gottfredson, 1996). As part of this selection process, she contended that individuals tend to eliminate potential jobs when they defy culturally acceptable prestige and sex-type roles. Since this rejection of possible jobs has potential to limit otherwise appropriate career options, solution-focused brief therapy might be an effective method for breaking these social barriers and helping clients pursue their true passions. One particular technique that might help clients focus on true passions rather than only culturally accepted jobs might be the miracle question. Let's discuss a case where complimenting and the miracle question, commonly used techniques in solution-focused brief therapy, might aid in this process.

Consider the female client whose Holland code states she would "fit" into the mechanical engineering field. Further, this client states that she likes mathematics and wishes she could find a job where this skill could be used. Despite this comment, the client's body language reveals conflict in selecting a male-dominated field such as engineering. It seems clear the client is eliminating job choices for reasons of gender rather than interest. How might the career counselor help the client refrain from eliminating jobs only because they cross gender roles?

Following are a few thoughts to help this client. First, the solution-focused career counselor might use the techniques of complimenting and the miracle question to help this client think beyond typical stereotypes. The sample counselor/client dialogue illustrates this premise:

Counselor: (*using a variation of the miracle question*) If you could use mathematics in the perfect job, what would that job look like? What would you be doing?

Client: I think I would be able to solve problems using math and create new products.

Counselor: (*complimenting*) I admire that you are willing to look at some new job responsibilities that you didn't list in your previous choices. Perhaps we could research some jobs that sound similar to what you described.

At this point, the career counselor might pull up some job duties and omit job titles to see if the client is interested in the job when the culturally sex-typed job titles have been omitted. By focusing on the miracle job responsibilities rather than the job label, the client may be empowered to pursue a previously uncomfortable choice and even learn more about the responsibilities of several previously excluded careers.

Krumboltz's Happenstance and Learning Theory

As you learned in Chapter 3, John Krumboltz believed career development is influenced by genetics, environment, learning, and task-approach skills (Krumboltz et al., 1976). Krumboltz also supported the premise that when given opportunities, clients make the most of them, a premise he called happenstance. As part of happenstance, Krumboltz believed in the importance of constant learning that eventually leads to future opportunities. In other words, clients do not have to plan for a career in advance for it to be fulfilling (Krumboltz, 2008).

SFBT techniques blend well with Krumboltz's contentions. For example, consider the client who is unhappy in their current job. This person may feel confused, angry, frustrated, and like a failure for spending too much time in the "wrong" job or choosing it to begin with. Since Krumboltz believed career learning helped generate unplanned events (Krumboltz, 2008), clients might be taught to view the time spent in previous jobs as beneficial steppingstones toward the next career opportunities. Solution-focused techniques can expand on these concepts.

Solution-focused complimenting, exception questions, coping questions, and the miracle question can be used to reinforce Krumboltz's contentions. First, the client might be complimented for learning previous skills. For example, after completing a questionnaire illustrating career skills the career counselor might say, "You mastered many important skills in that job (complimenting). I wonder how you see those skills working for you in your next job (exception question)."

The miracle question can also expand on the client's options. The career counselor might say, "If you were in the perfect job, what would you be doing? How would your day be different (variation of miracle question applied to career counseling)?" Once the client responds with a miracle job, the career counselor might say, "I wonder if we can research some opportunities that fit your desires with the skills your learned." In this way, solution-focused techniques reinforce the premise that opportunities are created from previous learning and never end if learning continues. Guided Practice Exercise asks you to consider how happenstance theory might fit with your own career experiences.

Guided Practice Exercise 10.3 Happenstance Theory in Your Own Life

Take a few minutes and discuss jobs you held in the past or college majors that, in hindsight, were not a fit. Did any of these jobs or majors contribute to learning experiences that brought you into the counseling arena today? Did any of your past jobs or experiences lead to another job or career path? Do you agree with John Krumboltz that learning should be constant and that every new skill has potential to lead to a new job? Why or why not? What genetic tendencies do you have that fit/do not fit certain careers? For example, some of us will never be professional basketball players because we are too short. What other examples can you describe?

Ginzberg and Colleagues' Developmental Model and Stages

As you recall from Chapter 4, Ginzberg, Ginsburg, Axelrad, and Herma created a model that discusses three career stages, fantasy, tentative, and realistic (Ginzberg et al., 1951). According to these theorists, the fantasy stage occurs between the ages of birth and age 10 and involves career development as a factor of play. This play gradually becomes more work-oriented toward the end of the stage. The fantasy stage is followed by the tentative stage, or transitional stage, which typically occurs between the ages of 11 and 18. During this stage, individuals begin to understand the concept of work while also becoming familiar with personal areas of interest, abilities, and values. Finally, the realistic stage emerges around the age of 18 and carries into young adulthood. The realistic stage is a time for integration into the work arena and involves further development of values and interests. During this stage, clients become more specific in their choice of careers and solidify work expectations and patterns (Ginzberg, 1972). Solution-focused brief therapy might be especially helpful when working with clients in the realistic stage who hate their current jobs and have forgotten that work can be both productive and fulfilling. The following section offers an example to help understand this concept.

Consider the client who says she is "absolutely miserable everyday" because she "hates her job." When asked what she might enjoy, she states, "Work is a four-letter word. No one I know likes going to work." It seems obvious to the career counselor that this negative mind-set is eliminating the motivation to find fulfilling work. The effective career counselor might remember Ginzberg and colleagues' first developmental stage, fantasy, and employ some unique solution-focused techniques. For example, this counselor might use a variation of the miracle question by saying, "I want you to pretend you are 5 years old and playing with your friends. You are having a wonderful time and pretending to have the perfect career. What are you doing and saying?" The career counselor listens for patterns and writes down any remarks or memories the client makes that elicit enjoyment as part of work.

Another variation of the miracle question that might be used to help the client includes a fantasy activity. In this activity, the counselor says, "I want you to pretend you are 4 years old and telling your friends what you do for work. This job is the exact opposite of what you do now, and you totally enjoy yourself. Tell me about this job." The client tells any story they would like. As the career counselor listens, again they jot down patterns that can be described to the client. Once the client begins to see that work can have enjoyable aspects, the job search can begin. Basically, this activity allows the career counselor to recycle the client back through the phases, fantasy, tentative, and finally, to realistic. Guided Practice Exercise 10.4 asks you to discuss your own career development through Ginzberg and colleagues' stages with the use of songs.

Guided Practice Exercise 10.4 Moving Through Ginzberg and Associates' Stages

Think about your own career development for a few minutes. On a sheet of paper create three columns. Label the first column "Fantasy," the second column "Tentative," and the third column "Realistic." Try to remember when you went through these stages. Create a list of songs you remember that depict your career development during each of these times. For example, you might list a song such as "Walk with the Animals" if you remember wanting to be a veterinarian as a young child. Discuss your songs with a partner and how your career development changed throughout this process.

Theory of Work Adjustment/Person-Environment-Correspondence

As you learned in Chapter 2, Dawis and Lofquist created a theory called theory of work adjustment. Up until the late 1900s it was known as the theory of work adjustment but is now more commonly referred to as the person-environment-correspondence (PEC) theory. Dawis and Lofquist (1991) believed work was far more complicated than simply moving through step-by-step tasks; it involved human interaction. These theorists argued that work was a continual interaction and individuals constantly strive to keep a positive relationship with their work environment (Dawis, 2004; Dawis & Lofquist, 1984). As part of this positive relationship, individuals have expectations for their work environments, and work environments have expectations for workers. When individuals are able to maintain a positive relationship with their work environment, they are happier and more likely to continue in that role. Overall, job satisfaction and perception of the work environment have potential to determine a person's longevity in a particular career.

A solution-focused approach integrates seamlessly with Dawis and Lofquist's (1991) theory of work adjustment/person-environment correspondence theory. Specifically, coping questions, scaling questions, and the miracle question can be very helpful when using this theory. These questions aid in a client's understanding of the specifics in a given job and may ultimately help them find a career with which they can have a positive relationship. A career counselor using a SFBT approach to Dawis and Lofquist's theory will help their client identify solutions for finding the ideal career rather than focusing on problems they have previously experienced.

Consider a woman struggling to find a new career path after spending many years at home with her children. Dawis and Lofquist (1991) believed a critical aspect of finding a good career fit was a person's ability to find and maintain a positive relationship with their work environment. For this reason, the miracle question may be a valuable technique to allow this woman to identify aspects of the work environment that may fit with her expectations. For example, the career counselor might ask, "If you were to wake up tomorrow and have an ideal career, what do you think would be some aspects of your job you would enjoy most?" Getting the client to imagine their idyllic career atmosphere and understand their preferred work environment is a beginning to choosing a career path and maintaining this positive relationship.

Similarly, asking scaling questions is another way SFBT techniques integrate seamlessly with this theory. Consider a recent college graduate who has multiple job offers and is nervous about accepting the "right" offer. Asking scaling questions can help this client compare various aspects of each offer and choose which might best fit with his expectations. For example, "Each of these offers has positive and negative aspects. They have different salaries, expected work hours, office dynamics, and commuting challenges. On a scale of 1–10, how important would you say salary is for you in determining your ideal job? Similarly, on that same scale of 1–10, how important are office dynamics and the people with whom you work?" In this example, scaling questions are used to help the client identify which aspects of the work environment are most important to him. As Dawis and Lofquist (1991) mention, it is important for individuals to understand their expectations of the work environment as well as to consider the expectations the work environment has for them. In the example given, this college student understands the expectations for each of the jobs offered to him. The career counselor is using scaling questions to help him also discover and understand the expectations found within the work environment. Case Exercise 10.3 asks you to determine which techniques you might use when working with a similar client.

Case Exercise 10.3 Selecting Techniques With Ariya

Ariya is a high school senior who cannot seem to decide which college to attend. She seems to change her mind every day, and she is afraid she is making the wrong decision no matter what. She says this is all so scary and that it just isn't fun thinking about it anymore. What solution-focused techniques would you use to help Ariya? Which career theories might be evident in her issues?

To fully integrate career theory with SFBT for this and other clients, however, it is also important to consider limitations and ethical issues that are evident in the solution-focused career counseling process. For this reason, we will discuss these issues in the next section.

Limitations and Ethical Issues

As with any theoretical approach, limitations are evident when integrating solution-focused brief therapy with career theories. As you have seen throughout this book and will see in the upcoming chapters, many theoretical approaches may be used to facilitate career counseling. While considering which tools to use, it is always critical to take time to develop a therapeutic relationship with your clients and understand their worldview and needs. It is equally critical to use the many theories and techniques learned in this book to find the best fit for your client. All counselors should work to fit the theory and techniques to their client(s) rather than try to make the client fit the counselor's preferred theory.

Primary ethical considerations for this chapter are related to well-being of the client, counseling plans, and counselors practicing within the boundaries of their competence (ACA, 2014). According to American Counseling Association (ACA) code of ethics , the primary responsibility of counselors is the welfare of their clients. Therefore, counselors integrating SFBT techniques into their career work should first and foremost look to provide services that take into consideration the clients' best interest. Concomitantly, counselors should only practice within the areas in which they are competent to practice. Therefore, counselors interested in adding a solution-focused angle to their career work should seek out continued areas for growth and understanding of this approach.

CASE STUDY

The following case demonstrates how solution-focused brief therapy might be integrated with Donald Super's developmental career theory when working with a client suffering from a job loss.

Liam is a 53-year-old Caucasian male who was employed in a factory for 32 years. This past year, the factory replaced Liam's assembly job with a specialized machine or robot. Liam enters your office and sits down.

Counselor: (*Beginning Miller's stage 1*) What do you hope to accomplish in our session today?

Liam: I am just lost. I haven't looked for a job or had training for 32 years. I am not good at anything and now even my old job can be done by a machine. Can you help me figure out what to do?

Because Liam's comments exhibit a sense of low self-worth and defeat and Liam is in a stage where he must recycle through Super's career development stages, the career counselor decides to integrate Super's premises with solution-focused brief therapy techniques.

Counselor: (*in response to Liam's first statement*) It sounds like you are going through quite a change right now. It takes a lot of courage to start on this new career adventure (*compliment*).

You will notice the counselor avoids the words "starting over" at this point and, instead, calls this a career adventure. This is intentional to help the client focus more on the positive, adventure-based aspects of career development rather than dwelling on negative and unchangeable job loss.

Liam: I hadn't really thought of it as an adventure. It seems hopeless at my age.

Counselor: This job loss might actually turn out to be a blessing. You have a unique opportunity to train and start on a career path you will enjoy (*reframe*).

Liam: Well, I must say I hated my last job. But I really need to get a job to pay my bills. Maybe you can just help me figure out some options.

Counselor: (*Beginning Miller's stage 2*) Then let's go ahead and get started. Tell me how you found your last job. What steps did you take (*exception question*)?

Liam: It was 32 years ago, so I just found a job opening in the newspaper, applied for the job, trained, and a few weeks later they called me to start.

Counselor: It sounds like you understand that it will take some research, networking, training, and leg work to find the next job also. The good thing about being 53 years old is that you know you can do this because you have done it before (*explaining the stages and exceptions previously accomplished; age reframe*).

Liam: I guess I can do this.

Counselor: If you had the perfect job, what would you be doing? Describe it to me (*miracle question*).

Liam: I would be working on cars. I always loved working on engines.

Counselor: On a scale from 1–10, how certain are you that you would like to work with engines (*scaling*)?

Liam: I would say an 8. I really miss getting to do this.

The client's self-defeating attitudes and cognitions are already improving at this point, so the career counselor can now infuse career counseling models and continue helping this client through the integration of solution-focused techniques. For example, the counselor identifies Liam's information needs and offers the client some assessments to help determine interests, values, life roles, and abilities. Per Miller's (2004) model and Hansen's (1984) sequencing model, the counselor also offers Liam feedback with regard to the assessments, develops a hypothesis, and assigns homework to be accomplished over the next week. To help Liam better tie exceptions to future success and understand these links, the counselor asks Liam to draw a career lifeline for homework where he will identify past jobs, events, and a history of choices that impacted his current path. Using this lifeline as a guide, Liam and the counselor's next session will synthesize the assessments and lifeline and create a goal and tasks that Liam will complete over the next month.

SUMMARY

SFBT is a theory of optimism (de Shazer, 1985). When using a solution-focused approach, words can become reality. The career counselor's role is often times that of a cheerleader, highlighting the successes of their clients and encouraging the client to build on the small successes they have already achieved. Counselors using a solution-focused approach believe the best way to affect change is to look for solutions to current problems rather than focus on the problem itself. As it relates to career counseling, a solution-focused approach would seek out times when individuals have found success in their work or have enjoyed their chosen career path rather than what they dislike. Key assumptions of SFBT are that small changes can bring about larger change, individuals have the strength within themselves to makes changes, and focusing on solutions is more effective than focusing on problems.

In this chapter, the authors reviewed basic foundational aspects of SFBT and ways counselors can integrate SFBT techniques into career counseling. Solution-focused techniques may be very helpful to career counselors who gravitate toward the work of Donald Super, Gottfredson, Krumboltz, Ginzberg, and Dawis & Lofquist. Coping, exception, and scaling questions are helpful techniques to aid counselors in understanding a client's current concerns. The same questions, in addition to using "the miracle question," are also helpful in turning the client's focus from problems to solutions. Career counselors routinely encounter clients who may find it difficult to see past the presenting career concern. Solution-focused brief career counselors believe seeing past the concern is critical for change to occur. Reframing statements, finding the exception to the problem, and building on small successes are important ways career counselors can integrate SFBT into their career counseling work.

Keystones

- SFBT integrates with career theory to help clients with vocational discernment and career development.
- Solution-focused techniques may be instrumental when helping clients who present with low self-esteem and career self-efficacy.
- As with all theories, SFBT has limitations that must be considered before integrating into career counseling sessions.

Author Reflections

While researching and writing this chapter it became unbelievably clear to me that all counselors are career counselors. I believe every counselor, working with every client, is engaged in some type of career-related work. I also believe the vast majority of counselors are integrative in nature, meaning they do not base their practice entirely on only one theoretical orientation. For these reasons, it seems only natural that counselors need to have the skill of integrating theories to fit a wide variety of client needs. I've gravitated toward a solution-focused mind-set for most of my 15 years in practice and believe it is a mind-set. By sharing this mind-set with clients, counselors share the expectation that change will occur. In fact, de Shazer and Berg and others believed change was inevitable and always occurring (de Shazer et al., 1986). A solution-focused mind-set is not getting "caught in the weeds"; it is the belief that you get what you are looking for. If you look for what is going wrong (i.e., focus on the problem) you will get more problems. If you look for what is going right (i.e., find solutions) you will find solutions. One of my favorite sayings, that I believe fits wonderfully with a solution-focused mind-set, is, "The grass is not always greener on the other side. The grass is greener where you water it." —Michael Moyer

I find career counseling to be the most exciting type of counseling. This goes back to my roots when I was working on my internship many years ago as part of my master's program. I was told to help the women at a homeless shelter find jobs. After my first visit, it became clear that these women would not be able to find a job unless they built their feelings of self-esteem and self-efficacy. They would not have the courage to select a job, let alone interview, without recognizing their own strengths. This is when I truly understood that career counseling and personal counseling are so related that they can't be easily separated. Needless to say, solution-focused techniques were crucial in building their career confidence. It also became clear that many of the career theories integrated beautifully in solution-focused techniques. I hope this chapter helped you understand that career counseling can be so much more than simply matching a job on a list with a person's interests. Career counseling can be multifaceted, and, yes, career counseling is a very important and often misunderstood form of counseling. I wish you the best in your career counseling future. —Janet Hicks

Additional Resources

The following resources provide additional information about the content provided in this chapter.

Useful Websites

American Counseling Association:

https://www.counseling.org/careers/aca-career-central/job-hunting-tips-resources

This site lists job resources and tips for a variety of clients as well as future counselors.

Solution Focused Brief Therapy Association: http://www.sfbta.org/

The Solution Focused Brief Therapy Association was founded in 2002 by Steve de Shazer, Insoo Kim Berg, and their colleagues. The association is dedicated to research, awards, and scholarship related to solution-focused brief therapy. Their most important work is to hold an annual conference to further the work of solution-focused practitioners.

Institute for Solution Focused Therapy: https://solutionfocused.net/

The Institute for Solution Focused Therapy is an organization dedicated to training practitioners on the use of solution-focused techniques.

Books

De Jong, P., & Berg, I. K. (2013). *Interviewing for solutions*. Brooks/Cole.

This book walks the counselor through solution-focused techniques, challenges, and types of clients.

References

American Counseling Association. (2014). *Code of ethics*. Author.

Brown, J. D. (2014). Self-esteem and self-evaluation: Feeling is believing. In J. M. Suls (Ed.), *Psychological perspectives on the self, Vol. 4* (pp. 27–59). Lawrence Erlbaum Associates, Inc.

Dawis, R. V. (2004). The Minnesota theory of work adjustment. In S. D. Brown & R. W. Lent (Eds.), *Career development and counseling* (pp. 3–23). Wiley.

Dawis, R. V., & Lofquist, L. H. (1984). *A psychological theory of work adjustment*. University of Minnesota Press.

Dawis, R. V. & Lofquist, L. H. (1991). *Essentials of person-environment-correspondence counseling*. University of Minnesota Press.

De Jong, P., & Berg, I. K. (2013). *Interviewing for solutions.* Brooks/Cole.

de Shazer, S. (1985). *Keys to solutions in brief therapy.* Norton.

de Shazer, S., Berg, I. K., Lipchik, E. V. E., Nunnally, E., Molnar, A., Gingerich, W., & Weiner-Davis, M. (1986). Brief therapy: Focused solution development. *Family Process, 25*(2), 207–221.

Gingerich, W. J., & Eisengart, S. (2000). Solution-focused brief therapy: A review of the outcome research. *Family Process, 39*(4), 477–498.

Ginzberg, E. (1972). Toward a theory of occupational choice: A restatement. *Vocational Guidance Quarterly, 20*(3), 169–176.

Ginzberg, E., Ginsberg, S. W., Axelrad, S., & Herma, J. L. (1951). *Occupational choice: An approach to general theory.* Columbia University Press.

Gottfredson, L. S. (1996). A developmental theory of circumscription and compromise. In D. Brown & L. Brooks (Eds.), *Career choice and development: Applying contemporary approaches to practice* (pp. 179–232). Jossey-Bass.

Hansen, J. C. (1984). *Users guide for the strong.* Consulting Psychologists.

Krumboltz, J. (2008). The happenstance learning theory. *Journal of Career Assessment, 17(2)*, 135–154.

Krumboltz, J. D., Mitchell, A. M., & Jones, G. B. (1976). A social learning theory of career selection. *The Counseling Psychologist, 6*(1), 71–81. https://doi.org/10.1177/001100007600600117

Miller, J. H. (2004). Building a solution focused model into career counseling. University of Canterbury, 1–16.

Nica, E., Manole, C., & Briscariu, R. (2016). The detrimental consequences of perceived job insecurity on health and psychological well-being. *Psychological Issues in Human Resource Management, 4(1)*, 175–181.

Seligman, L., & Reichenberg, L. W. (2010). *Theories of counseling and psychotherapy: Systems, strategies, and skills (3rd ed.).* Prentice Hall.

Super, D. (1953). A theory of vocational development. *American Psychologist, 8*(5), 185–190.

Super, D. (1978). Career exploration and planning. *Annual Review of Psychology, 29*, 333–372.

Winbolt, B. (2011). *Solution focused therapy for the helping professions.* Jessica Kingsley.

CHAPTER 11

Using Adlerian Techniques in Career Counseling

Mary G. Mayorga and Brian Le Clair

> *Man knows much more than he understands.*
> –Alfred Adler

Alfred Adler's (2010) view of human life was influenced by his belief that people not only grew but survived through social interest. He believed people needed to be part of a social group, believe in themselves, and have faith in society to do well in life. Through a *social interest* perspective, people could become aware of their own strengths, resources, and abilities.

Adler (2010) also believed humans are goal-directed beings and each person moves through life toward goals that attract them. It is this goal-directed view that moves people toward a future they create for themselves. According to Adler, people's behavior is purposeful, and a psychological gain is behind each person's actions.

When Adlerian techniques are used in career counseling, abstract concepts include the following: (a) purpose, (b) courage, and (c) encouragement (Adler, 2010). Career counselors might work with clients to help them determine the purposes behind their behaviors. Career counselors might also look for courage within clients that fuels them to move toward goals that encourage positive self-efficacy. Helping them to have a perspective of "I can" rather than "I cannot" may direct the clients' focus toward a willingness to contribute to their own career goals. Finally, career counselors need to have the innate ability to use encouragement as a way to help the client develop or increase their levels of self-esteem (Adler, 2010). Clients must believe in their ability to move in a forward manner and reach meaningful goals.

CHAPTER OVERVIEW

This chapter discusses the use of Adlerian techniques for conducting career counseling sessions with clients. Adlerian theory, its accompanying techniques, and application of theoretical techniques as applied to vocational discernment are discussed in connection to career development, career maturity, and career decision making.

LEARNING OBJECTIVES

After reading this chapter, you will be able to do the following:

- Understand Adlerian therapy and its techniques
- Understand how Adlerian therapy integrates with career theories
- Understand the application of Adlerian therapy and techniques with clients' facing career counseling/vocational discernment issues

Adlerian Therapy: Theoretical Background and Premises

Astute students of counseling and psychotherapy may notice that the inclusion of Adler's theoretical premises in academic texts is often meager, his mention being more like an afterthought or a historical footnote that rests at the bottom of the page. Contemporary textbooks rarely dedicate more than few paragraphs to Adlerian theories (Blair-Broeker & Ernst, 2019; Gazzinga, 2018; Myers & DeWall, 2018). For many devout practitioners of psychoanalysis, Adler is interpreted as being a rogue who departed from the core nature of the science, stepping aside from the guiding hand of Freud to sit on the sidelines of real psychotherapy.

Along with others such as Karen Horney and Carl Jung, Adler is usually identified as a *Neo-Freudian* (Gazzinga, 2018). These are theorists whose works still have Freudian underpinnings but whose benchmark contributions demonstrate a significant departure from Freud's original premises (Lundin, 1996). As such, Adler would never have described himself as a true devotee of Freud (Colby, 1951). For Adler, Freud's theories were too highly *deterministic*, meaning behaviors were set and highly predicated by a person's past or, in layman's terms, there was little of the leopard being able to change his spots. Adler found *determinism* to be counter to his own intuitions of the potential of the individual psyche (Adler, 2010).

In this light, the Adlerian approach, known as *individual psychology,* acknowledged the innate capacity of humans to consciously engage in choice and initiate change (Adler, 2010). This new psychological thinking created schools of thought acknowledging unresolved childhood psychosocial tension as being the etiology of neurosis and disordered behavior and greatly differed from Freud's previous focus on sex, sexual fixations, or gender (Adler, 2010; Horney, 1992; Lundin, 1996). In order to best understand Adler's theoretical premises, let's take a more in-depth look at his background.

Background

From 1902–1911, Adler was a regular attendee of Freud's "Wednesday Society," a discussion group of fellow analysts that met in Freud's home and were schooled by him so as to deepen their skills of his seminal approach to psychological treatment (Muhlleitner & Reichymayr, 1997). Freud had little tolerance for dissension. Deviation or disagreement with Freud's ideas was very often met with harsh criticism and removal from the group. Not surprisingly then, after 10 years of membership in Freud's circle, Adler voluntarily parted ways with him. In so doing, Adler retained a hint of Freudian flavor to his theories and techniques but, nonetheless, created his own branch of the psychoanalytic movement that augmented the growing eclecticism of psychology as a practical science (Dreikurs, 1950).

Adler was the second of six children born in 1870 to a Jewish Viennese grain merchant. Historically, Adler's childhood was punctuated by ill health, a delicate physique and subsequent accidents. His overall frailty prompted his parents to pamper and dote over him, which most likely influenced aspects of his writing and ideology (Lundin, 2015).

Adler is noted for several key concepts linked exclusively to his system. Some of these concepts closely parallel Freudian constructs, illustrating the reality that while Adler differed with Freud in significant areas, the Freudian influence in the creation of his own systems theory remained. It is hard to extricate Adler from Freud because it is likely that without Freud's influence we might not have the Adler we know of today.

Adler's theories were heartily welcomed by fellow colleagues and by laity, partially because they were not received as being distasteful. Freud's writings were awash in sexual constructs such as the *Oedipal complex* where the boy harbors a murderous wish toward his father so he may sexually possess his mother (Lundin, 1996). Such a notion was repellant to polite society and was impossible to scientifically validate. On the contrary, Adlerian theory was perceived as being prosocial and uplifting, drawing many adherents to his cause, partially because he was not Freud and partially because his constructs were so readily recognized as applicable and easily understandable (McWilliams, 1994).

Key Constructs of Adlerian Therapy

The following sections help you understand the premises of Adlerian Therapy so you are able to integrate these premises with career theories later in the chapter.

Inferiority Complex, Striving for Superiority, and Goal Setting

Conjecture has it that Adler's frailty as a youth prompted him to make efforts to rise beyond the physical limitations imposed on him by nature (Lundin, 2015). It is perhaps this reality that prompted his belief in growth via overcoming felt perceptions of inferiority (i.e., the *inferiority complex*) that motivate people to move away from a perceived lesser status toward a higher one (Adler, 2010). Whereas Freud constructed a reductive psychosexual growth model motivated by pursuit of pleasure, Adler ideated that, through assertion, people can rise above any genetic, cultural, or environmental limitations imposed on on them as they seek not pleasure but purpose and meaning (Lundin, 2015).

Adler later changed his inferiority complex to the more purposeful and relatable *striving for superiority* (Adler, 1929. Striving for superiority gives an individual permission to set goals that concretize efforts to move from an inferior echelon to a higher one. Readers might recognize this while considering their journey through undergraduate school. You moved slowly through each of the 4 years to finally be at the top, only to find yourselves once again at the bottom as you entered graduate school. Despite this lowered status, you set a goal to complete your graduate degree. This means your future is established by assertion in the present (i.e., your current goal setting to alleviate the feeling of inferiority moving you from a feeling of a felt minus to a felt plus). As you consider the eventual completion of your new degree you will find yourself on top again.

Striving for superiority sounds somewhat similar to Freud's writings on compensation. As you remember, compensation is overcoming a deficit in one area of life but overachieving in another (Corey, 2009). In comparison, Adler's contribution reflects more of a protracted lifelong dynamic, but it is difficult to not see the Freudian influence in this concept.

Sociality or Social Interest

Adler believed the key to working out life issues is through purposeful contact with others (Adler, 2010). He wrote extensively about the three ties that create unity and cohesiveness among healthy people: finding an occupation that will realistically fit the present environment, cooperation and association with others, and how we attend to marriage and family relationships (Adler, 2010).

Adler argued that healing work toward resolution of sensitive psychosocial or social-cognitive problems must manifest through some kind of social contribution (i.e., social interest; Corey, 2009). Adler (2010) wrote, "The man who meets the problems of human life successfully acts as if he recognized, fully and spontaneously, that the meaning of life is interest in others and cooperation" (p. 10). He felt collective human welfare was a high priority and that association and cooperation with others was an intrinsic part of eventual arrival at personal healing. Specifying social isolation as an element foreign to healing, Adler argued that salient treatment is augmented through human association (Sweeney, 2009). Regarding career counseling, Adler would most purposefully ask his client the question, "In what ways will your career search and choice lead you to make a meaningful contribution to you and to the lives of others?"

Fictional Finalism

Adler drew from the works of Hans Vaihinger (1911) who proposed the world could be viewed from an "as if" perspective. Vaihinger observed that we often function from the wisdom in broad beliefs that really have no basis in reality. He was not referring to delusions. He was referring to ideals such as such as, "Where there is a will, there is a way," or, "If you build it, they will come." Adler expanded Vaihinger's ideas and held that internalizing idealisms can actually be purposive in setting goals and can have an uncanny ability to help them come to fruition. Essentially, he proposed that people lived "as if" what they portend is true can become true.

Adler used the expression *fictional finalism* to refer to the power of internalized ideals that, throughout the life span, can operate both consciously and unconsciously. These ideals guide the person toward goal acquisition and mastery (Lundin, 2015). During the formative years, fictional finalism can help ease the sting of inferiority feelings and can be a unidirectional force, energizing efforts toward superiority. For those seeking to overcome matters of strained mental health, the use of fictional finalism allows pathology to be re-designated as an obstacle toward the attainment of more mature and fully functional mental health. Again, whereas Freud saw behavior as deterministic, Adler was more optimistic in his assessment of the person's ability to work toward healing and wholeness.

Lifestyle

Lifestyle or "style of life," as it is also known, is actually the collection of perceptions that children acquire by the age of 4 or 5 that helps them know how to react, to respond, and to interpret the social environment around them (Lundin, 2015). These perceptions can organize into thematic introjects with corresponding social-cognitive patterns that allow the child to react safely to ambient stimuli. These perceptions become crystalized as internalized convictions, cognitions, and messages regarding relationships to others. For the growing child, they serve as a compass. For example, the child who learns to persistently annoy their parent (in order to eventually break them down and receive concessions) might transfer this behavior to interactions with teachers and extended family. These convictions endure and take root in the landscape of personality.

Lifestyle would also include any fictional finalisms, areas of social interest, and strivings for superiority that create the global teleological experience of what it means to learn, grow, and survive. Adler might ask the client about their earliest memories or recollections of an event and would explore what assumptions may have run in the child's mind at that time. For example, clients considering a career choice in the medical field might be prompted to explore their earliest memories of doctors and hospitals. Pinpointing these memories could help re-establish a fictional finalism and generate thought and behavior toward eventual entrance into the medical field.

As you can see, knowing someone's lifestyle might help the career counselor bring about fictional finalism and career development for the client. With this in mind, Guided Practice Exercise 11.1 asks you to consider your own lifestyle regarding career development. Later in the chapter, we will examine ways to use this information as part of a career-related lifestyle analysis.

Guided Practice Exercise 11.1 Lifestyle

Take a moment and think about your childhood. What experiences did you have that influenced your decision to become a counselor? What were you told about counseling or helpers? Did you visit a helping professional? How might fictional finalism play into your own career role?

Now that we understand Adler's background and basic premises, let's take a look at how some of these contentions are implemented using specific theoretical techniques. Later in the chapter, we share how career theory integrates with Adlerian techniques. We will also share a case study whereby Adlerian techniques are integrated into a career counseling session.

Individual Psychology Techniques

Adler's approach to human behavior came from a holistic perspective that states that all behavior has a purpose (Carlson & Englar-Carlson, 2017). Adler also had several specific techniques that he used to help a person understand his or her personal view of the world. He believed that a person's view of his or her world was created and molded in the first few years of life and then molded in the initial social setting, which involved the family constellation (Lundin, 2015; Sweeney, 2009). Adler also highlighted the importance of social and cultural context in a person's life and how these two concepts impacted the development of the personality.

Because of this, an Adlerian career counselor considers a client's family constellation and its impact on the client's present lifestyle. The career counselor must also gauge a client's social and community interest to determine the impact on the client's career path and explore the client's personal belief system. This is important since some beliefs about life, self, and others may be accurate, while other beliefs may be inaccurate or faulty. According to Adler (Carlson & Englar-Carlson, 2017), belief systems are formed early in life through interpretation of early experiences and then are lived out by the client as if those beliefs are accurate.

One of the major goals of career counseling from an Adlerian perspective is to help increase or to help foster the client's social interest and community feeling or *gemeinschaftsgefuhl* (Milliren et al., 2007; Sweeney, 2009). Social interest and community feeling are terms that refer to an individual's awareness of being part of a human community and how an individual's attitude affects how they deal in the social world. It is important to remember that in Adlerian therapy these two concepts are highly significant.

These principles are evident in specific techniques used in Adlerian therapy and can be conducive to career decision making and exploration. Table 11.1 gives an overview of a few of these Adlerian techniques and their purposes. We will discuss specific techniques that bridge gaps between individual psychology and career counseling later in this chapter.

When using Adlerian techniques, it is important to remember that Adler emphasized subjectivity, in other words, how the client views his or her own life. For this reason, ties between client understanding, career decision making, and assessment are inseparable. In order to best understand assessment as part of these facets, we will first discuss the basic assumptions inherent in Adlerian career assessment and, next, discuss assessment-related techniques.

TABLE 11.1   **Additional Adlerian Techniques**

Technique	Description
Confronting	Challenges private way of viewing life or private logic.
Asking the question	Asks "What would be different if you were . . . ?"
Encouragement	Demonstrates that the counselor has faith in the client; encourages the client to feel good about self and others
Acting as If	Instructs the client to act "as if" they are the person they wish to be
Spitting in the soup	Points out certain behaviors that impede desired payoff
Catching oneself	Helps promote awareness of self-destructive behavior or thoughts
Task setting	Helps set short- and long-term goals and objectives
Push button	Encourages discretion and focus on helpful stimuli; focus is on creating desired feelings by concentrating on thoughts

Adapted from Sweeney (2009)

Assessment

Four basic assumptions underlie Adlerian career assessment and can be utilized when working with a client (Watkins, 1993). The first assumption is that a person (here, we can think of the person as the client seeking career counseling) is striving to move from feelings of inferiority toward superiority, perfection, or totality. The second assumption is a striving toward an individualistic unique goal developed by the individual (again, the client). The third assumption is the fact that although there is a goal that the client has, it is somewhat vague and not yet fully developed by the individual (the client). The fourth assumption is that the individual's goal is the final cause influenced by the personality structure of the individual. This entails having the counselor and the client look at the individual's life problems (work, love, friendship). This examination of life problems helps lead the individual toward a self-awareness of social problems and further looks at how they have impacted his or her work, love, and friendships. These facets also inversely affect the socialization of the individual.

Specific Techniques Conducive to Career Assessment

While several Adlerian techniques can be incorporated into career counseling, one particularly useful assessment technique involves analysis of the client's lifestyle. We will first look at the steps in analyzing an individual's lifestyle from an Adlerian perspective and then proceed to specific techniques that can be used to help enhance an individual's career direction.

Lifestyle Analysis

What exactly is an analysis of a client's lifestyle? In Adlerian writing, the lifestyle has been referred to by various names, such as the life line, or the life plan (Watkins, 1993). The Adlerian lifestyle analysis or assessment can provide a great deal of information about an individual's motivations, preferences, and general orientation toward self, others, and the world at large (Godot, n.d.). The analysis helps the counselor identify targets and client successes (Curtis, 2010).

Although the Adlerian lifestyle analysis is generally used within the scope of Adlerian therapy, it can also be adapted for utilization in career counseling. This is done by focusing on how the client believes his or her relationship with self, family, and society has impacted career choices throughout his or her life. Reflecting on this relationship information can help the client develop an expedient and comprehensive view of career paths that may have been previously overlooked.

As in all counseling relationships, it is important to establish a proper career counselor/client therapeutic relationship. This relationship ensures that the process involving career path assessment goes smoothly. Once the relationship has been established, and prior to conducting an Adlerian lifestyle assessment, several additional steps must fall into place as follows (Corey, 2019):

- Establishing the proper therapeutic relationship
- Choosing an appropriate assessment to explore the psychological dynamics operating in the client's life
- Using encouragement to help the client develop self-understanding and insight into life's purpose
- Working with and helping the client move toward new choices that can reorient and reeducate the client about self, others, and society

Once these steps are in place, the career counselor can begin focusing on the Adlerian lifestyle analysis/assessment and its concentration on the family constellation and early memory recollections. Both of these facets have a strong impact on a person's view of self, others, and society (Leong et al., 2001).

The Adler Graduate School has an excellent lifestyle assessment that can be used or modified as needed when working with a client. It consists of more than 30 pages of detailed information that can be used to help the client better understand what their present lifestyle represents and how it came to be. Because the assessment intends to help clients move in a positive direction, both in life and career, you may be interested in finding out more about this site. In this light, website information can be found at the end of this chapter in the section "Additional Resources."

Family Constellation

The family of origin has an immense impact on an individual's personality; therefore, assessing a client's family constellation is more than simply asking a few questions (Sweeney, 2009). In fact, the career counselor performs an intensive, comprehensive, and investigative assessment process. This process gives both the counselor and the client the most detailed picture as to how the family constellation is impacting the client's personality lifestyle.

The assessment process includes looking at members of family-of-origin relationships, birth order, sibling interrelationships, parental relationships, family genogram, school's influence on the life of the client, the client's attributes as a child, influential adult figures in the life of the client, and the client's own conclusions about life. As you can imagine, life, itself, is greatly influenced by the aforementioned areas of assessment, and because so many areas are assessed, the process can be exhaustive (Bartholow et al., 2006).

Birth Order

One specific area assessed as part of the family constellation assessment includes birth order and its characteristics. Adler believed birth order to be an important part of a client's early life developmental process. He contended that the client's birth order might influence their later life behavior (Shulman & Mosak, 1977).

An Adlerian overview of birth order and birth order characteristics has been adapted by Stein (2004) from Adler's (2010) book *What Life Could Mean to You*. Stein (2004) indicates there are 12 positions into which a child can be born. Stein (2004) also describes the family situation the child is born into, along with the child's characteristics as related to their birth order position. Let's review the birth order positions, along with a brief statement regarding connections between the child's birth order and personal characteristics.

A child can be born into the position of the following:

- *Only child.* This child may be timid or anxious and tends to receive a high percentage of parental attention. The child tends to mature early and is dethroned when the next child is born. For example, the child has to learn to share when the next child is born. Characteristics of only children include being overprotected and spoiled, liking being the center of attention, and difficulty sharing. This child prefers the company of adults and needs to be quickly recognized and promptly rewarded

- *Oldest child.* The oldest child must endure parental expectations, which are high, is given extra responsibilities, and is expected to set a positive example for younger siblings. Characteristics of this child include overemphasizing the importance of authority, rules, and laws such that the child may become authoritarian or strict. The oldest child can also become a "problem kid," unless encouraged. Further, this child tends to focus on the past and is pessimistic about the future

- *Second child.* The second child arrives late and must catch up. Because the older sibling is always ahead of second child, the second child often becomes competitive in nature. In fact, the second child wants to overtake the older child and may tend to become a rebel or try to outdo everyone. Competition may become rivalry.

- *Middle child.* The middle child is sandwiched in and may feel squeezed out of a position of privilege and significance. Characteristics of the middle child include the child being even-tempered and having a take-it-or-leave-it attitude. The child may have trouble finding their place in the birth pecking order or may become a fighter of injustice.

- *Youngest child.* The youngest child tends to have "many mothers and fathers" because the older children try to educate this child. This child always has an assigned place in the birth order and does not have to be concerned with being dethroned. Characteristics may include wanting to have a more influential place in the pecking order when interacting with the other children. This child has huge plans that may never work out and may stay "the baby" throughout life, along with being spoiled by the family.

- *Twin child.* Twins differ in that one child is typically stronger or more active than the other. Although they may be born only minutes apart, parents tend to see one twin as older than the other twin. A twin child may have identity problems and the stronger twin may become the leader of the "twins."

- *Ghost child.* This is a child who is born next in succession following the death of an immediate sibling. This position is labeled due to this child having a "ghost" in front of them. Because of loss and fear, the mother may become overprotective of this child. Characteristics of this child includes use of exploitive methods toward the mother due to her overprotective behavior. These children are also known to exhibit rebelling behavior and to loudly protest any comparisons made to the deceased child.

- *Adopted child.* The adopted child may be spoiled by parents, in part because they are grateful for having received a child. This spoiling may occur among adoptive parents in an effort to compensate the adopted child for the loss of their biological parents. Characteristics may include the child becoming spoiled and demanding. This child may develop resentment toward the biological parents or may idealize the unknown biological parents.

- *Only boy among girls.* This male child will usually spend inordinate amounts of time with women, especially if the father is away. This child may try to prove he is "the man of the house" or he may become effeminate.

- *Only girl among boys.* This female child will be faced with overprotective brothers and becomes used to managing these behaviors. Characteristics of this child includes becoming very feminine or a tomboy in an attempt to outdo the brothers. This child will also try to please her father.

- *Boy among all boys.* These young men may deal with unique issues. For example, if these boys' mothers wanted a girl, they may dress their boy as a girl. In response, this child may either capitalize on the assigned role or protest it vigorously.

- *Girl among all girls.* These young girls may be dressed as boys. As with the boy among all boys, these girls may either capitalize on the assigned role or protest it vigorously.

Certain adult traits can often be explained when assessing birth order position. Consequently, assessing a client's birth order is especially helpful in career counseling. The birth order assessment can help the client understand (a) reasons for low performance in their career path, (b) their inability to hold onto a job, or (c) their difficulty in establishing professional work relationships. Guided Practice Exercise 11.2 asks you to consider your own birth order with relationship to your career choices.

Guided Practice Exercise 11.2 Birth Order

As you read in the passage regarding birth order, Adler contended that birth order affected later life outcomes. Take a moment and think about your own birth order. Did you have siblings or were you an only child? Do you think your personality was shaped, in part, by the culture created by your birth order or by the lack of siblings in your home? How might this impact your career decisions today? Do you think it influences how you get along with others in the work environment?

Early Recollections

As a general rule, early recollections are not difficult to obtain. They refer to memories that occurred before the age of 8, are focused on a single, specific event, and can be clearly visualized by the client (Sweeny & Myers, 1986; Watkins, 1993). They are a useful and interesting manner in which to get to know a person (in this case the client) and the choices that they have made throughout their life, including career choices. Adler (2010) believed that early recollections were important and significant because they helped better understand the client as a human being.

According to Adler (2010), the early recollection of memories can help a client begin to understand the "story of his or her life." They show the style of life the client has lived in its simplest expressions. Those recollections will show if the client was pampered or neglected, if the client learned to cooperate or express rebellious behavior, if the client had problems with confrontation, or if the client struggled with confrontation, and so on. Therefore, early recollections are considered a wealth of information that can provide useful insight to the career counselor, and to the client as well (Stein, n.d.; Verger & Camp, 1970).

The following example illustrates how the use of early recollections might be used to uncover reasons for a client's behavior-related career impediments.

Counselor: You mention that you are having a hard time understanding your reasons for not doing well at your job. You state that you try hard to do a good job, but you also do not believe that you are doing your best. Some of our perceptions of ourselves may be impacted by our family of origin and, when we were collecting your family constellation information, you mentioned that you have a conflictual relationship with your mother. See if you can recall an early memory that involves an interaction between you and your mother before the age of 8 or so.

Client: Okay, I will try. Let me see. One of the first memories I have is when I was 5 years old. I was trying to learn to ride my tricycle. I was in the front of my house on the sidewalk trying to pedal my tricycle. My mother was standing on the front porch. As I tried to go forward, I found that it was difficult for me to pedal the tricycle. My mother began to criticize me by telling me that I would never learn to ride a tricycle unless I tried "really hard." I think 5 or 10 minutes went by with me trying to succeed, but I could not. All I remember wondering is why she didn't come down to help me. Instead, she stood on the porch and continued to berate me about my lack of success. I remember thinking I would never be good at anything.

As you can see, this early memory recollection begins to uncover possible reasons this client has been unsuccessful in doing well in his or her career.

The Integration of Adlerian Therapy With Career Counseling Theories and Models

Adler's techniques blend well with a number of career theories. Among these are Krumboltz, Super, and Roe's career theories as discussed in Chapters 3, 4, and 5 of this text. Their main tenets will be addressed in their connection to Adlerian approaches to career counseling in the sections that follow.

Krumboltz

Graduate students might notice that John Krumboltz appears to be a confluence of theories from Uri Bronfenbrenner, Albert Bandura, as well as Alfred Adler. Krumboltz (Krumboltz et al., 1976) believed that people are heavily influenced by what they see in others. Bandura (1977) is known for the development of social learning theory where people establish appropriateness of behavior based on behaviors modeled for them. Bronfenbrenner (2005) is noted for his theory of ecological psychology and broke influence down into specific brackets: broader, more cultural and era-specific systems called "macrosystems" and more individual, intimate domains called "microsystems." When looking at Krumboltz, a reader would find references to microsystemic genetic endowments and genetic abnormalities, which would exert influence on which careers would be realistic.

Krumboltz acknowledged the macrosystemic effects of being born into a certain period of time and certain places. As discussed in Chapter 3, he also identified happenstance theory, meaning that certain cataclysmic events outside our control would affect career choices (Krumboltz, 2009). Happenstance theory could be applied to changes wrought by war, a volcanic eruption, or a tsunami that wipes out a village. For example, it would be more typical of someone growing up in 18th-century Iceland to become a fisherman because the geography, the time period, and the empirical career options modeled before them would point to a career in harvesting fish. Similarly, someone growing up in the 1990s Silicon Valley might be inclined to seek out computer and software development work because the era and the area would complement the career choice pathway. However, someone growing up in Europe in the 1940s might have to select a military career because of political circumstances unraveling beyond the control of the average person. Guided Practice Exercise 11.3 asks to reflect on events occurring in your lifetime and how they led to your current career path.

Guided Practice Exercise 11.3 Happenstance

The text refers to several examples where a person might be more prone to end up in a particular career path based on life era and events. What events have you witnessed in your lifetime that affect your career choices? How are career paths different today than they were 10, 20, or 40 years ago? What facets influence career path besides just living with a certain time period?

Krumboltz stepped away from the psychoanalytic tradition of insight learning as the root of discovery, favoring learning derived from the environment to play a role in career selection. Thus, exposure to direct or indirect instruction of commercial fishing or software development might more heavily influence someone from 18th-century Iceland or 1990s Silicon Valley as they select a career. The overlay of different systemic influences coupled with modeling and instruction fuses together to synthesize the variables in place as people choose careers.

In relation to Adler, Krumboltz et al.'s (1976) theory is heavily dependent on sociality. As we have seen, Adler (1954) believed strongly in sociality, association, and cooperation with other human beings.

Krumboltz's identification of the strong role of sociality in career selection works off Adler's theory on the need for social influence necessary for healing and problem solving.

As we consider this, it is evident that Krumboltz also acknowledged Adler's work on the style of life. Innate patterns of thinking that fuse to form thematic patterns of thought and behavior are, to some degree, drawn from association with others and from self-generated cognitions. When self-referent beliefs are coupled with messages received from others and boost our felt sense of inferiority, enduring cognitive distortions can form that affect the style of life. Krumboltz referred to these as *faulty thinking*, and they are manifested by beliefs of inadequacy that become embedded in how potential is interpreted. For example, faulty thinking can form the bedrock of one's style of life and is recognized by expressions of self-negating beliefs that emphasize inability and inadequacy. Issues further arise in that faulty thinking also poses little acknowledgement of the possibility for change. From an Adlerian perspective, faulty thoughts infused into style of life could generate energy toward overcoming inferiority. Without help, however, these thoughts could cement that inferiority. The key to the door out of this would be association, modeling, and an emphasized message from others that options are still available. Case Example 11.1 asks you to consider ties between faulty thoughts and overcoming inferiority.

Case Example 11.1 The Case of Omar

Lenny is a 25-year-old woman who works nights as an admissions counselor in a hospital. Many nurses who work alongside Lenny tell her they think she would make an excellent nurse. Lenny would secretly love to go to nursing school and become a nurse but can't see this in her future. How might faulty thinking be impacting Lenny's stance?

Donald Super

Donald Super's (1957) work presents a developmental approach to career decision making that unravels throughout the life span. Similar to Erikson, discussed in Chapter 6, each stage involves a crisis that must be negotiated successfully before full transition to the subsequent stage is possible. As mentioned in Chapter 4 of this text, the growth stage encompasses the formative years up to about age 15 when vocational choice is first contemplated. When contemplating this stage, Adler would query what exact kinds of self-beliefs formed the self-concept, thus integrating into a person's own idiosyncratic style of life (Adler, 1954). These beliefs would then relate to career options a client could realistically consider. Exploring Adler's question of earliest memories could, therefore, help crystalize which beliefs about occupations became concretized in their developing self-concept and corresponding style of life.

The exploratory stage, usually up to age 25, goes beyond the growth stage in that it allows people to gain more information about career and assess to what degree a fit exists between self and vocation (Super, 1969). Knowledge of self is critical during this period, and self-awareness should expand as chronological age progresses. This phase is a lot like trying on suits at the mall: There will be constant exploration of different careers until a good fit is found.

From an Adlerian perspective, much emphasis is placed on the unconscious lure from early memories and whether the current choice matches the meaning of those early introjected recollections with the worker's life. Adler (2010) wrote, "It is our task to recognize the underlying motives, to see the way they are striving, what is pushing them forward, where they are placed, the goal of superiority and how to make it concrete. Will income, status, opportunity for growth and learning all be sufficient? Will they remain constant and will the current career choice continue to trigger a serious striving for superiority and or will that choice eventually deflate, flatten out and wither?" (p. 243). To make a meaningful contribution to the well-being of self and society, people in exploration must reassess throughout this stage or a return to a felt sense of inferiority where stagnation is at risk.

The establishment stage follows exploration and ends at about age 45 when one has finally committed to a chosen profession (Super, 1957). During this period of time, the worker proceeds with a fuller devotion to work, believing further entrenchment can maximize personal growth, opportunity, and welfare. This is reflective of Adler's concept of *private logic* or the idea that there is an unconscious teleological direction rendered by choices. These choices further propel the person toward career evaluation and choice, thus moving him or her closer to a felt sense of superiority.

The following two stages, maintenance (45–65) and disengagement (65+), parallel Eriksonian crises and examine whether career selection continues to foster generativity. If so, career selection allows a sense of social connectedness, contribution, and needs fulfillment. The maintenance stage follows the established choice (Super, 1969). Maintenance entails reaching a tenured, veteran status where there is visible accumulation of years of service. Disengagement speaks not to retirement but to the gradual shift of energy away from work toward life after work. This is seen as the natural stepping away from deep work commitment and addresses the introspective need to feel integrity once full retirement commences.

A key concept related to Donald Super is *searching*, which implies a continued hunt for alternatives if the current career fit isn't the best match. This is usually experienced during the establishment stage and is considered quite normal. Often people will change positions in a career field but remain in that same domain. For example, teachers might one day choose to become school counselors and/or later administrators. However, it is very normal to leave one field entirely and begin working in a new field altogether. Searching is analogous to Adler's construct of striving for superiority because searching necessitates course corrections in order to self-improve and self-actualize.

Ann Roe Career Choice and Development

Ann Roe (1957) is probably one of the more fascinating researchers we can link to in our review of Adler because, as discussed in Chapter 5, she expanded the theory of a more contemporary theorist, Abraham Maslow. Part of Roe's contribution to career counseling was to augment Maslow's hierarchy of needs by adding her observation of a person's need for beauty and need for information, the latter being most purposeful in the search for a career. She also argued that a person's career choice is partially a reflection of unmet social-emotional needs from the formative years. Strained or unsatiated social-emotional needs stem from the kind of rearing the child received from parents in the home environment. She believed that the most compelling unmet hierarchical need, as per Abraham Maslow, also plays a pivotal role in choice of occupation.

Roe (1957) conceptualized career choice as having its roots in early parent/child attachment dynamics and that occupational choice is related to the resulting personality and any personality deficits formed by the overarching parent/child attachment pattern exhibited during rearing. Roe identified three categories of potential parenting styles: (a) parental energy floods toward the child, (b) neglects the child, or (c) is in attunement with the child. Parents whose energy floods toward the child stifle creativity, independence, and initiative by being overwhelming and overprotective. They rob the child of growth opportunities by their overprotection and instill a sense of dependency toward the parents. Such parents do not recognize their restrictions, and protections damage the child and negatively affect their growing personality (Roe, 1957).

The second parenting/child attachment pattern category she wrote of pertains to child avoidance. Avoidant parents are either rejecting of their children, ignoring them altogether, withholding love and emotional affect, or simply neglecting them during the child-rearing process. (Roe, 1956) Such parents exhibit low emotional involvement toward their children who grow up unconsciously believing that minimal emotional attachment and involvement between families is healthy.

The third category of parenting involves creation of a home environment where children experience acceptance (Roe, 1956). Casually accepting parents show a convincible amount of love but do not go overboard and could perhaps show more. Loving and accepting parents are highly nurturing but establish an unquestionable form of warm, consistent acceptance. These parents know enough to set boundaries around the affection they display toward children so as not to emotionally overwhelm them. Loving, accepting parents also foster a sense of curiosity, initiative, industry, and independence among their children.

The most significant point to be made about Roe is that these attachment patterns exert an unconscious influence, culminating in the eventual inclination either toward interaction with other people or away from other people. She believed that the parenting style children experienced unconsciously spilled onto career choice. Per Roe (1957), occupations were reflective to the degree of comfort in social interactions experienced in the formative stages. Early parent/child interaction set the tone for occupations with either a low or a high level of interaction with others. Thus, the home environment, parenting styles, and early childhood experiences heavily influence eventual career selection.

Even novice counseling students should recognize the heavy Adlerian influence in Roe's writings. It can be argued that the style of life and corresponding lifestyle beliefs are acquired via the attachment and interaction kids experience with parents during early development. Faulty thinking and faulty self-statements most likely abound and can be linked to clients' earliest memories of parent/child interaction. As a result, exploring what early memories are still retained and the influence they exert on self-efficacy and career expectations would prove a worthy therapeutic pursuit from an Adlerian perspective.

Parenting exposes children to unique and differing environments. This and natural genetic inheritance may influence future career development. Roe (1956) argued that genetic inheritance plays an important role in career choice and argued that people move either toward or away from people. Roe also discussed parenting and the degree warm and nurturing parenting influences the child versus a cold rejecting style. Career counselors can integrate Roe's premises with Adler's techniques involving birth order, early childhood experiences, and family constellation to help clients understand how these facets impact career choice and development.

Limitations and Ethical Issues

As with all theories, limitations and ethical issues need to be taken into consideration when using Adlerian therapy in career counseling. Generally, when a client is seeking career counseling, it is not a long, drawn-out process. The client is looking for a way to regroup or change their career goals. The client may be in the middle of transitioning during mid-life and may not have 2 or 3 months to find employment. Consequently, Adlerian career counseling may not be appropriate for these clients.

Further, the family constellation is very detailed, and several visits may be needed to process all the information before a recommendation can be made by the career counselor. For this reason, some researchers differ on whether Adlerian therapy is or is not considered a form of therapy for a quick solution (Mosak & Maniacci, 2006). Others suggest a lack of empirical support for Adlerian therapy overall and tout the absence of a clear intervention model (Godot, n.d.). These limitations, including consideration of multicultural issues, need to be considered by the counselor when integrating Adlerian techniques with career counseling (Godot, n.d.).

The ACA (2014) Code of Ethics states that all counselors (including career counselors) become multiculturally competent when working with diverse populations. It is important to consider the best approach for the client. Therefore, ethical considerations when using Adlerian therapy in career counseling must be considered when working with a multiculturally diverse client. A multiculturally diverse client may hesitate to offer information through a family constellation. There may be issues of loyalty to family of origin that may not allow the client to speak of the "family." The early recollection of memories may, again, create a sense of betrayal to family of origin members. Therefore, it is imperative that a solid therapeutic relationship be established with the client before venturing into using any of the Adlerian techniques, especially the lifestyle analysis/assessment, birth order assessment, or early memory recollection technique.

CASE STUDY

The following case demonstrates how Adlerian therapy might be integrated when using the lifestyle analysis/assessment family constellation when working with a client who is having difficulty doing well at his or her job.

Jazmine is a 23-year-old Hispanic female who is presently employed at a child care facility. She has been employed in her position of primary caregiver for 2- and 3-year-old toddlers for 6 months, and during that time she has begun to experience stress and anxiety regarding her level of responsibility. She has decided to come see you because she thinks she needs to look for another job. Jazmine enters your office and sits down.

Counselor: (*beginning lifestyle analysis/assessment family constellation parental influence*) Tell me which family member has had the most influence on you when you were growing up.

Jazmine: I guess the one person who had the most influence on my life has been my mother. She criticized me about everything that I did. She still does. That is why I am here. Every time I see or speak with her, she tells me that I am not a good enough teacher to be working with young toddlers. I guess she is right. I am scared every time I go to work and by the end of the day I am so stressed out.

Jazmine's comments exhibit her parental influence (in this case her mother) that has influenced her own conclusions about who she is and what her capabilities are as a person. These comments help you as the counselor begin to see how Jazmine's belief system about who she is and how she views her capabilities are hampering her from enjoying her job.

Counselor: It seems the picture that you have of yourself and of your abilities has been created by a belief system that is not your own. This could be the beginning to seeing yourself through your own eyes rather than through the eyes of someone else, primarily your mother.

Jazmine: I have never thought of that before. I just have always believed that I do not have the capability (*inferiority*) to do well. I try (*striving for superiority*) but I never seem to believe it.

Counselor: You say that your mother has been critical of you when you were a child and continues to criticize you now as an adult. Share a time in your life when your mom criticized you.

Jazmine: Wow! It's interesting that you ask me that question. Last week I got home from work. I still live at home and believe me when I tell you that I do not like living at home. I never get any rest because my mom and I fight all the time. She starts in on me by telling me that I never clean my room, that I never do anything around the house, and that I should not have taken that job. She tells me that I will never amount to much of anything. I just wish she would like me better and stop telling me that I am not good at anything. When I am at work that is all I think about.

Counselor: It seems that your perception of who you are is not your own but has been given to you by your mother. You seem to have taken on the belief system that your mother has about you, rather than you developing your own belief system about who you are as a person. Have you ever thought about it from that perspective?

Jazmine: I never thought about the fact that my belief system was not my own. I just assumed she was right.

At this point in the counseling session Jazmine begins to see the influence that her mother has had on her own perception about self, others, and so forth. Through lifestyle analysis/assessment and family constellation the counselor can help the client see a clear picture of what is real and not real and help the client begin to determine how she wants to live her life as she moves away from her mom's belief system to one of her own.

SUMMARY

Adlerian therapy encompasses a holistic and optimistic view of the human condition (Eckstein et al., 2006). The career counselor operates in different roles: as someone who encourages, as someone who helps the client explore their career path, and as someone who helps the client clarify goals and expectations. Adlerian therapy and techniques can help the career counselor do just that with the client.

Keystones

- This chapter examined Adlerian therapy and included key constructs, including the inferiority complex, striving for superiority, and goal setting. The chapter also examined the three areas Adler believed impacted one's life. These three areas are looking at the self, others, and society, which, according to Adler, can have an immense impact on a client's personal development. This is especially true regarding the family constellation process, which includes the lifestyle analysis/assessment, looking at birth order, and recollection of memories.
- Different career counseling theories and models can be integrated with Adlerian premises in the career counseling process. Theories and models included in the chapter were Krumboltz, Super, and Roe.
- When theory, techniques, and career models are all integrated, the goal of the career counselor is to help the client reach career goals. When using the Adlerian career counseling approach, this means helping the client gain insight into their present and past lifestyle. Once this occurs the client can reeducate and reorient self in the direction of the chosen career path.

Author Reflections

Helping write this chapter has again reminded me why I enjoy Adlerian therapy so much. It allows a person to delve deeper in their personal psyche, along with the journey of discovering who he or she is. The techniques connected with Adlerian therapy, especially the lifestyle assessment and recollection of memories, bring to the forefront untapped issues that may have been dormant for a long time. As we remember from the chapter, Adler's goal was to help a client understand their motivation for their behavior. Using the lifestyle analysis and reviewing early recollections of the client can go a long way in helping the client get a "true" picture of the impact that family constellation had on the development of their personality characteristics and personal beliefs. This, in turn, continues to impact the client's belief of self, others, and society, all areas that impact career and career choices. Adler (1954) stated that the understanding of human nature seems to be indispensable to every man, and the study of its science, the most important activity of the human mind. Let us remember, as counselors, we strive to help our clients understand their own human nature as they progress through their life, including life's career path. —Mary G. Mayorga

As I have examined my own entry into the field of counseling, I've wondered if perhaps some faulty cognition either delayed me from choosing this field sooner or if too heavily engrained distorted self-beliefs wielded a too dissuasive influence from me choosing an entirely different career path. If you're like me and are questioning why you are even reading this book, Adler might be of some help to you. Think back to your own undergraduate abnormal psychology classes. Try to remember the little caveat the author included at the beginning of the text advising you not to diagnose yourself as you read the different chapters on disordered behavior. Self-diagnosis is an all too common problem among entry-level counseling students. Symptoms of psychopathology are often perceived in the self and, most often, these students get it wrong. These texts invite students to seek out the expertise of a competent therapist to guide them through any counter-transferal reactions they might generate as they read each chapter.

With that advice, the author was clearly offering an invitation to seek out sociality, association, and connection to accurately look at your feelings and reactions. Adlerian theory reboots the struggle between isolation and association and, in this case, an untrained student could easily self-pathologize if conclusions were drawn in silent withdrawal or retreat. Adler's gift to this field is that all healing is more productively negotiated through sociality. In other words, if you are questioning if you made the right choice to become a counselor, talk to someone! Please do not stew in a broth of dissonant seclusion. Adler teaches us that all healing and insight are generated through connection and association. Damaging self-doubt is obviated by social investment in others, and all healing and understanding embrace social connection at its core. —Brian Le Clair

Additional Resources

The following resources provide additional information about the content provided in this chapter.

Assessment

Bartholow, R. G., Willhite, R. G., & Brokaw, S. P. (2006). *Lifestyle assessment*. Adler Graduate School. www.transformcma.ca.
   This assessment depicts Adler's lifestyle assessment.

Websites

Alfred Adler Institute of Northwestern Washington: www.adlerian.us
   This site discusses Adler's concepts of birth order in greater detail.

References

American Counseling Association (ACA). (2014). *Code of ethics*. Author.

Adler, A. (1929). *MVTN*. University of Southern Carolina. Retrieved from https://onedrive.live.com/?authkey=%21APuI%2D-JNeeLiVKP4&cid=E7FF4FB363DE19FC&id=E7FF4FB363DE19FC%21500&parId=E7FF4FB363DE19FC%21498&o=OneUp

Adler, A. (1954). *Understanding human nature*. Fawcett World Library.

Adler, A. (2010). *What life should mean to you*. Martino.

Bandura, A. (1977). *Social learning theory*. Prentice-Hall.

Bartholow, R. G., Willhite, R. G., Brokaw, S. P. & Wolf (2006). *Lifestyle assessment*. Adler Graduate School. www.transformcma.ca.

Blair-Broeker, T., & Ernst, R. M. (2019). *Thinking about psychology* (4th ed.) (pp. 447–528. Bedford, Freeman & Worth.

Brennan, J. F., & Houde, K. A. (2018). *History and systems of psychology*. Cambridge University Press.

Brofenbrenner, U. (2005). *Making human beings human*. SAGE.

Carlson, J., & Englar-Carlson, J. (2017). *Adlerian psychotherapy*. American Psychological Association.

Colby, K. M. (1951). On the disagreement between Freud and Adler. *American Imago, 8*(3), 229–238.

Curtis, R. (2010). *Counseling theories: Adlerian therapy*. www.auburn.edu/cspd/fall04/counseling.

Dreikurs, R. (1950). *Fundamentals of Adlerian psychology*. Alfred Adler Institute.

Eckstein, D., Milliren, A., Rasmussen, P. R., & Willhite, R. (2006). An Adlerian approach to the treatment of anger disorders. In E. E. Feindler (Ed.), *Anger-related disorders: A practitioner's guide to comparative treatment* (pp. 257–276). Springer.

Gazzinga, M. (2018). *Psychological science*. Norton.

Godot, D. (n.d.). Adlerian career assessment & counseling. http://davidgodot.com/adlerian-career-assessment-counseling/

Hitchcock, S. T. (2004). *Karen Horney: Pioneer of feminist psychology*. Chelsea House Publishers.

Horney, K. (1992). *Our inner conflicts*. Norton.

Krumboltz, J. D. (2009). The happenstance learning theory. *Journal of Career Assessment, 17*(2), 135–154.

Krumboltz, J. D., Mitchell, A. M., & Jones, G. B. (1976). A social learning theory of career selection. *The Counseling Psychologist, 6*(1), 71–81. https://doi.org/10.1177/001100007600600117

Leong, F. T. L., Hartung, P. J., Goh, D., & Gaylor, M. (2001). Appraising birth order in career assessment: Linkages to Holland's and Super's models. *Journal of Career Assessment, 9*(1), 25–39.

Lundin, R. W. (1996). *Theories and systems of psychology*. D. C. Heath and Company.

Lundin, R. W. (2015). *Alfred Adler's basic concepts and implications*. Routledge.

McWilliams, N. (1994). Psychoanalytic diagnosis: Understanding the personality structure in the clinical process. Guilford.

Milliren, A. P., Evans, T. D., & Newbauer, J. R. (2007). Adlerian theory. In D. Capuzzi & D. R., Gross (Eds.), *Counseling and psychotherapy: Theories and Interventions* (4th ed.) (pp. 123–163). Prentice-Hall.

Mosak, H. H., & Maniacci, M. P. (2006). *Tactics in counseling and psychotherapy*. Brooks/Cole.

Myers, D. G., & DeWall, C. N. (2018). *Psychology* (12th ed.). Freeman & Worth.

Muhlleitner E., & Reichymayr, J. (2007). Following Freud in Vienna the psychological Wednesday Society and the Viennese Psychoanalytic Society 1902–1938. *International Forum of Psychoanalysis, 6*(2), 73–102.

Roe, A. (1956). *The psychology of occupations*. Wiley.

Roe, A. (1957). Early determinants of vocational choice. *Journal of Counseling Psychology, 4*(3), 212–217.

Shulman, B. H., & Mosak, H. H. (1977). Birth order and ordinal position: Two Adlerian views. *Journal of Individual Psychology, 33*(1), 114–121.

Stein, H. T. (n.d.). Questions and answers about classical Adlerian psychology. Alfred Adler Institutes of San Francisco & Northwestern Washington. www.adlerian.us

Stein, H. T. (2004). Adlerian overview of birth order characteristics. Alfred Adler Institute of Northwestern Washington. www.adlerian.us

Super, D. (1953). A theory of vocational development. *American Psychologist, 8(5)*, 185.

Super, D. E. (1957). *The psychology of careers: An introduction to vocational development*. Harper.

Super, D. E. (1969). Vocational development theory: Persons, positions and planning. *The Counseling Psychologist*, 1(1), 2–9.

Sweeney, T. J. (2009). *Adlerian counseling and psychotherapy: A practitioner's approach (5th ed.)*. Routledge.

Sweeney, T. J. & Myers, J. E. (1986). Early recollections: an Adlerian technique with older people. *Clinical Gerontologist, 4*(4), 3–12.

Vaihinger, H. (1911). *The philosophy of "as if."* Harcourt, Brace, and Co.

Verger, D. M., & Camp, W. L. (1970). Early recollections: Reflections of the present. *Journal of Counseling Psychology, 17,* 510–515.

Watkins, C. E. (1993). Psychodynamic career assessment: An Adlerian perspective. *Journal of Career Assessment, 1*(4), 355–374.

CHAPTER

Using Cognitive Behavioral Theory in Career Counseling

Nicole Noble and Logan Winkelman

You had to learn to feel as you do. And what is learned can be unlearned or modified.
—Albert Ellis

lbert Ellis firmly believed that people could impact their emotional state through their choices of thoughts and behaviors (Caserta et al., 2010; David & DiGiuseppe, 2010; Ellis, 1962, 2005). Rather than an individual's thoughts or emotions being the product of some external event or circumstance that occurred, Ellis (2010) proposed that emotions materialized as a result of one's beliefs about the event—not the event itself. Albert Ellis believed we can choose to think in a rational manner that promotes productive, functional thoughts and behaviors. With the premise that individuals can learn to think and feel in a rational, functional manner, Ellis created rational emotive behavioral therapy (REBT), which is a cognitive behavioral theory (CBT) (Ellis, 1962, 2005). Cognitive behavioral theories focus on both internal thought processes and external behaviors (Sheward & Branch, 2012). A central tenant to CBT is that cognitive and behavioral changes reinforce each other. Also, CBT assumes that through changing a pattern of thoughts or behaviors, lasting positive change can be achieved.

Because identifying and obtaining a meaningful career can be an inherently challenging process, engaging in productive thoughts and behaviors is essential to promoting career success (Sheward, 2016; Sheward & Branch, 2012). Due to the ability to reinforce productive thoughts and behaviors, the use of CBT in career counseling can be powerful in helping clients achieve their career goals. Using CBT in career counseling is beneficial because the process of finding a career or transitioning into a new career is full of the need to try unfamiliar activities, increase involvement in social/professional networking opportunities, focus intently on difficult tasks, and cope with a substantial amount of rejection. Further, utilizing CBT can aid clients in tolerating the uncertainty that is typically present in career development (Law et al., 2014). This approach empowers individuals to be in control of their emotional reality through recognizing the choice to practice thinking and behaving in a rational, positive manner, which impacts their careers in all stages of development.

CHAPTER OVERVIEW

This chapter focuses on employing CBT in career counseling. This chapter will begin with an overview of CBT, then connect common dysfunctional/irrational thoughts associated with career transitions, incorporate other career theories with CBT, and finally apply a case study to provide the appropriate context for this theory.

LEARNING OBJECTIVES

After reading this chapter, you will be able to do the following:

- Understand premises of CBT
- Identify examples of dysfunctional/irrational beliefs common among individuals experiencing a career transition
- Recognize how CBT can be integrated with other career counseling theories and models such as social cognitive career theories, learning theory and happenstance, and life span, life space theories
- Explore the use of CBT with case examples of clients experiencing career concerns

Cognitive Behavioral Theory: Theoretical Background and Premises

The origins of cognitive behavioral theory began with Stoic philosophers from Greece and Rome, including Epictetus, Socrates, Plato, and Marcus Aurelius (Beck, 1976; Ellis, 1962, 2005). Their writing suggested that much of human distress occurs not because of unfortunate external factors that befall an individual (Ellis et al., 2010), but rather because the individual has certain distortions of reality (Beck, 1976). The theory began to develop in the late 1950s and early 1960s with Albert Ellis and Aaron Beck. Albert Ellis constructed a theory of counseling originally called rational therapy (1961), which later developed into rational emotive therapy (1962), and finally rational emotive behavioral therapy (REBT) (2010). Ellis (2005) constructed his theory after reading classical philosophers and realizing that most of the philosophers he read "clearly pointed out that people partly constructed their own feelings of anxiety, depression, and rage" (p. 946). Ellis had personal reasons for developing his theory. Growing up he "was worried about innumerable performances and was preoccupied with succeeding at them and avoiding any risks of failing" (Ellis, 2005, p. 945). Similarly, Beck also began his theory as cognitive therapy (1976) and later added the behavioral component, cognitive behavioral therapy (CBT) (Beck & Emery, 1985). Both rational therapy and cognitive therapy originally involved some behavioral components, but the word *behavioral* was not added to the theories until later when both realized the importance of testing negative assumptions through a behavioral component (Beck, 1976; Beck & Emery, 1985; Ellis, 1962; Ellis & Harper, 1961).

CBT primarily asks individuals to question their automatic thoughts rather than simply assume these thoughts as fact. The individual is expected to question their thoughts and then test these thoughts through altered behaviors. By challenging cognitive distortions and engaging in behaviors that test the accuracy of these distortions, an individual is able to change their unproductive cognitive schemas, which are patterns of core beliefs about themselves, others, and the world (Beck, 1976; Ellis, 1962). Several key aspects to CBT are described in the paragraphs that follow.

Interactions Between Environment, Thoughts, Mood, Behaviors, and Physiology

The environment, thoughts, mood, behaviors, and physiology all impact one another. This means if you have a negative thought when you encounter a new environment, such as "This interview will be stressful," then your physiology (e.g., nervous system) may become stimulated. When your nervous system is aroused you may have an increased heart rate, have difficulty taking full deep breaths, and find it strenuous to collect your thoughts. Therefore, what began as a negative thought turns into a heightened physiological state. Next, your mood may become affected. For example, you may think, "I am very anxious right now; it may become impossible for me to answer these interview questions well." Finally, you may start shaking, stumbling over your words, and not behave in a confident manner throughout the interview. This is a common example of how the *CBT Five Areas Model* indicates that our "environment, thoughts, moods, behaviors, and physiology all interact to influence each other" (Sheward & Branch, 2012, p. 5).

CBT as a Brief Intervention

A brief intervention means that CBT is not a time-consuming therapy model that requires the client to participate in years of therapy, but rather asks the client to identify a clear specific concrete goal and works to rapidly make progress toward achieving that goal. After the goal has been achieved, the client now possesses the coping skills necessary to duplicate this approach with other issues they may experience in the future.

The Collaborative Process

A collaborative process between client and counselor allows the client to work with the counselor to identify dysfunctional or irrational thoughts and behaviors that impede their progress in achieving their goals. While Beck viewed the therapeutic process as collaborative and felt it required a strong therapeutic alliance based on acceptance and trust in order to achieve a goal (Beck & Emery, 1985), Ellis valued therapeutic genuineness and viewed errors in thinking as being more important to the client than that of maintaining positive feelings toward the therapist (Ellis & Harper, 1961). In contrast, Beck believed the client would accept feedback from the therapist more readily if the therapist remained approachable, collaborative, and warm throughout therapy.

Remaining Goal Oriented

Remaining goal oriented to solve a specific problem is imperative throughout the process of using CBT because the client needs to tackle one cognitive distortion at a time in order to combat thinking errors successfully. While using CBT, "the therapist may need to translate the patient's vague complaints into specific problems" (Beck & Emery, 1985, p. 180). This specificity assists the client so that they remain focused and ensures the intervention remains brief.

A Here-and-Now Focus

Focus on the here-and-now issues throughout career counseling sessions. Unlike previous interventions such as psychoanalytic therapy, CBT focuses on addressing thinking errors that are occurring in the present (Beck, 1976; Ellis, 1962, 2005). Rather than identifying the root cause of a cognitive distortion, CBT focuses on a present maladaptive thought and questions the validity and usefulness of that present thought. Let us explore a sample client's career situation and how the counselor might help them focus on the here and now in Case Exercise 12.1.

Case Exercise 12.1 John's Self-Esteem

John is approximately 22 years old and in his last semester of college. He is completing a BS in biology with a minor in chemistry. John scheduled a mock interview because he has been selected for a medical school interview; however, he feels discouraged and worried that his experience is not nearly as extensive as his peers. During the interview, John expressed that he doesn't think he will perform as well as the other candidates and, therefore, is worried he will not be selected. His answers tend to focus on his negative attributes rather than strengths. How might you help John reframe his negative thoughts? What techniques could you use to help John focus on the here and now rather than comparing himself to his peers? What other factors would you consider in your approach with John?

Homework Aimed at Changing Thoughts and Behaviors

Because CBT is a brief process geared toward fast improvements, the counselor using CBT will utilize homework in recognizing unproductive thoughts and challenge these thoughts through collecting alternative evidence to battle this thinking. Additionally, many of the homework assignments will be centered on changing one's behaviors. If a client experiences social anxiety, the counselor might suggest the client attend an event where they do not know anyone present. Through practicing changing one's behaviors, the client is able to overcome negative beliefs about the event by realizing it was not as bad as the client anticipated.

Teaching Coping Skills

Teaching the client skills necessary to cope with future issues in a healthy manner is necessary "because cognitive therapy is time-limited (and) many of a patient's problems will remain unsolved at the end of treatment. By the time treatment ends, the patient will have enough psychological tools to approach and solve problems on his own, knowing that the therapist is available for booster sessions if necessary" (Beck & Emery, 1985, p. 172). Guided Practice Exercise 12.1 asks you to consider ways you might help teach a client healthy coping skills.

Guided Practice Exercise 12.1 Healthy Coping Skills

As you read this chapter, you probably noticed that CBT can be very useful in helping clients develop healthy coping strategies to manage their irrational or unproductive thought and behavior processes. How might you implement CBT techniques to teach skills necessary to cope with future career issues in a healthy manner? Because CBT is typically time limited, how might you ensure your clients implement these new skills?

These salient characteristics of CBT make it an ideal approach when working with individuals experiencing career transitions. For example, career counselors using CBT can help their clients, who are likely to encounter challenging situations that may evoke irrational, dysfunctional beliefs, by countering those negative beliefs. Further, CBT allows the counselor and client to work together "to identify and correct maladaptive thoughts and behaviors that are maintaining a problem and blocking its solutions" (Beck & Emery, 1985, p. 180).

Because career transitions often threaten a person's ability to meet their basic needs (e.g., food, shelter, clothing, and safety; Maslow, 1943), individuals may experience heightened levels of anxiety and depression throughout career transitions. Fortunately for these clients, CBT has been empirically supported to be an ideal intervention to treat anxiety and depression along with many other issues (Beck, 2011). From CBT's early inception, it has been used for anxiety disorders and phobias, which may be some of the most common issues encountered in career counseling (Beck & Emery, 1985).

Many career counseling clients express the need to identify one career path at the exclusion of all others. CBT can be beneficial for these clients because they can challenge thoughts and behaviors that interfere with the ability to identify and focus on a single clear goal. Another typical concern for individuals regarding their career is the possibility of facing rejection when participating in career-related activities such as delivering a speech, participating in an interview, or attending a professional organization meeting. The CBT approach offers help to these individuals by reframing the situation. "When people suffer from social anxiety, they often believe that they will behave in a way that is unacceptable to others and that this, in turn, will lead to rejection" (Sheward & Branch, 2012, p. 93). A CBT counselor can challenge this cognitive distortion by asking the client to question whether an individual has to be accepted by others at all times in order to have a productive career. They can also recognize that one career rejection does not apply to all other jobs.

As is commonly the case for individuals concerned with an upcoming interview or presentation that will impact a person's career, "dwelling on the fear makes the threatening situation more salient and more imminent: that is, it brings a distant danger into the here-and-now" (Beck & Emery, 1985, p. 12). Therefore, if an individual avoids a potentially challenging and uncomfortable situation, such as attending a job interview, they will immediately feel a sense of relief at not having participated in the interview. This also means that despite not facing rejection or failure in this instance, they will unfortunately fear the next job interview even more intensely.

Specific Techniques

CBT touts several techniques a career counselor might use to help clients change their thoughts and behaviors. Continue reading to learn additional information on several of these techniques.

Disputing Irrational Beliefs

When transitioning to a new career or engaging in a behavior that may impact the course of a client's career, it is common for the client to experience thoughts that question their ability to appropriately cope with this new experience. These questioning thoughts may appear in the form of irrational beliefs. Irrational beliefs can be defined as unqualified automatic thoughts that include language such as "should," "must," or "ought" and are often generalized core beliefs regarding one's character. Table 12.1 shares Ellis's (1962) 11 original irrational beliefs from his work. This table also shares examples of irrational thoughts related to career issues, techniques, and examples to dispute these thoughts.

TABLE 12.1   **Irrational Beliefs for Career Transitions**

"**Irrational Idea No. 1**: The idea that it is a dire necessity for an adult human being to be loved or approved by virtually every significant other in his community" (Ellis, 1962, p. 61).	
Mind reading: Assuming others are thinking negatively about you	Fix: Identifying alternative explanations for others ambiguous behaviors
Example: "My boss has not spoken to me over the last few days; she must have disliked my report I submitted and not want to have to tell me."	Alternative thoughts: "Maybe my boss is busy and hasn't had time to review the report. Maybe she has something happening in her personal life and doesn't feel like socializing. Maybe she has a big project she is focusing her energy on completing."

"**Irrational Idea No. 2**: The idea that one should be thoroughly competent, adequate, and achieving in all possible respects if one is to consider oneself worthwhile" (Ellis, 1962, p. 63).	
Making demands: Thinking in a rigid manner with terms that express absolutism such as "should," "must," and "ought."	Fix: Appreciating the uncertainty and lack of control that many experiences require. View these experiences as a want, desire, or preference instead of a requirement.

Example: "I must figure out my major this semester so that I can graduate on time or I will have trouble getting my life back on track to achieve my goals."	Alternative thought: "If I am delayed in determining my degree by a semester or two, that will not have a significant impact on the course of my career. It would be better to put a little less pressure on myself now so I can have time and space to make a thoughtful, logical decision rather than rush into a degree that I'm not interested in pursuing."

"Irrational Idea No. 3: The idea that certain people are bad, wicked, or villainous and that they should be severely blamed and punished for their villainye" (Ellis, 1962, p. 65).

Labeling: Viewing self, others, or events negatively	Fix: Engaging in logical thought to reason that no one person or event is entirely negative
Example: "My coworker walked past me and did not smile or acknowledge me; he must just be a rude, self-absorbed person."	Alternative thought: "There are numerous reasons for him not to greet me in the hall; I don't have to label him based on that behavior."

"Irrational Idea No. 4: The idea that it is awful and catastrophic when things are not the way one would very much like them to be" (Ellis, 1962, p. 69).

Mental filtering/discounting the positive: Avoiding considering two sides to an issue and solely paying attention to the negative	Fix: Trying to look for situations that disconfirm your previously held belief
Example: "Although, I received some positive feedback on the progress I was making toward completing my long-term project, it's unlikely that I'll actually complete it on time and correctly, because I struggle with numbers."	Alternative thought: "The feedback I just received lets me know that I'm on track to complete the project."

"Irrational Idea No. 5: The idea that human unhappiness is externally caused and that people have little or no ability to control their sorrows and disturbances" (Ellis, 1962, p. 72).

Fortune telling: Engaging in negative predictions about the future due to lack of information	Fix: Adopting an attitude or waiting to see what the future will bring with the possibility of the future having positive outcomes and a sense of tolerance for the uncertainty of the current circumstances
Example: "I'll get a low paying job and struggle to make a living."	Alternative thought: "Even if my starting salary is less than I would like, I will work hard to hopefully raise it quickly."

"Irrational Idea No. 6: The idea that if something is or may be dangerous or fearsome one should be terribly concerned about it and should keep dwelling on the possibility of its occurring" (Ellis, 1962, p. 75).

Emotional reasoning: Interpreting events based on your emotions	Fix: Recognizing that it's normal to experience some apprehension aro vding a job or beings successful at work

(Continued)

TABLE 12.1   *(Continued)*

Example: "During my upcoming interview that will be held over dinner, I'll be nervous so I'm not going to order the right entree and I'm going to spill food on myself and be a complete embarrassment."	Alternative thought: "There is no perfect item to order and no perfect things to say and behaviors to engage in. My interviewers will know that I'm nervous, but as long as I remain polite and appreciate this opportunity that will go a long way toward helping me navigate this dinner successfully."

"**Irrational Idea No. 7**: The idea that it is easier to avoid than to face certain life difficulties and self-responsibilities" (Ellis, 1962, p. 78).

Low frustration tolerance: Not recognizing the long-term goal is worth some short-term discomfort	Fix: Considering the positive outcomes to engaging in a short-term discomfort
Example: "I don't have the time necessary to extensively study for the GRE."	Alternative thought: "While it's difficult to find the time and energy to study for the GRE, studying consistently for the next few months may allow me to earn a high score. Achieving a high score will increase my odds of being accepted into a graduate program that I'm interested in attending and make getting a scholarship a possibility."

"**Irrational Idea No. 8**: The idea that the one should be dependent on others and needs someone stronger than oneself on whom to rely" (Ellis, 1962, p. 80).

Dependency: Believing others are more capable than yourself and trusting their judgment over your own	Fix: Recognizing that others are more likely to share positive experiences about themselves and that you may be more likely to remember your negative experiences rather than your positive ones
Example: "I don't know what career path I should take; I'll just follow my career counselor."	Alternative thought: "While my career counselor knows about various career paths, they do not know about my interests, skills, personality, and values more than I do, I am better equipped to make this decision than they are."

"**Irrational Idea No. 9**: The idea that one's past history is an all-important determiner of one's present behaviors and that because something once strongly affected one's life, it should indefinitely have a similar effect" (Ellis, 1962, p. 82).

Overgeneralization: Using a few data points to make generalizations that distort your perspective	Fix: Recognizing that this experience maybe an isolated event(s) and does not necessarily have lasting implications
Example: "Because I did not receive this promotion, it is unlikely I will ever receive a promotion with this company."	Alternative thought: "I tried my best to receive a promotion this time; maybe next time an opportunity presents itself, I will have more experience, have made my intentions known, and demonstrated that I am capable of performing the additional responsibilities."

"**Irrational Idea No. 10**: The idea that one should become quite upset over other people's problems and disturbances" (Ellis, 1962, p. 85).

Personalizing: Believing that you are in some way responsible for the negativity of someone or something else	Fix: Acknowledging that not all negative outcomes are your fault and considering other contributing factors
Example: "The meeting today seemed more stressful on everyone; I wonder what I did to cause this heightened stress level?"	Alternative thought: "The team today did appear stressed, but that is to be expected with how close we are to the deadline. While I may have contributed to the stress in some ways, I am not solely responsible for it."

"**Irrational Idea No. 11**: The idea that there is invariably a right precise, and perfect solution to human problems and that it is catastrophic if this perfect solution is not found" (Ellis, 1962, pp. 86–87).

All-or-nothing/black-or-white thinking: Thinking things must happen or should happen in order to be fulfilled	Fix: Engaging in reality testing and trying to consider alternatives that are realistic and flexible
Example: "If I am not offered this job, I'll never be offered any job."	Alternative thought: "There are infinite opportunities and by trying for this position, I'll prepare myself further for future opportunities."

A career counselor may wish to simplify these 11 irrational beliefs by categorizing them. For example, DiGiuseppe (1996) divided them into the following categories: demandingness (DEM), awfulizing/catastrophizing (AWF), global evaluation/self-downing (GE/SD), and frustration intolerance (FI). In response to the categories, Ellis prosed that all irrational beliefs had demandingness (DEM) of self, others, and the world in common (Ellis et al., 2010).

Career counselors may wish to promote alternative rational beliefs in contrast to DiGuiseppe's (1996) four categories. For example, instead of *demandingness*, career counselors can encourage a focus on preferences. Instead of *awfulizing/catastrophizing*, career counselors can use anti-awfulizing and normalizing techniques. Rather than allowing clients to globally evaluate and engage in *self-downing*, they can work toward fostering unconditional self/other acceptance. Instead of *frustration intolerance*, career counselors can support fostering high frustration tolerance. As seen in Table 12.1, these alternative rational beliefs focus on normalizing unfortunate career experiences and increase acceptance of imperfect career experiences.

ABC

The *ABC model* stands for A, activating event (sometimes referred to as adversity); B, belief of the event; and C, emotional and behavioral consequences due to the belief of the event (Sheward, 2016; Sheward & Branch, 2012). The counselor can ask questions of the client to explore whether the client's thoughts are rational or irrational. By asking questions about the event, the counselor can help clients focus on rational thoughts surrounding stressful situations. We will explore this technique further in the case study at the end of this chapter.

Socratic Questioning

To aid in reality testing and increase a client's self-awareness regarding unhealthy thoughts and behaviors, a career counselor can ask *Socratic questions*. These Socratic questions can be designed to help the client recognize thoughts that preceded an event and resulted in an unproductive emotional consequence. Socratic questions might also help the client face demands requested of themselves, others, and their careers when facing negative and unproductive emotional consequences. Case Exercise 12.2 asks you to identify ways you might utilize Socratic questions with a client.

Case Exercise 12.2 Claire's Confidence

Claire is a 30-year-old secondary teacher candidate. She is preparing for the upcoming teacher job fair and has scheduled an appointment because she is concerned her shyness will be a detriment to her performance at the fair and in interviews. Claire is a very bright and creative young woman who easily shares information about her student teaching experience. However, Claire finds it difficult to approach and start conversations with unfamiliar people. Claire is very soft spoken, has difficulty making small talk, and says she comes across as unenthusiastic.

How might you integrate Socratic questions to help Claire identify some of her unproductive thoughts that might be contributing to her lack of confidence while networking? What other CBT techniques could you use to help Claire increase her self-awareness regarding the demands she places on herself and others?

Mock Interviews

Let's say you just received the notification that you have an interview next week for a position you have been dreaming about for years. What emotions are you experiencing? Excitement, nervousness, self-doubt? Practicing for an interview by role-playing sample interview questions with a career counselor offers the client a low-stakes opportunity to engage in a behavioral approach. This feedback can increase the client's self-confidence and improve their ability to remain present focused (Sheward & Branch, 2012). It can also alleviate the tendency to unnecessarily mentally rehearse the next response, self-monitor, and conduct a post-mortem of how the comment impacted the interviewer (Sheward & Branch, 2012). By participating in a mock interview, the interviewee can manage unreasonable expectations.

Counting Automatic Thoughts

When a client is unable to restructure or combat automatic thoughts due to a slurry of repeated anxious concerns, they may still be able to slow down cognitions simply by counting each thought. This process of counting provides the client with the ability to distance themselves from the thought and act as almost a silent observer of the thoughts. Without acknowledging whether the thought is true, the individual can accept that the thought has occurred and acknowledge that their emotional state is a result of the thought, although not necessarily accurate. This counting affords the client the ability to practice mindfulness instead of judging the negative thought and engaging in self-downing as a result of the thought.

Journaling Automatic Thoughts

A career counselor using CBT can assign the homework of recording automatic thoughts daily. In the journal of automatic thoughts, the client can have several columns focusing on "the situation, automatic thought, questioning the evidence, alternative therapy, re-attribution, de-catastrophizing" (Beck & Emery, 1985, p. 205). After the client collects and logs this information for several days, the counselor and client can discuss these automatic thoughts and engage in reality testing. By recording these thoughts, the client is able to recognize that the negative experience was not necessarily the cause of the negative thought. Next, the client is able to label the automatic thought as a false thought. Then, the client can gather data to question whether this automatic thought is true. Finally, the client can consider an alternative thought and work toward reattributing the reason for the situation and de-catastrophize the experience.

Induced Imagery

After a client has participated in mock interviews, to further address any anxiety the client has concerning the upcoming interview a career counselor might devote an entire session to induced imagery. First, the career counselor could invoke a state of calm through breathing and relaxation techniques. Following this technique the counselor may use imagery to positively alter spontaneous fantasies while conducting a walk-through of the interview. As part of this, the client might detail the day of the interview. For example, they may describe detailed aspects such as waking up ready and prepared for the interview, getting ready for the day, driving or traveling to the interview, walking into the building, greeting the receptionist, shaking hands with the interviewers, answering the interview questions comfortably, asking questions of the interviewers, thanking the interviewers, and, finally, leaving the interview. Vivid descriptions invoking the five senses should be used to help clients "recognize the specific details of a feared situation and then reality-test and correct distortions" (Beck & Emery, 1985, p. 212).

Recording Sessions

By recording a session with a client, particularly a mock interview, the client is able to witness their performance and challenge cognitive distortions. Invariably throughout a mock interview, most clients have thoughts at some point, such as "This is terrible. Others can tell I don't know what to say" or "What a horrible response to the question." After witnessing a recorded session, the client can challenge these negative thoughts and see for themselves that their performance was better than anticipated.

Using these techniques from cognitive behavioral therapy in career counseling can help clients understand their internal dialogue, search for themes, and restructure cognitions. Now that we have a firm understanding of these techniques, let us focus on the use of CBT when it is integrated with some of the career theories covered in the first section of this textbook. Specifically, we will cover the integration of CBT with social cognitive career theory (SCCT), happenstance learning theory (HLT), and Donald Super's life span, life space career theory.

The Integration of CBT With Career Counseling Theories and Models

Social Cognitive Career Theories

As mentioned in Chapter 3, SCCT is a relatively new and complex theory created by Lent, Brown, and Hackett (1994). It is heavily influenced by Bandura's (1986) general social cognitive theory, drawing from his concepts of self-efficacy and applying them to career development. SCCT is also influenced by other theorists such as Hackett and Betz (1981), who identified self-concept as a key factor in career development; Holland's (1985) personality typology; and Super's (1990) life span, life space theory; among others. By combining elements of existing career theories, Lent et al. (1994) created a comprehensive framework offering an integrative system of models (e.g., interest development, choice, and performance), which attempt to explain intrinsic and extrinsic factors that influence career development. These models seek to describe (a) how academic and career interests develop, (b) how educational and career choices are made, and (c) how academic and career success is achieved. Central to SCCT, Lent et al. (1994) posited that career development occurs as a result of self-efficacy, outcome expectation, and personal goals.

According to Lent et al. (1994) self-efficacy is influenced and developed through personal performance experiences, vicarious learning, social persuasion, and physiological states and reactions. The level of self-efficacy, that is the strength of self-efficacy, can therefore be increased through successful experiences in a certain domain and decreased by failure in a certain domain. It is important to note that self-efficacy according to Lent et al. (1994) is not universal and can fluctuate according to the specific domain or task. For example, a student majoring in a human services–oriented degree program may have high levels of confidence in their written, verbal, and listening abilities but may feel less confident in their abilities in the areas of math and science.

The second key concept, outcome expectations, is defined as beliefs about the consequences or result of performing a particular task or behavior (Lent et al., 1994). In other words, if an individual were to perform a certain task, what is their perception that they are to be successful in performing said task? Referencing the example in the previous paragraph, the student studying human services who has high self-efficacy in writing, speaking, and listening may expect to do well in tasks that involve these skills. According to SCCT, individuals are more likely to seek out and participate in activities they believe will result in desired outcomes. For instance, if an individual receives recognition or rewards for a certain activity or task, it is more likely that student is to seek out and engage in similar activities. Lent et al. (1994) posited that these two concepts, self-efficacy and outcome expectations, contribute to the formation of vocational interests, which, in turn, lead to engagement in activities that align with said interests. From this engagement in activities congruent with interests, performance outcomes develop. In other words, ultimate success in a particular activity is due in part to an individual's self-efficacy, beliefs, and outcome expectations.

The last key concept in SCCT is personal goals, which can be defined as an individual's intention to pursue and engage in an activity or reach a certain level of performance in an activity. These types of goals are also known as choice goals (e.g., a student pursuing a specific major) and performance goals (e.g., attaining a 4.0 GPA) and are usually consistent with one's personal perceptions of capabilities and expected outcomes. To summarize, an individual is likely to develop interests in activities when they believe themselves to be competent and receive desired outcomes. This combination of events leads to performance attainment and goal setting.

The Integration of CBT and SCCT

The following are considerations a career counselor might make to integrate CBT and SCCT into their approach with a client. For this example, we will consider a first-year undergraduate, first-generation college student who is seeking a degree in engineering. He states that his parents have encouraged him to pursue engineering because it lends itself to a steady and well-paying career. The student is worried about pursuing this degree because he expresses that he does not have the skill set necessary to be successful in the advanced math courses even though he has not taken any college-level math. He does mention that he has performed well in his high school math courses. While the student likes the idea of making "good money" after college, he has doubts about his interests and abilities in the field as he has never actually met an engineer, nor does he know what exactly his future job tasks might entail. Additionally, the student is struggling with the idea of having to "pick his career" so soon without an awareness of all the possibilities available and without taking any major-related coursework.

A career counselor might approach this client by first investigating the student's self-efficacy as it relates to math and discussing his outcome expectations. The career counselor could start by assisting in the development of positive self-efficacy by recognizing the student's previous performance during high school math courses. Next, the counselor might prompt the student to challenge his automatic thoughts or outcome expectations concerning his math ability by engaging in behaviors that test the accuracy of this belief. This might entail suggesting the student enroll in a college-level math course in the upcoming semester. Additionally, the counselor might also suggest learning opportunities to influence his self-efficacy and outcome expectations. For example, he could attend an upcoming engineering job fair hosted by his college where he could learn more about the field of engineering and future career opportunities. The counselor might assign the task of attending the job fair as homework. Completing an interest inventory might be another homework assignment the career counselor could assign. An interest inventory such as the *Strong Interest Inventory* (Herk & Thompson, 2012), could assist the student in clarifying and developing appropriate career goals in accordance with his interests.

Learning Theory and Happenstance

John Krumboltz (1993, 1994, 2009, 2011), creator of learning theory and happenstance, also known as the happenstance learning theory (HLT) believed learning is constant. As discussed in Chapter 3, Krumboltz also believed that unplanned events occur daily and have a significant impact on individuals' lives. Krumboltz defined these unplanned events as happenstance. The primary goal of this theory is to assist clients in helping them find and create satisfying careers and lives for themselves. HLT posits that the consequences of our daily actions cannot always be predicted, but ultimate success is dependent on a client's ability to optimize these unplanned events. HLT emphasizes four main tenets: taking action toward more fulfilling lives, not just a single career decision; fostering learning through assessments, not just job matching; promoting engagement in exploratory actions, not simply talking about past experiences and feelings; and focusing on real-world accomplishments outside of the counseling arena to foster self-efficacy.

Krumboltz (2011) offers a framework from which career counselors can work when implementing HLT. First, the counselor and client must clarify the goal. Contrary to traditional approaches, Krumboltz (2011) states it is not a counselor's role to help individuals choose career paths, but rather to help the clients "create more satisfying lives for themselves" (p. 48). The argument for this approach is that the world is ever changing, and counselors cannot be expected to recommend future occupations. They can, however, help clients find strategies to create more life satisfaction.

The next step a career counselor using this approach might focus on is the conveyance of empathetic understanding. Krumboltz (2011) states that counselors must understand not only the facts of an individual's situation, but their feelings about that situation as well. This must be accomplished or the counselor cannot truly help the client. This tenet echoes Carl Roger's (1958) person-centered approach touting the importance of empathy and unconditional positive regard. The next step Krumboltz outlines is to mutually brainstorm action steps. This process would include developing a list of possible or less possible actions to prompt the client toward more constructive behaviors to improve their situation. After the list is agreed on, the client will select one action to perform at a specific time.

Integrating HLT with CBT

CBT blends well with this approach particularly because of its action-oriented nature. For example, consider a nontraditional student who is coming back to school to get an advanced degree because she has recently been laid off. This client may feel stress of being let go from her job, believe she is out of place compared to the traditional students, and may have low self-efficacy regarding the events that have transpired. A career counselor integrating CBT and HLT might approach this client by first addressing some of her irrational beliefs about these unplanned events while also identifying how her previous job experience can be beneficial toward her new academic and future career goals. The counselor and client would then develop an action plan to help the client create small successful experiences, such as making an A in a course or updating her resume to restore her sense of self-efficacy. Guided Practice Exercise 12.2 asks you to consider what action steps you might assist a client develop that would foster learning and encourage action toward career self-efficacy and satisfaction.

Guided Practice Exercise 12.2 Using CBT With Krumboltz's HLT

As you learn in this chapter, CBT may integrate well with other career theories such as learning theory and happenstance. When integrating these two theories, how might you foster learning and encourage action toward career self-efficacy and satisfaction? For example, let's consider a nontraditional student returning back to school after having been laid off. What action steps might you suggest to this client to assist her in embracing happenstance and acting toward a goal?

Donald Super's Life Span, Life Space Career Theory

Donald Super's theory of career development was covered in Chapter 4. Because the following section considers the integration of Super's life span, life space theory when integrated with CBT, it may be helpful to review Chapter 4 as you read the section that follows.

Integration of Life Span, Life Space and CBT

Because of the developmental aspect of Super's career stages of self-concept, the life span, life space theory works particularly well with brief interventions that focus on promoting positive quick change in thoughts and behaviors such as CBT and SFBT. Super's life span, life space theory provides the client with the opportunity to explore the complexity and dynamic interaction between various life roles that occur throughout their career journey (Coogan & Chen, 2007). Specifically, in order to fully acknowledge the areas that impact an individual's career decisions, career counselors need to consider not only their client's work roles but also their other roles such as citizen, student, leisurite, and so on. (Herr, 1997). These roles carry with them undisputed negative thoughts that can be disputed through CBT.

As an individual's situation changes, their self-concept morphs in response (Super, 1953). This change occurs because people seek fulfillment in all roles in their life (Super & Hall, 1978). This fulfillment, or lack thereof, can help form positive thoughts and a higher-level self-concept, or the reverse can be true. Life span, life space theory helps explain that individuals who have difficulty forming a higher-level self-concept and locus of control may have difficulty in making career decisions (McInnes & Chen, 2011). Perhaps this is because negative cognitions run parallel to levels of self-concept.

To demonstrate how a career counselor can integrate Super's life span, life space with CBT, we will consider an international graduate student who is obtaining her PhD and who, upon graduation, wants to attain a faculty position at a research institution. After managing a small research lab and conducting several studies under the supervision of her faculty advisor, she is reconsidering her goals of working at a research institution. To add to the confusion, while researching, she also taught undergraduate courses and found that lecturing large groups everyday drained her energy. After several years of extremely long workweeks, she is finally graduating but is reconsidering her career goal. She wants to begin a family and does not want to be in such a stressful and competitive environment. Finally, because she is an international student, she must seek sponsorship from an employer to remain in the United States. Due to immigration laws, it is much easier for her to attain sponsorship from a university than from another industry. Our student finds herself anxious and ashamed of her changing career goals, is avoiding others, and is in a state of fear regarding her uncertain future.

Using developmental stages from life span, life space theory, let us first consider her shifting developmental stages. While she was conducting research and teaching courses, our student was in the early stages of establishing her career. Now that she does not wish to conduct research or teach, she finds herself in Super's (1953) stage of exploration where she is seeking new activities. Also, while completing her degree, several of her life roles may have impacted her self-concept. For example, the worker role was too large and stressful, and other roles were too small. She may now have negative cognitions leading to anxiety about positions that parallel a faculty position. Further, now that she has graduated, she is hoping to expand her life roles and add parent. This must be considered when helping with her developmental career needs.

When integrating Super's theory with CBT, you might first recognize the self-downing language she uses when discussing indecision about her career path. Then, you work with her on thought-stopping techniques and ask her to challenge her negative schemes by recording her thoughts. Next, you suggest she focus more energy and time on personal life roles for which she is currently pleased. You can further help her consider her life roles by proposing that she expand her professional network and participate in local professional organizations. In this way, she might learn more about alternative positions. Throughout your work together, the client can focus on negative self-talk and isolating behaviors and set concrete goals. Career counseling may help her remain focused and continue to explore alternative career areas. Guided Practice Exercise 12.3 asks you to consider how Super's life span, life space theory might fit with your own career experiences. Perhaps you share commonalities with the fictional student from this passage.

Guided Practice Exercise 12.3 Super's Life Span, Life Space Theory in Your Own Life

Reflect on the different stages of your life according to Super's life span, life space theory. What stage would you consider yourself to be in at this moment? Additionally, what life roles do you currently identify with? How have these roles influenced your career development? Last, how has your self-concept evolved over time? What were the contributing factors to this evolution? Did some of your past life roles affect your cognitions or self-concept about jobs?

Limitations and Ethical Issues

The use of CBT in career counseling can be difficult due to a few limitations. For example, one of the most notable limitations to using CBT in career counseling is that in order to successfully assist clients with negative cognitive schemes and unproductive behaviors, the clients must share their private, often embarrassing thoughts with their counselor. Because of the time constraints often involved in conducting career counseling, it can be difficult to develop strong rapport with clients and help them feel comfortable sharing these shameful thoughts.

Second, client improvements when using CBT commonly occur through strong time commitments and homework focused on challenging unproductive thoughts and behaviors. Again, due to the often brief nature of career counseling, homework involving the recording of thoughts and thought-stopping techniques may prove to be a difficult task for which to follow up. Finally, CBT focuses on promoting change through an individual's thoughts and behaviors and does not focus on societal problems or family issues that may be impacting the individual's career. Despite these limitations, CBT offers techniques and premises that aid clients. Now, let's turn our attention to such as case.

When working with a client facing career concerns, the following case demonstrates how a career counselor can use cognitive behavioral therapy.

Camille is a 26-year-old Caucasian female who is seeking a job in instructional design, which involves computer programing to create online teaching platforms. Camille is rapidly losing her hearing due to a genetic condition. You, the career counselor, had two sessions with Camille covering resume writing and how to apply for jobs. Camille is coming in for her third session.

Counselor: What would you like to work on today?

Camille: I keep worrying if I'll be able to handle a future full-time professional position. While I certainly learned a lot of information in my classes about my field, there is still tons of technical software I have only a basic knowledge of. What if I can't learn it all? How am I supposed to convince an employer to hire me if I don't believe I'll be able to keep up?

Counselor: It sounds like you are feeling anxious about two things. The first is your ability to perform the functions of the position. The second is the interview.

Camille: Definitely, I couldn't sleep last night because I just kept thinking, "Why did I pick such a difficult field?" I'm probably going to fail at it like I did that difficult software course that I was telling you about last week.

Counselor: Yes, I remember you telling me about that, but as I recall when you retook it you ended up making an A.

Camille: Well that was before I knew I was losing my hearing. It was difficult enough succeeding then; imagine how hard it will be to learn now if I can't hear what they are saying!

In addition to the typical feelings of anxiety that most new professionals have regarding establishing themselves in their career, Camille has the added pressure of coping with this medical issue that will impact how she interacts with others, including others at work.

Counselor: Let's explore your thoughts last night when you were having trouble sleeping. What were you telling yourself about your job search, your ability to contribute to the instructional design field, and your hearing loss?

The counselor wants to begin exploring thought processes that are contributing to the client's negative schemes. By starting the conversation with the most common career concern, finding a job, the counselor hopes to focus on coping skills before tackling the bigger issues of adjusting to life with a disability and seeking accommodations in the workplace.

Camille: I thought to myself, "You're never going to find a job, but if you do, then you're going to fail at it in an embarrassing way because of your hearing."

Counselor: Okay, let's evaluate each of those concerns using the A-B-Cs that we discussed last week. What is the A, activating, event about your finding a job?

Camille: I've been looking for a job for 2 months and haven't found one yet.

Counselor: Good. What is your B, belief, about this event?

Camille: That because I haven't found a job yet, that I won't find one.

Counselor: Is that a rational belief?

Camille: No. I am catastrophizing the situation. Just because I haven't found a job yet does not necessarily mean that I never will.

Counselor: Excellent. So because you have that irrational belief, what is the C, emotional consequence, to that belief?

Camille: I feel sad and scared about my future.

Counselor: It's no wonder you feel that way with those thoughts. Now let's go back to the B, belief, about the event. What would be a more rational belief?

Camille: That I have been searching for a position for a relatively short time, and I'm taking every step that I am aware of to improve my applications such as coming here, submitting more applications, and increasing my job search network through shadowing industry professionals.

Counselor: So, you have higher quality applications and you are submitting a higher quantity as well. You also are challenging your beliefs about your lack of competence in your field by meeting professionals and learning more about the work. So what is the C, emotional consequence, to this new belief?

Camille: I'm feeling more hopeful of my future.

Throughout this session, we can already see Camille becoming more confident and positive surrounding her future. Camille's fears concerning her ability to learn the field, provide for herself, and cope with her disability all still need to be addressed. During the course of career counseling, Camille may also wish to discuss disclosing her disability and seeking accommodations in the workplace. In this brief excerpt, we explored Camille's negative thoughts, but further work, such as assigning homework to improve her behavior, could also contribute to a new outlook regarding the challenges she is currently encountering. The remainder of this session might focus on disputing her thoughts about her competence and her disability. In the next session, the counselor should address disclosure of a disability and seeking accommodations. The Job Accommodations Network is a resource that would further assist with this concern and can be seen at the end of this chapter in the section "Additional Resources."

SUMMARY

CBT is a present, focused intervention that explores an individual's thoughts and behaviors. It focuses on changing patterns of thoughts or behaviors to positively impact emotions and physiological responses to stressful situations such as career transitions or other issues. Using CBT, change is solicited by exploring unproductive behaviors and beliefs that promote undue fear or concern about challenging situations. The career counselor's role centers on questioning automatic thoughts and compulsive, perpetuated behaviors so as to explore external and internal locus of control. While events may be outside the client's control, thoughts and behaviors are believed to be a choice inside the client's control.

Throughout this chapter, we provided elements of the framework of CBT as well as methods to integrate CBT into career counseling. Further, we described the career counseling theories of social cognitive career theories, learning theory and happenstance, and life span, life space, which can be incorporated into cognitive behavioral theories. Advantageous techniques for CBT in career counseling are recognizing irrational beliefs, using the ABC model, asking Socratic questions, conducting mock interviews, counting automatic thoughts, journaling automatic thoughts, inducing imagery, and recording sessions. Cognitive behavioral career counselors seek to promote change through reinforcing positive thoughts and behaviors.

Keystones

- CBT can assist individuals with their career development and career concerns.
- Techniques that promote changing an individual's negative cognitive schemes and unproductive behaviors may be instrumental for individuals experiencing concerns such as anxiety, depression, or lack of motivation for their career.
- CBT requires discussion of personal thoughts and behaviors, which may be challenging for a career counselor providing a very brief intervention with a client.

Author Reflections

An individual's identity and belief about themselves, their lives, and their future is impacted profoundly by their career. I fundamentally believe that in order to feel successful, a person must have a project that is challenging and can benefit others if only in a small way. While a certain level of feelings of self-doubt and anxiety are unavoidable for new professionals or for individuals embarking on a taxing task, an individual can decide not to dwell on negative thoughts and instead appreciate their inherent value as a human being. In every type of job, an individual can choose to see the greater meaning of their work and value their contribution to society. Every moment a person is engaged in productive work, they are choosing to remain focused and believe in themselves and their ability to succeed. CBT promotes the idea that our identities are changing from moment to moment and that we only need to have a current positive thought or engage in a present productive behavior in order to aim toward our goals and be triumphant. —Nicole Noble

Cognitive behavioral theories are some of the most popular in the mental health field; however, when researching for this chapter, it was enlightening to see the utility CBT has in the career counseling arena. As outlined in the chapter, CBT in career counseling integrates well with many other career counseling theories. I believe career counseling is a crucial component to mental health counseling and is often overlooked, particularly regarding the significant psychological distress career concerns can cause when facing issues such as job loss. This example speaks to how careers are so inherently ingrained into our identities and well-being; it is hard to imagine any type of mental health counseling without also considering career counseling factors. Likewise, career counseling should be practiced from the same theoretical and evidenced-based stance as that of other mental health counseling roles, with the same cultural, ethical, and individualized considerations. It is my hope that this textbook demonstrates the necessity for quality trained career counselors and how fulfilling the role of a career counselor can be. —Logan Winkelman

Additional Resources

The following resources provide additional information about the content provided in this chapter.

Useful Websites

The Albert Ellis Institute: http://albertellis.org

The Albert Ellis Institute was established in 1959 and promotes emotional and behavioral health through research practice and training.

The Beck Institute: https://beckinstitute.org/

The Beck Cognitive Behavior Therapy Institute provides training, therapy, research, and resources for CBT.

Job Accommodation Network (JAN): https://askjan.org

The Job Accommodation Network provides information for individuals with disabilities about workplace accommodations, the Americans with Disabilities Act (ADA), and the Rehabilitation Act. It also serves as a free source to receive confidential guidance on disability employment issues.

Books

Sheward, S., & Branch, R. (2012). *Motivational career counselling and coaching: Cognitive and behavioural approaches.* SAGE.

This book walks the counselor through using cognitive behavioral theory and techniques for clients with career concerns.

References

American Counseling Association. (2014). *Code of ethics.* Alexandria, VA: Author.

Bandura, A. (1986). *Social foundations of thought and action: A social cognitive theory.* Prentice Hall.

Beck, A. T. (1976). *Cognitive therapy and the emotional disorders.* International Universities Press.

Beck, A. T., & Emery, G. (1985). *Anxiety disorders and phobias: A cognitive perspective.* Basic Books.

Beck, J. S. (2011). *Cognitive behavior therapy: Basics and beyond* (2nd ed.). Guilford.

Caserta, D. A., Dowd, E. T., David, D., & Ellis, A. (2010). Rational and irrational beliefs in primary prevention and mental health. In D. David, S. J. Lynn, & A. Ellis (Eds.), *Rational and irrational beliefs: Research, theory, and clinical practice* (pp. 172–194. Oxford University Press.

Coogan, P. A., & Chen, C. P. (2007). Career development and counselling for women: Connecting theories to practice. *Counselling Psychology Quarterly, 20*(2), 191–204.

David, D., & DiGiuseppe, R. (2010). Social and cultural aspects of rational and irrational beliefs: A brief reconceptualization. In D. David, S. J. Lynn, & A. Ellis (Eds.), *Rational and irrational beliefs: Research, theory, and clinical practice* (pp. 49–61*).* Oxford University Press.

DiGiuseppe, R. (1996). The nature of irrational and rational beliefs: Progress in rational emotive behavior theory. *Journal of Rational-Emotive & Cognitive-Behavioral Therapy, 14*(1), 5–28.

Ellis, A. (1962). *Reason and emotion in psychotherapy.* Citadel Press.

Ellis, A. (2005). Why I (really) became a therapist. *Journal of Clinical Psychology, 61*(8), 945–948. https://doi.org/10.1002/jclp.20166

Ellis, A., David, D., & Lynn, S. J. (2010). Rational and irrational beliefs: A historical and conceptual perspective. In D. David, S. J. Lynn, & A. Ellis (Eds.), *Rational and irrational beliefs: Research, theory, and clinical practice* (pp. 3–22). Oxford University Press.

Ellis, A., & Harper, R. A. (1961). A guide to rational living. Prentice-Hall.

Herk, N. A., & Thompson, R. C. (2012). Strong Interest Inventory manual supplement. Myers Briggs Foundation. https://www.psychometrics.com/wp-content/uploads/2017/05/strong-manual-supplement-occupational-scales-2012.pdf

Hackett, G., & Betz, N. E. (1981). A self-efficacy approach to the career development of women. *Journal of Vocational Behavior, 18*(3), 326–336.

Herr, E. L. (1997). Super's life-span, life-space approach and its outlook for refinement. *The Career Development Quarterly, 45*(3), 238–246.

Holland, J. L. (1985). *Making vocational choices: A theory of vocational personalities and work environments* (2nd ed.). Prentice-Hall.

Krumboltz, J. D. (1993). Integrating career and personal counseling. *The Career Development Quarterly, 42*(2), 143–148.

Krumboltz, J. D. (1994). The Career Beliefs Inventory. *Journal of Counseling & Development, 72*(4), 424–428.

Krumboltz, J. D. (2009). The happenstance learning theory. *Journal of Career Assessment, 17*(2), 135–154.

Krumboltz, J. D. (2011). Capitalizing on happenstance. *Journal of Employment Counseling, 48*(4), 156–158.

Law, A. K., Amundson, N. E., & Alden, L. E. (2014). Helping highly anxious clients embrace chaos and career uncertainty using cognitive behavioural techniques. *Australian Journal of Career Development, 23*(1), 29–36. https://doi.org/10.1177/1038416213517371

Lent, R. W., Brown, S. D., & Hackett, G. (1994). Toward a unifying social cognitive theory of career and academic interest, choice, and performance. *Journal of Vocational Behavior, 45*(1), 79–122.

Maslow, A. H. (1943). A theory of human motivation. *Psychological Review, 50*(4), 370–396. https://doi.org/10.1037/h0054346

McInnes, T., & Chen, C. P. (2011). Chronic career indecision: Amalgamate career development theories and action research perspectives. *International Journal of Action Research, 7*(1), 80–100.

Rogers, C. R. (1958). The characteristics of a helping relationship. *The Personnel and Guidance Journal, 37*(1), 6–16.

Sheward, S., & Branch, R. (2012). *Motivational career counselling and coaching: Cognitive and behavioural approaches.*

Sheward, S. (2016). *CBT for career success: A self-help guide.* Routledge.

Super, D. (1953). A theory of vocational development. *American Psychologist, 8*(5), 185.

Super, D. E. (1990). *A life-span, life-space approach to career development.* In D. Brown, L. Brooks, & Associates (Eds.), *Career choice and development* (pp. 197–261). Jossey-Bass.

Super, D. E. & Hall, D. T. (1978). Career exploration and planning. *Annual Review of Psychology, 29*, 333–372.

CHAPTER 13

Using Spiritual, Art, and Sand Tray Techniques to Help With Career Discernment

Julie Merriman, Mary Mayorga, Michelle Corvette, Tom Knowles-Bagwell, and Janet Hicks

The best and most beautiful things in the world cannot be seen or even touched-they must be felt with the heart.
—Helen Keller

The opening quote reminds all of us that, as holistic beings, we must often venture beyond things right in front of us if we are to achieve our full potential. Spirituality, art, and play are mediums that have the potential to uncover personal beliefs and reach into the heart and soul of our clients. Since a person's career plays such an important life role, finding this missing piece and using it to heal past career hurts can be vital. Those who understand themselves, exhibit self-efficacy, and are self-regulating have better chances of finding career fit and happiness (Maree, 2016). This chapter discusses methods that are often overlooked when assisting clients and gives us innovative methods for reaching into these client domains. Let us delve into three of these unconventional methods: spirituality, art therapy, and sand tray therapy, as we learn practical ways to help clients with career-related issues.

CHAPTER OVERVIEW

This chapter discusses the use of spirituality, art, and sand tray therapy when conducting career counseling sessions with clients. Techniques are discussed with regard to vocational discernment, career development, and decision making. Limitations are included to ensure an understanding of what is and is not appropriate when using these techniques. Cases and examples are included to illustrate the practical integration of these facets with career counseling.

LEARNING OBJECTIVES

After reading this chapter, you will be able to do the following:

- Understand the origins and background of spirituality, art, and sand tray therapies as part of the vocational counseling process
- Understand new and often unconventional spiritually related techniques for working with clients from all ages
- Understand how art therapy and sand tray therapy can be mediums for impacting a client's career development

Spiritual Practices That Guide Vocational Discernment

Let us begin by discussing spiritual practices with regard to career development. Before we delve into our first topic involving spiritual practices, however, it is important to understand the definition of spirituality and how it applies to career development. Let us examine these aspects.

Spirituality, when examining career development, includes vocational discernment and can be defined through the lens of work value (Wheat, 1991). This includes exploring whether levels of spirituality influence levels of intrinsic and extrinsic work values (Dudeck, 2004). It may also include personal valuing, experiencing or expressions of a larger context or structure in which to view one's life, an awareness of and connection to life itself and other living things, as well as a reverent compassion for the welfare of others (Hood & Johnson, 2002).

Another way to look at spirituality and its impact on a person's career choice is a *calling*. We can think of the word "calling" as a passion or need to do something that fills a person with a deep satisfaction regardless of prestige, money, or power (Dik et al., 2009). In the sections that follow, we will discuss this "calling," along with some basic origins and premises of spirituality that lend themselves to vocational counseling. Once we cover spiritual practices used in career counseling, we will then turn our attention to discovering the career-related practices of art and sand tray therapies.

Overview of Spiritual Practices in Counseling

From the beginnings of civilization, humans have typically assumed the roles they were assigned by the happenstance of their birth, being taught the knowledge and skills necessary for their gender and the role of their family in society. There are many sources that demonstrate how people have chosen or been assigned to a career based on their gender and their role in society, including biblical stories. For example, the story of Ezekiel represents someone who was born into one station of life, the priesthood of Jerusalem, and transforms into another role or vocation, in this case that of prophet to the people of Israel.

Thus, it was during the rise of Christianity that the term *vocation* began to be used to distinguish whether a person lived a life within marriage in the secular world or as a religious person. Consequently, the concept of vocation is rich and has a long and valued history and has its roots in early religious figures (Gregg, 2005). These religious figures include major biblical figures such as Abraham to major figures in the reformation such as Luther and Calvin.

It is important to note that selection of persons for these *vocations* in religious life by families was not unique to the religions of the West, but were also present in Hinduism, Buddhism, Taoism, Shinto, and indigenous spiritualties (Smith, 1991). All of these spiritual beliefs also shaped societal roles by influencing individual values as to what was deemed a "proper" or "improper" career as well as through a person's perception of their calling. One such example of this shaping and finding a calling occurred during the Industrial Revolution.

The Industrial Revolution in Europe and North America during the late 18th and early 19th centuries transformed societies in dramatic ways, including the emergence of new roles in society and the severing of the connection between the family and one's vocation or *career*. As a result of this disengagement, many people of faith began to seek guidance from their traditions as to the selection of paths on which to embark in their careers. The central question of this search was and still is, "What am I put on this earth for?"

As society moved forward, spirituality and religion in career development became primarily focused on understanding the degree for which spirituality and religiousness affected the way individuals navigate career-specific tasks (National Career Development Association, 2006). This navigation of career tasks with regard to spiritual and religious ties is still important today. For this reason, a few career-related spiritual techniques are described in the next section.

Specific Techniques and Integration With Career Counseling Theories

Modern societies, particularly in the West, are characterized by more variety and freedom with regard to decisions of one's vocation and career path (Fox, 1994). Further, the spiritual traditions have resources that may be implemented in service to those who are seeking discernment in this area. Let's look at four such resources, two in the area of assessment and two that may be used in the discernment process.

First, *spiritual autobiography* is a tool often used by spiritual directors and spiritually integrated psychotherapists and counselors to aid persons in the clarification of their sense of "calling" or vocation in life. The spiritual autobiography differs from the standard psychosocial history in its focus on the presence and role of the holy or the sacred in the unfolding life of the individual. Adrian van Kaam (1975) referred to this as the ordinarily occurring "spiritual directors" that are found in a person's life, giving shape and form to that unique individual. The value of the spiritual autobiography as a tool for vocational assessment is its attention to the unique forming of the system of meaning and values that this individual embodies and is seeking to give expression to in his or her vocational decisions.

A second resource for assessment that comes from the spiritual traditions is the *Enneagram*. This is a personality typology that draws on spiritual traditions and is associated with persons as widely ranging as Pythagoras, Gurdjieff, and Oscar Ichazo (Riso & Hudson, 1996). Its value in vocational discernment centers around its identification of personality styles as expressed in passions, virtues, ego fixations, and holy ideas, as well as the way in which all the types are dynamically related in such a way as to reveal wisdom to the individual inquirer when properly accessed. It should be noted that the Enneagram is a complicated instrument that requires advanced training to implement competently in practice.

The third resource that the spiritual traditions offer is a technique that may be called *spiritual conversation*. Much like the competent psychotherapeutic conversation, the spiritual conversation is characterized by accurate empathetic engagement, unconditional positive regard and client focus. Unlike the typical psychotherapeutic conversation, however, the spiritual conversation attends to the presence and role of the sacred in the life of the client. The objective of the spiritual conversation is to aid the client in connecting with the sacred in her or his life more closely or to remove career obstacles to that connecting that may emerge along the way.

Finally, one of the most popular techniques appropriated from the spiritual traditions as applied to the counseling field is *mindfulness meditation*. The usefulness of this technique in the medical and psychotherapeutic fields has been researched and documented extensively (Brown et al., 2015). In the task of vocational discernment, mindfulness meditation is of value as a way of clearing the mind of mental clutter that distracts from achieving clarity of vision regarding the question, "What am I put on this earth for?" It also is a way of soothing the anxiety that accompanies the raising of such a question. It is important to let the client guide you as to whether they would like to use spiritual practices as part of counseling. Spiritual practices are used only in conjunction with multicultural and ethical standards of practice. Guided Practice Exercise 13.1 asks you to consider how you might use meditation and/or other spiritual techniques to help your clients facing career challenges.

Guided Practice Exercise 13.1 Spirituality

Suppose your client wants to discuss spiritual beliefs as part of the career counseling session. Which techniques as described in this section might you feel comfortable using? Discuss how you might use each technique based on client issues as appropriate/not appropriate. What additional training might you need to best use these practices? When would you avoid discussing spirituality or using spiritual techniques to assist a client? Be sure to review the ASERVIC competencies listed in the "Additional Resources" section of this chapter as you formulate your answers.

Art Therapy

Art therapy is defined as a mental health profession utilizing creative processes to improve and enhance the physical, mental, and emotional well-being of individuals of all ages and backgrounds (Gussak & Rosal, 2016). By developing a range of creative expressions, art therapy may help individuals and groups resolve conflicts/problems, cope with depression, increase self-awareness and self-esteem, develop interpersonal strategies, manage behaviors, reduce stress, and achieve career-related insights. Before delving into career-related issues, let's discuss the basic foundations of art therapy that lead to better understanding of art-related career techniques.

Theoretical Overview

As early as World War II, art therapy was used with veterans and children through the work of Franz Cizek, Florence Cane, and Viktor Lowenfeld (Gussak & Rosal, 2016). Cizek posited that children's artworks could reveal the inner workings of the mind in a spontaneous manner. Similarly, Cane developed methods that included movement and sound in addition to two-dimensional art such as painting to help children freely create images and foster creativity. Lowenfeld (1957), in his groundbreaking book, *Creative and Mental Growth*, argued that a child's intellectual development was integrally correlated to creative development. This synergy between art and psychology became accepted as a field of research and application.

With the founding of the American Art Therapy Association in 1969, shared knowledge from professionals working in the field developed standards of art therapy education and practice. By 1975, *Guidelines for Education and Training* were established by the association, and master-level education programs were created as part of university curriculums (Rubin, 2016). So, what does art therapy look like? How is it done?

Art therapy embodies the process of art making to facilitate reparation and recovery through a form of nonverbal communication with thoughts and feelings. Thus, the therapist's focus is on the therapeutic needs of the person to express themselves and not on any artistic merit or end product. Art therapy is an exploration of connecting the creative processes of expression with the ability to share experiences through image or art making. In the process of making art, decisions about which colors are appealing, which textures are enjoyable, and how to navigate a blank page or space helps a client increase their self-confidence, esteem, and ability to express themselves. By being absorbed with the tasks at hand, an individual may experience *flow* (engagement to the point of being in a near meditative state) and well-being (Csikszentmihalyi, 2009). Thus, art making allows a connection to inner selves and the others in the world, which may help in overcoming feelings of isolation and depression that impede career development. Through the processes of making choices and being creative, self-awareness to colors, light, and details around us begins to reshape how we see ourselves, allowing us to have an identity separate from our illnesses, diseases, and other issues impacting career development.

Art With Children

Children often are unable to verbally articulate experiences such as crisis, violations, abuse, trauma, or stress that impact the career development process (D'Amico, 2017). Art therapy is one way of allowing a visual communication without words to construct a safe space for their career fantasies, feelings, and experiences. For example, children may express ideas related to Ginzberg et al.'s (1951) stage of fantasy (as covered in Chapter 4) during art exercises. These revelations can be discussed and used to further children's ideas, career exploration, and development. When guided by a counselor, children are often able to develop imaginative narratives about elements located in a visual exercise that reveal significant details about their feelings, perceptions, and worldviews. Case Exercise 13.1 asks you to consider the use of art with a child having difficulty expressing career fantasy.

Case Exercise 13.1 The Case of Jenny

Jenny is an 8-year-old girl who, when asked to describe her career desires, states, "I don't know." It seems clear that Jenny is confused and unable to verbally describe her fantasy. How might you use art to help Jenny better understand career possibilities? What activities would you have her do and why? It may help to review the previous sections as you answer.

Art With Families

Because career happiness affects the family system and the family system impacts career development, group, family, and couple art therapy may be helpful when used in conjunction with individual career counseling (Malchiodi, 2012). Group, family, and couple art therapy are forms of nonverbal communication and expression where the benefits of social support within a group help create an overall supportive environment. Family art therapy, in particular, offers a shared learning community in which family members are asked to express themselves through visual art making to understand interpersonal dynamics and explore ways to interact more effectively. The opportunity for communication, interaction, negotiation, and observation among family members during the art making allows for curative potential to emerge, which addresses decision making, instilling hope/support, permitting interaction, seeing universality (others have similar problems/experiences), sharing mutual concerns, and reflecting altruism (positive and active exchange). Family issues and their impact on career development will be discussed in greater detail in Chapter 14.

Integration of Art With Career Counseling Theories and Models

Marriage and family therapists, counselors, educators, health professionals, social workers, psychiatrists, psychologists and others utilize art therapy with children, adults, and families. Since art therapy is a synthesis of multiple disciplines such as art, psychology, medicine, and education, there are numerous approaches that have emerged over the last 60 years (Clark, 2017; King, 2016; Malchiodi, 2012; Rappaport, 2009; Rubin, 2016;). Psychoanalytic, analytic, object relational, humanistic, cognitive behavioral, mind-body, solution-focused, narrative, expressive, and multimodal approaches have been developed and integrate well with career theories. This is by no means an exhaustive list of approaches, but rather an attempt to highlight some of the more articulated approaches in vocational discernment. In practice, most professionals use more than one model or theory in their work, depending on the client, setting, or situation.

Psychoanalytic and Analytic Art Therapy and Ginzberg and Colleagues

This approach is based on Freud's idea that art expression is a reflection of the art maker's unconscious and the Jungian concept that art could bring out the internal world of an individual if the conscious and unconscious were in dialogue with each other in a psychic equilibrium. It was developed from statements in therapy where the client alludes to the idea that they do not know how to say it, but they could draw it. The approach has potential to reveal unconscious career fantasies as described by Ginzberg et al. (1951) in Chapter 4.

Object Relational Art Therapy and Ginzberg and Colleagues

This approach developed from observations with children, objects, and meaning making. Winnicott's (1953) *transitional space* (where no clear distinction exists between inner/outer reality) and *transitional objects* (where an actual object such a blanket becomes imbued with meaning beyond what it is in reality) emerged as concepts to help children bridge subjective and objective realities. This process might be helpful when working with youth transitioning from Ginzberg et al.'s (1951) fantasy to tentative stages as career development goes from subjective to concrete.

Humanistic Art Therapy, Super, and Maslow

These approaches centered around models of existential therapy, person-centered therapy, Gestalt therapy, and transpersonal therapy and allowed life problem solving, self-actualization, and self-transcendent outcomes to assist the individual in transforming themselves into authentic expressions through art modalities. The humanistic approach relies on creativity as a means of experiencing and actualizing human potential as a healing agent. Donald Super's (1957) premises based on the development of self, as discussed in Chapter 4, may coincide with this approach as biological and psychological factors are transformed into authentic career expressions.

Expressive Art Therapy and Multimodal Art Therapy and Diversity

These approaches permit the ability to cross disciplines to better serve the client. Expressive art therapy allows for the integrative and therapeutic use of art, music, dance, movement, drama, poetry, and writing to link back to cultural and traditional world healing practices. By fostering awareness, emotional growth, and enriching relationships with others, clients are able to explore unknown facets of themselves, their careers, and their communities through nonverbal communications and achieve insights. Multimodal or intermodal approaches allow moving from one art form to another to be acceptable and encouraged. Integrative art activities combining art making and movement offer creative experiences through which individuals are able to express career-related thoughts, feelings, cultural strengths, and emotions nonverbally. In this way, diverse groups, such as those mentioned in Chapter 7, can embrace the curative potential of the creative process and potentially strengthen career decision making and motivation.

Career-Related Art Therapy Settings

Art therapy is adaptable to numerous situational contexts and settings. The list that follows offers some of the programs where art therapy coincides with career development and job-related issues.

Schools

Behavioral intervention coupled with educational and career goals pave the way for helping students of all ages with managing social skills, emotional concerns, cognitive abilities, career discernment, and behavioral barriers. An assessment tool called the *Levick Emotional and Cognitive Art Therapy Assessment* is available to help guide counselors (Levick, 2009). Since art therapy is often facilitated with students who have already experienced challenges in general education settings, using an assessment tool may help in addressing students' social, emotional, behavioral, and cognitive success relating to academia as well as career development.

Rehabilitation Centers

Working with a team of physicians, nurses, therapists, pathologists, case managers, and so on, an art therapy approach requires collaboration among everyone involved with the patient/client. Due to the average duration of stay hovering between 2 weeks and 1 month, it is imperative for open communication with all members of the team to help focus on how art therapy may be utilized in a given time constraint. Likewise, patients have varying medical and mental health concerns. Some of the approaches with art therapy may help reduce anxiety, engage in other rehabilitation activities, manage chronic pain, become reoriented to time/place, improve motor coordination, increase motivation, and allow for self-reflection and awareness and an overall increase of well-being, all factors tied to attaining or maintaining gainful employment and/or mastering life skills (Cox, 2016).

Prisons

Art therapy offers inmates unique connections to their inner emotions of pain, loss, and depression, as well as expressions of hope for the future. Since inmates may avoid therapy programs where weaknesses and vulnerabilities might be perceived, it becomes tantamount to observe and respect the privacy and rules of the correctional facilities (Gussak, 2013). Art therapy may be approached as a means of "sale" in the formation of murals, craft shops, decorated letters, tattoos, and so on as to accommodate the benefits of creation in prison systems. There are a limited number of art tools that are permitted in correctional facilities, which will establish precedent for the counselor. Art therapy offers inmates the ability to diminish pathological symptoms, mitigate instinctual impulses, and improve mood and socialization needed for job placement upon release. See Chapter 7 to review these specific issues as faced by ex-offenders in greater detail.

Specific Techniques

Art therapy requires a toolbox of supplies, creative immersion activities, and the ability to be flexible based on the setting, participants, and objectives (Buchalter, 2017; D'Amico, 2017). The following outlines considerations of supplies, two-dimensional projects, three-dimensional projects, photography, mixed media/collage, digital media, and reflective image journaling.

Supplies

Materials for art therapy are adjusted according to skills, concepts, age appropriateness, mindfulness, and settings. By considering the activity and outcome, the client will be able to be observant, descriptive,

TABLE 13.1 **Art Therapy Materials**

Generic Art Materials	Specific Materials
Boxes	Shoeboxes, various sized boxes (extra small to medium)
Brushes	Assorted sizes with synthetic brush (small, medium, large), sponge brushes (small)
Clay	Modeling clay, ceramic clay, Sculpey
Collage	Feathers, buttons, found objects (umbrella, small mirror, whistle, toys), dried flowers, magazines, newspapers, glitter, beads, ribbons, stickers w/animals, faces, ocean creatures
Cups	Small plastic cups, stackable for water
Drawing materials	Graphite pencils, colored pencils, charcoal pencils, charcoal sticks, assorted markers (thin-fine tip and thick-broad tip), chalk pastels, oil pastels, crayons
Glues	Glue sticks, Elmer's glue
Media	Camera/phone, computer
Nature	Twigs, branches, sticks, rocks, stones, shells
Painting	Poster paints (tempera), acrylic paint, watercolors (most paints may be purchased in sets of colors: red, yellow, orange, blue, green, purple, brown, black, white)
Palettes	To mix paint in try a small/medium muffin tin, aluminum pie plates, plastic paint tray
Paper	Assorted sizes of white paper, colored paper (construction), watercolor paper, colored tissue paper, recycled cardboard, poster board, tinfoil, butcher paper to protect surfaces, small sketchbooks, journals (for recording thoughts/reflections)
Scissors	Children's safety scissors and regular adult scissors
Soap	Dishwashing liquid soap, hand soap (bar)
Sponges	For cleaning and for painting textures
String	Twine, various colors of yarn
Tape	Masking tape, scotch tape, blue painter's tape

participatory, open-minded, nonjudgmental, and actively engaged in the creation of art therapeutic images or creations. Table 13.1 details specific materials that might be used when incorporating art into career counseling.

Techniques

Art therapy is about providing insight and visual understanding through expressions of creativity. Interpretations, assessments, and diagnosis are not the focus and are not typically conducted during art therapy. As illustrated in the following widely used career therapy techniques, the emphasis is on insights of meanings, possible visualizations of the problems, concerns or issues, symbols used to represent such situations, and visual progress while working through images or creations.

Technique 1: Free drawing or scribbles. Using paper, pencils, markers, oil pastels, or other dry mediums, work as quickly as possible to help the client create a free drawing or scribbles that channel their inner connections to their emotions about job issues or placement. A prompt might be, "What emotions are closer/further from you today?" or "Which colors are able to speak to you about your emotions?" Allow enough time and guidance for the client to create lines, forms, and shapes on the paper. Then slow down the process and begin to help them see if any spontaneous objects or forms are being visualized. See if they could slow down and then go back into the drawing with one color and perhaps fill in around some of the shapes to help them stand out more. This exercise may also be repeated using the nondominant hand and/or both hands.

Technique 2: Mandala creations. Using drawing or painting materials and paper, have a sheet with a round circle drawn in the center of it, about 8 to 10 inches in diameter. Prompt the client by asking them to focus on a career-related problem and have them begin by selecting colors to express their reflection. Encourage lines, shapes, circles, abstractions, and personal expressions of color to emerge from the first prompt and then, about halfway through, ask the client to imagine their own transformation of healing from the problem and encourage them to try a new color of expression and mark making within the mandala. This technique may help them to visualize their "sacred circle" and center themselves from within.

Technique 3: Creating a safe space. This activity may be useful for clients expressing anxiety about job interviews or when giving career presentations. Using a variety of materials, select the ones appropriate for your client to express their concept of a safe interview or job space on a sheet of paper or even in clay. Allow them to draw what a safe space would look like, items found within the area, and colors that could help them feel better. Discuss with them their thought process and ask them to walk you through the space. This technique may increase feelings of security and trust through information sharing and centering.

Technique 4: Create a self-soothing image book or "how I see myself versus how the world sees me." This activity may be especially helpful for clients who have difficulty maintaining employment or who have anxiety about how they are perceived in interviews or in the job setting. Using collage materials or even media/camera-based materials, allow the client to have two sheets of paper to cut, tear, and glue and have them create one image of how they view themselves and another image of how they believe those at work view them. A possible venue for discussion at the end includes unpacking how they experience the two images side by side and how they might begin to construct ways of working toward feeling whole or complete. A variation includes having the client capture photographs of themselves in both forms of viewing themselves and having a discussion about the images.

Technique 5: Feeling maps to help with trauma or depression. This activity may be especially helpful for clients facing depression after job loss, who faced sexual harassment trauma, or outside traumas impacting the client's career. Using the drawing or painting materials, prompt the client to create a map of their inner feelings and emotions concerning their problem. Ask them to explore anger, sadness, fear, joy, love of others, and love of self. See if they could use a different color for each area of the map/feeling and then see if they could connect the parts to the whole. Discussions help cognitively reprocess thoughts and allow for the emotional control necessary for job exploration and attainment or even necessary legal follow-through.

Technique 6: Building a mountain. Using drawing or painting materials, have a client create an image of a mountain or mountains representing career impediments. Once complete, ask the client to move the mountain or to change it so that it is no longer in the way. In a group setting, encourage personal approaches from each person and free expressions of creativity.

Technique 7: Symbolic tree. This technique may assist clients needing improved self-efficacy or self-esteem in order to follow through with job exploration, interviewing, and placement. One such example might include those recently leaving abusive relationships and, thus, needing immediate income and job placement. Because these clients may have internalized negative self-defeating thoughts based on their previous environments, use drawing materials and have the client draw a tree that represents themselves. Prompts might include "What type of tree is it?" "Is it tall/short, strong/weak?" "Does it have roots?" "Has it weathered many storms?" Allow them to add to it or to take away for the drawing as you discuss it with them. Discuss positive aspects of their drawings that relate to personal strengths and abilities.

Technique 8: Meaningful mask. Using a premade mask, painting, and collage materials, encourage the client to create a mask that they feel represents how they are feeling or what they wish the world could see about them. Allow them to express their creativity with additional mixed media and try the mask on near the end of the technique. This helps foster an awareness of inner strength and may allow for reflection of where they were to where they hope to be one day.

Sand Tray Therapy

Now let's turn to another creative method for assisting clients with career development, sand tray therapy. We will start with a theoretical overview and move to more specific information regarding how to use this medium with clients.

Theoretical Overview

Sand tray therapy is a form of play therapy that helps a client move past resistance by tapping deeply into one's subconscious psyche (Eberts & Homeyer, 2015). When using sand tray therapy as a method, clients are given a set of given miniatures in a tray of sand (e.g., sand tray) and asked to arrange them with counselor facilitation. The symbolism of the miniatures may be powerful and, often, surprising to the client. To best understand these symbolic techniques, let's turn our attention to the history and background of sand tray therapy.

History of Sand Tray Therapy

Sand trays and their therapeutic application date back to the late 1920s. However, it was not until the 1950s that Swiss Jungian analyst, Dora Kalff, named it *sand play* and developed it as a Jungian modality. Kalff was introduced to sand tray play studying under the British pediatrician Margaret Lowenfeld, who originated a modality she called *world play* (Labovitz Boik & Goodwin, 2000). Originally, world play involved children playing with miniature toys in sand and water during counseling sessions and, later, developed into the world technique described later in this chapter.

Kalff (1980) expanded on the original idea of world play and modified it by developing another modality of sand play based on Jung's theory. She wanted to promote healing and wholeness by engaging the psyche of the child during sand play (Labovitz Boik &-Goodwin, 2000). According to Badenoch (2008), Kalff was spot on in her theory as sand play, now known as sand tray therapy, has been found to be neurologically sound: "[Sand tray therapy's] notable ability to awaken and then regulate right-brain limbic processes can make it a powerful way to address painful, fearful, disassociated experiences" (p. 220).

Modern Sand Tray Therapy

Today, sand tray therapy is used with a wide range of clients, from children to the elderly, and with individuals, couples, families, and groups (Homeyer & Sweeney, 2005). Over the last 10 to 15 years, the modality has become popular with an increasing number of mental health professionals (Homeyer & Sweeney, 2011). It is easy to understand the rise in popularity as one considers how many senses are engaged with this modality, its applicability to career counseling, its relevance to all ages, and its freedom to choose from among the two dominant approaches, world view and sand tray.

The World Technique

Today, the "World Technique" (Lowenfield, 1979) represents a psychodynamic viewpoint, allowing for the counselor to actively interpret and verbalize perspectives of the client's sand tray creations and processes. The counselor offers regular feedback for each choice the client makes in miniatures, placement, and manipulation (Isom et al., 2015). Feedback is made up of questions and statements such as, "You put the horse there?" "You did that differently this time?" or "You worked really hard to get that just like you wanted it."

The Sand Play Approach

The sand play approach places the client as the expert in constructing and determining meanings and creates a safe space for the client's expression (Kalff, 1980). In essence, the sand and counselor are the container for the client's emotions, thoughts, and feelings. The counselor is an observer making very few, if any, interpretations. The focus is on facilitating meaning of the finished sand tray. This means the counselor's role is to help a client discuss the significance of choices made during the building of the sand tray (Homeyer & Sweeney, 2005). Once the client has created the tray, a statement like "Tell me about what you created" prompts the processing of the tray.

Sand Tray Logistics

Sand tray therapy requires proper training and supervision along with numerous tools. To conduct sand tray therapy, a counselor needs a shallow, rectangular sand tray, measuring 28 1/2 inches by 19 1/2 inches and 3 inches deep filled with sand of any desired colors. The sand tray usually has a medium-blue lining made out of either sheet metal or plastic so that, by shaping and moving the sand away, the client can create a blue patch that can represent a river, lake, or ocean.

Miniatures are also used in sand tray therapy. Although the number of miniatures from which clients may select varies, there are rarely fewer than 300 options available and they are purposely selected by the counselor (Landreth, 2002). These miniatures are grouped via shelving, and the client is free to unhurriedly choose as few or as many as desired. Further, these miniatures are used to represent a variety of emotional themes, conflictual elements, work activities, and roles as related to career development. Because career selection includes an element of hope, items such as wishing wells and magic lamps might be included as well as a variety of employment-related buildings.

Steps in the Process

Homeyer's and Sweeney's (2011) six-step protocol for sand tray therapy sessions includes the following steps: (1) room preparation; (2) introduction to client; (3) creation of the sand tray; (4) post-creation processing; (5) sand tray cleanup; and (6) documenting the session (Homeyer & Sweeney, 2011). The therapeutic work begins in stages 2, 3, and 4, with silent communication between the counselor, client, and sand tray along with the interaction of feelings, minds, awareness, metaphors, and meaning. During steps 2, 3, and 6, space is created for the client to expand in self-awareness. Steps 1 and 6 are completed without the client. Step 5 is usually completed once the client leaves; however, this depends on theoretical and/or philosophical considerations of the counselor (Eberts & Homeyer, 2015). Issues revealed during the sand tray session can be processed with the client as related to career decision making, values, interest, self-efficacy, and other factors.

Sand Tray With Children

For children, sand tray therapy has special benefits. Children often lack the vocabulary to put their feelings and experiences into words. By placing his or her world in the sand tray, the child can express that which cannot be put into words (Homeyer & Sweeney, 2011). The imaginations of children come to life as they build their trays, thus offering the ability to uncover Ginzberg et al.'s (1951) career fantasies (see Chapter 4). These fantasies can then be discussed and explored.

Sand Tray With Adults

While the literature on using sand tray therapy with adults for career counseling is sparse, research regarding the use of sand tray with career reflection shows promise. Mayes, Mayes, and Williams (2004) conducted a study using sand tray therapy to facilitate career reflection in teacher and administrator education to examine reasons for entering the profession. These authors examined the dynamics motivating an individual's decision to enter the profession and the purpose leading to the choice (Mayes et al., 2004). Sand tray therapy was employed to help explore these decisions at deep levels. The study inferred that sand tray therapy helped the participants experience greater self-awareness, empathy, and fulfillment in their work.

Sand Tray With Families

Homeyer and Sweeney (2005) inform that studies about the use of sand tray therapy for issues in family counseling is sparse; however, there are documented cases of success in the familial arena (Isom et al., 2015). Research suggests sand tray therapy is an effective approach for families as it contains accessibility and developmental considerations and is culturally inclusive (Isom et al., 2015). Frequently, families seeking therapy struggle with communication and adults may bring issues to work. Resolving these issues through sand tray therapy encourages problem-solving and coping strategies that affect the entire system, including the job environment (Homeyer & Sweeney, 2005).

Integration of Sand Tray Therapy With Career Counseling

Sand tray therapy may be a remarkable tool for clients stuck in old patterns of non-helpful problem solving and for those needing insight into a number of career processes and may assist clients with career decision making. Sand tray therapy allows a venue for the client to create new perspectives by presenting possibilities in a three-dimensional vision field (Homeyer & Sweeney, 2005). This method allows for exploration of internal and external factors, such as career desires and employment opportunities, and may support clients' career decisions. As part of this process, counselors need to empathically and relationally facilitate symbolic and metaphorical communication (Markos et al., 2008). Thus, over time, growth and awareness created during sand tray sessions are reviewed and processed by clients with the counselor's assistance, potentially leading to decision making about life and career issues (Markos et al., 2008).

Sand tray therapy can also be used to help process and make meaning of clients' interest inventories and other career assessment tools, career goals and challenges, family challenges, self-view, and culture (Swank & Jahn, 2018). Values, interests, personality, and skills revealed on inventories are especially important to contemplate during sand tray career exploration. Super (1957) regarded interests as a marker of underlying values and advocated for interests and values to be contemplated together in career decisions.

Career Counseling Solution-Focused Sand Tray

One modality integrating solution-focused brief therapy (as discussed in Chapter 10) with career counseling and sand tray therapy includes a treatment called career counseling solution-focused sand tray (CCSFS) thearpy. CCSFS uses client strengths as part of the problem-solving process. The client can process career dilemmas being experienced while choosing a career, changing a career, or overcoming unhappiness in a career. The synthesis of sand tray with solution-focused theory and techniques has the potential to create a richer experience for a number of career clients who need help beyond that offered through traditional talk therapy.

Solution-focused (SF) and sand tray therapies share underlying principles that stress resiliencies, strengths, and possibilities without the restrictions of traditional talk therapy. Both SF and sand tray therapies empower clients to be experts of their lives by building on areas of strengths while appreciating areas of resistance (Taylor, 2009). Both therapies focus on interpersonal processes, not necessarily techniques. These interpersonal processes are paramount during career counseling as a client is trying to discover not only a career fit, but also his or her purpose in life (Taylor, 2009).

When implementing CCSFS, the career counselor relies on the three methods used in SF to discover and enhance strengths while forming client goals. These SF methods, as discussed in Chapter 10, are complimenting, relationship questions, exception-finding questions, and scaling questions. These techniques can be illustrated by utilizing miniatures in the sand tray while also integrating SF techniques into the process (Berg & De Jong, 2005). Each of these SF techniques is briefly reviewed in Table 13.2.

TABLE 13.2 **Solution-Focused Techniques**

Technique	Example	Description/Purpose
Direct compliments	The career counselor might say to a client who is unemployed due to a layoff, "I'm impressed by your upbeat attitude and the number of career surveys you completed this week."	Compliments in CCSFS serve to increase the client's feelings of empowerment. A direct compliment discerns what actions the client is taking in the course of their career that are successful. This type of compliment has to be specific and based on career facts that the client may or may not grasp.
Indirect compliments	An example of an indirect compliment might be, "I'm curious what your wife would say about the things she thinks are your strengths."	A counselor supports the client in recognizing strengths or resistances by pondering what others may say or notice about him or her. The counselor would rely on indirect compliments to clarify strengths conducive to particular career fields.
Self compliments	The client might say, "I really did do that well."	Positions the client as the expert of their strengths, successes, and resistances (Berg & De Jong, 2005).
Direct relationship questions	A career counselor might ask a client about the challenges of meeting the requirements for becoming a lawyer by saying, "Tell me who might be the first person to comment when applying for law school. What comments would he or she make?"	Helps the client understand how they perceive others' viewpoints and behaviors about career challenges. CCSFS utilizes questions to help clients understand behaviors and how changes in those behaviors affect their relationship with their career.
Relationship challenge question	The career counselor would ask a question similar to this: "What will it take to prove to your [insert name of significant support person] that you can make a decision about your career and begin pursuing this career?"	The client is required to prove him- or herself to the significant person with a challenge. The career counselor is working to help the client recognize strengths that will help the client with the career challenge.
Significant support person relationship questions	A client wanting to be a lawyer might be asked, "I would like for you to imagine what [insert name of significant support person] will say once you get accepted into a law school."	Places emphasis on the client's significant support person's point of view. This helps the client recognize the beliefs they hold about this person's support.

(Continued)

TABLE 13.2 *(Continued)*

Technique	Example	Description/Purpose
Exception questions	The career counselor might ask the client to create (in the sand tray) a time when theyfelt less anxious about their career. The client delves into many details such as where they were, who they were with, and what they were doing when they experienced the exception.	The counselor inquires what the client would like to be different about their career, how this shift in career perspective could make a difference, what it would be like to have this modified career perspective, and if the client is experiencing any of these altered career perspectives (Taylor, 2009).
Scaling questions	The career counselor uses a scale of 1 to 10, asking the client, "On a scale of 1 to 10, with 1 being in a miserable career and 10 being in a dream career, what number do you think you are at currently?"	Used to develop goals by gauging motivation, successes, and feelings in relation to career; assesses the intensity of the current career dilemma and then helps to organize career strategies for improving the situation (Taylor, 2009).

Adding the Sand Tray: Session Steps

The following is the process used when conducting a five-step CCSFS session: define (1) career dilemma, (2) exceptions, (3) goals, (4) feedback, and (5) assess progress. When utilizing CCSFS, the counselor relies heavily on client/counselor nonverbal communications. Formal training in sand tray therapy is necessary before using this approach.

Step One: Define Career Dilemma

In CCFSS the career counselor invites the client to create the career issue by selecting a few miniatures that are relevant to the client, by placing these selected miniatures in the sand, and by continuing the process while adding additional miniatures (Homeyer & Sweeney, 1998). As the client creates this sand tray, the counselor offers a nonjudgmental presence while observing the client's body language. Minimal verbal interactions take place in the form of tracking, paraphrasing, and reflecting on content and feelings (Taylor, 2009). The counselor uses minimal questions and seeks to create a therapeutic relationship.

The few questions the career counselor utilizes intend to find what and who is significant to the client. The counselor is looking for past successes and patterns in the language the client uses to discuss the presenting career issue. While using the client's language, the counselor goes deeper by asking the client to teach him or her about the underlying meaning (Taylor, 2009).

The counselor never assumes the meaning of the miniatures, as the sand tray world is very unique for each client. The counselor uses questions to evoke deeper meaning and client understanding about the sand tray. In CCSFS, the questions are tied to past, present, and future career issues and the feelings associated with these. The counselor acknowledges problems but does not spend much time on them (in an effort to diminish the client's awareness of negative experiences). The goal in CCSFS is to underscore strengths, coping mechanisms, and solutions to be utilized in one's career (Taylor, 2009).

Utilizing a *career genogram* (a client-drawn graphic depicting family and ancestral careers) during a sand tray session may help a client who is struggling to articulate a career dilemma. In CCSFS, the counselor instructs the client to build a genogram depicting his or her career. The client does this by selecting miniatures that represent family or ancestral career relationships and ties them to various aspects of career: enjoyment of work, desired work hours, wages, atmosphere, type of work, purpose of work, creativity at work, socializing, and so on. The counselor can challenge the client to shift the sand tray genogram to represent a dream career. By doing this, the client is able to visualize what could be different and how this change could lead to a happier career (Taylor, 2009). Guided Practice Exercise 13.2 asks you to consider how a career genogram via sand tray might help a client.

Guided Practice Exercise 13.2 Career Genograms in the Sand

What types of career issues might improve through the use of career genograms via sand tray therapy? Do you think ancestral careers affect our current career aspirations, motivations, and drives? How might a family member's presence in a career affect a client's self-efficacy in that career?

Step Two: Exceptions

In CCSFS the career counselor is looking for exceptions to career problems. The career counselor listens and watches for exceptions (i.e., times the problem may not have occurred).

To learn more about exceptions used in this step, review the techniques in Table 13.2.

The career counselor uses exception questions to find out what was helpful in reducing career anxiety, what it feels like to have career clarity, who notices the change, who provides support, and other details to help the client rehearse and process the exceptions. While the counselor is helping the client figure out how they can repeat these successes, he or she is observing clues about the client's strengths, challenges, and resistances.

Step Three: Goals

CCSFC is dependent on setting goals that are comprised of the following details: (a) are specific, measurable, achievable, realistic, and timely (smart);(b) are described in a career context; (c) contain solution-based language including the career issue(s); and (d) illustrate the client's career values (Taylor, 2009). The best goals are set by the client using client language and perspective of the career dilemma, including actual career accomplishments and coupled with desired career goals. The career counselor will use a variety of questions: exceptions (discussed in previous section), scaling, and miracle (discussed in this section and in Table 13.2).

Scaling Questions

Using the sand tray, the counselor will invite the client to choose a miniature that represents the scaled number and then build a sand tray using the miniature. Next, the counselor asks, "What would it take for your career to move to an 8?" The client is then invited to select a miniature to represent this new number.

Finally, the client is asked to illustrate this change in the sand tray. Taking the client through this process assists the client in initiating momentum toward resolving the career dilemma.

Another approach to career scaling questions is to ask the client to create three different scenes representing three career events occurring during the previous week. The counselor challenges the client to scale each of the career scenes and process the elements that made the scenes successful, focusing on the most minute details. This technique depends on skillfully posed questions that aid in understanding how these successes can materialize. Finally, counselor and client discuss the possibility of including these successes as part of career goals (Taylor, 2009).

Miracle Question

Once a client has defined his career dilemma, the career counselor will ask the miracle question (see Table 13.2). The client is persuaded to consider what his or her life will be like once he or she finds his or her dream career. The answer he or she formulates easily lends itself as a goal for career counseling. The miracle question enables the client to crystalize his or her perspective of career struggles and find solutions. Using the miracle question in unison with sand tray therapy strongly facilitates the process by inviting the client to create what his or her world would look like if he or her was living his or her dream career (Taylor, 2009).

CCFSS helps a client create a psychological map in the sand tray for career success by rehearsing behaviors required to make big decisions and, perhaps, altering behaviors that have previously gotten in the way of career success (Taylor, 2009). Through this, the client's sense of being in control of their career is amplified. The sand tray provides the career counselor with a visual psychological "map" of cognitions that translates to better preparation and client support in reaching career goals.

Step Four: Feedback

Toward the end of the CCSFS session, the counselor will take about 5 minutes to gather thoughts and reflect on what the client built in the sand tray, take photos, jot down a few notes, and, finally, meet with the client to share this feedback (Taylor, 2009). While providing the feedback and suggestions, the counselor uses the sand tray as an illustration. This part of the session allows the client to fully appreciate that the counselor has been present and attending during session as the client worked on their career issues. In an effort to enhance client self-awareness, the counselor intertwines client strengths with the feedback from the sand tray.

The suggestions the career counselor provides hinge on how the client perceives him or herself in relation to the career dilemma and illustrate whether exceptions exist. If clients feel discouraged, counselors compliment clients regarding determination to tackle the career dilemma. If the client struggles to own the career issue, an observational suggestion is best. An observational suggestion is having the client observe an assigned task during the week. For example, the counselor makes a reference to the client's sand tray theme and asks the client to observe when they notice the theme at work or in day-to-day life during the week (Taylor, 2009).

Step Five: Assess Progress

During step five, the CCSFS counselor assesses for successes and provides positive reinforcement (Taylor, 2009). In this step, the counselor is helping the client recognize growth and resistance. It is important for the client to recognize and internalize growth, no matter the size. Moreover, it is equally important for the client to recognize and own resistance.

During this step, a career counselor takes time during a session to discuss with the client what he or she believes to be better about the client's career situation. Then, to reinforce the improvement, the counselor invites the client to build a scene of the improvement in the sand tray. The counselor utilizes scaling questions to help the client with his or her evaluation of career improvement. The client is asked about the exception to the career dilemma, explains what is different, and then illustrates the exception in the sand tray. Finally, the client is asked to show in the sand tray how he or she is able to "do" the exception to the career dilemma (Taylor, 2009). Again, the counselor is seeking to amplify success and help the client internalize positive outcomes. Now let's turn our attention to Case Exercise 13.2 as we apply sand tray therapy with a fictional client.

Case Exercise 13.2 The Case of Omar

Omar, age 30, comes to you for help finding a new job. He says he hates his job and fights constantly with his wife because he is stressed and unhappy. He is very quiet and responds to questions using one-word responses. You are unsure if culture, interest, or values are playing a role in Omar's unhappiness. He says he doesn't trust assessments. How might art or sand tray be helpful with Omar?

CASE STUDY

The following case demonstrates how a series of CCSFS sessions might be used when working with a fictional client, Paul, who is suffering from burnout, job misery, and lack of clarity on life's purpose. Paul is a 31-year-old Caucasian male who is employed as a manager at a national car rental agency. Paul changed majors numerous times in college but finally graduated with a bachelor's degree in psychology. He has never been clear about what he wants to do with his life and thus his career path. As he had to pay bills, he took a job as a manager working long hours with no days off and, quite frankly, hates everything about the job. He ends up in your office defeated, burned out, miserable, and has no idea what his purpose is in life.

Sensing that Paul does not trust himself and is full of anxiety, the counselor makes sure Paul feels safe and comfortable. The counselor then takes him through a 15-minute guided meditation exercise to set the stage for open communication while imparting instinctual trust and anxiety reduction. She then introduces him to CCSFS and, once he feels ready, leads him into the sand tray room. Paul creates his first sand tray based on overcoming a career issue and processes it with the counselor.

Counselor: You really worked hard building that tray and processing, Paul. I can see a very different light in your eyes, and your face seems more relaxed.

Paul: That was really cool. I've never gone that psychologically deep before.

Counselor: *(Step 2 exceptions)* Now we are going to manipulate the tray a bit as we search even deeper. Is that okay with you?

Paul: Sure, I'm in.

Counselor: So, I would like for you to create in the sand tray a time when you felt less defeated and had less anxiety about your career.

The counselor sits quietly with Paul as he thinks and makes changes in the tray.

Counselor: You were really in deep thought as you worked in the tray. Tell me about this shift you created.

Paul: It was weird, seemingly out of nowhere, I remembered a time in high school when I attended a fireman camp. Funny, I used to want to be a fireman. The lure of money sent me in another direction.

Counselor: Interesting. Tell me more about that, who was with you, what kind of feelings do you remember. Who supported you in this?

Paul tells the counselor very positive, upbeat memories. His whole being lights up as he gives her the details. The counselor makes note of this.

Counselor: *(Step 3 goal)* I appreciate how hard you are working on your career issues, Paul. I would like to ask you to pretend you have gone to sleep and when you wake in the morning, a miracle has occurred. You are waking to get ready for your dream job. In the sand tray, I want to invite you to build what your world looks like now and what is involved with your career.

The counselor is present with Paul as he contemplates this. Paul begins to build his miracle question sand tray that will lead to goals for career counseling.

Paul: *(While processing miracle question tray)* You know, I keep going back to the fireman thing. That is the last time I felt any joy or excitement about the idea of work. This tray is all about becoming a fireman. That is what was different about the day; I felt a sense of purpose at the thought of helping others, ha, kinda like a hero.

Counselor: That really provides a lot of clarity for you. To help clarify, let's draw a timeline of career events starting with this good memory you found from high school. Would that be okay?

Paul: I am not much of an artist, but so far all of this has helped, so yeah.

The counselor gives Paul art supplies and instructs him to draw a timeline of significant career events, beginning with high school. After the timeline is drawn, she has him label each event with a feeling. The counselor is trying to help Paul uncover goals for his career by tapping into several expressive arts.

Counselor: Paul, based on the activities we've done thus far, I am wondering what you feel your goal should be in our time as we work together?

Paul: I would not have believed it before we started all of this, but I really think I want to look into being a firefighter, EMT, or police officer. I want to serve my community and others. It is crazy, but I feel like that has been what is missing in my career. I just saw no purpose for what I was doing.

Counselor: *(Step 4 feedback)* Well, those are very specific career directions; I think you can find a lot of information to help you make your decision. When we first started working together you were very anxious and defeated in reference to your career. We began teaching you meditation and expressive art techniques to help you gain a deeper understanding of you and what you wanted for your life. You have been able to tap into your old dream of serving others and discovered this is very important to you. You told me, when we first met, you felt no purpose in your life. As you have worked it has become clearer to you that you want to explore the possibility of being a firefighter, EMT, or police officer. This is huge. Tell me how you are experiencing this new purpose.

Paul: I feel so much more at peace. I really think the meditation is helping and working with the expressive stuff has taught me so much about me. I guess I'm more self-aware.

Counselor: Absolutely. So, by our next session, I want you to have explored all that it takes to be a firefighter, how to apply, the pay scale, and every detail you can find. In the weeks to come, you will do the same for EMT and police officer. How does that feel?"

Paul: I think that is a great way to spend my time. I'm actually excited.

During the last session, the counselor and Paul assess progress through the sand tray. Paul realizes that he will pursue a career as a firefighter. He and the counselor process the details involved with this. Paul realizes he may have to move to be hired with a department and is at peace with this.

Limitations and Ethical Issues When Using Spiritual, Art, and Sand Tray Techniques

A number of limitations and ethical codes must be considered when using spiritual, art, and sand tray techniques. The primary limitation in the use of these practices as part of the process of vocational discernment centers around the competence of the practitioner. While some may view these resources as a matter of common sense, their misuse in practice can lead to serious damage to the client and unintended long-term consequences. Professional codes of ethics in all mental health disciplines prohibit practicing beyond one's competence and also tout practices furthering confidentiality, professional conduct, and duty to warn (ACA, 2014; Art Therapy Credentials Board, 2011; British Association of Art Therapists, 2011). Because of the potential subconscious psychological power involved in these modalities, the career counselor needs to understand the client's mental health history to ensure a fit with other presenting mental health issues. Finally, because both art and sand tray require many supplies, the career counseling office would need to be equipped with art and sand tray materials before use.

SUMMARY

Spiritual, art, and sandtray techniques offer unique approaches a client can use to holistically assess and process the often tumultuous work of choosing a career path, changing a career, and managing a career.

Keystones

- A number of techniques such as spiritual autobiographies, the Enneagram, and mindfulness meditation can be used to integrate spirituality into career decision making.
- Art and sand tray therapies, such as CCSFS, offer nonverbal modalities for assisting clients as they process thoughts, values, career interests, and other career-related factors.

Author Reflections

Mayes, Mayes, and Williams (2007) recommend keeping a photographic record of each client's sand tray. From my experience doing trays with career clients, I agree this is helpful. Clients are intrigued by pictures of their trays, enjoy discussing the pictures with friends and family, and find increasing significance over time. I have especially found that clients are able to sustain growth and appreciate bearing witness to their career growth and progress through CCSFS. They report enjoying the building of sand trays and, before processing them, had no idea how deeply the metaphor tapped into their subconscious. I believe the bottom line for any career counselor is finding efficacious processes that facilitate client growth. —Julie Merriman

Additional Resources

The following resources provide additional information about the content provided in this chapter.

Counseling Division Resources and Websites

Association for Spiritual, Ethical, Religious, Values in Counseling: http://www.aservic.org/resources/spiritual-competencies/

This site lists the competencies counselors use to ensure compliance with the ACA Code of Ethics and standards of practice when integrating spirituality into sessions.

Association for Play Therapy: https://www.a4pt.org/

This site is the homepage for the national play therapy organization.

Sandtray Therapists of America: https://www.sandplay.org/

This site is the homepage for the national sand tray therapy organization.

Homeyer, L., & Sweeney, D. (1998). *Sandtray: A practical manual.* Royal Oak, MI. Self Esteem Shop

The reader is encouraged to examine the writings of well-known and experienced practitioners and researchers such as Homeyer and Sweeney, including those regarding the specifics of sand tray and selection of miniatures.

References

American Counseling Association (ACA). (2014). *ACA code of ethics.* Author. https://www.counseling.org/resources/aca-code-of-ethics.pdf

Art Therapy Credentials Board. (2011, March 4). *Code of professional practice.* https://www.atcb.org/resource/pdf/2011-ATCB-Code-of-Professional-Practice.pdf

Berg, I. K., & De Jong, P. (2005). Engagement through complimenting. *Journal of Family Psychotherapy, 16*(1–2), 51–56.

British Association of Art Therapists. (2011). BAAT code of ethics and principles of professional practice. Retrieved from https://www.baat.org/Assets/Docs/BAAT%20CODE%20OF%20ETHICS%202019.pdfBrown, K. W., Creswell, J. D., & Ryan, R. M. (2015). *Handbook of mindfulness: Theory, research and practice.* Guilford.

Clark, S. M. (2017). *DBT-informed art therapy: Mindfulness, cognitive behavior therapy, and the creative process.* Jessica Kingsley.

Cox, C. (2016). Art therapy in rehabilitation centers. In D. E. Gussak & M. L. Rosal (Eds.), *The Wiley handbook of art therapy,* (pp. 451–459). Wiley.

Csikszentmihalyi, M. (2009). *Flow: The psychology of optimal experience.* HarperCollins.

D'Amico, D. (2017). *101 Mindful arts-based activities to get children and adolescents talking: Working with severe trauma, abuse, and neglect using found and everyday objects.* Jessica Kingsley.

Dik, B. J., Duffy, R. D., & Eldridge, B. M. (2009). Calling and vocation in career counseling: Recommendations for promoting meaningful work. *Professional Psychology: Research and Practice, 40*(6), 625–632.

Dudeck, J. M. (2004). The influence of spirituality on the career development of college seniors: An examination of work values. *College of Student Affairs Journal: Special Issue on Faith, Spirituality, and Religion on Campus, 23*(2), 185–195.

Eberts, S., & Homeyer, L. (2015). Processing sand trays from two theoretical perspectives: Gestalt and Adlerian. *International Journal of Play Therapy, 24*(3), 134–150. http://doi.org/10.1037/a0039392

Fox, M. (1994). *The reinvention of work: A new vision of livelihood for our time.* HarperCollins.

Ginzberg, E., Ginzburg, S., Axelrad, S., & Herma, J. (1951). *Occupational choice: An approach to a good theory.* Columbia University Press.

Gregg, C. M. (2005). Discover "vocation": An essay on the concept of vocation. *Journal of College and Character, 6*(1). https://doi.org/10.2202/1940-1639.1411

Gussak, D. (2013). Art therapy in the prison subculture: Maintaining boundaries while breaking barriers. In P. Howie, S. Prasad, & J. Kristel (Eds.), *Using art therapy with diverse populations: Crossing cultures and abilities.* (pp. 328–337). Jessica Kingsley.

Gussak, D. E., & Rosal, M. L. (Eds.). (2016). *The Wiley handbook of art therapy.* Wiley.

Homeyer, L., & Sweeney, D. (1998). *Sandtray: A practical manual*. Royal Oak, MI. Self Esteem Shop

Homeyer, L. & Sweeney, D. (2005). Sandtray therapy. In C.A. Malchiodi (Eds), *Expressive Therapies* (pp. 162–183). New York: The Guilford Press.

Homeyer, L., & Sweeney, D. (2011). *Sandtray therapy: A practical manual*. Routledge.

Hood, A. B., & Johnson, R. W. (2002). *Assessment in counseling* (3rd ed.). American Counseling Association.

Isom, E., Groves-Radomski, J., & McConaha, M. (2015). Sandtray therapy: A familial approach to healing through imagination. *Journal of Creativity in Mental Health, 10*(3), 339–350. https://doi.org/10.1080/15401383.2014.983254

Kalff, D. (1980). *Sandplay: A psychotherapeutic approach to the psyche*. Sigo Press.

King, J. L. (2016). *Art therapy, trauma, and neuroscience: Theoretical and practical perspectives*. Routledge.

Labovitz Boik, B., & Goodwin, A. (2000). *Sandplay therapy: A step-by-step manual for psychotherapists of diverse orientations*. Norton.

Levick, M. (2009). *Levick emotional and cognitive art therapy assessment: A normative study*. Author House.

Lowenfeld, V. (1957). *Creative and mental growth* (3rd ed). Macmillan.

Lowenfield, M. (1979). *The world technique*. Institute of Child Psychology.

Malchiodi, C. A. (Ed.). (2012). *Handbook of art therapy* (2nd ed). Guilford

Maree, J. (2016). *Career counseling matrix*. Randburg, South Africa, JVR Psychometrics.

Markos, P., Coker, J. & Jones, W. (2008). Play in supervision. *Journal of Creativity in Mental Health, 2*(3), 3–15. https://doi.org/10.1300/J456v02n03_02

Mayes, C., Mayes, P., & Williams, E. (2004). Messages in the sand: Sandtray therapy techniques with graduate students in an educational leadership program. *International Journal of Leadership in Education, 7*(3), 257–284. https://doi.org/10.1080/13603120410001694540

Mayes, C., Mayes, P., & Williams, E. (2007). Sandtray therapy, reflectivity and leadership preparation. *International Journal of Leadership in Education, 10*(4), 357–378. https://doi.org/10.1080/13603120701370777

National Career Development Association. (2006). *Spirituality, religion, and career development: Current status and future directions*. Retrieved from https://www.thefreelibrary.com/Spirituality%2c+religion%2c+and+career+development%3a+current+status+and...-a0152571591

Parsons, F. (1909). *Choosing a vocation*. Boston: Houghton Mifflin.

Rappaport, L. (2009). *Focusing-oriented art therapy: Accessing the body's wisdom and creative intelligence*. Jessica Kingsley.

Riso, D. R., & Russ, H. (1996). *Personality types: Using the Enneagram for self-discovery*. Mariner Books.

Rubin, J. A. (2016). *Approaches to art therapy: Theory and technique*. Routledge.

Smith, H. (1991). *The world's religions: Our great wisdom traditions*. Goodreads.

Super, D. E. (1957). *The psychology of careers*. Harper & Row.

Swank, J. M., & Jahn, S. B. (2018). Using sandtray to facilitate college students' career decision making: A qualitative inquiry. *The Career Development Quarterly*, 66, 269–277.

Taylor, E. (2009). Sandtray and solution-focused therapy. *International Journal of Play Therapy, 18*(1), 56–68. https://doi.org/10.1037/a0014441

van Kaam, A. (1975). *In search of spiritual identity*. Dimension Books.

Wheat, L. W. (1991). *Development of a scale for the measurement of human spirituality* [Unpublished doctoral dissertation]. University of Maryland.

Winnicott, D. W. (1953). Transitional objects and transitional phenomena: A study of the first not-me possession. *International Journal of Psychoanalysis, 34*(2), 89–97.

CHAPTER 14

Marriage, Couples, and Family Therapy: Treating Vocational Issues Systemically

Lynn Jennings, Eva Gibson, and Stephen Jennings

We are made wise not by the recollection of our past, but by the responsibility for our future.
—George Bernard Shaw

George Bernard Shaw understood that true wisdom means we have the ability to learn from our past so that we might avoid repeating mistakes in the future. By doing this, we create more a responsible and transformative future. "The past influences the present, and together, the past and present influence the future" (Patton & McMahon, 2006, p. 154).

When assisting clients to formulate meaning through the construction of positive career futures, it is important to consider life themes that emerge based on past and current experiences. These experiences include interpersonal influences, family influences, societal influences, and geographical influences, which envelop the person's life span: past, present and future. By understanding the systemic interplay between these factors, we are able to move forward in a manner that takes on responsibility for our future. Let us read more about a systems approach to career theory, how it integrates with family counseling, and its application in career counseling sessions.

CHAPTER OVERVIEW

This chapter discusses the embedded nature of career theory, systems theory, and family counseling. Specific techniques and approaches are discussed, along with vocational factors that impact the entire family system. A case study gives a practical example as to how a career counseling session might look when considering vocational issues through a systemic lens. A discussion of the synthesis of the theory with career counseling theories is included.

LEARNING OBJECTIVES

After reading the chapter, you will be able to do the following:

- Understand how systems theory integrates with several career theories you read about in the first part of this text (e.g., Donald Super's developmental theories, theory of work adjustment and PXE fit, Krumboltz's learning theory and happenstance, and social cognitive career theory)
- Understand the relationship between career issues and family concerns
- Apply this integrated model with clients' facing career counseling issues

Systems Theory and Integration With Vocational Counseling

Systems theory, first developed by Bertalanffy (1972) in the 1960s, was originally created to explain the impact of the environment, processes, and interactions on an organism. The theory was then broadened to include other fields such as psychology. In this context, an individual is not merely a sum of his or her parts but is best understood after accounting for patterns of interrelationships. Applied to therapy, the systems approach is often equated with family therapy as it not only focuses on the individual client but on the impact of the family unit as well (Lebow, 2014). This approach also allows for consideration of other influences from the environment on the development of the client.

Systems theory has expanded into a framework (STF) that can also be applied to career development. In this context, individual, social, and environmental factors influence career selection (Patton & McMahon, 2014). As the individual experiences continuous interactions with external factors, these processes influence the career development path. This approach is informed by constructivism in that reality is constantly being shaped in response to stimuli. All forms of work are encompassed in this framework, to include paid and unpaid labor. Work is understood as a major influence in our lives and is a source of identity (McMahon, 2017; Patton & McMahon, 2014).

Key elements of systems theory include the following:

- Wholes and parts
- Patterns and rules
- Acausality
- Recursiveness
- Discontinuous change

- Open and Closed systems
- Abductions
- Stories

In terms of career development, the application of STF requires the consideration that career decision making cannot be segmented into individual decisions, but rather as an understanding of career behavior as a whole. In lieu of focusing on specific discrete concepts, such as traits, this framework examines the context of development. This particular approach also focuses on patterns or webs of interrelationships. These rules of conduct govern communication and societal norms. Considerations such as these are addressed in STF. While typical human reactions assume causative effects of stimuli, the systems framework stands in stark contrast to that assumption. In this construct, human behavior is viewed as complex and attempts to directly link cause to effect are unsuccessful.

In a similar manner, the terms *recursive* or nonlinear best describe the path of development in this approach. Just as the path of causality is obscure, so is the feedback (and feed-forward) mechanism. In this system, learning opportunities come from multiple directions and growth does not occur in a linear fashion.

Discontinuous change is also viewed as a key element in this doctrine. While change occurs on a recurrent basis, it is categorized as discontinuous as it may shift to a new form of functioning rather than continuously along the same trajectory. This typically occurs when previous forms of functioning are no longer effective.

STF is often described as an open system in that individual development is impacted by the surrounding variables and factors. Abductive reasoning plays a major role in the development of this position as well. This process involves the exploration of patterns and the comparison of similar occurrences. This experience can then lead to the element of story in which the client examines significant connections and constructs a narrative based on their interpretation.

STF focuses on both the content and process of career development (Patton & McMahon, 2014). Relevant influences include the following:

- The individual system
- The contextual system
- Interactions between the individual and contextual system
- Change over time
- Chance

The emphasis on the individual and unique qualities is a key construct of this approach.

STF centers on sense of self and the intrapersonal influences within each individual. Influences include variables such as gender, ability, race, values, personality, sexual orientation, aptitudes, and interests.

As we do not live in a vacuum, the contextual system is also integrated in this paradigm. The contextual system has further been broken down to a social system and an environmental-societal system. The social system represents close connections, which inform the individual, such as peers, family, and community groups.

The environmental-societal system represents broader influences such as political decisions, the employment market, and even geographic location. The interactions between the overall contextual system and individual system are viewed as ongoing and consistently influence each other, lending to a dynamic process of development. This constant evolution over time influences and changes decision making and career progression. As to be expected with transition, unpredictable events, or chance occurrences, arise without notice. STF considers unplanned events as natural occurrences that impact the individual. Let us look at a sample client's career issue and consider how using the STF model could assist her in deciding on a possible career change.

Case Exercise 14.1 Shelly's Career Exploration

Shelly is a 50-year-old woman who has an exciting but highly stressful career. It has become increasingly stressful over the past year and has placed some tremendous stress on her and her family. She is feeling discouraged and disheartened by the impact of the stress on her family. Utilizing the STF model, what are some ways that Shelly can identify forms of ineffective functioning, in her current situation, and develop a new form of functioning, allowing her to remain in her current job and also lessen the negative impact on her family, or help her to decide to explore a new career direction?

Now that we have an understanding of the systems approach and how it can be applied to career counseling, let us examine the relationship between this approach and other relevant theories.

Integration of Career Theories and Models With Family Counseling

Donald Super's Developmental Theories

As previously discussed, Super's developmental theory (1957) includes all activities in all interacting life roles (Samide et al., 2014). These roles include work and non-work aspects (Zacher et al., 2018). As activities ebb and flow, career choices are impacted by self-concept, internal variables (such as values/interests), and well as external variables (such as the job market).

Alone we can do so little; together we can do so much.
—Helen Keller

Super's stage development model is somewhat similar to the dynamic structure of STF in that change is constant and expected. For example, Super further defined career as all the constant and expected activities that take place in life roles as these roles interact with and inform one another. Although these roles are ever present, role selection, bandwidth (time dedicated), and intensity are fluid. As clients move through the various stages in this process, it is essential to have a solid understanding of the personal values as they assist in the exploration of possibilities.

The use and reinforcement of counseling goals is important in this process and includes the following:

- Assessment of career maturity and strengthening of deficits
- Examining and reinforcing self-concept
- Recognizing relevant life roles
- Determining interests/skills and disbursing them across life roles

Systems therapy has the potential to reinforce these goals through the application of consultation, collaboration, and coordination (James & Gilliland, 2003). Consider the example of a recently retired military veteran preparing to transition into a new career. In the community, resources and agencies may be available to offer guidance and services to service members and dependents. After assessing career maturity, the counselor may be able to connect the client to local resources to strengthen deficits and/or specific skills. This consultation and collaboration may prove to be especially valuable for the client and family as they may not be knowledgeable about potential services available. The counselor may also work with the client to examine self-concept as well as life roles beyond that of a soldier. Through the use of coordination, the counselor may help the client create a manageable action plan as the veteran begins to apply skills to new roles. Guided Practice Exercise 14.1 asks you to consider how Super's developmental model integrates with STF and how it can be applied in a manner that impacts the family as a unit.

Guided Practice Exercise 14.1 Integrating Super and STF in Working With Career Exploration in Families

Review Super's theory from Chapter 2. What techniques were not mentioned in regard to integrating Super's theory with STF in this chapter? How would those techniques be applied when working with families?

Theory of Work Adjustment and P-E Fit

As discussed in Chapter 2, the theory of work adjustment, or person-environment (P-E) fit or person-environment-correspondence (PEC) theory, was created to meet the needs of vocational rehabilitation clients. This theory was designed to help increase and improve services to this particular population by changing the paradigm from career development and choice to vocational adjustment (Dawis et al., 1968). The P-E fit model goes beyond assessing individual abilities and work factors and strives to capture the nature of person and their environmental interactions (Chartrand, 1991). The questions that guide this theory include "1). What kinds of personal and environmental factors are salient in predicting vocational choice and adjustment? and 2). How is the process of person and environment best characterized?" (Chartrand, 1991, p. 520).

P-E fit theory considers the person and environment to be reciprocal in that each influences the other. P-E fit and work adjustment considers the concept of suitable and unsuitable fit when considering career exploration and choice. A suitable fit would indicate that the person and the environment are both satisfied in the work context, and a positive work adjustment has occurred in the person and environment. An unsuitable fit would indicate poor work performance, dissatisfaction with the job, and poor work adjustment in the person and environment.

In this concept, as well, is the idea of satisfaction (person's satisfaction with their work) and satisfactoriness (environment's satisfaction with the person's job performance), which speaks to the importance of the interaction between the person and environment, and work adjustment as an integral part of work success.

This theory fits well with STF, in that both theories focus on internal and external factors in career exploration, decision making, and adjustment. Integrating these theories from a family perspective is also a good fit. In the construct of the family, STF and P-E fit are complimentary approaches for identifying the needs of the individuals in the family and then integrating them into the family construct. By doing this, potential exists to develop satisfaction and satisfactoriness as it applies to the family and the family's impact on career exploration.

Family support may influence career development as part of P-E fit. If the family is experiencing satisfaction as a unit, the career seeker (within this family) is likely to be more satisfied with personal career choice, to have positive work adjustment and positive family support, and may also have increased support during challenging moments in this selected career choice. The opposite can also occur. Where there is dissatisfaction, the challenges of the career choice can be overwhelming to the career seeker and may systemically influence the family unit. This may subsequently lead to family dissatisfaction and diminish family support during difficult career decisions and issues, causing poor work adjustment. Let us look at a sample client's career issue and consider how using the theory of work adjustment and P-E fit model integrated with STF could assist her in deciding on a career.

Case Exercise 14.2 Bobbi's Decision

Bobbi is a 40-year-old woman who has been a stay-at-home mom for several years. She has a bachelor's degree and feels the need to get back into the work force. She has some ideas on what she would like to do, but it may require her to get a higher degree at some point. She enjoys helping people and problem solving. Utilizing the process of the P-E fit and work adjustment model, how can exploring individual abilities, work factors, her personal nature, and her environmental interactions help Bobbi make vocational decisions for her future and the future of her family? What types of adjustment issues may she be able to anticipate? What other considerations will she need to take into account, specifically regarding the impact of her vocational choices on her family?

Krumboltz's Learning Theory and Happenstance

As you may recall from the earlier exploration of Krumboltz's theory in Chapter 3, this approach emphasizes the fact that individuals filter events through observations and generalizations (Krumboltz, 2009). These generalizations are shaped by positive reinforcement and role models. Unexpected events are welcomed as new opportunities for growth and uncertainty are acceptable and viewed as constructive (Kim et al., 2016; Rice, 2014). Desired skills include curiosity, persistence, flexibility, optimism, and risk taking.

The systems approach can be nicely applied to Krumboltz's (2009) happenstance theory as it encompasses Brofenbrenner's (1979) ecological systems theory. As the counselor and client work to define the problem and set goals, an exploration of factors in Brofenbrenner's (1979) ecosystems (e.g., *microsystems*, influences in the immediate environment such as family members; *mesosystem*s, connections just outside the immediate environment such as between family and church; *exosystem*s, links between two or more settings such as extended family and neighborhoods, *macrosystems*, most distant influencers such as culture and political systems; and *chronosystems*, links to the constancy of time) might be pursued. Once pursued, these factors have the potential to merge with chance events and future preparation, thus adding credence to Krumboltz's (2009) contention that new opportunities often occur unexpectedly through chance, including through ecosystem influencers.

Consider the case of a recently divorced mother of three who is attempting to reenter the workforce after staying home with her children for a number of years. After goals have been established, the counselor can assist the client in exploring connections and relationships that have the potential to generate job openings. The alliance then devises a feasible action plan while also generating alternatives. As touted by both STF and Krumboltz (2009), the counselor and client then anticipate the potential for unexpected events (Ryan & Tomlin, 2010). For example, will she need additional education to achieve her overall goals? If so, what is the plan to accomplish this while still providing for her children? If a future opening has been shared by an influencer, what will she need to do to best prepare?

As part of STF, the client will consider her microsystem or immediate family and their needs. This means probable consequences to these plans should be explored, leading to further examination of the selected approach. For example, if a traditional class schedule is not an option when raising children and concurrently pursuing needed training, what other educational possibilities exist? STF implies the consideration of the entire family system as part of the decision-making process. In this case, perhaps the counselor and client can explore online classes so that needs of the entire family system are met. Once a final career decision is made, the counselor can assist the client in applying the process to new problems. Guided Practice Exercise 14.2 asks you to consider how Krumboltz's learning theory and happenstance integrate with STF and how they can be applied in a manner that impacts the entire family system.

Guided Practice Exercise 14.2 Integrating Krumboltz and STF in Individuals and Families

Review Krumboltz's theory from Chapter 2. What techniques were not mentioned in regard to integrating Krumboltz's theory with STF in this chapter? How would those techniques be applied when working with families versus individuals?

Social Cognitive Career Theory

As previously learned about social cognitive career theory (SCCT) in Chapter 3, this approach proposes the utilization of individual agency demonstrated as how people's ability and motivation influence their own environment (Zacher et. al., 2018). This concept borrows from Bandura's social cognitive theory and the triadic reciprocal model, which assert that bidirectional influences occur among individual characteristics, contextual characteristics, and behavior. SCCT was established as a rejection of the trait approach and contends that behavior may not be stable across circumstances as reactions are triggered by varying stimuli (Kell, 2018).

Key elements of this approach include self-efficacy, outcome expectations, and goals. These constructs empower people to exercise agency in a fluid manner as new information is constantly introduced (Ezeofor & Lent, 2014). Environmental considerations, both as supports and barriers, can help facilitate or impede self-direction. SCCT posits that people develop desires to pursue tasks that parallel self-efficacy and outcomes expectations. Actual implementation is contingent on environmental factors, supports, and barriers. Application of this approach offers an examination of specific cognitive meditators that impact behavior and decision making, specifically in career development (Patton & McMahon, 2014). SCCT considers race and gender as socially constructed variables and encourages counselors to examine these factors as needed as they may impact perspective and opportunities.

SCCT may be integrated with the systems approach to help clients resolve problematic issues. For example, consider the client who is an African American male. He is currently employed but has repeatedly been overlooked for promotions and reports constant microaggressions directed toward him at work. His frustrations from work are beginning to impact his relationships at home, and the tension is growing.

Using the systems approach, the counselor may want to explore the following questions: "How does his context inform his behavior?" "How does his behavior impact the context?" Counselors using this modem need to critically examine the various relationships, interactions, and context to best support the client and family unit. In an effort to be culturally responsive, the counselor must also consider the impact race has on his experience and perception. In this example, the counselor may want to help the client evaluate current career satisfaction, identify supports, weigh the supports against the challenges, and then reassess goals. You may wish to review Chapter 7 as you consider the integration of cultural and career issues in this instance.

Guided Practice Exercise 14.3 asks you to consider how social cognitive career theory integrated with STF can be applied in a manner that will help you reflect on your career exploration and on decisions that have impacted your family unit.

Guided Practice Exercise 14.3 Integration of SCCT and STF in Career Exploration Within the Family

Think about your career exploration and development for a few minutes. In what manner did you, or in retrospect, could you, utilize the integrative work of SCCT and STF to critically examine the various relationships, interactions, experience, and context to best support yourself and your family. What aspects would you change? What aspects would remain the same?

The Relationship Between Career Issues and Family Concerns

As discussed in this chapter, family concerns and career issues are intertwined. In fact, Frizelle (2014) states that "the family is the most significant predictor of career choice" (p. 24). Greenhaus and Callahan (1994) postulate that occupational choice is highly influenced by family concerns as seen in the past, present, and unforeseen future.

Just as family values serve as a large influence on career exploration and career choice, the reverse may also be true. Shifts in work location, work hours, and other factors may affect the family system. This may explain research inferring that young workers seem to be shifting from traditional job roles to roles more focused on life, work, and family balance. For example, millennials often place more emphasis on time off to spend with friends and family, will quit if needs are not met, are more motivated by enjoyable work than money, and expect life balance regarding combinations of career, marriage, and family (i.e., *work-life balance*; Johnson, 2015).

This "work-life balance" is an issue often touted when discussing career and family issues. For example, due to peer pressure, or in some cases choice, women have been more likely to choose professions that allow for a balance of family and work. Contrary to past generations, young male workers are now increasingly choosing vocations where they can more easily combine work and family, along with their partners (Johnson, 2015; Smithson, 1999).

When considering work-family concerns, environmental support, family support, job opportunities, attitudes, and values play a large role in developing career interests. For example, in a 1996 study, organizational employment was weighed against self-employment among MBA graduates. Organizational employment was chosen significantly over self-employment due to the issues of workload, assumed barriers to work-life balance, and family and leisure concerns (Kolvereid, 1996). The concept of being self-employed brought forth concerns of a person being overworked due to large workloads, allowing less time for work-family balance, decreasing the importance of personal values, and increasing the importance of work values. This was perceived to lessen the family and environmental support given to the self-employed person, thus negatively impacting the family. Meanwhile, organizational employment was perceived as allowing for paid sick and vacation time, reasonable insurance, steady work hours, and so on—all of which were thought to more positively impact the family. These thoughts and ideas were found to favor the employee and the employee's family in the long term. This was true even when considering other possible financial benefits often experienced regarding self-employment.

Ultimately, career choice and family systems are inseparable entities. Each influences the other. Every vocational decision impacts the family either in a positive or negative manner. Career choice is something that needs to be considered through a careful process, including internal factors, environmental and family factors, values, attitudes, relationships, abilities, and support. Now let's turn our attention to Case Exercise 14.3 where we discuss the case of Mario and the interrelationship of issues between his job and family.

Case Exercise 14.3 Mario's Family Issues

Mario enters career counseling full of despair because he hates his job and his family is not functioning well as a result. Every day Mario tries to please his boss, who expects him to work 12-hour days. It seems the harder Mario works the less pleased his boss is with his performance. He knows the constant anxiety and frustration is coming home with him at night. Mario states that his wife, Zelda, is constantly complaining that he is fussy, never around, and hard to live with. Mario says he must find a new job or his marriage is in jeopardy.

What are some career issues that are impacting Mario's relationship? As Mario's career counselor, what are some things you can do to help him with career development? What other issues may Mario need to address outside career counseling?

Limitations and Ethical Issues

Due to STF theory's integrative style, practical application, and overall usefulness, especially in the area of career choice, limitations and ethical issues would likely lie within the career counselor and not within the process. For this reason, training is important for career counselors. This training might include an understanding of differences between the career counselor's role and the role of the marriage and family counselor. The American Counseling Association's (2014) Code of Ethics (A.6.d.) states that counselors inform clients of changes in counseling roles, offer informed consent, and discuss anticipated consequences. The ACA code also states that counselors explain the purposes, procedures, goals, and other such information with clients (A.2.b.). Further, counselors are to work only within areas where they have competence (A.11.a.). For this reason, clients facing both career and family issues may need referrals to family counselors. Family counselors can help resolve marital and family concerns as you, the career counselor, concurrently assist with career development.

Career counselors might also be trained in the use of quantitative and qualitative measures so that they are best able to assist a person with decision making. It is important to use individualized processes that are unique to each person, allowing for diverse values, beliefs, personal, and environmental factors. See Chapter 8 for more information regarding career assessment measures.

Due to the fluid nature of STF and its ability to adjust to individual needs, it is difficult to foresee limitations, even in the ever-changing world in which we live. Ongoing research to move this theory in the direction that will continually meet the needs of the future generations should be encouraged to allow this theory and practice to grow in its usefulness and effectiveness regarding career counseling. Guided Practice Exercise 14.4 asks you to consider the case of Shondra. In this case, you will discern an ethical response to a client facing marital issues.

Case Exercise 14.4 Ethical Considerations

Shondra is a new counselor recently hired to serve as a career counselor for her university. After stating that her role in the setting is that of career counselor and going over informed consent, it becomes clear that her client, Ryon, is having problems in his marriage. Ryon asks Shondra if she can help him work on his marriage issues while she helps him find a job. What should Shondra do if she wants to act ethically in this situation?

CASE STUDY

The following case study demonstrates how STF might be integrated with Super's developmental theory when working with a wife attempting to reenter the workforce after her husband has been diagnosed with a terminal illness.

Sarah is a 32-year old Hispanic female who has been a stay-at-home mom for the past 10 years. This past year, her husband, Carlos, was diagnosed with a terminal illness and can no longer work. They have two children who are in elementary school. Sarah enters your office and sits down.

Counselor: Hi Sarah. What do you hope to achieve during our time together today?

Sarah: I am not sure. I need to work. I need a job, but I don't know where to start. My husband is sick and cannot work. I have been a stay-at-home mom for the past 10 years and I don't know what I am good at, other than cleaning my house and taking care of my kids.

Since Sarah has been out of the workforce for 10 years, she is exhibiting a sense of low self-esteem and fear of the unknown. The use of systems theory can be applied to her situation through the application of consultation, collaboration, and coordination. The first step is to determine career maturity in order to connect the client with the appropriate resources.

Counselor: It sounds like you are in a big life transition right now. The good thing is about transition is it gives us the opportunity to try new things, or explore things we felt we were unable to look into before an opportunity like this.

Sarah: You know, I never thought of it that way. Hmmm. That's an interesting perspective. I have always wanted to be a teacher, so I could work the same work hours as when my kids go to school.

Counselor: What type of postsecondary education do you currently have?

Sarah: I have an associate's degree in general studies.

Counselor: That's great. You might consider talking to the local school system and finding a job in the school system to fulfill your desire to work the same hours as your children attend school. If that works out well, then you can look at taking classes and the local university to be able to get your teaching degree.

Sarah: This may sound crazy, but I never even considered working for the school. That is a good plan. I will call the regional office today and fill out an application.

This consultation and collaboration process can prove to be valuable for this client and her family, as she does not seem to be knowledgeable about where to start in the process of obtaining a job, nor a career. Having guidance and direction through the process can help to lessen the fear of the unknown and connect her to tangible resources to help her achieve her goal of becoming a teacher.

Sarah: You mentioned attending the local university to get my teaching degree. What do you know about that? The structure of the classes, and so on? I don't know with my husband's illness and my children being the age they are if I can attend night classes.

Counselor: The bachelor's degree programs offer many online classes that you can take, and some of the programs are fully online. Once you get settled in your job and your new routine, you need to call the university and make an appointment to visit with the Education Department and inquire about their program.

Sarah: That is great idea! I will do that. One step at a time.

Through the use of coordination, the counselor helped Sarah develop a manageable action plan as Sarah began to look toward applying new skills to her new role as a person in the workforce.

The client's fear of the unknown along with her lack of work experience has already begun improving. In future sessions with this client, the counselor will work with the client on examining her self-concept and life roles beyond that of a stay-at-home mom while integrating work-life balance into the action plan for the client and her family. Due to her husband's illness, the age of her children, and cultural expectations, she will need to remain aware of the internal and external factors that can cause change to occur in her plan and reassess the plan as necessary to manage those changes.

SUMMARY

In the recent past, career counseling morphed from a narrow focus to a much more broad focus, allowing integrative theories to emerge to meet the needs of the ever-changing world. With this, traditional roles, attitudes, and values have also been modified to meet this generation's paradigm shift from work focus and work identity to work-life balance, family concerns, and leisure. STF moves away from the trait-factor theoretical approach and into a problem solving–type approach. By doing this, the focus becomes an individualized process that takes into account the individual and the family when helping with career decision making.

Change over time, and chance, also play a role in career development, as unexpected changes can occur. As stated by Krumboltz (2009), this change can alter the course of an intended direction, either temporarily or more long term. Our past, present, and future are linked, and they influence decision making in all areas of life. STF was designed to be used in an integrative manner with other career theories to aid in career exploration and decision making in an ever-changing world.

When integrating STF with other career counseling theories, we find compatibility in individual and family contexts. Knowing that career concerns and family concerns are inextricably linked helps us to view these contexts through the lens of integrated theoretical models more easily. When looking at integrating STF with Super's developmental theory, we find a good blend consisting of interacting life roles and the expectation that change is ever constant. When applying the integration of STF with Super's developmental theory with family counseling, the roles of consultation, collaboration, and coordination play a vital role in creating a manageable action plan for the individual and their family (James & Gilliand, 2003).

When integrating STF with P-E fit and work adjustment, the focus is on internal and external factors and good vocational adjustment. In the context of family counseling, when utilizing this integration of STF and P-E fit, needs of the individuals are identified and integrated in a family construct that helps the family move forward in an interdependent, positive manner. STF and Krumboltz's model come together to define problems and set goals and factors included their microsystem, mesosystem, exosystem, and macrosystem. This applies well to family counseling as we help families and the job-seeking individual create an action plan, generate alternatives, and anticipate unexpected events. Once this is established, families can move forward and adjust when new information or job changes come their way.

SCCT was established as an alternate to trait and factor theory. STF is born out of a need for looking at career behavior as a whole and not in parts, thus these theories are complimentary to one another. The integration of these theories can help clients resolve issues by looking at the relationship between work, home, and family and the impact each has on the other. Evaluation of relationships, interaction, and context must be considered to make a plan that best supports the individual and the family as a unit.

Career and family systems are interwoven entities that rely on one other and influence the other in ways that are inseparable. Family and career decisions ultimately have an impact on the individual's career development and therefore cannot be viewed from a divided perspective. Thus, it is important to view career decisions and family systems from the lens of internal and external factors, values, attitudes, relationships, abilities, and support so that success in both areas can be achieved.

Keystones

- Key elements of systems theory include wholes and parts, patterns and rules, acausality, recursiveness, discontinuous change, open and closed systems, abductions, and stories.
- Counseling goals, according to Super's theory, include assessing career maturity and strengthening deficits, examining and reinforcing self-concept, recognizing relevant life roles, determining interests/skills, and disbursing them across life roles.
- P-E fit model assesses individual abilities and work factors while striving to capture the nature of a person and their environmental interactions.

- Krumboltz's theory emphasizes that individuals filter events through observations and generalizations; unexpected change is constructive; and desired skills include curiosity, persistence, flexibility, optimism, and risk taking.
- Key elements of SCCT include self-efficacy, outcome expectations, and goals. These constructs empower people to exercise agency in a fluid manner as new information is constantly introduced.

Author Reflections

While writing and researching this chapter, it became increasingly clear to me that we engage in career counseling with all of our clients: young and old, individual, couple, and family. Utilizing integrative counseling methods are very much the norm in counseling practices and in academic settings. In our practice, we typically utilize a systems-based approach due to our work with children and families in crisis. Utilizing this framework, we are able to consider multileveled issues at hand, internal and external factors, the family's past, present and future, and then develop a plan of action that allows each member of the family to move forward individually, while also functioning positively as a unit. —Lynn Jennings

This particular theory strongly resonates with my personal approach to counseling. I believe that clients are impacted by many factors and we have to consider the influence of these factors on the journey of the client. Use of STF encourages the counselor to view each individual from a unique perspective and create a personalized assessment and agreed plan of action to meet the particular needs of the client. This comprehensive process allows for the consideration of issues specific to the individual. I connect best with clients when I know their stories as it helps me assist them in identifying themes, goals, and opportunities for growth. I am convinced that each person is the expert in their own life, but I can be more effective in our interactions if I listen to their story and help them discover aspects not previously considered. STF reminds me of the words of Dr. Martin Luther King, Jr., "We are caught in an inescapable network of mutuality, tied in a single garment of destiny. Whatever affects one directly, affects all indirectly." Although I may be in the client's system for a brief period of time, my hope is that our experience together serves to strengthen him or her along the journey. —Eva Gibson

Additional Resources

The following resources provide additional information about the content provided in this chapter.

Useful Websites

https://www.careers.govt.nz/resources/career-practice/career-theory-models

This site lists job databases, resources, courses, and tools for a variety of clients and future counselors.

Organizations

National Career Development Association: ncda.org

    This organization is a division of the American Counseling Association and offers memberships and helpful resources for career counselors.

International Association of Marriage and Family Therapists: iamfconline.org

    This organization is a division of the American Counseling Association and offers membership and resources to counselors working with couples and families.

Career Resources: Preparing Workers for Life: https://careerresources.org/

    This site offers resources to help families through career development.

References

American Counseling Association. (2014). *Code of ethics*. Author.

Bertalanffy, L. (1972). The history and status of general systems theory. *Academy of Management Journal, 15*(4), 407–426.

Brofenbrenner, U. (1979). *The ecology of human development*. Harvard University Press.

Chartrand, J. (1991). The evolution of trait and factor career counseling: A person x environment fit approach. *Journal of Counseling and Development 69*(6), 518–525.

Dawis, R. V., Lofquist, L. H., & Weiss, D. J. (1968). *A theory of work adjustment: A revision*. University of Minnesota Press.

Ezeofor, I., & Lent, R. L. (2014). A social cognitive perspective on assessment in career counseling: The case of Tiodore. *Career Planning and Adult Development Journal, 30*(4), 73–84.

Frizelle, K. (2014). *A qualitative exploration of the career narratives of six south African Black professionals* [Master's thesis, University of KwaZulu]. Digital Theses.

Greenhaus, J. & Callahan, G. (1994). *Career management* (2nd ed.) Dryden Press

James, R. K., & Gilliland, B. E. (2003). *Theories and strategies in counseling and psychotherapy* (5th ed.). Allyn and Bacon.

Johnson, M. (2015). *Stop talking about work life balance*. Work Solutions Review. https://meaganjohnson.com/wp-content/uploads/2015/04/Stop-Talking-about-work-life-balance.pdf

Kell, H. J. (2018). Unifying vocational psychology's trait and social-cognitive approaches through the cognitive-affective personality system. *Review of General Psychology, 22*(3), 343–354. https://doi.org/10.1037/gpr0000146

Kim, B., Rhee, E., Ha., G., Yang, J., & Lee, S. M. (2016). Tolerance of uncertainty: Links to happenstance, career decision self-efficacy, and career satisfaction. *Career Development Quarterly, 64*(2), 140–152. https://doi.org/10.1002/cdq.12047

Kolvereid, L. (1996). Organizational employment versus self-employment: Reasons for career choice intentions. *Entrepreneurship Theory and Practice, 20*(3), 23–31.

Krumboltz, J. D. (2009). The happenstance learning theory. *Journal of Career Assessment, 17*(2), 135–154.

Lebow, J. L. (2014). *Couple and family therapy: An integrative map of the territory*. American Psychological Association.

McMahon, M. (2017). Work and why we do it: A systems theory framework perspective. *Career Planning and Adult Development Journal, 33*(2), 9–15.

Patton, W., & McMahon, M. (2014). *Career development and systems theory: Connecting theory and practice* (3rd ed.). Sense Publishers.

Rice, A. (2014). Incorporation of chance into career development theory and research. *Journal of Career Development, 41*(5), 445–463. https://doi.org/10.1177/0894845313507750

Ryan, C. W., & Tomlin, J. H. (2010). Infusing systems thinking into career counseling. *Journal of Employment Counseling, 47*(2), 79–85. https://doi.org/10.1002/j.2161-1920.2010.tb00092.x

Samide, J. L., Patrick, J., Eliason, G., & Eliason, T. (2014). *Career development across the lifespan for community, schools, higher education, and beyond.* Information Age Publishing.

Smithson, J. (1999) Equal choices, different futures: young adults talk about work and family expectations. *Psychology of Women Section Review,* 1,2, 43–57.

Zacher, H., Rudolph, C. W., Tordorovic, T., & Ammann, D. (2018). Academic career development: A review and research agenda. *Journal of Vocational Behavior, 110,* 357–373. https://doi.org/10.1016/j.jvb.2018.08.006

CHAPTER

Building Career Counseling Programs

Stephan Berry, Sally McMillan Berry, and Mary Claire Dismukes

> *Go confidently in the direction of your dreams; live the life you have imagined.*
> —Henry David Thoreau

Words that speak to the significance of our individual hopes and dreams resonate with most of us. Thoreau understood the courage needed for individuals to pursue their dreams and set forth a challenge to live life to the fullest. However, in addition to mustering the necessary courage to embark on a particular life path, fulfilling dreams also requires self-knowledge and practical guidance. Whether someone is a bright-eyed adolescent fresh from high school graduation or a mid-life adult bound for a new career path, crucial questions need to be answered: How do I know if I am well suited for a particular type of work? How does this career align with what is important to me? Once I know what I would like to do, how do I prepare? How can I obtain tuition? Where do I begin?

Fortunately, most K–12 schools, colleges, and universities, to varying degrees, are equipped with resources and expertise to guide and assist students in their career decision-making processes. However, due to the cultural shift toward increased assessment and high-stakes testing, limited public school funding, and increasing numbers of college-bound students, many school counselors are so overwhelmed with other duties that it is difficult for them to fully meet the career counseling needs of their students (Sanders et al., 2017). To compound matters, the multi-faceted work of career counseling continues to expand as our rapidly changing digital world presents novel demands requiring new and increased preparation.

Individuals who require career counseling need services that not only address academics and technical concerns but also strategies that integrate with personal dispositions. Flexibility remains key, as economic and cultural changes point to the reality that today's children and adolescents will one day be employed in work that has not yet come to fruition. As career paths change and individuals of all ages are asked to adjust, the self-knowledge and critical thinking necessary to successfully adapt increases in importance. The importance of building sound, research-based career counseling programs in K–12 and college and university settings can't be overemphasized. Individuals of all ages need well-placed guideposts along their unique and changing life paths. Guided Practice Exercise 15.1 asks you to look at your own career journey from the beginning to where you are now.

Guided Practice Exercise 15.1 Your Career Development Process

Think back to your own career development process. Recall the earliest instances of people or events you remember that shaped your view of the world of work and describe their effect on you. What were the things the schools that you attended did or did not do for career development? What could your school have done to be helpful in developing your career?

CHAPTER OVERVIEW

This chapter will examine how to create an effective career counseling program in K–12 institutions, colleges, and universities, and for working adults within the community. In this chapter, the framework and strategies needed to develop an effective career counseling program will be explored at the elementary, middle school, and high school levels. However, career counseling does not stop once someone has graduated from high school. Consequently, programs and interventions available to college students and working adults will also be explored.

LEARNING OBJECTIVES

After you complete this chapter, you will be able to do the following:

- Demonstrate how the American School Counseling Association's (2012) national model can be used in the development of a school's career program
- Explain the steps for creating a program at the elementary, middle school, or high school level
- Identify ways to assist college students and working adults with career development

Career Counseling and the ASCA National Model

Career counseling is one of the main functions of today's school counselor. The American School Counselor Association (ASCA, 2017) emphasizes this saying: "School counselors implementing comprehensive programs strive to have an impact on student growth in three domain areas: career development, academic development, and social/emotional development" (p. 1). As one of the three domains that school counselors impact, school counselors are at the forefront of preparing and implementing college and career preparedness interventions. What can school counselors do to impact the students with whom they work? Answers to this question can be found in the ASCA (2012) national model.

The ASCA (2012) national model was created to assist school counselors in the development of a comprehensive school counseling program that focuses on student achievement. This model provides the outline and structure to guide a school's efforts in crafting an effective school counseling program. School counselors who use this framework find great utility as to how the model guides their efforts, especially in career development. The model is composed of four components: foundation, delivery system, management system, and accountability. The purpose of each of the four sections is to provide guidelines for use in constructing a comprehensive school counseling program.

The foundation section offers a best practice framework for constructing three programmatic areas: program focus, student competencies, and professional competencies. Contained in the program focus section are guidelines for writing professional belief statements about programmatic student benefits, a vision statement to inform desired student outcomes, and a school counseling mission statement. The mission and vision statements are then used as the North Star for informing what the school counseling program's goals will be.

The next section of the foundation component, student competencies, provides a framework for describing the knowledge, skills, and attitudes students will obtain from the emergent program. These competencies are detailed in ASCA's (2014) *Mindsets and Behaviors for Student Success: K–12 College- and Career-Readiness Standards for Every Student*. This work contains 35 standards in three domains: academic development, social/emotional development, and career development. In terms of career development, these standards help students to "1) understand the connection between school and the world of work and 2) plan for and make a successful transition from school to postsecondary education and/or the world of work and from job to job across the life span" (ASCA, 2014).

In addition to the ASCA (2014) *Mindsets and Behaviors*, the National Career Development Association (NCDA, 2004) has established their own list of career development standards titled the *National Career Development Guidelines* (NCDG) *Framework*. Many states have also mandated standards for career development programs, so let's look at factors to consider when determining programmatic standards—in terms of knowledge, skills and attitudes—when creating a new program in Guided Practice Exercise 15.2.

Guided Practice Exercise 15.2 Selecting Program Standards

The *ASCA Mindsets and Behaviors for Student Success: K–12 College- and Career-Readiness Standards for Every Student* describes the knowledge, skills, and attitudes students should acquire from the school counseling program. How would you determine which standards should be part of the career counseling program? How many standards would be a reasonable number to attempt? Why? Would the process be different if you were at an elementary school as opposed to a high school?

It is incumbent for counselors to keep up to date on trends so they can develop research-based programs that work effectively in the contexts of their institutions. The delivery system component of the *ASCA National Model* contains career counseling guidance on individual student planning, responsive services, and system support. ASCA (2016) recommends a student–to–school counselor ratio of 250:1, but the national average is almost double this at 464:1, which indicates the critical need to use the guidance curriculum's mechanisms to reach all students with greater efficiency. Examples of this include classroom career guidance lessons taught by counselors, teachers, and others and activities such as career fairs, SAT/ACT prep courses, and parent workshops. In individual planning, the counselor helps the student develop both their short- and long-term educational and career plans by cooperatively analyzing career assessments, advising on career choice, or making plans for postsecondary life. Career advisement and career-based small group counseling sessions can also be conducted as part of the responsive services.

A third component of the *ASCA National Model* is the management system, which uses annual agreements, organizational assessments, action plans, and other tools to manage school counseling programs. The career program is continually evaluated through ongoing assessment and this data is used to discover programs' major strengths, areas in need of development, and short- and long-term goals for improvement (ASCA, 2012). The program planning tools in the management system ensure the career counseling program is purposeful and well–thought out before any action is taken.

The accountability component is the final section of the model and details how school counselors must be accountable for their expenditures of time and resources to their stakeholders. School counselors are responsible for collecting data to monitor the effectiveness of career interventions, to evaluate and improve career programs, and to provide concrete evidence to stakeholders regarding the efficacy of their career programs. By implementing each component of the *ASCA National Model*, counselors can be equipped to build a career counseling program that effectively meets the needs of all students.

Building Career Counseling Programs in Elementary Schools

The query "What job should I pursue?" has been around for as long as people have been working. For decades, top career theorists have recognized that career development begins in early childhood (Gottfredson, 2002; Super, 1980), which means that elementary-level school counselors also shoulder the responsibility of building career counseling programs. The National Office for School Counselor Advocacy (NOSCA, 2012) describes their responsibilities as "creat[ing] early awareness, knowledge and skills that lay the foundation for the academic rigor and social development necessary for college and career readiness" (p. 2). Understanding students' developmental stages is the first step in creating a college and career program in an elementary school.

Developmental Stages

Most students in elementary grades are between the ages of 6 and 12, which Erik Erickson's theory of psychosocial development places in the industry versus inferiority stage—a time characterized by the need to learn and master tasks. Through mastering tasks, children, in turn, gain self-confidence (Kail &

Cavanaugh, 2018). Failure to master these tasks leads to feelings of inferiority, which hinders children's development at multiple levels, thereby weakening their later success and decision making. This makes it especially important to consider young students' cognitive capabilities when designing interventions. Indeed, significant cognitive development occurs during the elementary years, which Piaget depicted, in part, through his description of two stages: the concrete operational stage from ages 7–11 and the formal operations stage from ages 11 and above (Kail & Cavanaugh, 2018). Cognitive abilities mature as thoughts become more logical and objective as one transitions from one stage to the other. It is during this stage that children develop the ability to take on the perspective of others and role-playing different occupations can take advantage of this development. Further insights on developing elementary interventions can be gleaned from Linda Gottfredson (2002) and Donald Super (1980).

Gottfredson's (2002) theory of career development says career decision making is based on the process of circumscription and compromise. Circumscription is the process of eliminating jobs based on one's self-concept while compromising is adjusting one's career aspirations to the external realities of the world. The elementary years span two of Gottfredson's stages: orientation to sex roles (ages 6–8) and orientation to social values (ages 9–13). In the orientation to sex roles stage, children learn about the world of work and determine some jobs are for men and some are for women based on gender stereotypes. Later in the elementary years the orientation to social values stage begins as children begin to classify jobs in social status terms such as education level, income, and lifestyle, as well as sex type. During this stage, jobs are circumscribed because they do not meet acceptable social value criteria or are perceived as out of reach based on ability level, education, or other criteria.

Super's (1980) growth stage spans elementary school and lasts until around age 14. The major tasks for children are to develop their self-concepts and their concepts of work. Super breaks down this growth stage into the substages of fantasy (ages 4–10) and interest (ages 11–12). In the fantasy stage, behavior relevant to career development is motivated by fantasy in role-playing. In the interest substage, behavior relevant to career development is linked to personal likes and dislikes. Incorporating these developmental stages while creating a career counseling program will increase the effectiveness of any intervention.

Program Goals

Thoreau's quote that begins this chapter directly applies to what a career counseling program should do: point people in the direction of their dreams. This raises the question, "How do we help someone determine that direction?" It begins with determining the direction and goals of the career counseling program by an advisory board made up of counselors, teachers, administrators, parents, and community members. The advisory board may use the ASCA mindsets and behaviors, state standards, and the NCDA's guidelines framework to develop their goals. In 2011, the NCDA suggested the following goals for elementary school career programs: (a) make the classroom a workplace reflecting today's work world; (b) teach productive work habits like preparing, arriving on time, and doing your best; (c) help students see the connection between academics and work; (d) use community volunteers when possible; (e) stress career awareness not specific occupations; and (f) decrease career stereotyping by using nontraditional role models. It would be infeasible, if not impossible, to meets all the goals suggested by these organizations, so advisory boards must be thoughtful and discerning in selecting what goals they wish to adopt.

Implications for Elementary-Level Practice

Super (1980) stated it is crucial to provide a setting in the elementary years where the child's curiosity can be encouraged; therefore, career activities must be especially engaging, interactive, at times even whimsical, to elicit questions and interest. The most authentic way to achieve this is by infusing career counseling activities into the entire curriculum. All faculty and staff should be involved in these activities because it sends a message to students that their careers are significant. An additional benefit of inclusive faculty and staff involvement is that when students hear from multiple perspectives, they are better able to entertain new life possibilities. Finally, communicating about career programs is essential for whole school and for parental and stakeholder buy-in. When all involved know what is being done and why, they are more likely to see how it aligns with the mission of the school and to support programmatic efforts.

Career Counseling Activities

While there are numerous methods of delivering career information, classroom guidance lessons are one of the most effective. Not only can these lessons be delivered by a variety of people (school counselors, classroom teachers, school staff, or community members), but high-quality lessons are readily available through career lesson databases that many states make available online. Since students learn differently, most databases provide lessons that integrate multiple learning styles. For example, activities include listening to career-related books (auditory), creating career maps (visual), and role-playing (kinesthetic). Additionally, there are numerous platforms on the Internet where teachers, counselors, and other professionals can come together and share their ideas for career development.

Effective career-oriented instruction for elementary-aged students may also be implemented outside a classroom. For example, field trips can provide opportunities for children to experience what the "real world" of work looks like. Prior to a trip, students should engage in activities that define what they want to know, what they expect to see, what skills are needed at a work place, what education is necessary for a job, and other questions pertinent to the trip. After the trip is concluded, follow-up activities need to be conducted to reinforce the learning.

Career fairs are time-honored traditions in career development and can be well worth the time it takes to plan. Networking with other schools who have successfully put on a career fair and adapting their format can make the process of planning the fair much easier. Formats differ, as they can take place in a single classroom or throughout an entire school, and they can be completed in 1 day or require a whole week of activities. No matter what the format of the career fair, planning it can be challenging; however, in terms of student engagement, stakeholder buy-in, and school productivity, they can be worth the effort.

An effective way to document student growth that occurs through programmatic activities is by creating career development portfolios, which are a collection of artifacts tracing students' career activities throughout their academic years. Ideally, portfolios should be started in elementary school and then passed on to subsequent schools when students transition to a different campus. At the elementary level, it should contain samples of career-related projects with the understanding that additional items such as student resumes, interest assessment results, grade transcripts, extracurricular activities, career goal lists, and other pertinent career-related information will be added as appropriate in later years.

Parental Involvement

Parents play a central role in career development processes as children form their first impressions of work by observing their own parents. Parents are a significant influence in a child's career development (Ginevra et al. 2015), which makes them an authentic choice for collaborating with schools in career development. For example, teachers might ask students to research their family's job history by completing a *family tree* or *ecogram* listing the occupations and educational experiences of family members. The information gained from the assignment can, at times, provide insight into possible career needs and assets of individual students. While parents can provide career information as volunteer classroom speakers, school counselors can provide opportunities for parents to receive career-related information at parent-teacher organization meetings or during parent conferences. School counselors can provide career information to parents via brochures and newsletters or by posting information on the school websites. While the importance of creative collaborations is not lost on most teachers and counselors, beginning an entire career counseling program from scratch can be a daunting task. Let's look at Case Exercise 15.1 where Jacob is faced with this exact task.

Case Exercise 15.1

Jacob is a 24-year-old recent school counseling graduate who had just obtained his first job in a new K–12 school district. Jacob is the only school counselor in the district. The district is comprised of an elementary school (K–5), middle school (6–8), and high school (9–12) with a total student population of just over 1,000 students. The superintendent of the school system has a strong interest in helping students' career development and asks that Jacob focus on building the career counseling program in his first year. If you were in Jacob's shoes, what would you say to the superintendent about his request? What would be your first steps in developing the program? What would be your biggest challenges and opportunities in developing the program?

Building Career Programs in Middle School

The middle school years, typically grades six through eight, are a time for students to begin to refine their interests, discover their aptitudes and abilities, and clarify their values in relation to their careers. Middle school counselors design opportunities for students "to explore and deepen college and career knowledge and skills necessary for academic planning and goals setting" (NOSCA, 2012, p. 2). Successful career counseling in middle school is critical since students will be asked to commit to a plan of study after completing the eighth grade. Middle school is also when adolescents may have their first paying job such as mowing yards or babysitting. All of these factors highlight the need for schools to provide high-quality career interventions.

Developmental Stages

Middle school marks a time of rapid change—often more than at any other stage of life. For example, as the physical bodies of most undergo extreme transformations, so too do their relational worlds. Peers, instead of parents, become the most influential relationships. In this time of new independence—often marked by intense confusion and uncertainty—it is not unusual for an adolescent's self-concept to shift in possibly negative and frequently novel directions.

Erickson's stage of identity versus role confusion includes the years from age 12 to 18. The main task of adolescents in this stage is to develop a sense of who they are, in other words their self-concepts. It is during this stage that adolescents begin to experiment with many different behaviors, such as dressing differently or developing new friendships, to establish their identities. If successful, the adolescent will emerge from this stage with a solid knowledge of who they are and the ability to stay true to their values and beliefs. However, when adolescents can't or don't want to discover an identity, they emerge from this stage with role confusion, which complicates their efforts to pinpoint a career path. When adolescents lack self-identity knowledge, it is not uncommon for them to approach the quest for a fulfilling career path—one that complements their strengths, interests and values—in an ineffective or haphazard manner. Understanding where adolescents are in their development aids counselors in determining if students are making appropriate progress.

Piaget's stage of formal operational thought begins around age 12 and extends all the way into adulthood. During this stage, abstract thinking develops, gradually replacing the concrete thinking that typifies the elementary school years and the ability to use deductive logic and an ability to attribute cause and effect logic to situations begins. Two key cognitive changes occur that can have a significant impact on adolescents' career development are perspective taking and the ability to plan systematically. The ability to take on new perspectives enhances career development because the adolescent who has this ability can increase the number and types of occupations they can see themselves in. Planning systematically allows students the chance to chart their career paths, with assistance from others, in a logical manner. The career development process is greatly assisted by these traits.

Middle school marks the end of Gottfredson's stage of orientation to social values and begins the stage of orientation to the internal, unique self around age 14. Adolescents are still circumscribing occupations at this time, but these occupations are now being eliminated due to the adolescents' increased knowledge of their interests, values, beliefs, and self-concept. One area of concern during this time is that the adolescent may circumscribe some occupations too hastily because they have not given much thought to the possibilities in that particular occupational area. This potential pitfall can be minimized by encouraging a thorough investigation of an occupational area before it is circumscribed.

Adolescents begin to enter the last part of Super's growth stage during middle school. Super places students in the interest substage within the growth stage as they enter middle school, and it is in middle school where they also transition to the capacity substage. By this time, students have developed a sense of their interests and have begun to investigate career possibilities for themselves. This progression leads to the recognition of one's capacity where one's ability level becomes the basis for vocational thought.

Program Goals

Having successfully accomplished the goal of becoming aware of careers and their significance, students enter the stage of their career development where exploring careers becomes the primary focus. It begins with the student developing a positive self-image. Without a positive self-image, the student may limit themselves unfairly due to inaccurate feelings of inadequacy or incompetence. A positive self-image is built on a realistic assessment of who they are as a person and what their interests and abilities are, thus guiding a student in learning who they are and what they can do. When a student begins to understand their interests and abilities, they will be able to see the connection between these characteristics and the world of work. Thus, students should be provided with meaningful opportunities to explore their unique interests and abilities, which will then allow them to set tentative career goals. It should be explained to students that these goals are not final but are just a starting point and can be updated, revised, or completely changed as the student learns more about themselves.

It is during middle school that students should also begin to determine if college is a necessity for their postsecondary plans. Students need to be clear that college is just one means to a career and that other paths, such as joining the military or entering the world of work directly out of high school, do exist. However, if postsecondary education is a possibility, they need to be educated as to the distinctions between universities, community colleges, and technical or vocational schools, along with information regarding the admissions requirements and process. Normally, students are asked, if not required, during their eighth-grade year to select their courses for high school, and knowing what careers are available to them will make these choices easier (Center on Standards & Assessment Implementation, 2016).

Implications for Middle School–Level Practice

Middle school is the time when career counseling becomes much more focused and intentional in its delivery. States such as Pennsylvania and Texas have developed career development standards that must be met in middle school. In Texas, the "Texas Essential Knowledge and Skills" (TEKS) sets the outcomes students in Texas are expected to master (Texas Education Agency, 2017). TEKS focuses on two areas in relation to careers: career investigation and college and career readiness. An example of a career investigation standard from TEKS for an eighth-grade student is "the student investigates job-seeking skills. The student is expected to: (A) identify the steps for an effective job search; (B) describe appropriate appearance for an interview; and (C) participate in a mock interview" (Texas Education Agency, 2017, p. 2), while an example of an eighth-grade college and career readiness standard is "the student recognizes the impact of college and career choices on personal lifestyle. The student is expected to: (A) prepare a personal budget reflecting the student's desired lifestyle" (p. 4). Whoever designs the career program in a school must make sure their program meets all the standards a state may require.

Many of the strategies used in elementary school are just as applicable to the middle school, but other strategies are available that will enhance the effectiveness of the middle school program. One useful strategy for helping middle school students with career development is the assigning of a faculty member to meet with and track the student throughout their middle school career. The Georgia Department of Education (2008) has created a program, Teacher as Advisor, that serves as the main delivery system for its career development activities. Each faculty member who is assigned to a student should be given the state standards for career development and the professional development training needed to serve as the student's career development contact. The individual attention provided by programs like this can greatly enhance the continuity of a student's career development. Guided Practice Exercise 15.3 asks you to examine the differences in these types of programs.

Guided Practice Exercise 15.3 State Career Programs

The Georgia Teacher as Advisor framework serves a career guide for use by Georgia teachers. Find your home state's guide and one other state's guide and compare them to the Georgia framework. How are they similar and how do they differ? What are the strengths and weaknesses of each? What issues do you think you would encounter if you were to implement one of them into your school? What other activities, resources, and strategies would you need in order to make your program the best it could be?

Career Counseling Activities

There are a multitude of methods schools can use to enhance the career development of middle school students. Classroom guidance remains a primary vehicle for guiding students along their career paths. Some states consider the middle school years to be so vital to a student's career success that career classes have been created by the state to be used at the middle school level. If schools do not offer a career class, the use of a career curriculum infused throughout many subject areas is still a fundamental intervention.

Students need to begin the process of narrowing down their interests, and this can be accomplished by completing formal interest inventories such as the *Strong Interest Inventory (SII)* (Harmon et al., 2012) and the *O*NET Interest Profiler* (U.S. Department of Labor, n.d.). These free interest inventories can assess the student's interest, and this information can then be placed in the student's career portfolio.

Career fairs in middle school are a great way to provide a large number of students with useful career information. More tasks are involved with a middle school fair than an elementary fair because of the change from creating career awareness to promoting career exploration. You can prepare career speakers beforehand by sending out a list of questions that may be asked, important information to cover, the general expectations, along with a schedule and map of the event. Preparing the students includes composing a list of questions to ask prior to the fair and creating individualized student schedules of who to visit and at what time.

For many students and parents, middle school is the time when they begin to make college plans, and several strategies can be used to inform them about post–high school educational opportunities. The career fair is an ideal time to invite recruiters from universities, community colleges, and technical/trade schools to inform students and parents of what the schools have to offer. Students can also visit local colleges and universities to get firsthand information about the college. This is also a good time to hold *parent workshops* on college issues, such as admission requirements, costs, and programs offered at each university, and to detail the college experience.

The task of exposing students to a wide variety of occupations continues during the middle school years. Guest speakers in the classroom remains a good intervention, especially if the information they provide is new or disrupts stereotypical career views. *Job shadowing* is another way to expose students to the real world of work. This experience differs from the career field trips in that instead of just visiting the site and asking questions, the students actually observe the person performing their job. Students are still encouraged to ask the person they are shadowing questions and to record the answers and observations in a journal, which will then be added to the student's portfolio. A lot of intensive work goes into planning activities for middle school career development. Let's turn our attention to Case Exercise 15.2 and see how you can help Jacob plan one particular event.

Case Exercise 15.2

Jacob is approached by the principal of the middle school at the same school district in Case 15.1 and was told the principal's previous school had conducted highly successful career days each year. The principal inquires as to when Jacob will be doing a career fair and what activities he has in mind. How would *you* go about developing a career fair for a middle school? What outcomes from the career fair will need to be achieved to consider it a "success"? What resources will you need to implement a career day that meets the expectations of the principal and the career development needs of the students?

Parental Involvement

Middle school students face several important decisions, and parental input and support are needed to make the best possible decisions. Parents need to be made aware of information about their child's career interests, aptitudes, and abilities, ideally in a conference with the student, their parents, teachers, and counselor. This conference would also be an opportune time to discuss the student's academic progress, career needs, and courses to take in high school. ASCA (n.d.) has created a guide, *Middle School Career Conversations*, which provides a template for conducting this discussion. The counselor can conduct parent workshops on topics such as transitioning to high school, accessing college resources, financial planning for college, and other topics. The school's website should also be kept up to date with links to college and career resources for both parents and students.

Building Career Programs in High School

High school marks the transition to the career planning stage and may be the last time most students will be exposed to formal career counseling. Whether a student chooses to go straight into a career or begins postsecondary education, the career decisions made during this time can have lifelong repercussions. Fortunately, career programs and school counselors can "create access to college and career pathways that promote full implementation of personal goals that ensure the widest range of future life options" (NOSCA, 2012, p. 2).

Developmental Stages

Having made it through the turbulent middle school years, high school students may anticipate smooth sailing, but major changes still lie ahead—especially in terms of career development. Students remain in Erickson's stage of identity versus role confusion in high school, but hopefully they have clarified who they are and what they want to do with the rest of their life. It is important students have a firm idea of their identity, including career aspirations, in order to meet the challenges of Erickson's next stage, intimacy versus isolation, when they graduate high school. High school students also remain in the same stage of Piaget's cognitive development during high school as they did in middle school, formal operations. Nonetheless, the adolescent's ability to use abstract thought, take the perspective of others, and think about the future continues to increase. These increased abilities enhance the student's ability to make career decisions.

In high school, a student will move from Super's growth stage to the exploration stage, ages 14–24. The role of student takes on additional significance as one tries to develop a realistic self-concept and occupational preference by exploring occupational options and trying out different roles. The exploration stage is composed of two substages: the tentative substage from ages 15–18 and the crystallization of preference substage from ages 18–24. The tentative stage is when one begins to form an occupational preference by narrowing down possible jobs fields until a tentative career goal is established. At the end of the high school years, the crystallization of preference stage begins, especially if the student decides to enter the world of work directly out of high school and foregoes any postsecondary education or training. Gottfredson's stage of orientation to the internal, unique self also continues. Adolescents continue to search for their careers, but the process is more purposeful now. Students become more aware of who they are and what is important to them and begin to align this information with occupations they are willing to explore. Students move from a process of eliminating what they know does not suit their identities to making decisions based on personal preferences.

Goals

The goal of career counseling in high school is to prepare students for life in the postsecondary world through career exploration. Many goals from elementary and middle school carry onto high school and mark the culmination of years of time and effort working on these goals. These goals include awareness of their career interests, continued development of the knowledge, skills, and competencies needed for postsecondary life, and creation of a career plan that will guide the student during and after high school. Students who don't accomplish these goals face major obstacles in creating and sustaining a successful, meaningful career.

While proper planning is an essential part of career counseling, it can be just as important to scaffold students toward a healthy and realistic perspective of early adult life. Students may enter high school with a distorted picture of how easy life will be once they are free of the shackles of parental and school supervision. These students may need to develop an understanding of the self-discipline needed to be successful in college or living on their own. In contrast, some students may be overwhelmed knowing they will no longer have the degree of parental or school support for which they have become accustomed. These fears might be paralyzing for some, so they might develop self-management skills that alleviate this anxiety. Creating a realistic view of the challenges students will encounter after graduation will further students' ability to make these school-to-school or school-to-work transitions successfully.

Implications for High School–Level Practice

High school represents the last opportunity someone may have to benefit from intentional career planning services, so it is incumbent on schools to meet a student's needs in order to enter the postsecondary world, whether it be getting a full-time job, joining the military, or entering into postsecondary education, or other options. When a student enters high school, a lot of personal career-related information has been accumulated, and that information only increases in high school. Schools need a repository where they can easily store and update this information. Fortunately, online programs such as Naviance (www.naviance.com) and Kuder (www.kuder.com) make this possible. Many states require the school to meet with individual students at least annually in high school for career planning. These online programs can make this process efficient by providing every student's information to the counselor at the touch of a keystroke. During these meetings, career plans can be updated as needed and assessed as to whether the student's academic and career plans still line up.

Career Counseling Activities

Just like many of the goals of the middle school career program are in sync with the goals of high school, many of the career activities are in also in sync. Activities from middle school that can be used at the high school level include conducting career assessments, going on field trips to businesses or universities, job shadowing, attending career fairs, and participating in mock job interviews. Classroom guidance lessons continue to be an important tool, but now they focus on issues such as graduation requirements, SAT or ACT preparation, college culture, locating and applying for jobs, resume writing, or other areas related to the world of work or postsecondary education and training.

Extracurricular activities outside of the regular school day such as participation in Future Farmers of America, the robotics team, or academic competitions can contribute to a student's career development in significant ways. The experience of having a part-time job is another experience that can provide students with invaluable information about the requirements and expectations of the work world. If a student is unable to have a part-time job, internships and volunteering are other ways of gaining this type of vocational experience. Another task the school counselor must undertake is providing students who have chosen to attend college with the information they need. This process begins with providing information on what programs are offered at each college that match the student's career interest. Keeping students and parents updated on deadlines is also critical, as missing a deadline can create a major disruption to the admission process. School counselors often advertise when tests, such as the PSAT, SAT, and ACT, will be given and offer related testing information. Students can also be given the chance to meet with and learn about the college experience from college, university, or technical school recruiters when they come to campus.

Parental Involvement

Parents still play a key role in career development during high school even though their child is moving toward a state of independence. Whatever postsecondary path a student takes, parents need to be kept up to date with pertinent information, especially if academic problems arise that may interfere with graduation. Even in the best of circumstances, choosing and enrolling in a college, university, or technical school can be a confusing, frustrating process. School counselors would be wise to hold a series of workshops for parents that explain different issues regarding college such as admission requirements, the application process, deadlines, paying for college, scholarships, and federal student loans. Schools can encourage students to attend college by holding an event such as College Application Day (Week or Month) and publicizing it to the community. Frequently, colleges and universities will waive application fees when applications are submitted in conjunction with these events. Just like the ceremonies held when student athletes sign paperwork for athletic scholarships, schools can hold ceremonies that publicly celebrate a student's selection and acceptance into the college of their choice. Keeping parents informed can head off potential problems and ease the school-to-work or school-to-school transition for students.

Thus far, this chapter discussed numerous activities school counselors can implement as part of their career development program. To further aid school counselors, additional activities and resources for each grade level are available in the appendix of this textbook. Now let's discuss career development when working with students in higher education.

Career Counseling in College

It has often been said that education is the key to the American dream. While this is debatable, college graduates still have the greatest prospects for employment according to the U.S. Bureau of Labor Statistics. The unemployment rate stands at 2.1% for college graduates and 4.3% for high school graduates (U.S. Bureau of Labor Statistics, 2018). The debate comes into play as it relates the investment in higher education. Higher education is exceedingly expensive, but most Americans believe one is still better off with a degree than without (Fishman et al., 2017). Prospective students have access to vast amounts of data and are making decisions on where to attend college based on their perceived outcomes. As a result, college career centers are more visible than ever and occupy a critical role in preparing students to achieve their dreams. According to the National Association of Colleges and Employers (NACE, 2016), "The primary purpose of career services is to assist students and other designated clients in developing, evaluating, and/or implementing career, education, employment, and entrepreneurial decisions and plans" (p. 5). As the quote implies, career services in higher education are designed to support a student throughout the entire career development process. College career centers serve a wide range of stakeholders who play a role in a student's career development. In accordance with the accreditation standards set by the Council for the Advancement of Standards in Higher Education (CAS) and NACE, students are the primary stakeholder. A student's interaction with the career center begins before they arrive on campus. Students should be collecting data on which field or major to study. Their decision of what to study can have a lasting impact, as some college majors pay more than $3.4 million than other majors over a lifetime (Carnevale et al., 2015).

Career Centers

Career centers serve an important role in providing data on the career outcomes of graduates, as well as labor market information, to assist both prospective and current students in career decision making. A student entering a college career center may receive this assistance in a variety of ways, including individual career counseling and assessment, group education, and access to alumni and industry representatives who share insights about their particular area of expertise. Some may view college career centers as one-stop shops for all things career related. This flawed view limits the potential of the career center to reach all students enrolled at a given institution, however. Career counselors must also serve as educators to the wider campus community and increase their overall potential for impact.

Partnering With Stakeholders

Faculty serve as important partners in college-level career education, from facilitating student learning in the classroom or in internships to having career conversations with advisees. Career counselors can educate faculty on issues such as labor market outcomes for graduates or how to close industry-based skills gaps. Students may be more inclined to speak to a faculty advisor with whom they have an existing relationship than a career counselor they have never met. Faculty are trained to be teachers but are not trained in career conversations—and this is where the career counselor can provide support to the faculty member in facilitating this conversation.

Organizations employing graduates serve as important stakeholders to career centers, as strong employer partnerships lead to positive career outcomes for students. Employers also play an important role in a student's experiential education through internships and sharing career advice. The career center can connect students to employers through online platforms, career fairs, mentoring programs, and hosting employers on campus for career education programming. In some cases, this will be facilitated by a career counselor, and in other cases it will be facilitated by a member of the employer relations team in the career center.

Families are increasingly more involved in their student's education (Association for the Study of Higher Education, 2015). Some parents want to ensure a positive return on their investment, while others are being asked by students to weigh in on career decision making. College is a time when the relationship dynamic between a student and parent changes (Association for the Study of Higher Education, 2015). No matter the reason, career centers can help parents understand meaningful ways to support their students. A parent might expect to meet with the career center at orientation and hear from them throughout their child's academic experience via newsletters and campus programming. Parents also have the capacity to serve in another role—connecting career center staff to hiring managers at their respective organizations.

As you can see, the career center plays a pivotal role in stewarding relationships with important stakeholders. This is done by all members of a career center staff, from the career counselor to the director. A career counselor might benefit from training in individual interventions as well as program development and marketing. This is where cross-institutional partnerships come in—providing continued professional development for all members of a career development team. Organizations like the National Association of Colleges and Employers, the National Career Development Association, and their regional counterparts provide standards of practice and ongoing training opportunities. These associations also serve as standard bearers on ethical issues and common areas of practice. Educational institutions may also form consortiums to combine resources and provide streamlined opportunities for employer/student connections.

From faculty referrals to alumni mentors, career counseling is truly a team approach. Building college career counseling programs requires much time spent out of the office meeting alumni, faculty, and employers and building partnerships. These relationships will not only support the program but will be utilized to impact a greater number of students than you could ever see through an individual session. Career counselors in higher education focus on the outcomes of all students who attend the institution, not just the ones who opt in.

Career Counseling for the Working Adult

Career transition is a common theme for the working adult. Gone are the days of an individual (historically, a White man) getting a job out of high school, trade school, or college and staying with that company for the entirety of his career. As each new generation enters the workforce, opportunities change. This happens as a result of economic, political, and individual factors. During 2007–2009, the Great Recession caused a loss of 8.7 million jobs, and many fields that once provided a great deal of job security, such as banking, law, education, or government, saw enormous changes (Mischel et al., 2012). Many workers in these fields found themselves out of work, for reasons completely beyond their control. Diversity and inclusion efforts have also drastically changed the workforce, and evidence continues to be collected on the link between diversity and financial performance (Hunt et al., 2018). Jobs that were traditionally embodied by a particular gender are now more open. These factors influence workforce and hiring trends at the macro level and may show up in the context of a career counseling session.

Individual factors may cause an adult to seek career counseling. For example, a career they once found interesting is no longer an option. The plant closes, the corporation downsizes, or the client is fired. Another client may seek career counseling because they never found work interesting and they are ready for a change. Some may have taken a leave of absence to raise a child and are now ready to reenter the workforce. Finally, a client may want to retire and seeks career counseling to develop a transition plan out of the workforce altogether.

There are a number of career development theories that address the complex issues faced by a working adult. Schlossberg's transition theory provides a framework for guiding clients through transitions, anticipated or otherwise. Krumboltz's happenstance learning theory emphasizes teaching the client to take action, explore their curiosities, and develop new skills for success. Bright's chaos theory of careers takes into account the changing nature of the workforce and practical strategies for managing change. These are just a few highlighted examples of the many theories that can address the complex issues facing a working adult. As the last few paragraphs have demonstrated, the working adult population cannot be characterized in one way. Your theoretical approach should take into consideration multiple factors, and your client should serve as the guide. Let's now take a look at Case Exercise 15.3 and discuss what strategies you would use to assist John in his current situation.

Case Exercise 15.3

John has been working in real estate for the last 15 years. For the first 10 years, he loved the entrepreneurial nature of the work. Real estate had a degree of risk that kept him going. While he couldn't guarantee a property would sell, he found a rhythm of what worked for most clients, and the more risks he took, the bigger the payoff. After he got married, the job began to wear on him and his partner. The financial risks and unpredictable nature of the hours made it difficult to budget. They were anxious to start a family and needed a steady income. John didn't know where to turn and was referred to a career counselor in private practice. You need to develop a plan of action with John, so what information do you need to learn first? Would you use an assessment? If so, why? Which strategies will be the most effective?

SUMMARY

Building a best practices–based career counseling program requires an enormous amount time and creative energy if it is to be done effectively. Since children begin to form their impressions of the work world and how they fit into it by observing their parents, career counseling should begin early. Therefore, programs should begin in elementary school and extend across middle and high school, and even into college and the workplace. Career programs exist for everyone—from kindergarten-age students to senior adults looking for a new challenge in the vocational world.

Keystones

- Career counseling programs in public schools follow a path from career awareness in elementary school to career exploration in middle school to career exploration in high school.
- The school counselor may be in charge, but developing and maintaining a career counseling program also takes the involvement of teachers, parents, administrators, and community members to be successful.
- After high school graduation, many students can take advantage of their university, college, or vocational schools' career centers, which, working in conjunction with stakeholders, can provide services to direct and further students' career choices and preparation.
- Mature, working adults may find the need for career counseling due to dissatisfaction with a current position or due to economic factors. Fortunately, career theories, research, and resources are available to address these circumstances.

Author Reflections

Children at an early age are often asked, "What do you want to be when you grow up?" When met with that familiar query when I was a child, I had no idea what to say, but I recall hearing my friends respond with answers such as doctor, firefighter, teacher—or whatever was considered cool on TV. By the time I was in junior high school I knew a little bit about what interested me but did not understand the importance of uncovering and considering personal skills, aptitudes, and values when choosing a career. At some point during my adolescence, the vague idea that I might like to be a psychologist emerged, not because I knew anything about what that career might entail, but because I had great respect for my church league basketball coach who was a psychologist.

Throughout my secondary years, I did not receive career guidance at my high school, which severely hampered me when I went to college. Without a career focus, I struggled for the first few years as an undergraduate; after all, it is difficult to move forward when you do not know where you are going. After a series of mishaps and false starts, my life direction became clear, and once it did, my path through college became much easier. Unfortunately, my experience was not unique—either then or now. With the rising costs of tuition, entering college with little viable career choice input is a problem that neither individuals nor our society can afford to ignore. —Stephan Berry

"Dr. McMillan, may I speak with you a minute?" Pausing amid gathering the numerous books, folders and tote bags that inevitably accompany me to every class, I made quick eye contact with Yvette, a pleasant young woman in her early 20s who was working toward secondary English certification. "I need a faculty mentor for a research project I am conducting on the work of a school counselor. Would you be interested?" Delighted by the prospect of equipping an undergraduate to conduct research, I agreed to help Yvette with a qualitative design. However, as the semester progressed, her enthusiasm waned noticeably, and as we talked one evening, it became clear that Yvette was not merely overextended, she was deeply discouraged. After conducting field observations and interviews at a local high school, she realized that school counselors not only have limited contact with individual students, but they also have few opportunities to offer life or career counseling. Blinking back tears, Yvette confided, "When I was in high school, I needed help. I needed someone to guide me in deciding where to go to school and what to major in. I am the first one in my family to go to college, so no one at home could tell me anything. Everything has been so hard, so I thought that if I eventually became a school counselor, I could help people like me make decisions about what they wanted to do. Then, I could help them to get scholarships. But that doesn't seem to be important in high schools. I think I might need to do something else." Her dilemma touched my heart, and still does. Yvette understood the importance of sound and consistent career counseling in schools because she knew the negative impact a lack of it has on the lives of those who need it most. Through the gift of this young woman's life lens, I had the opportunity to see that a well-developed school counseling program is not a frill or a special privilege. Rather, it is a matter of individual and societal equity. —Sally McMillan Berry

Additional Resources

The following websites contain information, activities, and games for students of various ages.

Elementary

Exploring Career Clusters in Elementary School: https://vacareerview.org/pro/toolkits/toolkits/exploring-career-clusters

Child-friendly site that allows exploration of the career clusters

Kids Work!: https://www.knowitall.org/series/kids-work

An interactive career exploration composed of virtual workplaces

Middle School

My Future: www.myfuture.com

Whatever your future holds this website provides tools and resources to plan it.

High School

CareerOneStop: http://www.careeronestop.org/ExploreCareers/Learn/career-profiles.aspx

U.S. Department of Labor site containing career information and free career assessments

O*Net Online: https://www.onetonline.org/

Comprehensive occupational finder

References

American School Counselor Association. (n.d.). *Middle school career conversations*. https://www.schoolcounselor.org/asca/media/asca/Publications/MSCareerConversations.pdf

American School Counselor Association. (2012). *ASCA national model: A framework for school counseling* (3rd ed.). Author.

American School Counselor Association. (2014). *The ASCA mindsets and behaviors for student success: K–12 college- and career-readiness standards for every student.* Author.

American School Counselor Association. (2016). *Student-to-school-counselor ratio 2015–2016*. https://www.schoolcounselor.org/asca/media/asca/home/Ratios15–16.pdf

American School Counselor Association. (2017). *The school counselor and career development* [Position Statement]. https://www.schoolcounselor.org/asca/media/asca/ PositionStatements/PS_CareerDevelopment.pdf

Association for the Study of Higher Education. (2015). Family engagement and involvement in college. *ASHE Higher Education Report 41*(6), 34–44.

Carnevale, A. P., Cheah, B., & Hanson, A. R. (2015). *The economic value of college majors*. https://1gyhoq479ufd3yna29x7ubjn-wpengine.netdna-ssl.com/wp-content/uploads/The-Economic-Value-of-College-Majors-Full-Report-web-FINAL.pdf

Center on Standards & Assessment Implementation. (2016, September). *High school graduation requirements in a time of college and career readiness*. https://files.eric.ed.gov/fulltext/ED570363.pdf

Fishman, R., Ekowo, M., & Ezeugo, E. (2017). *Varying degrees: New America's annual survey on higher education*. New American Foundation. https://na-production.s3.amazonaws.com/documents/Varying-Degrees.pdf

Georgia Department of Education. (2008). *Georgia teachers-as-advisors framework.* https://www.georgiastandards.org/Programs/Documents/Teachers-As-Advisors_Framework-R_FINAL_3-5-08.pdf

Ginevra, M. C., Nota, L., & Ferrari, L. (2015). Parental support in adolescents' career development: Parents' and children's perceptions. *Career Development Quarterly, 63*(1), 2–15.

Gottfredson, L. S. (2002). Gottfredson's theory of circumscription, compromise, and self creation. In D. Brown (Ed.), *Career choice and development* (4th ed.) (pp. 85–148). Jossey-Bass.

Harmon, L. W., Hansen, J. C., Borgen, F. H., & Hammer, A. L. (2012). *Strong Interest Inventory and technical guide.* Stanford University Press.

Hatch, T., Greene-Wilkinson, D., & Holcomb-McCoy, C. (2014). *The use of data in school counseling: Hatching results for students, programs, and the profession.* Corwin.

Helwig, A. (2004). A ten-year longitudinal study of the career development of students: Summary findings. *Journal of Counseling and Development, 82*(1), 49–57. https://doi.org/10.1002/j.1556-6678.2004.tb00285.x

Hunt, V., Prince, S., Dixon-Fyle, S., & Yee, L. (2018). *Delivering through diversity.* McKinsey & Company. https://www.mckinsey.com/~/media/McKinsey/Business%20Functions/Organization/Our%20Insights/Delivering%20through%20diversity/Delivering-through-diversity_full-report.ashx

Kail, R. V., & Cavanaugh, J. C. (2018). *Human development: A life-span view.* Cengage.

Mischel, L., Bivens, J., Gould, E., & Shierholz, H. (2012). *The state of working America* (12th ed.). Cornell University Press.

Morgan, L.W., Greenwaldt, M. E., & Gosselin, K. P. (2014). School counselors' perceptions of competency in career counseling. *The Professional Counselor, 4*(5) 481–496.

National Association of Colleges and Employers. (2016). *Professional standards for college and university career centers.* https://www.naceweb.org/uploadedfiles/files/2016/publications/product/professional-standards/2016-nace-professional-standards-for-college-and-university-career-services.pdf

National Career Development Association. (2004). *National Career Development guidelines (NCDG) framework.* https://www.ncda.org/aws/NCDA/asset_manager/get_file/3384?ver=16587

National Career Development Association. (2011). *Standards.* https://www.ncda.org/aws/NCDA/pt/sp/guidelines

National Office for School Counselor Advocacy. (2012). *Elementary school counselor's guide: NOSCA's eight components of college and career readiness counseling.* College Board. https://secure-media.collegeboard.org/digitalServices/pdf/advocacy/nosca/11b-4383_ES_Counselor_Guide_WEB_120213.pdf

Sanders, C., Welfare, L. E., & Culver, S. (2017). Career counseling in middle schools: A study of school counselor self-efficacy. *Professional Counselor, 7*(3), 238–250.

Super, D. (1980). A life-span, life-space, approach to career development. *Journal of Vocational Behavior, 16*(3), 282–298.

Symonds, W. C., Schwartz, R., & Ferguson, R. F. (2011). *Pathways to prosperity: Meeting the challenge of preparing young Americans for the 21st century.* Harvard University Graduate School of Education.

Texas Education Agency. (2017). *Chapter 127: Texas essential knowledge and skills for career development, subchapter a., middle school.* http://ritter.tea.state.tx.us/rules/tac/chapter127/ch127a.pdf

U.S. Bureau of Labor Statistics. (2018, May 10). *Unemployment rate 2.1 percent for college grads, 4.3 percent for high school grads in April 2018.* https://www.bls.gov/opub/ted/2018/unemployment-rate-2-1-percent-for-college-grads-4-3-percent-for-high-school-grads-in-april-2018.htm?view_full

U.S. Department of Labor. (n.d.). *O*NET interest profiler.* https://www.mynextmove.org/explore/ip

Epilogue

Layla Bonner, Cassandra Riedy, and Janet Hicks

Now that you have read this book, we hope that you expanded your knowledge and understanding of key theoretical orientations and practices in career development and counseling. We also hope you found practical applications for the concepts that were presented. After reading practical information such as that covered in this text, career counselors often ask two basic questions: "Are these practices efficacious?" "Which of these theories or techniques should I use if I want to focus on specific multicultural counseling issues?" Because of these questions, this epilogue hopes to help you understand these realms so that you are prepared to move forward, select the most appropriate strategies, and help clients. Let's begin by discussing multicultural career counseling and development and then we will move to concepts related to ensuring the effectiveness of career counseling.

Selecting Multiculturally Sound Career Techniques

The National Career Development Association (NCDA) established the "Minimum Competencies for Multicultural Career Counseling and Development" (NCDA, 2009b). These competencies address the expectation that career counselors and other mental health clinicians be prepared to "promote the career development and functioning of individuals of all backgrounds" (NCDA, 2009b, p. 1). Counselors are specifically expected to develop the skills to satisfactorily respond to the needs of clients from diverse backgrounds in individual or group career counseling. Counselors are also expected to select culturally appropriate resources such as assessments and interventions that address the needs of diverse populations. Finally, ethically, practitioners must remain up to date on multicultural issues and research concerning the career development and counseling of diverse populations (NCDA, 2009b). Research provides us with several considerations when career counseling diverse groups. Literature suggests the career counselor identify and tailor interventions that focus on a client's identity, environmental contexts, biculturalism, social learning, and the counselor's self-awareness.

Based on our review of the literature, we recommend that you select and utilize those interventions that facilitate the exploration of the cultural identity of your clients and its relationship to their career outcomes (Arthur & Popadiuk, 2010; Leong et al., 2010; Kerka, 2003). For example, how might a college student's culture, ethnicity, or religious beliefs influence the major they declare (Arthur & Popadiuk, 2010)? How do these cultural expectations affect the client's motivation and wellness? How can you engage the client's family or support systems in the career counseling process? Has the client experienced any shifts in the cultural identity that might impact their vocational aspirations (Arthur & Popadiuk, 2010)? It becomes important, then, to help clients to make choices that are consistent with their identity, the intersection of identities, and their cultural/familial expectations (Arthur & Popadiuk, 2010; Leong et al., 2010).

An exploration of cultural identity should also include assessment of the client's worldview, racial saliency, and level of acculturation (Flores & Heppner, 2002; Kerka, 2003). You can do more harm than good when advising a client who holds a collectivistic worldview if you focus solely on self-interests, personal values, and independence in vocational discernment as these areas may counter cultural values (Leong et al., 2010). Interventions rooted in social cognitive career theory are also recommended as being helpful when working within these domains (Chartrand & Rose, 1996; Flores & Heppner, 2002).

Career counseling interventions should also facilitate an honest exploration of the cultural and environmental contexts of the client and their impact on career development and attainment (Arthur & Popadiuk, 2010; Chartrand & Rose, 1996; Leong et al., 2010; Kerka, 2003). Questions to consider might include the following: What are the client's external barriers and influences? Are these influences real or perceived regarding the client's career opportunities? How do contextual variables create limiting beliefs and limited opportunities for work experiences that foster the development of self-knowledge and self-efficacy (Kerka, 2003)? Has the client internalized the beliefs of damaging social forces (Chartrand & Rose, 1996)? These questions may bring forth answers that illustrate why clients need to identify external influences. Further, answers may explain the interactions these influences have with personal characteristics and behavior (Chartrand & Rose, 1996).

We encourage you to especially focus on the role of issues such as racism/discrimination, sexism, poverty, and other social ills that may negatively impact a client's self-efficacy beliefs and career outcomes (Flores & Heppner, 2002). Career accomplishments based on meritocracy may not be the reality for clients from diverse backgrounds (Kerka, 2003). Consequently, occupational expectations might be limited. As the clinician, it is also important to develop interventions that help clients identify coping skills for such circumstances (Kerka, 2003).

Interventions That Assist With Biculturalism

Clients from diverse backgrounds may also benefit from interventions that help them explore the role of biculturalism in their career development and process and identify personal resources or strategies that enhance their agency and power when interacting within the macrosystem or dominant culture (Diemer, 2007; Rice, 2010). Research examined the perspectives of African American men and how they flow between a predominantly White occupational world and their own culture of origin (Diemer, 2007). Participants indicated that alternating between the two worlds was stress inducing (Diemer, 2007). Some of their stressors included tokenism, discrimination, a fear of individuals in their culture of origin who may perceive them as having lost their Blackness, and finding a comfortable balance between engagement with the dominant culture and their culture of origin. Participants described using interpersonal or bicultural skills such as *code switching* (selecting diverse methods to communicate based on culture) when engaging with the dominant culture (Diemer, 2007). For this reason, it is important to help clients from diverse backgrounds develop and use effective, cognitive, and interpersonal coping skills when they are interacting in the dominant culture (Diemer, 2007; Rice, 2010).

Working on Yourself as Counselor

A cultural formulation approach also suggests that counseling interventions include an emphasis on the cultural dynamics between client and therapist (Arthur & Popadiuk, 2010; Byars-Winston & Fouad, 2006;

Leong et al., 2010). Specifically, as a counselor, it is critical that you reflect on your own metacognitions and cultural awareness. Remain up to date and informed about the cultural values and expectations of your client's cultural group while also maintaining the understanding that within-group differences exist (Leong et al., 2010). To use a euphemism, avoid painting your clients with a broad brush. No matter where you find yourself in the career counseling process with your client, examine your internal processes. For example, during the relationship building stage, ask yourself, "What are the gaps in my knowledge about the client's context?" (Byars-Winston & Fouad, 2006, p. 195). When exploring the client's career concerns, ask yourself, "Are there career issues I am willing to address more than others? Are there issues I am avoiding? What are my own thoughts and reactions about the possible impact of cultural variables on career issues?" (Byars-Winston & Fouad, 2006, p. 195).

Multicultural Considerations When Selecting Career Assessments

When selecting career assessments, be certain the assessment includes normative data on cross-cultural samples (Flores & Heppner, 2002). If instruments have not been normed on diverse populations, use them with caution (Flores & Heppner, 2002). Finally, when selecting interventions, ask yourself, "On what basis am I determining how helpful my interventions are?" (Byars-Winston & Fouad, 2006, p. 195).

Specific Multicultural Career Counseling Techniques

A *strengths-based career counseling* (SBCC) approach was found to increase the self-esteem and use of strengths among participants from a diverse group (Littman-Ovadia et al., 2013). Three months after the SBCC, participants also reported more success in gaining employment. The SBCC approach included specific interventions such as role identification, reframing, and finding exceptions. Participants responded to exception questions in order to find positive solutions to problems they identified in their career development process (see Chapter 10). They also implemented more novel interventions such as polyvocality, metaphorical sign posting, and sentence completion techniques to help clients identify and process their strengths in career counseling (Littman-Ovadia et al., 2013).

Polyvocality is a technique in which the interviewers encouraged clients to utilize their social capital and embrace the voices of supportive others regarding their personal strengths (Littman-Ovadia et al., 2013). For example, the interviewer asked, "If your best friend were here, what would he mention as your greatest strength?" (Littman-Ovadia et al., 2013, p. 408).

Researchers also used an intervention called the *metaphorical sign-posting technique*. This technique involves the use of imagery that helps the client and counselor identify variations and levels of growth and change in the client's career exploration and development process (Littman-Ovadia et al., 2013). For example, in using the metaphor of the gears of a manual transmission, the counselor might ask, "What precipitated the change from second to third gear?" (Littman-Ovadia et al., p. 408). The metaphorical signpost helps clients to assess current and future strengths that will be useful in their career development and attainment.

Finally, the *sentence completion technique* invites the client to complete a sentence such as, "I am more likely to achieve my goal of (client's expressed goal) if I am a(an)____ person" (Littman-Ovadia et al., p. 408). This technique invites clients to make a connection between their strengths and accomplishing their goals (Littman-Ovadia et al., 2013).

In short, these guidelines should be considered when perusing the techniques described in this textbook so that you can select a best fit for your client. With regard to best fit, the second question we pondered at the beginning of this epilogue regarded the effectiveness of career counseling overall. Follow along as we discuss this important consideration as we consider the appropriateness of career techniques and career counseling overall.

The Efficacy of Career Counseling and Career Strategies

How do we determine if career counseling is effective? How do we know that the theories and interventions counselors employ positively impact their clients? What does progress look like for career counseling clients? The answers to these questions vary according to the conceptualizations of efficacy, impact, and progress a clinician or researcher applies. As discussed, ethical and competent counselors or researchers are aware of their conceptualizations and the impact of their worldview on perceived success. They make intentional choices about how to determine efficacy, explore variables appropriate to their choices, and then potentially disseminate the results in order to further the profession and the well-being of clients.

Effectiveness Measured by Client Success

In the process of assessing career counseling, counselors or researchers first identify the lens through which they view success and how to evaluate success according to that lens. Career success is one potential lens through which to view the efficacy of career counseling. Categorizations for potential assessments of career success include objective or subjective variables.

Examples of objective career success include readily observable variables such as increases in salary, managerial level, and promotions after entering career counseling (Pan & Zhou, 2015). When applying objective career success as the lens of efficacy, progress for clients looks like higher pay, elevated status at work, and promotions. Measuring subjective career success is not directly observable but instead necessitates time spent understanding the client's estimation of his, her, or their career experiences since entering counseling, including self-referent comparisons to personal goals and beliefs and other-referent comparisons to societal standards or cultural norms (Abele, 2011).

When employing subjective career success as the lens of efficacy, clients are positively impacted when they estimate themselves to be more closely aligned with personal goals and beliefs or with the societal and cultural standards that they have internalized. Qualitative assessments, such as narrative assessments, would prove beneficial in determining career counseling's impact on subjective career success (McMahon, Watson, & Lee, 2019).

Effectiveness Measured by Client Well-Being

Another potential lens to employ while evaluating career counseling is client well-being regarding alleviation of symptomology (Robertson, 2013). Potential symptoms include career-related symptoms such as difficulty making decisions, lack of motivation, and maladaptive behaviors in response to adjustment as well as symptomology impacted by and impacting career such as distress intolerance, anxiety, and general life dissatisfaction (Masdonati et al., 2009; Oliver & Spokane, 1988; Robertson, 2013). Client progress through the lens of career-related symptomology could be indicated by improved decision-making abilities, increased motivation, and greater adaptability. Quantitative assessments in the field of career counseling such as the *Career Adapt-Abilities Scale* can illuminate progress regarding career-related symptomology (Maree et al., 2018). Client progress through the lens of more holistic symptomology could be indicated by improved distress tolerance, decreased anxiety, and greater life satisfaction. Both quantitative assessments such as the *Brief Symptom Inventory* and the *Beck Depression Inventory* as well as qualitative assessments such as client self-report could provide evaluation of overall symptom abatement.

Counselor Self-Reflection

Finally, rather than looking solely to the client in career counseling evaluation, it is important that career counselors possess the ability to self-reflect and engage in both self-evaluation and supervision, when appropriate. Instruments like the *Career Counseling Self-Efficacy Scale* and the *Counseling Self-Estimate Inventory* exist to garner counselors' estimation of their impact on the client and ability to foster progress (Larson et al., 1992; Perrone et al., 2000). The Career Counseling Self-Efficacy Scale measures a counselor's sense of his or her therapeutic process and alliance skills, vocational assessment and interpretation skills, and multicultural competency skills, while the *Counseling Self-Estimate Inventory* measures a counselor's sense of his or her micro skills, process, ability to work with difficult client behavior, cultural competence, and awareness of values (Larson et al., 1992; Perrone et al., 2000). A competent counselor seeks supervision when self-reflection encourages consultation with other professionals (NCDA, 2009a). Supervision on a regular basis provides an external layer of evaluation that ensures the well-being of the client and the positive impact of the counseling professional (NCDA, 2009a).

Multiple factors will impact the lens through which a career counselor views his or her impact on clients' progress and the method of evaluation that he or she selects. It is integral to competent and ethical practice that a career counselor be aware of the impact of his or her worldview on his or her perception of impact and progress. Worldviews are an amalgamation of years of experience, beliefs, attitudes, motivations and goals, spirituality and religious culture, societal culture, and various aspects of identity such as race, ethnicity, gender, sexual orientation, and socioeconomic status. They form the complex foundation on which counselors ground their theoretical orientation and practice. The theoretical orientation to which career counselors subscribe will impact their conceptualization of both clients' progress and their impact on clients' progress. The NCDA (2009a) states that a theoretical orientation is essential for competent counseling. An extension of this integral competency is career counselors' awareness of the influence of theoretical orientation on their clients and themselves throughout the counseling process, including its impact on the lens through which they view their impact and their clients' progress. As well, competent and ethical counselors will stay abreast of current research and apply evidence-based practices when appropriate, including in the process of evaluating the counseling process, clients' progress, and their impact and efficacy in counseling.

Evidence-Based Practices

As the body of literature generated by research into career counseling grows, more and more theoretical orientations and interventions are being substantiated as evidence-based practices. Current career counselors well versed in current research have a large toolbox with which to serve their clients. For example, cognitive behavioral therapy and solution-focused brief therapy can be practiced with the confidence and insight delivered by extensive research detailing effective interventions (David et al., 2018; Franklin et al., 2011). Coinciding with the evidence mounting in support of particular theoretical practices is the increasing research in support of the efficacy of therapeutic factors common to the majority of theoretical orientations (Blow et al., 2007). Research publications authored by Todd W. Leibert and Dunne-Bryant (2015, Mark Hubble and colleagues (1999), and Michael Lambert (1992) speak to empirically supported efficacy of common factors that transcend theoretical orientation, including the therapeutic alliance, empathy, trust, and facing fears. In fact, a clinician's practice is not competent or ethical should he or she focus solely on executing evidence-based interventions without attention and effort spent on the therapeutic relationship (Norcross & Wampold, 2011).

Researchers employ quantitative, qualitative, and mixed methods in order to gather insight into the practice of career counseling and its impact on clients. Popular quantitative methods include a variety of scales, questionnaires, and inventories. Examples commonly used include the *Vocational Certainty Scale*, the *Working Alliance Inventory*, the *Career Decision Difficulties Questionnaire*, and the *Satisfaction with Life Scale* (Cardoso & Sales, 2018; Masdonati et al., 2009; Robertson, 2013). Narrative analysis is an example of a qualitative method that aligns with the current trend in career counseling of employing narrative techniques and is pioneered by Mark Savickas (Blustein et al., 2005).

Because career counseling is not a cookbook approach, only you, the expert counselor can determine which strategies are the best fit for your client. Nonetheless, we hope the information in this epilogue prepares you to select the best possible strategies and to integrate the information provided in this book with the needs of your clients. Most of all, we wish you well in your future counseling related career!

References

Abele, A. E., Spurk, D., & Volmer, J. (2011). The construct of career success. *Zeitschrift Für Arbeitsmarktforschung, 43*(3), 195–206. https://doi.org/10.1007/s12651-010-0034-6

Arthur, N., & Popadiuk, N. (2010). A cultural formulation approach to career counseling with international students. *Journal of Career Development, 37*(1), 423–440. https://doi.org/10.1177/0894845309345845

Blow, A. J., Sprenkle, D. H., & Davis, S. D. (2007). Is who delivers the treatment more important than the treatment itself? The role of the therapist in common factors. *Journal of Marital and Family Therapy, 33*(3), 298–317. https://doi.org/10.1111/j.1752-0606.2007.00029.x

Blustein, D. L., Kenna, A. C., Murphy, K. A., DeVoy, J. E., & DeWine, D. B. (2005). Qualitative research in career development: Exploring the center and margins of discourse about careers and working. *Journal of Career Assessment, 13*(4), 351–370. doi:10.1177/1069072705278047

Byars-Winston, A. M., & Fouad, N. A. (2006). Metacognition and multicultural competence: Expanding the culturally appropriate career counseling model. *The Career Development Quarterly, 54,* 187–201.

Cardoso, P., & Sales, C. M. D. (2019). Individualized career counseling outcome assessment: A case study using the personal questionnaire. *Career Development Quarterly, 67*(1), 21-31. https://doi.org/10.1002/cdq.12160

Chartrand, J. M., & Rose, M. L. (1996). Career interventions for at-risk populations: Incorporating social cognitive influences. *Career Development Quarterly, 44*(4), 341-353. https://doi.org/10.1002/j.2161-0045.1996.tb00450.x

Cohen-Scali, V., Rossier, J., & Nota, L. (Eds.). (2017). *New perspectives on career counseling and guidance in Europe: Building careers in changing and diverse societies.* Springer.

David, D., Cristea, I., & Hofmann, S. G. (2018). Why cognitive behavioral therapy is the current gold standard of psychotherapy. *Frontiers in Psychiatry, 29.* https://doi.org/10.3389/fpsyt.2018.00004

Diemer, M. A. (2007). Two worlds: African American men's negotiation of predominantly White educational and occupational worlds. *Multicultural Counseling and Development, 35*(1), 2-14.

Flores, L. Y., & Heppners, M. J. (2002). Multicultural career counseling: Ten essentials for training. *Journal of Career Development, 28*(3), 181-202.

Franklin, C., Trepper, T., McCollum, E., & Gingerich, W. (Eds). (2011). *Solution-focused brief therapy: A handbook of evidence-based practice* (1st ed.). Oxford University Press.

Hubble, M. A., Duncan, B. L., & Miller, S. D. (1999). Introduction. In *The heart and soul of change: What works in therapy* (pp. 1-19). Washington, DC: American Psychological Association.

Kerka, S. (2003). *Career development of diverse populations.* Eric Clearinghouse on Adult Career and Vocational Education (ED482536).

Lambert, M. J. (1992). *Psychotherapy outcome research: Implications for integrative and eclectical therapists.* Basic Books.

Larson, L. M., Suzuki, L. A., Gillespie, K. N., Potenza, M. T., Bechtel, M. A., & Toulouse, A. L. (1992). Development and validation of the counseling self-estimate inventory. *Journal of Counseling Psychology, 39*(1), 105-120. https://doi.org/10.1037/0022-0167.39.1.105

Leibert, T. W., & Dunne-Bryant, A. (2015). Do Common Factors Account for Counseling Outcome? *Journal of Counseling & Development, 93*(2), 225-235. doi: 10.1002/j.1556-6676.2015.00198.x

Leong, F. T., Hardin, E. E., & Gupta, A. (2010). A cultural formulation approach to career assessment and career counseling with Asian American clients. *Journal of Career Development, 37*(1), 465-486. https://doi.org/10.1177/0894845310363808

Littman-Ovadia, H., Lazar-Butbul, V., & Benjamin, B. A. (2013). Strengths-based career counseling: Overview and initial evaluation. *Journal of Career Assessment, 22*(3), 403-419. https://doi.org/10.1177/1069072713498483

Maree, J. G., Cook, A. V., & Fletcher, L. (2018). Assessment of the value of group-based counselling for career construction. *International Journal of Adolescence and Youth, 23*(1), 118-132. https://doi.org/10.1080/02673843.2017.1309324

Masdonati, J., Massoudi, K., & Rossier, J. (2009). Effectiveness of career counseling and the impact of the working alliance. *Journal of Career Development, 36*(2), 183-203. https://doi.org/10.1177/0894845309340798

McMahon, M., Watson, M., & Lee, M. C. Y. (2019). *Qualitative career assessment: A review and reconsideration* doi:https://doi.org/10.1016/j.jvb.2018.03.009

National Career Development Association (NCDA). (2009a). *Career counseling competencies.* https://www.ncda.org/aws/NCDA/pt/sd/news_article/37798/_self/layout_ccmsearch/true

National Career Development Association. (2009b). *Minimum competencies for multicultural career counseling and development.* https://www.ncda.org/aws/NCDA/pt/fli/12508/false

Norcross, J. C., & Wampold, B. E. (2011). Evidence-based therapy relationships: Research conclusions and clinical practices. *Psychotherapy, 48*(1), 98-102. https://doi.org/10.1037/a0022161

Oliver, L. W., & Spokane, A. R. (1988). Career-intervention outcome. *Journal of Counseling Psychology, 35*(4), 447–462. https://doi.org/10.1037/0022-0167.35.4.447

Pan, J., & Zhou, W. (2015). How do employees construe their career success: An improved measure of subjective career success? *International Journal of Selection and Assessment, 23*(1), 45–58. https://doi.org/10.1111/ijsa.12094

Perrone, K. M., Perrone, P. A., Chan, F., & Thomas, K. R. (2000). Assessing efficacy and importance of career counseling competencies. *Career Development Quarterly, 48*(3), 212–225. https://doi.org/10.1002/j.2161-0045.2000.tb00287.x

Rice, D. (2010). *African American women in the workplace: Models of career development.* Adult Education Research Conference. https://newprairipress.org/aerc/2010/roundtables/13

Robertson, P. J. (2013). The well-being outcomes of career guidance. *British Journal of Guidance & Counselling, 41*(3), 254–266. https://doi.org/10.1080/03069885.2013.773959

Appendix

Career Activities for K–12 Students

Goal: Career readiness and awareness about higher education

Possible Primary School Activities (Grades K–2)

1. Students wear favorite college/trade school's apparel on a special designated day.
2. Teachers post signs indicating schools they attended and host question-answer sessions about their school experience and preparation.
3. Students create posters that describe themselves and their career interests.
4. During "show and tell," students describe jobs depicted on an artistic collage created from pictures cut from magazines or newspapers.
5. Students bring memorabilia from a family member's career or university experience to show and tell.
6. Host "dress-up days" where students dress like those who hold certain jobs.
7. Decorate cans or jars students can use to store savings in and start their "college fund." Discuss the importance of saving for this purpose.

   (For specific activities by grade level, see McKeesport Area School District, 2018).

Possible Elementary School Activities (Grades 3–5)

1. Host guest speakers and field trips so students learn about a variety of careers.
2. Decorate classroom doors to depict a variety of universities, colleges, or trade schools. Include student-researched information on the decorations such as maps, number of students enrolled, majors, and any other interesting information.
3. Choose or rank favorite jobs from a given job list.
4. Give each child a different fact about a university or job and a sheet listing all universities/jobs described. Students go around the room asking questions of other students until they match each fact (person) with the job or university name. They write the name of the person holding the fact card beside the job listed.
5. Introduce students to computer websites such as Whyville.net and the O*Net as their development allows.

   Specific Activities by grade level can be seen at the following source:
   (For specific activities by grade level, see McKeesport Area School District, 2018).

Possible Middle School Activities (Grades 6–8)

1. Attend a career night where a variety of universities are in attendance.
2. Decorate classroom doors to depict a variety of universities, colleges, or trade schools.
3. Host shadowing events such as "Take Your Child to Work Day" or other variations of this activity.
4. Create an advertisement for a particular university, college, trade school, or job. Present the ad to the class.
5. Create a career collage depicting jobs in a particular career cluster.
6. Write a sample letter of interest for an actual job posting that interests the student.
7. Write a sample resume for a specific job. Research the job using the O*Net.

   (For specific lesson plans and activities, see Layton, 2019).

Possible High School Activities (Grades 9–12)

1. Host scholarship events where particular scholarships are revealed or explained.
2. Students take the O*Net assessments and use Holland codes to find and explore career interests, determine skills, values, and other facets.
3. Students take the Myers–Briggs assessment and discuss personality types and how they tie to job fit or misfit.
4. Attend career nights where universities set up booths and distribute information.
5. Host an evening to learn about the FAFSA for parents and students.

   (For additional activities for all levels, see ACT Center for Equity in Learning, n.d.)

References

ACT Center for Equity in Learning. (n.d.). *College and career awareness activities for elementary and middle school students*. https://www.acenet.edu/Documents/College%20and%20Career%20Awareness%20Activities%20for%20Elementary%20and%20Middle%20School%20Students%201.0.pdf

Layton, S. (2019, December 12). *Career exploration lesson plans for middle school*. Applied Educational Systems. https://www.aeseducation.com/blog/best-career-exploration-lesson-plans-middle-school

McKeesport Area School District (2018). K–5 career readiness lesson plans. https://www.mckasd.net/site/handlers/filedownload.ashx?moduleinstanceid=2246&dataid=2465&FileName=K-5%20Career%20Readiness%20Lessons.pdf

Index

About the Editors

Janet Froeschle Hicks, PhD, LPC, is a licensed professional counselor and certified school counselor who currently serves as professor and director of mental health counseling at Belmont University in Nashville, Tennessee. Before becoming a professor, she worked as a lead school counselor where she implemented comprehensive school counseling programs (with an emphasis on career development issues) in the K–12 setting. She was inducted into the American Counseling Association Fellows in 2015 and is listed as an expert on the *Psychology Today* website where she authors a professional child- and family-focused blog entitled *Raising Parents*. She is a board member for the international group SAFE (Stop Abuse for Everyone); has served as a media expert at national and state levels on topics related to child, adolescent, and family counseling; and serves professionally through many volunteer activities. For example, Dr. Hicks served as special events chair for the International Association of Marriage and Family Counselors and research committee co-chair for the Texas Counseling Association, and she currently serves as president elect for the Tennessee Counseling Association.

Dr. Hicks has researched and written over 70 publications and presented numerous times on topics related to career, child, adolescent, family, and school counseling. She currently serves as a reviewer for the *Journal of Women and Minorities in Engineering*, and her work has appeared in journals such as *Professional School Counseling, Journal of Creativity in Mental Health, Middle School Journal, Journal of School Counseling, The Family Journal*, and *International Journal of Play Therapy*, among others. In addition, her work has been demonstrated in invited presentations at the American Counseling Association Conference & Expo as well as in *Counseling Today* articles. She has received numerous awards, including induction into the 2015 ACA Fellows, 2008 and 2009 High Plains Counseling Association Outstanding Counselor award, the 2010–2011 Texas Tech University Hemphill Wells New Professor Excellence in Teaching award, and 2014 Barney Rushing Outstanding College Research award.

Brandé Flamez, PhD, LPC, NCC, is a licensed professional counselor and clinical professor at Lamar University. Dr. Flamez is also the CEO and founder of the nonprofit SALT (Serving and Learning Together) World Inc., which provides donations and volunteer services to developing countries. Her clinical background includes working with children, adolescents, and families in community-based and private counseling settings. Dr. Flamez is active in the counseling profession. She has served on the American Counseling Association (ACA) Governing Council for the International Association of Marriage and Family Counselors (IAMFC), ACA Finance Committee, and ACA Investment Committee and has chaired the ACA Publications Committee. Dr. Flamez is the past president for the Association for Humanistic Counselors (AHC), past president for IAMFC, secretary of AHC, and currently chairs the AHC Bylaws/Ethics Committee. She also serves internationally as the secretary to the Congress for EADD and is on the Izmir Democratic University Scientific Committee.

Dr. Flamez is on the editorial board for *The Family Journal* and the *American Journal of Family Therapy*. She has provided over 100 presentations and training workshops to professional groups throughout the United States and internationally. Her scholarly contributions include more than 35 coauthored book chapters and journal articles. Dr. Flamez is the coauthor or coeditor of seven textbooks currently used in clinical training programs throughout the USA including, *Counseling Assessment and Evaluation: Fundamentals of Applied Practice, Diagnosing Children and Adolescents: A Guide for Mental Health Practitioners, A Counselor's Guide to the Dissertation Process: Where to Start and How to Finish*, and *Marriage, Couple, and Family Therapy: Theory, Skills, Assessment, and Application*. She is the recipient of 20 national awards and four international awards, which demonstrates her dedication to advocacy, leadership, and research in the field of counseling.

Mayorga, Mary, PhD, LPC, is a counselor educator at Belmont University in the department of Clinical Mental Health Counseling. She has worked as a therapist in substance abuse, domestic violence, and sexual assault. She has also worked with at-risk adolescents and families in crisis. She has published numerous articles on conflict resolution, multicultural diversity, and wellness behavior and has written several chapters in various counseling textbooks. In her private practice, she works with clients suffering from trauma-related issues, life issues, and school and career concerns. Her main research interest is on wellness behavior among counselors.

About the Contributors

Aimienoho, Eniye, MA, graduated with her Master of Arts degree in Mental Health Counseling from Belmont University in 2020. She is interested in working with clients struggling with life issues, social and diversity issues, relationship concerns, and depression and anxiety. She received her Bachelor of Science degree in Psychology from High Point University.

Awbrey, Brandon, PhD, LPC, is an assistant professor in the department of Psychology and Counseling at Hardin-Simmons University. He worked as a career counselor at a rural community college and is a former president of the Texas College Counseling Association. In private practice he mainly focuses on emerging adults and men's issues. His other research interests include mindfulness-based interventions, ethics, technology concerns in counseling, and creativity in counseling.

Berry, Stephan, PhD, LPC, is an assistant professor at Troy University. He is a former special education teacher and school counselor and has also worked in addiction treatment centers, psychiatric hospitals, and outpatient counseling programs. He has published articles on bullying and articles and a book chapter on solution-focused brief therapy. His research interests include school crisis management, bullying, and solution-focused brief therapy in schools.

Bonner, Layla, PhD, LMFT, NCC, is an assistant professor in the Mental Health Counseling program at Belmont University. She received her PhD from Trevecca Nazarene University in 2018. Her research interests include African American relationships, marriages and families, and multicultural competence in counselor education. Prior to becoming an assistant professor, she worked as a counselor in the school and university setting.

Brown, Dara N., LPC, LSOTP, obtained her bachelor's degree in psychology from Temple University in Philadelphia in 2009, her master's degree in mental health counseling from Kutztown University of Pennsylvania in 2012, and her PhD in counselor education and supervision from Texas Tech University in Lubbock, Texas, in 2016. Her work experience is focused on treatment with sex offenders in residential civil commitment, state and jail incarceration, and outpatient probation and parole as well as community and inpatient mental health and crisis work. Dr. Brown is a licensed professional counselor and licensed sex offender treatment provider in Texas as well as a certified sex offender treatment provider in Virginia. Her research interests include effective sex offender treatment, offender recidivism, community reintegration for offenders, suicide intervention, and effective policies and procedures for inpatient and residential treatment programs.

Corvette, Michelle, PhD, currently serves as assistant professor of art at Belmont University. She holds two PhDs, one from University of London, Goldsmiths, in visual arts research and another from the University of Tennessee, Knoxville, in educational psychology. Her research interests include social intervention art, a practice of giving back to the community through art; diversity and inclusion research; and art therapy. She is especially interested in helping youth and families facing career and educational issues, such as bullying and mental health, through creative outlets.

Dennis, Garrik, MA, obtained his master's degree in mental health counseling from Belmont University in 2019. As an Army veteran, his interests include assisting veterans and active duty troops with career and educational issues. He currently works as lead instructor for Vets2PM.

Dickson, Cody W., PhD, LPC, LMHP, NCC, is an assistant professor and chair in the Department of Counseling at Wayne State College in Nebraska. He has worked in community mental health services, as a counselor within the criminal justice system, and in private practice. He has worked with clients of diverse ages and backgrounds as a behavioral health and career counselor and vocational trainer. He works with several academic and community programs to address behavioral health career development needs in rural Nebraska. His research interests include life span and identity development, consultation and service collaboration, advocacy, and contemplative practices.

Dismukes, Mary Claire, LPC, is director of the Office of Career and Professional Development at Belmont University. She has worked with college students her entire career: as career counselor, fundraiser providing access to education, advisor to student leaders, and volunteer coordinator. Her other research interests include leadership development, spirituality and vocation, workforce development, and human resources.

Gibson, Eva M., EdD, is an assistant professor of psychology at Austin Peay State University. Prior to becoming a counselor educator, she spent 11 years in the public school system as a licensed school counselor. During this period, she focused on the academic, career, and social/emotional development of students and often consulted with parents to help meet the needs of the family unit. Other research interests include interventions for at-risk students and marginalized populations.

Green, DeAnna, PhD, LPC, CSC, is an assistant professor of counseling and school counseling program coordinator at Sam Houston State University. Prior to becoming a counselor educator, she spent 9 years as a school counselor at both the elementary and secondary levels working on comprehensive school counseling programs, including youth career development. Her research areas include school counseling, career counseling, first-generation college students, youth counseling, and strategies for serving at-risk populations.

Humphreys, Krystal, PhD, LPC, is an assistant professor of counseling at Grace College. She has worked as a teacher and counselor in schools, as a counselor at a safe house for survivors of sex trafficking, as a counselor at a child and adolescent partial hospitalization facility, and a counselor in a women's clinic.

She has published numerous articles on human trafficking, non-suicidal self-injury, and resiliency among adolescents in military families. In her areas of practice, she works with various clients whose circumstances have affected their outlook on their current and future careers. Her research interests include generational changes among children and adolescents and their relation to sex trafficking vulnerability, the effects of military life on adolescent mental health, and how career choice is impacted by trauma.

Jennings, Lynn, PhD, LPCS, LSOTP, is in private practice in Amarillo, Texas. She is an adjunct faculty at Texas Tech University and associated faculty at Denver Seminary. In her private practice she works with children, adolescents, and adults in the area of crisis, trauma, physical and sexual abuse, and career development. Her research interests include middle school and high school bullying, secondary traumatic stress in counselors and other helping professions, and treating abused and traumatized children and adolescents.

Jennings, Stephen, PhD, LPCS, LSOTP, is in private practice in Amarillo, Texas. He, along with his wife, Lynn, own Jennings Counseling and Associates and have been serving the Texas Panhandle for the past 15 years. Stephen is adjunct faculty at Texas Tech University as well as associated faculty at Denver Seminary. His therapeutic focus is marriage and family therapy, co-parenting for divorced and blended families, and career development across the life span.

Knowles-Bagwell, Tom, DDiv, LPT, is currently associate director and associate professor in Belmont University's Mental Health Counseling program. He is a graduate of Vanderbilt Divinity School with both the Master of Divinity and Doctor of Ministry degrees. He is licensed as a clinical pastoral therapist in Tennessee and is an ordained minister in the Christian Church (Disciples of Christ). In addition, Tom is certified as a diplomat in the American Association of Pastoral Counselors and is a certified sexual addiction therapist through the International Institute for Trauma and Addiction Professionals.

Le Clair, Brian, PhD, LMFT, is a licensed marriage and family therapist in private practice in the Los Angeles, California, area. He has worked for the Los Angeles Unified School District for 30 years while concurrently operating a private psychotherapy practice. He has published several articles on cyberbullying and instigators of bullying as well as articles on the link between human trafficking and pornography consumption. In his private practice, he works with individuals and couples whose lives have been adversely affected by pornography abuse and sexual addiction. He runs groups for men in recovery from the abuse of pornography and associated trauma. His other research interests include awareness of laws and ethics among novice counselors, the changing acceptance of shifting sociopathology, age of onset of addictive behaviors, and best practices and strategies for treating established addictions.

Merriman, Julie, PhD, NCC, LPC-S, RPT-S, graduated with her PhD in counselor education and supervision from Texas Tech University in 2011. She has over 21 years experience working with clients in the field. Currently, Julie serves as associate dean and associate professor at Tarleton State University where she teaches graduate-level counseling courses. Dr. Merriman is also past president of the Association for Play Therapy.

McMillan Berry, Sally, PhD, was formerly an associate professor in curriculum studies and literacy in the College of Education at Texas Tech University. Prior to her tenure at TTU and her current position as the English Department director at Trinity Presbyterian School, she worked as a middle and high school English teacher in Louisiana and served in the Louisiana Department of Education's Bilingual/ESL department. Her publications and research interests include education narratives, qualitative research, adolescent literacy, and 19th-century women writers. She is primarily interested in the role that narrative plays in informing student identities.

Moyer, Michael, PhD, LPC-S, is professor and associate chair in the Department of Counseling, Health, and Kinesiology at Texas A&M University, San Antonio. He received his master's in counseling and doctorate in counselor education and supervision from Texas A&M University, Corpus Christi. Throughout his tenure as a counselor educator, Dr. Moyer has taught various courses; however, he most often enjoys teaching courses related to ethical and legal issues in counseling, practicum, and counseling techniques. Some of Dr. Moyer's primary research interests include ethical decision making, non-suicidal self-injury, and counselor education. In additional to his teaching, research and involvement in professional organizations, Dr. Moyer maintains a small private practice and specializes in working with individuals who self-injure. Outside of work, Dr. Moyer enjoys being outside and spending time with his wife and three children.

Noble, Nicole, PhD, LPC, is an assistant professor of counselor education at Texas Tech University (TTU) and a licensed professional counselor in the state of Texas. Previously, she was an associate director of the Career Center at TTU. She holds a doctorate (counselor education), a master's degree (school counseling), and a bachelor's degree (psychology) from TTU.

Ossoff, Leslin, MA, graduated with her Master of Arts in Mental Health Counseling from Belmont University in 2019. She has experience working with a variety of clients and issues. Currently, she works as program therapist for Yellowstone Boys and Girls Ranch in Montana.

Riedy Rush, Cassandra, MA, is a doctoral student and research assistant in the counseling department at George Washington University. As a counselor, she has primarily served women in the Tennessee prison system and substance use facilities. She has presented research findings and innovative counseling practices on the national, state, and regional level. Her publications have addressed various topics such as cross-generational counseling and the impact of substance use on families. Her current research focuses on health disparities experienced by individuals of various races, ethnicities, and sexual orientations.

Waltz, Macy, PhD, LPC, is a licensed counselor and an adjunct faculty in the department of Psychology and Counseling at Lubbock Christian University. She has worked with children, adolescents, and adults at a counseling center and medical clinic. Her research interests include stress on individuals, counseling different generations, bullying, human trafficking, and crisis counseling. When counseling she works with clients suffering from various issues including depression, anxiety, abuse, PTSD, marital conflict, divorce, grief, and career guidance. Her other research interests include spirituality and counseling, EMDR, and postpartum.

Wardle, Elizabeth Ann, PhD, LPC-S, RN, is a clinical mental health counselor who graduated from Texas A & M University, Corpus Christi with a PhD in counselor education. In addition to being a registered nurse, she has taught at Del Mar College, the University of Houston-Victoria, and Texas A & M University, Kingsville. She has provided supervision for licensed professional counselor interns. Her academic experience includes grant writing and civic engagement projects, in addition to presentation at the local, regional, state, national, and international levels.

Winkelman, Logan, PhD, is an assistant professor and program director of the Clinical Mental Health Counseling program at Texas Tech University Health Sciences Center School of Health Professions and a licensed professional counselor in the state of Texas. Prior to her role at the TTU Health Sciences Center, she was an associate director of the career center at Texas Tech University (TTU). She holds a doctorate (counselor education and supervision), a master's degree (counselor education), and a bachelor's degree (human development and family studies) from TTU.

Printed in the USA
CPSIA information can be obtained
at www.ICGtesting.com
CBHW081547081024
15567CB00031B/833